MICROSOFT INTERNET Explorer 3.0
FrontRunner

MARY MILLHOLLON

LUANNE O'LOUGHLIN

TONI ZUCCARINI

CORIOLIS GROUP BOOKS

Publisher	Keith Weiskamp
Project Editor	Toni Zuccarini
Cover Artist	Scottsdale Color Graphics
Cover Design	Gary Smith of Performance Design
Interior Design	Michelle Stroup
Layout Production	Kim Eoff
Proofreader	Marisa Pena
Indexer	Luanne O'Loughlin & Kirsten Dewey

Trademarks: Any brand names and product names included in this book are trademarks, registered trademarks, or trade names of their respective holders.

Text copyright © 1996 Coriolis Group, Inc. All rights under copyright reserved. No part of this book may be reproduced, stored, or transmitted by any means, mechanical, electronic, or otherwise, without the express written consent of the publisher.

Copyright © 1996 by The Coriolis Group, Inc.

All rights reserved.

Reproduction or translation of any part of this work beyond that permitted by section 107 or 108 of the 1976 United States Copyright Act without the written permission of the copyright owner is unlawful. Requests for permission or further information should be addressed to The Coriolis Group, 7339 E. Acoma Drive, Suite 7, Scottsdale, Arizona 85260.

The Coriolis Group, Inc.
7339 E. Acoma Drive, Suite 7
Scottsdale, AZ 85260
Phone: (602) 483-0192
Fax: (602) 483-0193
Web address: http://www.coriolis.com

1-57610-006-5: $29.99

Printed in the United States of America

10 9 8 7 6 5 4 3 2 1

Contents

Introduction xv

Chapter 1   In the Beginning... Oh, Never Mind!   1

What's the Internet and What's the Big Deal?   2
   internet vs. Internet   2
   What's a Network?   2
   So, What's the Big Deal?   3
Whose Idea Was This Internet Thing, Anyway?   4
What in the World Is the World Wide Web?   7
What's an Online Service?   9
   America Online   10
   CompuServe Information Service   10
How Does MSIE Fit into the Internet Picture?   10
What's a Web Page?   11
   The Home Page Component   12
   Understanding Links   12
What's the Difference between a Web Page and a Web Site?   13
What's Up with All Those Dots and Coms Everyone's Always Talking About?   14
Is Learning How to Surf Really a Prerequisite?   16
When's the Best Time to Explore the Internet?   16
Chapter in Review   16

Chapter 2   MSIE Up and Running   21

Installing MSIE   22
The MSIE Browser Window   24
Menu Bar   25
   File Menu Commands   26
   Edit Menu Commands   29
   View Menu Commands   29
   Go Menu   31
   Favorites Menu   32

      Help Menu   33
      Local File Menus   34
  MSIE Toolbar   34
  Address Box   35
  Links Toolbar Button   35
  Display Window   36
  Status Bar   37
  URLs and the Address
     Text Box   38
      The Protocol   39
      Server Name   40
      Directory Path and File Name   40
      Common Protocol Designations   41
      Local File URLs   47
      Using Partial URLs   48
  Pointing to a Site   49
  Viewing an Error Message   50
  Chapter in Review   52

Chapter 3   MSIE Extras   53

  Taking Advantage of Windows Compatibility   54
  Speeding Up Performance   55
  Introducing Added Interactivity with ActiveX, ActiveMovie, and More   58
     ActiveX   58
     ActiveMovie   60
  Communicating Online   61
     Microsoft Internet Mail and News   61
     Microsoft NetMeeting: Conferencing Software   62
  MSIE Is Multilingual   63
     Foreign Language Versions of MSIE   63
     International Extensions   64
     Rating the Sites   65
     How Do Ratings Work?   66
  Browsing with Maximum Security   67
     Trusted Code   68
     Secure Channel Protocols   69
     CryptoAPI   70
  Introducing Smart Caching   70
  Using a Proxy Gateway? Not a Problem   71
  Chapter in Review   73

Chapter 4 Getting to Know the MSIE Options 75

View|Options 76
General Card 77
   Multimedia 77
   Appearance 78
   Toolbars 80
   Fonts 80
Connection Card 81
   Dialing 81
   Proxy Server 82
Navigation Card 83
   Customize 83
   History 85
Programs Card 86
   Mail and News 86
   Viewers 86
   Default Setting 87
Security Card 87
   Privacy 88
   Certificates 89
   Active Content 89
Advanced Card 90
   Ratings 91
   Temporary Internet Files 92
   Cryptography 95
   Additional 95
Local File Properties 96
Chapter In Review 98

Chapter 5 Customizing Your MSN Start Page 101

Customizing Your Start Page Links 101
Welcome to the MSN Start Page 102
   Personal Preferences Options—Page 1 104
      Who Are You? 104
      Special Place for the Kids 105
      Music to Surf By 105
   Services Options—Page 2 106

Contents

  Investment Savvy 107
  Sports Scores and Statistics 108
  This Week at the Movies 109
  Music to your Ears 110
  Family Planning and Parenting 110
News and Entertainment Options—Page 3 111
  Daily News with MSNBC 111
  Time for Television 113
  Comic Relief on the Web 114
  Keeping Up on Computer Technology 115
  Playing with Politics 115
  Rain or Shine Weather Report 116
Internet Searches Options—Page 4 117
  Internet Searches 118
  Great Sites 119
  Keep Track of Your Favorite Links 120
Viewing Your MSN Start Page 123
Chapter in Review 124

Chapter 6 MSIE and America Online 125

Downloading AOL and Explorer 126
  For Current Members Only 127
  Downloading from the AOL Web Page 127
Installing AOL 3.0 and Explorer 128
  Installing AOL from CD-ROM 128
  Installing AOL from the Downloaded Program 129
  Installing Explorer from CD 129
  Installing Explorer from the Downloaded Program 129
  The Windows 95 Difference 130
Jumping Online 131
  The AOL Toolbar 131
  Favorite Places 136
  Testing the AOL/MSIE Integration 137
AOL's Internet Features 139
  Mail 139
  FTP 139
  Gopher 139
  Newsgroups 140
Getting Online Support 142
Indispensable Features 142

Hyperlinks 142
Buddy Lists 143
FlashSessions 143
Parental Controls 144
Free Areas 145
Chapter in Review 146

Chapter 7 Microsoft Internet Explorer and CompuServe 147

The Parts 148
Setting Up Explorer for CompuServe Users 148
   Preparations 149
   Going through the Motions 150
Establishing a PPP Connection to CompuServe 154
   Installing and Configuring the Dial-Up Scripting Tool 155
   Sorting Your Unmatched (Win) Socks 157
Running Microsoft Internet Explorer 158
   Taking Your Browser out for a Test Drive 159
Switching Providers 160
Mail and News Features 161
Getting Online Support 162
Chapter in Review 163

Chapter 8 Microsoft's Essential Services Directory 165

Using the Essentials Directory 166
   Home Reference 168
   Financial Information 175
   Phone & Address Look-Up 180
   Travel Tips 186
   Writer's Reference 190
   Publications Searches 196
   Movies 199
   Music 201
Chapter in Review 204
   Home Reference 205
   Financial Information 206
   Phone & Address Look-Up 208

Travel Tips 208
Writer's Reference 209
Publications Searches 210
Movies 211
Music 211

Chapter 9   Today's Links to Microsoft's Best of the Web Picks   213

MSIE's Today's Links Button   213
The Surf Stories Page   214
The Pick of the Day   215
More Links   216
  Basic Viewing Habits 216
  Arts & Entertainment 218
  Business & Finance 219
  Fun & Interests 220
  Computers & Technology 220
  Sports & Health 221
  Travel & Leisure 222
  Previous Picks 222
  Stale Surf 223
MSN Sitemap   224
Chapter in Review   230

Chapter 10   Searching and Search Engines   231

Understanding How Search Engines Work   231
  Keywords 233
The Big Six   234
  Alta Vista 234
  Excite 236
  Infoseek 238
  Lycos 240
  Magellan 243
  Yahoo 245
Other Search Engines   247
  SavvySearch 247
  search.com 250

WhoWhere? 251
Chapter in Review 251

Chapter 11 Your Favorites Folder and the History List 253

Your Favorites' Parts   254
   Nature of a Favorite Link   254
   Some Exploration Tools   255
   Pointing Particulars   256
Making History   257
Favorites: Extraordinary Tours de Force   258
   Viewing Your Favorites Folder   261
   Organizing Your Favorites Folder   264
   Filling the Favorites Directories with URLs   267
   Filling the Favorites Subdirectories with URLs   269
   Deleting Favorites Links   271
   Shifting Your Favorites Directories   272
   Saving Links in a Different Folder   272
   Importing Netscape Bookmarks   272
Chapter in Review   273

Chapter 12 Shortcuts: Beyond the Favorites Folder 275

Surfing Fluidly Using MSIE Shortcuts   276
The Right-Click Trick   276
   Using the Right-Click Quick Menus   276
   Accessing the Title Bar Quick Menu   277
   Accessing the Address Box Quick Menu   278
   Accessing the Text Quick Menu   280
   Accessing the Graphic Quick Menus   286
   Accessing Web Page Menus   289
   Keyboard Commands   293
   Using the Drag-and-Drop Feature   296
Storing and Finding Your Links   297
   Desktop Links   297
   More Favorites Folders   300

The History Folder: Your Last 300 URLs   300
Chapter in Review   301

Chapter 13   Finding and Downloading Files   303

Zipping and Unzipping   304
Public Domain, Shareware, and Freeware   304
Finding the Files You Want   305
   Search Engines   308
   Doing It on Your Own   314
Chapter in Review   317
Other Useful Sites   317

Chapter 14   Microsoft Internet Mail   319

Using the Microsoft Internet Mail Service   320
   The Toolbar   321
   Addressing Mail   322
   Using the Address Book   323
Setting View Options   325
   Previewing Your Mail   326
   Sorting Your Mail   327
Making Mail Work for You   328
   Customizing Your Replies   328
   Checking Mail Automatically   329
   Composing Mail Offline   330
   Volumes of Mail   330
   Sending and Receiving Mail   331
   Setting Your Priorities   333
   Keeping Your Mailroom Neat   334
   Signatures: Adding Your John Hancock to Your Messages   334
Organizing with Folders   336
   Inbox Assistant   337
HTML   338
Sending Attachments in Internet Mail   339
Import   340
Export   340
Message Formats   340
Simple Shortcuts   342
Working With Listservs   342

    Roadmap to Mailing Lists   *343*
Microsoft Internet Mail vs. Windows
    Messaging   344
    Changing to Microsoft Internet Mail   *345*
Who's on First?   345
Chapter in Review   346

Chapter 15   Microsoft Internet News   347

Getting Started with Microsoft Internet News   349
    Searching for Topics   *350*
    Viewing Subscribed Newsgroups   *353*
Newsgroup Netiquette   353
Previewing Messages   354
Managing the News   354
    Sorting Posts   *355*
    Reorganizing Your View   *355*
    Speed Reading   *356*
    Internet News Folder   *357*
Posting to Newsgroups   358
    Quotes in Posts   *360*
News vs. Mail   362
    Signature   *362*
    Reply Address   *362*
    Include Original Message in Reply   *363*
    Read, Check for New Message Every X Minutes   *363*
Offline News   363
Cross-Posting Your Messages   364
Just the FAQs, Ma'am   366
Chapter in Review   368

Chapter 16   Multimedia, MSIE, and the Web   369

Frames   370
    Floating Frames   *370*
    Pop-up Frames   *371*
    Frame Exploration   *373*
Audio: Surfing with Sound Waves   373
    MIDI Files   *373*
    Sound Clips   *373*

xii Contents

RealAudio 375
Animated Graphics 376
   Animated GIFs 376
Video and Mixed Media 380
   ActiveMovie 378
   Shockwave 379
   QuickTime 380
   VDOLive 380
Multimedia Programming Tools 381
   Java 381
   ActiveX 383
The Future: Surfing in 3D 385
   WorldView 385
   Alpha World 386
Chapter in Review 387

Chapter 17 Creating Your Own Web Page 389

Introducing HTML 389
   HTML Editors 390
Writing HTML 392
   Creating Backgrounds 392
   Text Formatting 397
   Creating Links to Other Sites 400
   Using Images 401
   Adding Marquees 405
Chapter in Review 408
Other Resources 408

Appendix Writing Great HTML 411

Index 439

Acknowledgments

I was going to keep this simple, but…Thanks: to Archie & Shiela (m&d), for life, love, and their continuing support—including sending me off to college with my first computer (a Kaypro 2!); to grandma Jill, my favorite poet; to AJ, Tim, and Julie (now maybe you'll call sometime!); to Chris & Matt (the two best friends a girl could have) for making this insane world a lot more fun; to Stephanie, but don't tell her I said that; to Joycie and Jefe for the best morning tea and coffee break emails around; to Toni and Luanne for all their hard work through alpha…beta1…beta2…(!); and to Ron and Keith for giving me the opportunity to write this book. Special thanks: to Cale for making everything possible (YSTB), and finally, to the little guys who remind me everyday of what life's all about: Robert and Matthew.
Mary Millhollon

As always I'd like to thank Tom and Carly for their patience and understanding along the twisty road called writing a book. Carly particularly loves seeing her name in print and this provides another opportunity. Thanks also to my great email friends (Jane, Donna, Connie, Julie, Mike, Valerie, and all). Your tidbits and missives keep me at the computer! I'd be remiss if I failed to thank Toni and Mary for their efforts. It was great being part of the team.
Luanne O'Loughlin

I'd like to thank Karl for his patience and support (and allowing me to vent) while I was writing this book. You helped more than you know. And of course, to my parents, for encouraging me to write. Thanks for always supporting me (and, as Mary said, for giving me my first computer—a Commodore 64). And thanks to my coauthors, Mary and Luanne. You guys were great to work with, and made this three-way process surprisingly easy.
Toni Zuccarini

We really appreciate everyone at the Coriolis Group for making this book as smooth a process as possible. Special thanks to Kim Eoff, for doing a great job laying out the book, and for her helpful suggestions and flexibility. Thanks also to Keith Weiskamp, who gave the three of us the chance to write this book in the first place.
From all of us

The first guy in the door has to turn on the lights.

That's true whether you're the first member of a team to adopt a new technology, or whether you're doing it all by yourself. Being "first" means that you have no one to ask for help—and that you must find the light switch on your own.

There are undeniable benefits to being a technology frontrunner: Those first in the door can set the standards, test new approaches, and be first to market with major products. There could be millions of dollars lying on the table, waiting for the first hand that learns how to grab them.

We at Coriolis Group Books created the FrontRunner Series so that you'd have help on Day One: the day you bring that new technology product home and crank it up. This will be true even if Day One for you is Day One for the product, too. We've built working relationships with the technology leaders in our industry so that our teams of analysts and writers can be working as soon as new technology is out of the labs. When it comes to a new technology product, you're not all alone anymore. The Front Runner is here to help.

Our goal is to provide you with the best possible information on new technology products the day they're released to the public. Not "soft stuff" or hot air, either—just real, useful, practical information that you can put to work right away. We hope that this book gives you whatever additional power you need to make that final sprint over the line—and on to outstanding success in your study or business.

Jeff Duntemann

Introduction

The Microsoft Corporation has a flair for approaching an area of computing and setting new industry standards—look how Microsoft set the pace in the world of word processing. Not one to sit and veg on the couch, Microsoft is at again. There's no doubt that Microsoft's Internet Explorer 3.0 will dramatically shift how the world views the Internet. The Microsoft Internet Explorer (MSIE) introduces the prospect of complete desktop interactivity, integrating your hard drive, disk drives, local networks, intranets, and the Internet. This shift in focus is forcing popular Internet browsers, such as Netscape, to play catch-up.

Not only is MSIE giving Netscape (and other browsers) a run for its money, but MSIE is teaming up with online services, becoming the Internet client for the two most popular services around: America Online and CompuServe. America Online, while retaining its traditional interface, makes full use of Microsoft's powerful features, such as Java support and ActiveX technology. CompuServe, on the other hand, embraces MSIE wholeheartedly—interface and all.

Microsoft Internet Explorer 3.0 FrontRunner is *the* companion reader for anyone interested in learning more about Microsoft Internet Explorer 3.0, online services, and the Internet. This book starts with a short question and answer chapter addressing common Internet questions (including the ones no one wants to ask, such as, "What's the difference between the Internet, the World Wide Web, and an online service?"). Next, the *FrontRunner* details how you can easily download and customize your free copy of MSIE. Before you know it, you'll be a pro with "advanced" topics such as Internet security issues and Web page rating controls. From there, the book takes you all over the world, introducing you to hot MSIE features and cool Internet sites. You'll learn how to:

- communicate with other netizens using Microsoft Internet Mail and Microsoft Internet News
- surf the Internet with confidence and quickly find the information you want and need
- download documents effectively and safely
- interact with America Online and CompuServe using MSIE
- personalize your start page and create your own home page (yes, they're two different things)
- access the Microsoft Network areas open to you as an MSIE user
- put an end to plug-ins by using ActiveX technology

Prior to the appearance of MSIE 3.0, we (Toni, Mary, and Luanne) were Netscape junkies. After using MSIE and learning about its features, we realized that people needed to learn about MSIE's innovations—innovations sure to change how people interact with the Internet forever. We wrote this book hoping you would fall in love with MSIE's simplicity and ease of use as much as we did. No more plug-ins; no more hunting around the Internet for browser extras. Thanks to Microsoft's ActiveX technology, everything you need comes packaged with Microsoft Internet Explorer 3.0. We've gone the extra mile to show you MSIE's multimedia capabilities in Chapter 16, and in Chapter 17, we show you how to create your own home page. In fact, we've even included a complete HTML reference in the Appendix, featuring a section on Microsoft's newest extensions! (And don't worry if you don't know what HTML is—we'll tell you.)

This book is for you if you're interested in getting the most out of the Internet and want to keep abreast of the latest and greatest technology around. So pack your bags, it's time for an Internet exploration—*Microsoft Internet Explorer 3.0 FrontRunner* will take you wherever you want to go.

In the Beginning... Oh, Never Mind! 1

The Internet doesn't slice, dice or chop; it doesn't turn on when you clap (at least not yet); and it doesn't taste like mom made it. It's not a gimmick, it's the Internet, and it's here to stay.

I was going to write a big comprehensive chapter about the history of the Internet, with a detailed discussion of the evolution of the browser, but my editor said she was so sick of reading about the evolution of the browser that she didn't think she could stand to read another version. With that in mind, I bagged the browser story idea and, instead, decided to answer some common questions about the Internet and the World Wide Web. In some places, I may get a little carried away; for example, I couldn't resist giving a quick run-down on the history of the Internet (I think it is kind of interesting, but feel free to skip over the summary if it is going to put you to sleep). All-in-all, I think this chapter will help you to form a mental picture of what the Internet and the World Wide Web are all about. Of course, the technology will seem vague, but it will all become much more clear as we work our way through this book. Mainly, at this point, I want you to feel comfortable with the terms and technology that we will be using as we voyage into the electronic realm of the Internet. We have a lot of fun stuff to cover, so let's get started.

What's the Internet and What's the Big Deal?

First off, before we start to talk about anything, I have to make sure you know the difference between an internet and *the* Internet (notice the capital "I"). Now, you probably think you know the difference, but bear with me for just a paragraph, or two, then we'll talk a bit about who started this whole Internet mess.

internet vs. Internet

According to the Computing Dictionary, an *internet* is any set of computer networks interconnected with *routers* (routers are devices that forward traffic between computer systems). Appropriately vague, you might say. In contrast, the definition for *Internet* is the world's largest computer network. Neither of these definitions will make sense without knowing the definition of a network (one more definition, then I'm done with defining for a while).

What's a Network?

Basically, a computer network is a bunch of computers hooked together one way or another (how's that for non-technical?). Computer networks have been compared to TV networks, but that isn't exactly accurate. TV networks are one-way; Computer networks are two-way (or, more accurately, multiple-way). In a computer network, Computer A sends a message to Computer B; Computer B then contacts Computer C, or D, or E, etc. to get information concerning Computer A's request; then Computer B sends a reply back to Computer A. Now that I think about it, computer networks are more like calling your mom than watching a sitcom. In other words, you can call one source, your mom, to find out the latest news, a.k.a. family scoop. Your source (mom) in turn has contacted or will contact other sources (family members) so that you can get the latest news via a single phone call. (Of course, when using a computer network, you save yourself from answering the stream of questions that mom designed to help her provide your information to the rest of the clan.) To complicate this discussion further, technology now allows Computer A to send messages simultaneously to Computers B, C, D, and E (four is not the limit, it is just my limit for this discussion). In other words, you can simultaneously have your mom on one phone and your mother-in-law on another (this is called crazy if you're using the phone and *multithreading* if you are using a computer system. We'll talk more about multithreading in a later chapter).

Anyway, to get back on track, the Internet is the world's largest computer network—a worldwide network of networks freely exchanging information.

So, What's the Big Deal?

OK, so now you have a vague mental image of the Internet, but, so what? Is there anything out there that you'll find useful or interesting? Let's pretend this book is a cheesy magazine for a second: *Are your computer relationships tired and stale? Take this Internet test to find out if you need an Internet connection in your life:*

- Do you use a telephone, write letters, chat with friends, listen to the radio, watch the news, conduct research, read magazines, or seek a job? If you answered yes to any of the options, the Internet is waiting for you.

- Are you an activist, student, stockbroker, writer, designer, engineer, scientist, musician, business professional, or sports fanatic? If so, the Internet wants to keep you abreast of cutting-edge information.

- Do you garden, work, ride a skateboard, check the weather, play a sport, collect trains, own a pet, or have a family? Yes? You need to look toward the Internet.

- Do you like music, reading, games, automobiles, sailing, Star Wars, traveling, or history? If not, then you'll still like the Internet.

- Do you like shopping from home, ordering pizza delivery, or watching the Discovery channel? Regardless of your answer, you'll find a comfortable spot in front of the Internet.

- Do you like to fool around, enjoy creativity, and can appreciate the clever? Of course you do, hence the Internet will definitely appeal to your sensibilities.

- Are you six-feet-under? If not (and I hope not), then you will (and I mean *will*) find something useful or entertaining on the Internet. (By the way, if you *are* six-feet-under, than all I have to say is that my publisher did an incredible job marketing this book!)

Here are your test results: The Internet has information relevant to your work, lifestyle, hobbies, research, travels, and talents. In fact, the Internet stores so much information that you'll access data you didn't even know you wanted.

Alrighty then, we've determined your eligibility. Now, let's see who can be held accountable for today's Internetmania.

Whose Idea Was This Internet Thing, Anyway?

The United States Government, of course! At least, that's the short answer. For a little more detail, read on. A case can be made that the Internet was born in 1858 with the laying of the Atlantic cable. The Atlantic cable was established to carry instantaneous communications across the ocean for the first time. Of course, the cable was a technical failure (it only worked for a couple days), but it laid the groundwork for the cables of 1866. The cables of 1866 were completely successful and remained in use for the next century.

The Internet can also be blamed on Russia's 1957 launching of the Sputnik satellite. With the Cold War escalating, President Eisenhower felt compelled to create the Advanced Research Projects Agency (ARPA) to counter Sputnik. Within 18 months, ARPA developed the United States' first successful satellite. Several years later, ARPA began to work on computer networks and communications technology.

With the Cold War in full swing, the 1960s brought growing governmental concern as to how the country could communicate after a nuclear attack.

ARPA had a solution. ARPA created a non-centralized computer network with links from city to city. The network was specifically designed to avoid creating a primary target for enemies and to reroute computer messages when parts of the network were destroyed. By 1969, ARPANET (the name of ARPA's network) was in place. ARPANET started small, connecting three computers in California with one in Utah, but it quickly grew to span the country.

During the 1970s, ARPANET was wildly successful, growing rapidly as computer stations were added to handle the load. Universities across the country wanted to join the foray; scientists and researchers quickly began to rely on ARPANET as a collaboration tool. And it wasn't long before leisure activities, such as chatting and emailing interest groups, made their appearance.

The 1980s brought more rapid advancement. In 1983, the military portion of ARPANET broke off to form MILNET. The two networks remained connected, thanks to a technical scheme called Internet Protocol (IP). Technically, a *protocol* is a set of formal rules describing how to transmit data across a network. You can think of a protocol as a language used between computers. IP enabled Internet traffic to be routed from one network to another. While there were only two networks at the time, IP was designed to allow for tens of thousands of networks. Additionally, IP was designed so that any computer on the network was just as capable as any other. This may not seem especially notable to you, but at the time, most networks consisted of a few large central computers and quite a few smaller terminals, which could only communicate with the central systems (not with other terminals). As popularity expanded, the need for a common computer language to control the information flow became necessary, so TCP/IP (Transmission Control Protocol over Internet Protocol) was dubbed the standard computer language for computers linked to the network. TCP/IP linked the parts of the branching network (which was becoming quite complex) into what soon became known as the Internet.

In 1986, the National Science Foundation (NSF) created NSFNET, a network connecting college campuses. Initially, NSF set out to create five supercomputers to work in conjunction with ARPANET, but the plan didn't work so NSF built its own, faster network to connect their five supercomputers. By 1989, NSFNET had gained most of ARPANET's networks. By June 1990, after nearly 20 years of service, ARPANET officially shut down without any noticeable effect—NSFNET had completely taken over.

In the early 1990s, NSFNET exploded. It became clear that while the interactive network idea was flourishing, the supercomputer home-base idea was not going to work. NSF, however, wasn't phased by the turn of events. By that time, NSF was so entrenched in the network side of things that NSFNET prevailed without its original purpose of supplying supercomputer access to academicians. Other events of the early 1990s included the first dial-up service in 1990 and the introduction of the World Wide Web in 1991 by CERN (the European Laboratory for Particle Physics in Geneva, Switzerland). The World Wide Web was an enormous step in making the Internet's information widely available. By 1993, the World Wide Web enjoyed a 341,634 percent annual growth rate in service traffic. 1994 ushered in the first cyberbank. And in 1995, NSFNET reverted back to being a research network, leaving the Internet in its now familiar form, with commercial networks handling the traffic.

1995 was a big year. By then, the Internet was completely supported by interconnected network providers. Literally, the Internet belonged to everyone and no one. Traditional online dial-up systems (like AOL and CompuServe) jumped on the bandwagon, providing customers Internet access as part of their service package. And, 1995 also marks the re-entrance of the government into the Net, as the Secret Service and Drug Enforcement Agency (DEA) bore the fruits of their first Internet wiretap by apprehending three people who were illegally manufacturing and selling electronic devices.

1996 brings you Microsoft's Internet Explorer (MSIE)—the browser/application that will combine your Internet travels and desktop applications into one big interactive computing package. We'll be getting into that—that's what this book is all about.

Well, my dear reader, there's the condensed version of the Internet story. Now for your next question: *If that's the Internet, what's the World Wide Web?*

What in the World Is the World Wide Web?

Time for a short story. (I hope you don't mind—it's much shorter than that rundown on the Internet I just gave you).

Once upon a time, a long time ago, there lived a spider of unusual intellect named Jim. Jim met up with the lead ant at the time, Donna. The ants, as usual, were incredibly successful, so Jim tried to convince Donna to incorporate other bugs into the ant's workgroups. Donna agreed to the plan, and soon Jim and Donna recruited grasshoppers, flies, earthworms, and spiders to become partners in the venture. The bugs thought it was a splendid idea, so they got together and created an elaborate labyrinth of anthills, spider webs, burrows, and tunnels. The system was in place; it looked perfect; it was time for the work to begin. Much to the bugs' disappointment, chaos ensued. While all the connections were in place, flies had a hard time navigating the tunnels, grasshoppers found it difficult to stay in line, earthworms were just too heavy to walk across the spider webs, and of course the ants' expectations were much too high to be met by any of the other bug groups. What the bugs had was a network. What the bugs needed was something or someone who could cross all mediums of the network safely—they needed a universal bug.

This story is (of course) the perfect analogy for our Internet/World Wide Web discussion. The Internet is the infrastructure for transmitting information—an infrastructure made up of computers, phone lines, and information bases, called *servers* (rather than anthills, spider webs, and tunnels). Unfortunately, just as spider webs couldn't support the earthworms, not all computers could support all computer file formats appearing in the Internet. It would have been impractical to include every available protocol for understanding the various document formats in all computers. We needed our own universal bug. We needed an information system that would support all (or most) of the protocols in existence on the Internet. We got the World Wide Web.

The main information system on the Internet today is the World Wide Web (also referred to as simply "the Web" or WWW). Nowadays, when you deal with the Internet—you'll most likely deal with the Web.

Specifically, the Web is a system for organizing, transmitting, and retrieving information of all types. The Web was originally conceived and developed at the CERN laboratory in Switzerland by Tim Berners-Lee. Originally, the Web was aimed at the High Energy Physics community, but it attracted a great deal of interest and quickly spread beyond that arena. Currently, the Web is the most advanced information system on the Internet, and it is equipped to embrace many future advances, including new networks, protocols, and data formats (including the much talked about Java).

Central to the idea and organization of the Web are *hypermedia documents*. Hypermedia documents are documents consisting of text, graphic, audio, and video files that may be traversed in a non-linear fashion using *links*. Links can take you from section to section within a Web document, or they can enable you to jump from one document to another with minimal limitations (more on links later in this chapter). Aside from linking capabilities, hypermedia documents can contain nontextual material as well as plain text. While the Web was originally intended only to link text documents, it is now possible to transmit pictures, audio clips, and even movies stored in a variety of electronic formats. In addition, the Web can support documents written in PostScript, ASCII, and HTML, among other languages.

So seamless are the links between hypermedia documents that users literally follow these pathways around the world without ever knowing the actual file location. Although these documents are truly hypermedia, containing information in various formats, they are almost always called hypertext documents. In this book, I use the term *hypertext*, but keep in mind that Web-based documents are always hypermedia in nature.

Before I close out this section, I want to point out one more item of interest about the Web. Electronic Web files are transmitted using the client/server model. This means that one system serves the request of another (client) system. Clients are fancy names for browsers. MSIE is your client. Servers are programs normally located on remote machines that respond to incoming client connections and provide a service. Currently, any user accessing information on the Web must use a client, and any information made available on the Web must be done through a server. In other words, a browser asks the server for a document (asking for a document is accomplished by either clicking on a link or sending a query for a particular Web document), then the server finds the document and hands it to the browser for viewing. The document resides on the client's machine only as long as the document is being viewed.

The Internet picture should be making more sense to you. First, there is the infastructure of the Internet. Then there's the World Wide Web—an electronic web of files. So, the next logical question is this: What are those online services that beg for business and continually send free disks in the mail?

What's an Online Service?

The job of an online service is to make your life easier. Basically, online services offer easily accessible connections to chat groups, business news, sports, and other information. Online services offer their members everything on the Internet plus a selection of goodies licensed by the service itself, then wrap it all up into a pretty, easy-to-use package. Online services take care of most of the technical details for members, too—leaving you the freedom to point and click on services you want to obtain. If you don't want to take the time to configure your own settings or find your own information, you may want to subscribe to an online service. This book includes two chapters on online services—America Online and CompuServe—but also contains enough information to make you knowledgeable enough to find the information you want and need without using an online service. Following, are short descriptions of two online services that have agreed to include the Microsoft Internet Explorer as part of their online services package.

America Online

America Online (AOL) is an online service provider based in Vienna, Virginia. According to Morgan Stanley, America Online became the largest and fastest online service in the world in October of 1995. The latest figures put AOL's membership at more than 5.5 million members, adding over 300,000 subscribers per month. AOL offers its subscribers electronic mail, interactive newspapers, magazines, conference capabilities, software libraries, computing support, investment advice, online classes, and games. In October 1994, AOL made the Internet available to its subscribers by providing FTP capabilities, and in May of 1995, AOL gave members full Internet access, including a gateway to the World Wide Web, as part of the online services package.

CompuServe Information Service

CompuServe Information Service (commonly referred to as either CompuServe or CIS) is the next largest online service after AOL. CompuServe has a base of over 4.7 million subscribers, and adds approximately 200,000 members per month—mostly overseas. CompuServe includes a wide variety of information and services to its members, including bulletin boards, online conferencing, business news, sports, weather, financial transactions, electronic mail, travel and entertainment data, and online computer publications.

How Does MSIE Fit into the Internet Picture?

By now you might be getting an idea how MSIE—a browser, a.k.a. client—fits into the Internet picture. MSIE, one of today's hottest browsers, enables Internet users to view multiple information formats on the Internet. MSIE is a far cry from the first browser developed at CERN. The CERN browser was a character-based (that is, non-graphic) browser. CERN wasn't being lazy when they created text-only processing. Virtually, all Internet-related programs were character-based until very recently. The reasoning was strictly practical because almost everyone accessing the Internet was using a non-graphical (text-based) terminal over a relatively slow modem.

The character-based Web browser from CERN was not a lot of fun to use and tended to be cryptic in operation. As a consequence, few network administrators put their information into Web-browsable format until the official introduction of the Mosaic browser in early 1993. Upon Mosaic's release, there were perhaps 100 Web servers in the world. Since that day, there has been an explosion in the number of Web server sites and in the volume of information contained on those sites. Web-related Internet traffic has been growing at a phenomenal rate. One demographic survey revealed that of the 37 million people aged 16 and over in the United States and Canada who have access to the Internet, 18 million have used the Web in the past three months. And as far as browsers, despite Mosaic's early start, MSIE and Netscape are the top contenders in the Web Browser Wars.

Looking at the wonderful capability of MSIE, it is incredible to believe the technology is so new. Now, instead of viewing text-only documents on the Web, we can click on a link that points to supplemental documents that may reside halfway around the world or in the next room. And, as I mentioned earlier, MSIE makes it possible to translate graphics, videos, animation, audio, applets (more about those later), and formatted text files easily and quickly. Figure 1.1 displays the MSIE browser pointing to the Microsoft Network Start page.

What's a Web Page?

Information on the Web is organized into *pages*, which are blocks of data identified by an Internet address. All documents published on the Web are called *Web pages*. Each Web page is usually stored on a Web server as a hypermedia document designed to be viewed by clients or browsers. Hypermedia pages are created and stored in *Hypertext Markup Language (HTML)*. We'll cover HTML in much more detail later in this book.

The choice of the term "page" for a Web document is unfortunate. Most computer users associate a page with what they see on the screen. Such is not the case with most Web "pages," which may be quite long. Substitute the word "document" in your head when you see the term "page," at least until the whole Web world begins to make sense. You may move through the page, as you would with any other Windows document, by moving the

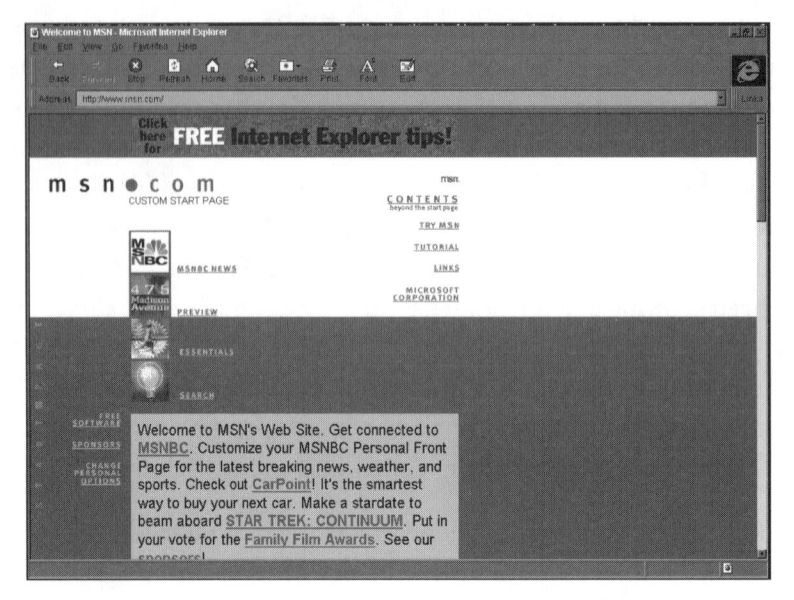

Figure 1.1 A look at Microsoft Network's start page using the Microsoft Internet Explorer.

scroll bar pointer with the mouse or by pressing the Page Up or Page Down keys, depending upon which direction you wish to travel. You can use the back and forward toolbar buttons (see the arrows at the top of the MSIE browser window shown in Figure 1.1) to move to the previous or next page. You can also use menus and Web addresses (more about those in this chapter, as well as subsequent chapters) to visit other pages.

The Home Page Component

A home page is a Web page with a special function. A home page is simply an HTML document that serves as the first document transmitted by a Web server when you access a Web site. It may all sound slightly confusing to you now, but if you stick with this book, you'll be creating your own home page by Chapter 17.

Understanding Links

After you open MSIE, you'll see that certain areas of text in the document view area are underlined, have a different color, or both. These items are *links* (technically, *hyperlinks*) to other resources and locations. Other resources may be textual or they may contain multimedia information.

The purpose of document links is to provide a nonlinear way for you to access information. Gone are the days of sequential processing and presentation. Now you can go where your interests lead you.

A hyperlink has two components: an *anchor* and a *reference.* The anchor is the displayed screen presence of the link (which may be either text or graphics), whereas the reference is the full Internet address of a document or service. You see the anchor as a link whenever the page is displayed; for the most part, references remain hidden. When the cursor strays over an anchor, its reference can be read in the status bar at the bottom of the screen. When you click on a displayed anchor, MSIE reads the reference address shown in the status bar, fetches the Web site, and automatically displays the document, plays the audio, shows the movie, accesses the newsgroup, runs the animation, or displays the graphic.

Now, when someone tells you they've found a cool Web page, you'll have an idea of what they are talking about. But what if they tell you they found a cool Web *site?* Is there a difference? Read on.

What's the Difference between a Web Page and a Web Site?

Anytime something is published on the Web, the information must physically be stored on a computer somewhere. This location is called the Web site. A Web site can be anywhere in the world. There are three basic components of a Web site: a computer, an Internet connection, and a really big hard disk. Ideally, the Web site should be connected to the Internet 24 hours a day in order for users to be able to access the Web site information at will.

Usually, the Web site's main mission in life is to transmit information. This is where the server part of the client/server model comes in (remember we briefly discussed MSIE as a client/server model). The Web server is specialized software that transmits information, such as a Web page, from a Web site to a user's computer.

What's Up with All Those Dots and Coms Everyone's Always Talking About?

To the uninitiated, all those wwws, dots, and coms flying around today probably sound meaningless and confusing. Never fear, they aren't as bad as they sound. Believe it or not, these items make up the addresses of Internet sites. As you may have noticed, most Internet addresses contain the WWW acroynym, indicating that the document is part of the World Wide Web network. Following is a typical Internet address:

http://www.microsoft.com

You use an Internet address to view a particular Internet document by typing the address into the Address box of your browser. The Internet address, more commonly known as a Universal Resource Locator (URL), can tell you a lot about a file. For example, the *http* portion of the address indicates that the document needs to be transmitted using the *hypertext transport protocol* (remember, a protocol is the language one computer uses to communicate with another).

We'll talk more about URLs and protocols in Chapter 2. For now, check out Table 1.1, which shows the six protocols most commonly used by Internet surfers.

After a URL's protocol designation, comes the URL's domain name, such as the **www.microsoft.com** in our example. The *dot-coms* are URL suffixes (commonly called top-level domains) that tell you what type of site the URL accesses. Table 1.2 contains a list of the common top-level domain abbreviations.

Looking back to our example URL, we can see now that **http://www.microsoft.com** indicates a commercial organization.

All of this might not make a whole lot of sense right now, but don't worry. We'll go into much more detail about URLs and protocols in a later chapter. For now, feel comfortable knowing that all those dots and coms actually make sense, and that they are parts of an URL that you can use to call up a Web page.

Table 1.1   File Protocols

Protocol	Definition
http://	Hypertext Transfer Protocol. The client-server protocol used on the World Wide Web for the exchange of HTML documents.
https://	Hypertext Transfer Protocol, Secure. The client-server protocol used on the Web for the exchange of HTML documents passing through a security connection (Secure Sockets Layer).
ftp://	File Transfer Protocol. A client-server protocol used to send and retrieve files from one computer to another over a TCP/IP (Transmission Control Protocol over an Internet Protocol) network.
gopher://	A protocol used to access a distributed document retrieval system originating from the Campus Wide Information System at the University of Minnesota. Many hosts on the Internet now run Gopher servers. Gopher has been largely superseded by the World Wide Web.
news:	A prefix used to indicate a newsgroup or bulletin board site, where users can hold discussions, as well as post and read articles.
telnet://	The Internet standard protocol used to log on to a remote system.
wais://	Wide Area Information Servers. A protocol used to access a distributed information retrieval system similar to Gopher and the Web.
file://	The protocol used to indicate that the path leads to a file on your hard drive.

Table 1.2   Top-Level Domain Abbreviations

Abbreviation	Meaning
com	Commercial organization
edu	Educational institutions
gov	Government institutions
int	International organizations
mil	Military sites
net	Networking organizations
org	Anything else

Is Learning How to Surf Really a Prerequisite?

Well, no, not really. I hope you haven't bought your board and wet suit already. What you need to learn is how to explore and control the waves, seas, and oceans of Internet information to help you get where you want go. If you follow along with this book, you will be able to surf better than a majority of Internet users—in fact, you'll be surfing with the pros, taking advantage of Internet and World Wide Web features that often go unnoticed by the untrained Internet eye.

When's the Best Time to Explore the Internet?

Now!—especially since you have this book in your hands. This book was written and designed to be a hands-on guide and resource. You can refer to this book on an as-needed basis, or you can read through it and join in on the expeditions. If you include this book in your explorations, you're sure to visit quite a few outstanding sites—many of which can take you to other sites beyond the scope of this book. Sure you could learn some of the information in this book by trial and error, but why waste your time? We've done a lot of footwork for you.

Chapter in Review

A short Chapter in Review section appears at the end of every chapter in this book. Sometimes new information is added in this section, other times it's a chance to chat, but most of the time the Chapter in Review encapsulates some of the topics and ideas presented in the chapter. I won't spend any more time explaining this concept, I'll just do it.

In this chapter, we covered the Internet from its earliest beginnings. You saw that the difference between the Internet and the World Wide Web is that the Internet is the actual hardware network, while the Web is an electronic web of files using the Internet. The Web uses the client/server model, in which the client, such as the MSIE browser, asks a Web site (the server) for a file, then the Web site finds the file and returns it to the client using specialized software called Web server software.

We also took a look at online services, which are networks that provide their members with access to information on private networks, as well as access to the Internet.

Our discussion then answered the basic questions any new Internet user would have. We defined such terms as Web page, Web site, home page, links, and URL (now you finally know what all those dots and coms mean).

Just about anyone can find information of interest on the Internet. MSIE simplifies your quest by providing you with cutting edge Internet tools. In addition, MSIE integrates desktop capabilities with browser features, thereby taking your system one step closer to the completely integrated workstation of the future. The more you understand the Internet, the World Wide Web, and MSIE, the more benefits you'll reap from the technology, and the more fun you'll have as you surf.

1982
TCP/IP established as the common protocol.

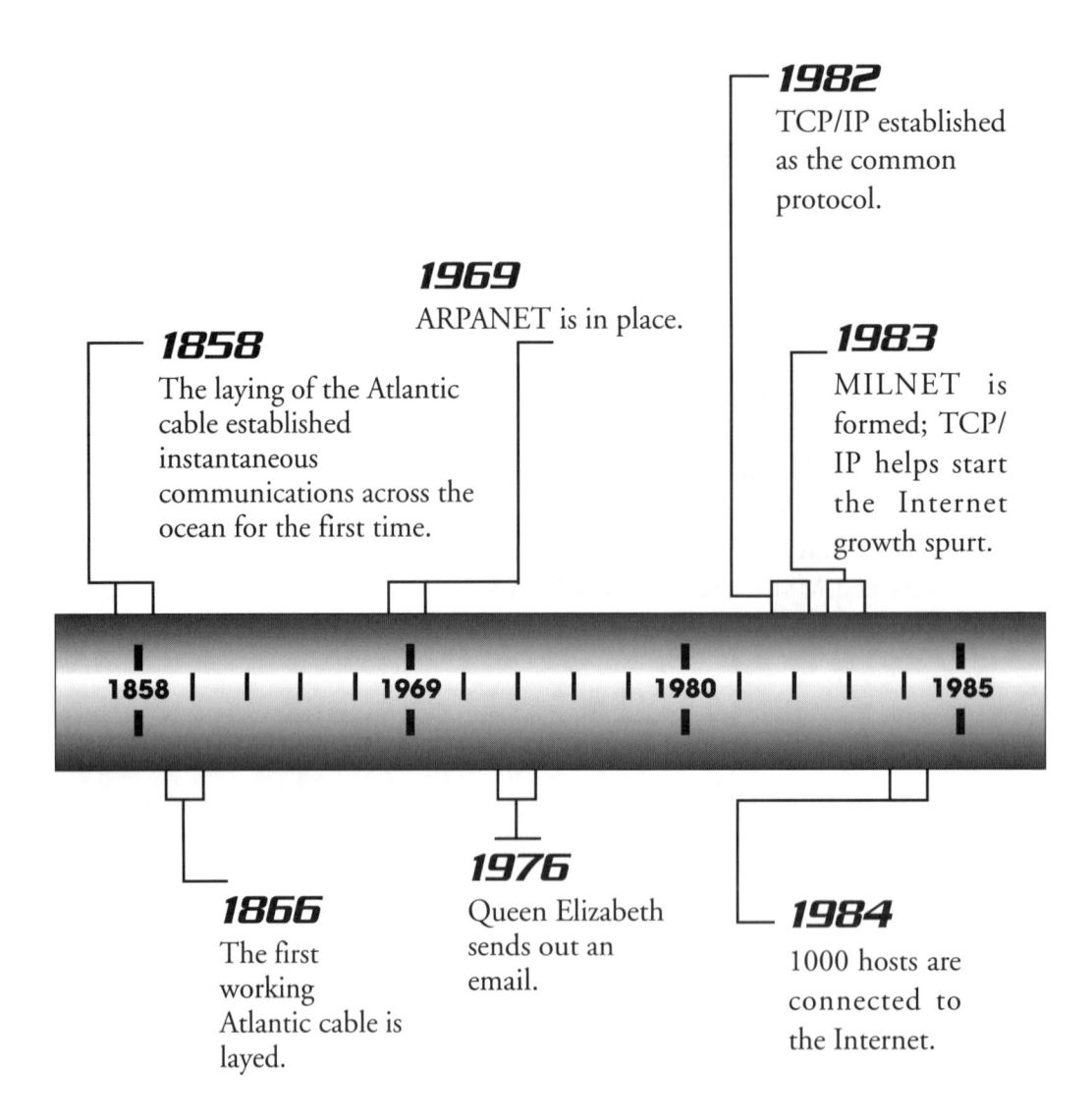

1969
ARPANET is in place.

1983
MILNET is formed; TCP/IP helps start the Internet growth spurt.

1858
The laying of the Atlantic cable established instantaneous communications across the ocean for the first time.

| 1858 | | | 1969 | | | 1980 | | | 1985 |

1866
The first working Atlantic cable is layed.

1976
Queen Elizabeth sends out an email.

1984
1000 hosts are connected to the Internet.

In the Beginning...Oh, Never Mind!

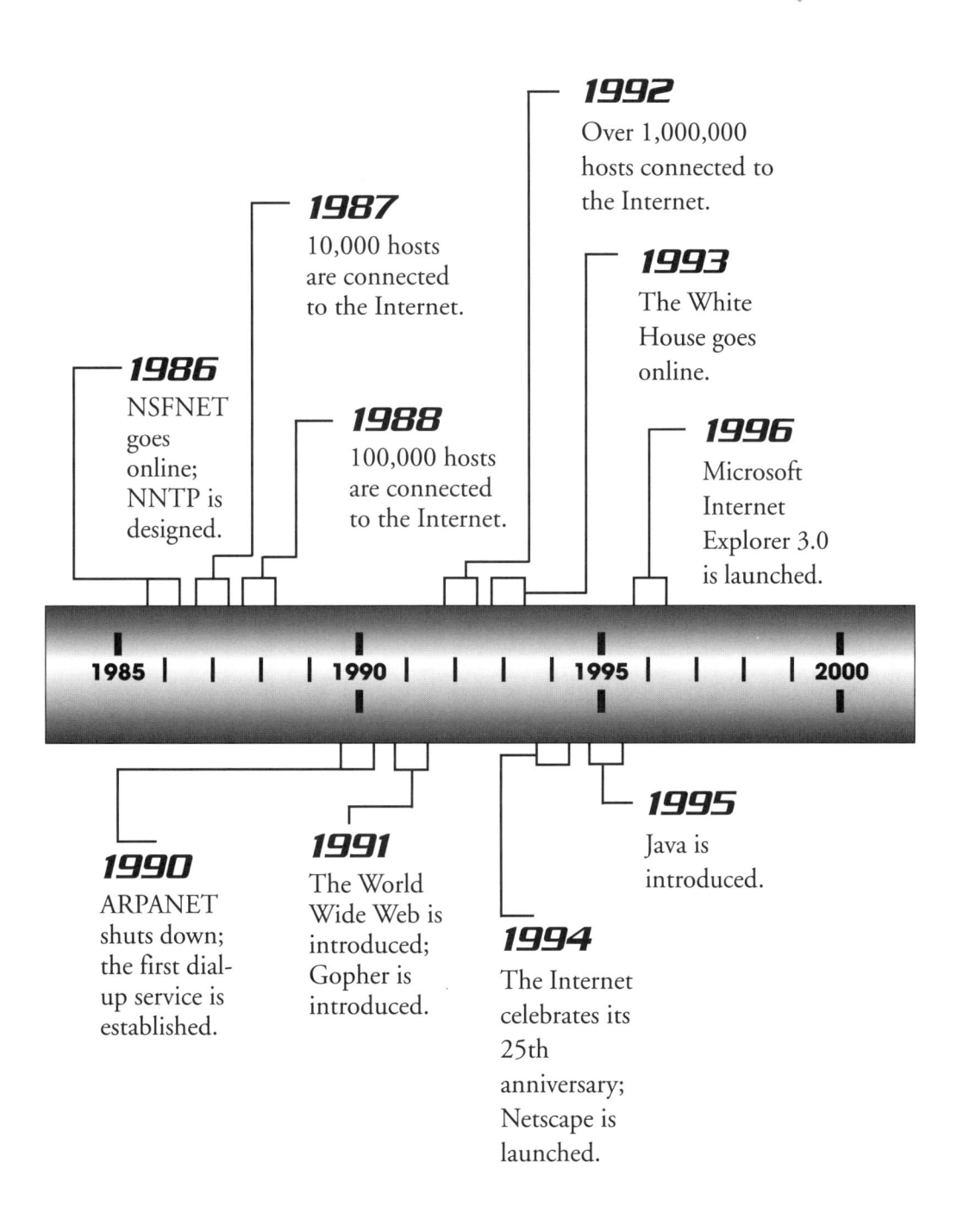

1986 NSFNET goes online; NNTP is designed.

1987 10,000 hosts are connected to the Internet.

1988 100,000 hosts are connected to the Internet.

1992 Over 1,000,000 hosts connected to the Internet.

1993 The White House goes online.

1996 Microsoft Internet Explorer 3.0 is launched.

```
| 1985 |   |   | 1990 |   |   | 1995 |   |   | 2000
```

1990 ARPANET shuts down; the first dial-up service is established.

1991 The World Wide Web is introduced; Gopher is introduced.

1994 The Internet celebrates its 25th anniversary; Netscape is launched.

1995 Java is introduced.

MSIE Up and Running

2

Try building a house constructing the roof first. You could do it, but there's an easier way. The same rings true for MSIE. Build a solid foundation, and you'll have the browser you've been looking for.

*C*onsider your Internet Explorer a shell application for all your computing needs. Now, think of the places your computing needs take you: desktop, disk drives, CD-ROM drives, local area networks, intranets, and the Internet. All Internet browsers take you to the Internet; some browsers enable you to access certain desktop files; MSIE does all that and more. In fact, MSIE is so flexible, I have a hard time calling it an Internet browser at all—the term is much too limiting. As you'll soon discover, MSIE is *the* application of choice for users who want to experience the future of true computing interactivity.

As with most things worthwhile, you need to lay some groundwork before you can reap the full benefits of MSIE (you knew there had to be a catch!). That's the sole purpose of this chapter's existence—to help you create a firm foundation for your Internet/MSIE experience. Now, you may be thinking that laying groundwork sounds kind of dull and dry, and maybe you'll just skip over this chapter. Wait! I beseech you. For your sake, I have sincerely tried to avoid putting you to sleep in this chapter. Not only do I point out all the basic features of MSIE and give you an overview of what types of sites are on the Internet, but I've thrown in some cool tips, a top-of-the-line multimedia site, and, if you stick with me long enough, I've included a pretty cool game using Java technology. How's that for bribery? OK, the choice is yours—you're more than welcome to read on.

Installing MSIE

First things first. Do you have the latest version of MSIE on your desktop? If not, there are a couple ways you can get it.

If you have an online service provider, such as America Online or CompuServe, MSIE probably comes with your package. If you have any installation questions, call your online service representative. Installation is also covered extensively in Chapter 6 (AOL) and Chapter 7 (CompuServe).

If you already own a version of MSIE, or if you're downloading it for the first time, you're in luck. You can easily download the latest version of MSIE from the Microsoft Internet Explorer download site at **http://www.microsoft.com/ie/download**.

Once you access the Internet Explorer download page, display the version you wish to download in the drop-down list box, then click on the Next button. Follow Microsoft's prompts until you arrive at the actual MSIE download page. You should see a Web page with a number of executable file links (files ending with the .exe extension) to the latest version of MSIE. Click on the link closest to your location. If that link is busy, click on another (all in all, it doesn't really matter which site you use to download MSIE). Soon you should see a dialog box asking if you would like to Open MSIE or Save it to disk.

If you are upgrading your MSIE version, select the Open document option when queried—opening the document will update your current version of MSIE automatically. If you are an MSIE newbie, select the Save As option to save MSIE to your hard drive. For more about downloading, see Chapter 13.

Finding MSIE After You Download
If you have trouble finding the downloaded MSIE file, click on the Start button in your Windows 95 taskbar, point to Find, click on Files Or Folders, then search for the name of the file you just downloaded.

After MSIE downloads, if you're an updater, you've just successfully upgraded your version of MSIE. The next time you open MSIE, you'll be working with the latest version. If you're an MSIE newbie, you'll need to pay a visit to the Internet Connection Wizard before you can use MSIE. Here's how to contact the Wizard:

1. Ensure that you have your:

- Service provider's name
- Account name
- Password
- Dial-up telephone number
- Domain Name System (DNS) server address
- IP address and submask (may not be required)
- Email address information (if you want to use MSIE Internet Mail)

    You can get all of this information from your Internet Service Provider. (Examples of ISPs are MCI, Primenet, and Earthlink. Don't be alarmed if I didn't mention your ISP, there are literally millions of ISPs out there).

2. Double click on the MSIE icon on your desktop to install MSIE.

3. Access the Internet Connection Wizard by clicking on your Windows 95 Start button and choosing Programs|Accessories|Internet Tools|Get on the Internet. The Internet Connection Wizard will walk you through the process of connecting to the Internet. If you can't find the Internet Connection Wizard, use your Windows 95 Start button and run a search for *Internet Wizard*. Scroll through your search results until you find the Get on the Internet file or shortcut. The introductory Internet Connection Wizard dialog box displays in Figure 2.1.

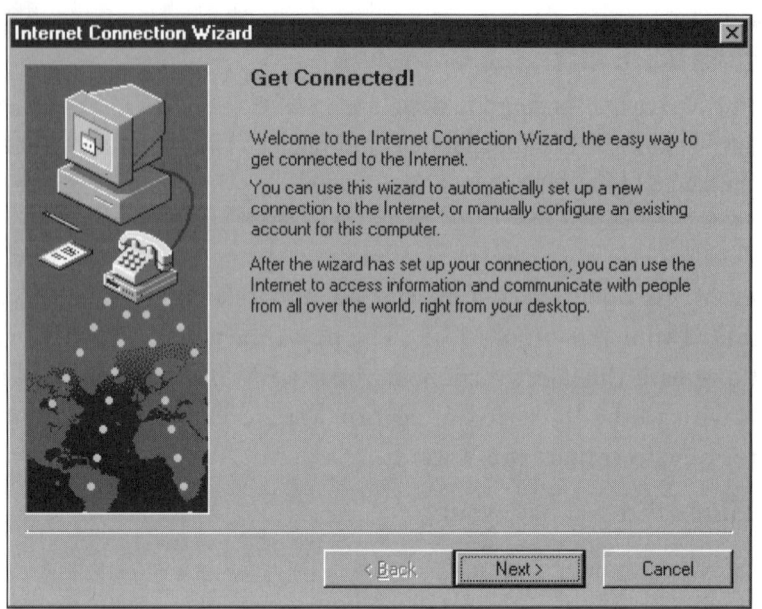

Figure 2.1 Meeting the MSIE Setup Wizard.

See that wasn't so bad! Now, double click on the Internet Explorer icon on your desktop; let's take a gander at the parts of the MSIE window.

The MSIE Browser Window

The folks at Microsoft based the MSIE interface on basic Windows design principles, making the MSIE window feel very familiar to most PC users. Figure 2.2 displays the MSIE window and its components.

Notice the typical Windows features: title bar, window sizing buttons, menu bar, toolbar, display window, and scroll bar. Additionally, MSIE displays an Address box, a Links toolbar button, and a status bar as parts of the browser window. I'm assuming you are already quite familiar with Windows, so I won't bore you with a discussion covering title bars, window sizing buttons, and scroll bars. On the other hand, I'm willing to venture into mildly interesting (and definitely informative) discussions about MSIE's menu bar, toolbar, Address box, Links toolbar button, display window, and status bar. We'll be dealing with MSIE's components throughout this book, so we may as well start off on the right foot by being clear on how to

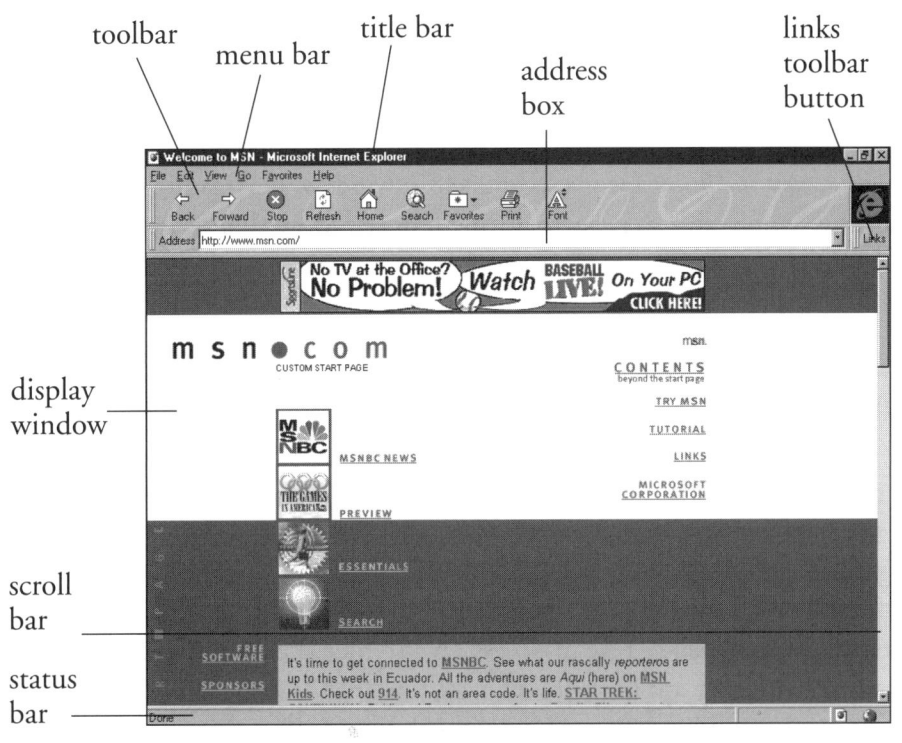

Figure 2.2 The Microsoft Internet Explorer window has components that will be familiar to Windows users.

use MSIE's components. Let's start at the top and work our way down. The first item on our agenda is a discussion of MSIE's menu bar.

Menu Bar

Like most Windows applications, MSIE offers a myriad of ways to execute commands. As you probably know, every Windows application comes equipped with a menu bar—MSIE is no exception. I'm going to run through the menu commands quickly. Don't feel the need to memorize them; I'm just listing the commands so you know the capabilities of MSIE. Later, when you're surfing the Net, you can pull down the menus or refer back to this chapter section when you are trying to find a particular command. As with all software applications, the more you use MSIE, the sooner you will become adept at using the available options.

File Menu Commands

The File menu, shown in Figure 2.3, contains commands similar to those you find in the File menu of all Windows applications.

File|New Window—Opens a second MSIE window. This feature is extremely useful when you are performing lengthy downloads (more about downloading in Chapter 13) or when you want to view more than one Internet site at a time.

Displaying Links in Their Own Windows

Here's a cool keyboard shortcut. If you want to view a link in a separate window, it's a snap: just hold down the Shift key while you click on the link.

File|Open—Displays the Open dialog box, as shown in Figure 2.4. You use the Open dialog box to access an Internet site by entering the site's Address information in the text box. Using the Open dialog box is similar to using the Address box located beneath the MSIE toolbar.

File|Save As File—Saves the current Web page to your hard drive according to the path and name you give the file. When you execute the File|Save As

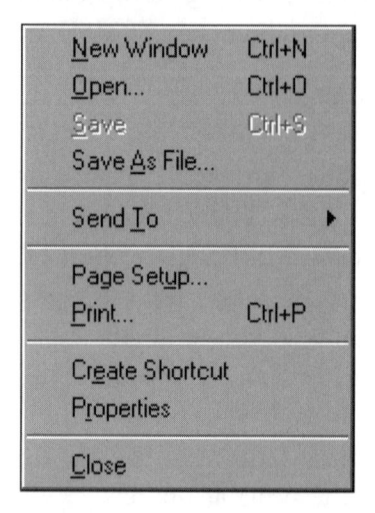

Figure 2.3 Viewing the File menu.

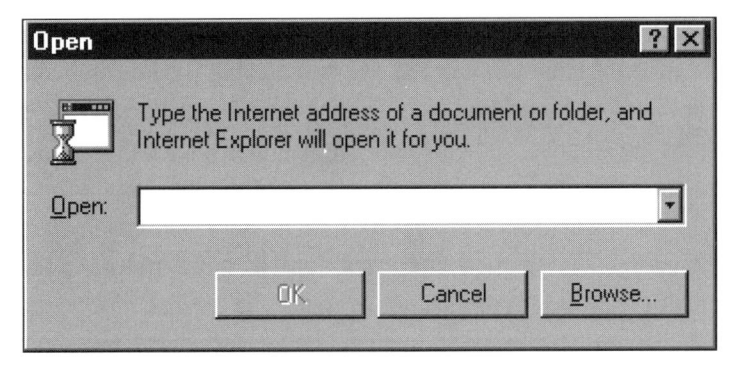

Figure 2.4 The Open dialog box allows you to access an Internet site.

File command, the Save As dialog box appears. The Save As dialog box is the same as those in most Windows programs.

You use the Save As dialog box to specify where you want to save a copy of the current Web page displayed on your screen. You can also specify what you want to name your copy of the Web page. When you save a copy of a Web page, you are only saving the text on that page. If you want to save the pictures, you will have to save each picture individually. (Each Web page has an Internet address, and each object on the page is a separate component with a unique Web address.)

File|Send To—Enables you to transmit a shortcut to the currently displaying Internet page. A shortcut is a link to a Web page. A link does not contain a copy of the Web page, rather it stores the Internet address of a site. When you click on the link, MSIE will open and call up a copy of the requested page. You can use the File|Send To command to send a shortcut to a disk, fax machine, an email recipient, or to your Windows 95 briefcase.

File|Page Setup—Allows you to specify your printed page settings. This option is very similar to the Windows Page Setup option.

Sharing Addresses

Someday we might have a paperless society, but in the meantime, there's a lot of cool stuff on the Internet that you'll want to share using the good old-fashioned

medium called paper. If you share a printed version of a Web document, you can make it easier for others to visit the site by including the Internet address in the header or footer on the printed copy. To do this, first copy the address displayed in the Address box (right-click in the Address box, then click on Copy). Next, while in MSIE, execute the File|Page Setup command. When the Page Setup dialog box appears, click on the Headers/Footers button. You'll see boxes indicating four locations on the printed page where you can place the Interent address. Paste the address into the box of your choice by clicking in the box, then pressing Ctrl+V.

File|Print—Prints the current Web page, which could consist of any number of actual pages of paper. For example, one Web page could print as many as 20 hard copy pages.

When you print a Web page from within MSIE, you can also choose to print a table of links that specifies the Internet addresses of all the links on the Web page. In addition to seeing the underlined links on your printed page, a table appears at the end of the document delineating the addresses of the links appearing on the Web page. To print a table of links, turn on the option to Print shortcuts in a table at the end of a document.

Printing Links with a Black and White Printer

If you are using a black and white printer, you may want to change your link colors to black before printing. Other colors may not display when you print, leaving large blank spaces in your printed document in place of link text. To change the color of links, display the General card in the View|Options menu and change the designated link colors to black by clicking on the color boxes. The Options cards are discussed in more detail in Chapter 4.

File|Create Shortcut—Creates a shortcut to the current Web page on your desktop. After creating a shortcut, you can click on the icon and go directly to the designated Web page.

File|Properties—Displays a General properties card and a Security card, providing information about the currently displayed site (we'll talk more about Property and Security cards later in the book).

File|Close—Closes the Microsoft Internet Explorer browser.

Edit Menu Commands

The Edit menu, shown in Figure 2.5, displays the basic edit commands available for use in MSIE.

Edit|Cut, Edit|Copy, and *Edit|Paste*—The Cut, Copy, and Paste commands in MSIE perform in the same manner as the Cut, Copy, and Paste commands in Windows applications. Cut and Copy will appear "grayed-out" unless text or another page element is selected. Generally, the only area where you can paste information while surfing the Net is in the Address box. Many times it is easier (and less error prone) to paste an Internet address, rather than retyping it in the Address box.

Edit|Select All—Selects all the text on the current Web page, including the picture placeholder text that is hidden beneath pictures. If you select all, copy, then paste a Web page's information into a Word file, you would view all the page text, plus picture placeholders such as <PICTURE>, wherever a graphic appears on the Web page.

Edit|Find (on this page)—Searches through the text on the page for a specified term. Executing the Edit|Find (on this page) command displays the Find dialog box.

View Menu Commands

The View menu, shown in Figure 2.6, assists you in setting your view options.

View|Toolbar—Toggles the display of the MSIE toolbar, which includes the toolbar, Address box, and Links toolbar. A check mark next to the Toolbar command indicates that the toolbar is currently displayed.

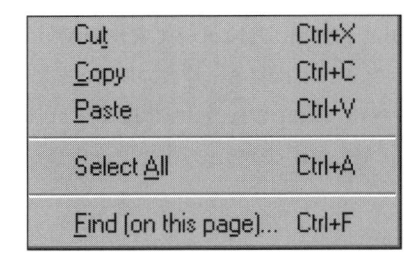

Figure 2.5 **The MSIE Edit menu provides commands for editing within MSIE.**

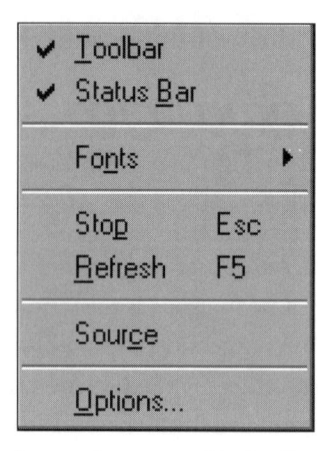

Figure 2.6 Setting your viewing preferences with the View menu commands.

View|Status bar—Toggles the display of the status bar, located at the bottom of the MSIE window. A check mark next to the Status bar command indicates that the status bar is currently displayed.

View|Fonts—Allows you to view the text on a Web page in one of five different, preset sizes. Clicking on the View|Fonts options enables you to select from the Largest to Smallest text size available (really—that's what the options are called: Largest, Large, Medium, Small, and Smallest). Not all Web pages are designed the same; this option helps ease the eyestrain when text seems too large or too small for your system's monitor (or your tired eyes).

View|Stop—Immediately stops MSIE from accessing a link, site, or current process, such as downloading a file or opening a large graphic. This command is useful when a process is taking much longer than you anticipated, and you are ready to quit the command and move on. (MSIE hopes to become so fast, that impatience will no longer be a major concern.)

View|Refresh—Displays the most recent version of a Web page. Sometimes MSIE will display a saved, or *cached*, version of a file (more about caching—pronounced *cashing*—in Chapters 3 and 4). A cached file can be outdated. Refreshing your display will download a fresh copy of the page from an Internet site.

View|Source—Displays the Hypertext Markup Language (HTML) used on the currently displayed Web page. Viewing source code is a good way to improve your HTML skills. If you see a cool Web page, you can view the source code and learn the HTML tags used to create the effect (you can learn more about HTML in Chapter 17 and the Appendix).

View|Options—Displays the General, Connection, Navigation, Programs, Security, and Advanced option cards. Chapter 4 discusses each card's features in detail.

Suppressing the Display of Web Page Items
If you have a relatively slow modem, you can shorten the time it takes to display a page by preventing MSIE from downloading graphics, sounds, videos, and animation. To speed up browsing, execute the View|Options command, then click in the Multimedia section of the General tab to turn off the features you prefer not to open during your Internet explorations.

Go Menu

The Go Menu, shown in Figure 2.7, provides directional assistance during your Internet explorations.

Go|Back—Displays previously visited sites during a browsing session.

Go|Forward—Displays the next site (if you have gone back at least once during a browsing session).

Go|Start Page—Displays your designated start page.

Go|Search the Web—Displays the MSN Internet Searches page. You use the search page to look for Web documents that match search criteria you indicate. Chapter 10 is dedicated to explaining how to use the Internet's search features and how to get the most out of your searches.

Go|Today's Links—Displays Microsoft's Surf Stories page, home of MSN's Web page picks of the day and sites of the week. Chapter 9 takes you on a comprehensive tour of the MSN Surf Stories page.

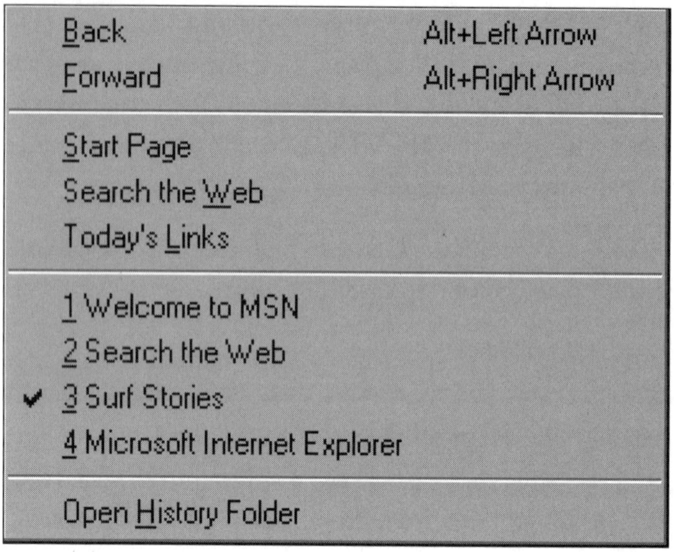

```
         Back                  Alt+Left Arrow
         Forward               Alt+Right Arrow

         Start Page
         Search the Web
         Today's Links

         1 Welcome to MSN
         2 Search the Web
      ✓  3 Surf Stories
         4 Microsoft Internet Explorer

         Open History Folder
```

Figure 2.7 The Go Menu provides commands to guide your MSIE adventures.

Go\History List—Displays a list of the sites visited during your current session. This list clears and restarts each time you open MSIE. The sites are listed in the order that you visit them, and a check mark appears next to the page MSIE currently displays. The History list in Figure 2.7 shows I started at the Welcome to MSN page, moved to the Search the Web page, visited the Surf Stories page, went to the Internet Explorer page, and finally returned to the Surf Stories page (notice the check mark). In Chapter 11, we discuss different ways you can use your History list to speed up your Internet browsing.

Go\Open History Folder—Opens your History folder, which is stored in your Windows folder by default. The History folder saves links to up to the last 300 sites you've visited. Unlike the History list, the History folder retains the information after you close MSIE. We'll talk more about the History folder later, in Chapter 12.

Favorites Menu

The Favorites menu is the home of all the Internet sites and pages you want to save for future reference. Some sites you'll access frequently enough to memorize their addresses, but for the most part, you're better off saving links to sites you like in your Favorites folder. Chapter 11 discusses how to create and manage your Favorites folder. Aside from your future Favorites list, there are only two commands listed under this heading.

Favorites\Add To Favorites—Creates a link in your Favorites folder to the currently displayed Web page. If you find a Web site or two that you want to save before you read Chapter 11, feel free to click on the Add To Favorites option. Accept all the default options for now—in Chapter 11, I'll show you how to organize the Favorites you've collected along the way.

Favorites\Organize Favorites—Opens your Favorites folder, allowing you to rearrange and edit the hierarchy of your favorite links.

Help Menu

The Help menu in MSIE is very similar to Help menus found in all Windows applications, except the MSIE Help Menu adds a twist of Internet.

Help\Help Topics—Displays the Help Topics: Internet Explorer Help dialog box containing the Contents, Index, and Find help cards. You use the Help feature just as you would in any Windows application.

Help\Web Tutorial—Takes you to Microsoft's Internet Tutorial. The tutorial is a friendly, albeit shallow, introduction to the Internet. Of course, you can check it out if you wish, but you'll find everything in the tutorial (plus a whole lot more) right here in this book.

Help\Microsoft on the Web—Opens a second menu which lists commands that will take you to a number of Microsoft pages, including: *Free Stuff, Product News, Frequently Asked Questions, Online Support, Send Feedback, Services, Search the Web,* and the *Microsoft Home* pages.

Help\About Internet Explorer—Displays a short summary about the version of MSIE you are currently running. This is helpful if you are not sure if you are using the latest version of MSIE.

Our quick rundown on MSIE menu option commands is complete. That wasn't too painful, was it? I have one more item to discuss concerning the MSIE menu bar, and then we'll move on to a review of the MSIE toolbar buttons.

Local File Menus

As I mentioned earlier (and as I'm sure to mention again), you can access local files using MSIE. When you are viewing a local configuration, the File, Edit, View, and Help menus appear the same as they appear in your Windows Explorer application. The Go and the Favorites menus display the same as when you were accessing Internet documents—this makes returning to a Web page from a local file a snap. With that said, we're now ready to review the MSIE Toolbar.

MSIE Toolbar

Currently, the MSIE toolbar consists of nine buttons (I say *currently*, because MSIE can change at the drop of a hat). Each of the buttons is a visual representation of a menu command, so I won't go into too much detail here. I've included the menu command in parentheses after each description in case you want to refer to the command definition for more detail. Remember, you can hide your toolbar by turning off the View|Toolbar command.

[Back] Displays the site you visited previously (Go|Back).

[Forward] Displays the next site; you have to have gone back at least once before you can use this button (Go|Forward).

[Stop] Immediately stops the current process (View|Stop).

[Refresh] Refreshes the current page by downloading the latest version from the Internet (View|Refresh).

[Home] Returns you to your start page (Go|Start Page).

[Search] Displays the MSN Internet Searches page (Go|Search the Web).

[Favorites] Opens your Favorites folder (Favorites|Organize Favorites).

Displays the Print dialog box (File|Print).

Cycles through the five available font sizes (View|Fonts).

Address Box

Time to wake up!—the lists are over for the moment, and the Address box is an MSIE window element that you'll want to hear about.

Most likely, you'll use the Address box every time you open your browser. The Address box is where the current page's Internet address displays. You can move to another site by typing a different address in the Address box. You can copy, alter, and edit an Internet address in the Address box. Plus, you can click on the drop-down arrow located on the right end of the Address box to view a history of the sites you've visited in the recent past. (The drop-down list doesn't display all 300 sites saved in your History folder, but it does show more than the few sites displayed in your History list.) You'll use the Address box throughout this book as you access cool sites and learn how to surf the Internet like a pro.

Links Toolbar Button

No, it's not a typo—The Links *button* really is a *toolbar*. If you click on the MSIE Links button (which is how the MSIE displays the Links toolbar by default), you should see the MSIE Links toolbar appear in the area where the Address box once shined, making the Address box appear as a button. Figure 2.8 shows the effect on the MSIE toolbar area after clicking on the Links button.

This is where I get to tell you that you can customize how your toolbars display. You can move the Links toolbar and Address box by clicking on the words *Address* or *Links*, then dragging the element to another area in the toolbar section. Figure 2.9 shows the Links toolbar displaying beneath the Address box, and Figure 2.10 shows the Address box embedded in the MSIE toolbar.

Another way you can customize the Links toolbar is to reassign the Links buttons. You can reassign each button to link to a different Web page. I'll show you how to do that in Chapter 4. For now, I recommend you wait until you see each button's offerings before reassigning the links.

Figure 2.8 Clicking on the Links button displays the MSIE Links toolbar.

Experiment with the different toolbar display options and see what works best for you. Following is a quick review of the five default Links buttons.

Today's Links—Displays the MSN Surf Stories page. In Chapter 9, we'll review the Surf Stories page in detail.

Services—Displays the MSN Essentials Directory—a one stop shop for many of your Internet research needs. Chapter 8 covers every major link included in the Essentials directory. (I guarantee you'll know more about what you can find in the Essentials directory from reading Chapter 8 than if you sat down and spent an entire day clicking on all the Essentials directory links. Knowing where to find the appropriate information on the Internet is key to your Internet success.)

Web Tutorial—Opens the MSN Tutorial (the same tutorial accessed using the MSIE Help menu). It's a friendly feature that will seem extremely simplistic after your review of this book.

Product Updates—Takes you straight to the Microsoft Internet Explorer home page.

Microsoft—Displays—you guessed it—Microsoft's home page.

Display Window

The MSIE display window is not your average Windows window…well, actually it is, it's just that you can use it for a whole lot more than viewing document pages. You'll soon learn that you can use the MSIE window to

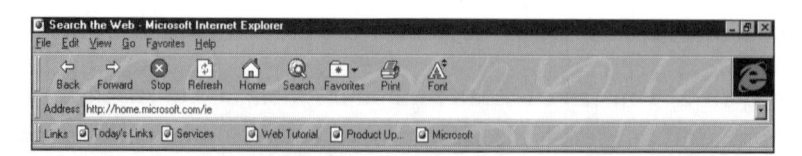

Figure 2.9 Moving the Links toolbar.

Figure 2.10 Embedding the Address box in the MSIE toolbar.

view Web pages, videos, local files, and graphics; you'll explore pages using frames (a technology enabling a single Web page to be divided into multiple, interactive sections); you'll use applications within the window to play music and games; and you'll manage your desktop files and folders without so much as minimizing the MSIE display window. Eventually, Microsoft will incorporate the MSIE display window into the Windows operating system—combining all your computer applications into a single interface. The concept is fascinating and a little bit exciting (now I *know* I'm really turning into an Internet geek!). That's about as far as I want to venture into a discussion on the display window right now. I'll show you lots of window tricks throughout this book.

Status Bar

Remember how under the View menu options you could toggle your status bar on and off? I suggest you keep your status bar turned on. It's full of good data. Whenever my status bar gets turned off for one reason or another, it drives me crazy—I catch myself looking for my little friend every few seconds.

There are a few informational elements in the status bar—which you can't tell by looking at it when it is inactive. First, the status bar displays link information. Whenever you move your cursor over a link, either the actual address hidden in the link or a shortened description of the address of the link displays in the status bar. When you click on a link, the status bar gives you a status report (imagine that!) on the search and retrieval process entailed in accessing a link. As a linked site opens on your system, a bar chart displays in the right corner of the MSIE status bar, indicating the percentage of the Web page element that is downloaded (this is helpful when large graphics are being opened). Also in the right-hand corner of the status bar is a small globe, which appears when you aren't actively dowloading Internet documents. You use the globe to indicate which International language extension MSIE should apply to documents written in foreign languages.

We'll talk more about International extensions in Chapter 3. In Figure 2.11, the status bar indicates that MSIE is opening the Web page's background music and the bar chart shows that the music file is almost completely downloaded (in addition, you can see by the graphics placeholders that there are still a few pictures that need to come in before the download is complete).

That status bar is a pretty handy tool, if you ask me. Oh, and if you want to take a look at the Open Mind site displayed in Figure 2.11, the Internet address is **http://ourworld.compuserve.com/homepages/OpenMind/OPENMIGB.HTM**.

Fortunately, the next section is all about Internet addresses—after you read that section, come back here and copy the Open Mind site address into your Address box. The Open Mind site is a great repository of cutting-edge Internet multimedia technology—it's really worth the visit.

URLs and the Address Text Box

When viewing a Web document with MSIE, you will often see links to other Internet documents. Links, usually displayed as underlined text in a

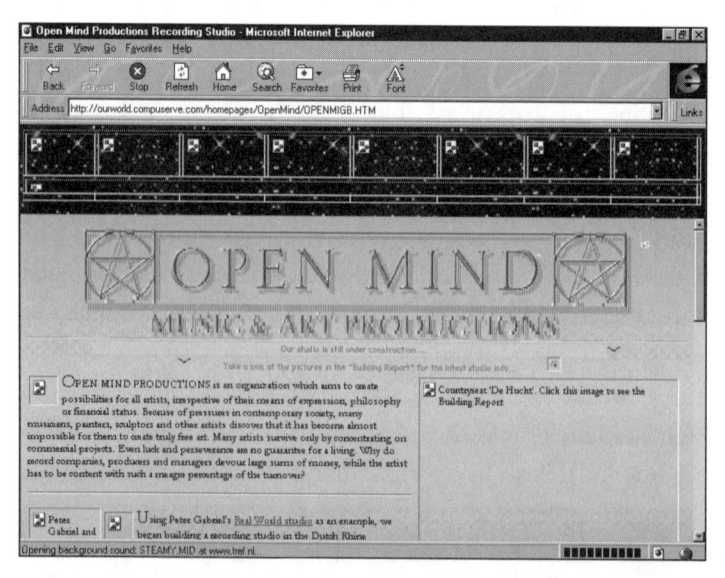

Figure 2.11 The status bar displays helpful information during your Net travels.

color other than the page's text color, contain hidden information MSIE uses to locate another Internet site. The hidden information is an Internet address—also called a *Universal Resource Locator*, or URL.

Think of URLs as standardized pointers to Internet resources. In Web terms, an Internet resource might be a picture, sound, video, animation, text file, or any combination of these. URLs also point to Internet resources other than Web documents, enabling you to perform Gopher, Telnet, and FTP processes (we'll address Gopher, Telnet, and FTP in just a second). A URL can fetch the latest postings from a favorite newsgroup, point to a local file found on your desktop, or access a file on a locally networked machine.

In many cases, it's convenient to conceptualize a URL as the Internet equivalent of the standard DOS pathname and file name. The major difference, of course, being that a target file may reside on a server located anywhere in the world. The general concept underlying a URL is: If it's somewhere out there on the Internet, you can point to it. In this section, we will explore some common URL formats.

In Figure 1.1 in the last chapter, you viewed the Microsoft home page. The figure has the URL for the home page displayed in the Address box, located below the MSIE toolbar. Let's say you were surfing the Net and wanted to return to Microsoft's home page. One way to do this would be to enter the following URL into the Address box:

http://www.microsoft.com

Entering this URL would bring you back to Microsoft. Let's look at a few URL fundamentals. A URL can be divided into four basic sections: protocol, server name, directory path, and file name. Let's dissect these components.

The Protocol

The protocol is the first part of a URL, and it tells the browser what type of document is being requested. In our example, the protocol is the "http://" prefix. The acronym *HTTP* stands for *Hypertext Transport Protocol*. HTTP is the most popular protocol on the Internet.

A protocol is a standardized language used by both the server and client (MSIE is a client, the software that transfers a file to your desktop is a server). As we saw in Chapter 1, if computers don't speak a common language, then data transmission cannot happen. It's similar to traveling to a foreign country such as Germany. You speak English and the Germans speak German. If neither of you understands the other's language, then you couldn't communicate very well. Turning up the volume or repeating yourselves wouldn't help matters much at all.

The idea behind a protocol is to have one language that is commonly recognized by all computers hooked up to the Internet. Some of the common Web protocols, in addition to HTTP, are Gopher, Telnet, FTP, News, and File. A colon and two forward slashes separates the protocol from the remainder of the URL.

Server Name

The second part of the URL, "www.microsoft.com" in our example, is the Internet address that contains the server software name (also known as a *host* name or *domain* name). This address contains several levels. The "com" part in this example is called the *top-level domain* and indicates that the site is a commercial organization. The "microsoft" portion is commonly called the *domain* and indicates, in our example, that this site is the Microsoft site. The "www" portion indicates the document is part of the World Wide Web structure.

Directory Path and File Name

Some URLs continue with a *directory path* and a *file name* of the target file. For example:

http:// www.microsoft.com/ie/personal/default.htm

In this example, "ie" is the directory, "personal" is a subdirectory, and "default.htm" is the file name. The ".htm" (sometimes appearing as ".html" and other times not appearing at all) extension marks the file as a standard Web hypertext document. The acronym *HTML* stands for *Hypertext Markup Language*, and it is the standard coding language used to format hypermedia documents so that they can be viewed on the Internet. We will talk more about HTML later.

> **Using the "/" in a URL**
> Slight controversy exists over using a terminal "/" (forward slash) in URLs. Some Web servers strictly enforce the URL standard that states that a URL should be terminated with a /. If MSIE hangs up when given a URL with a terminal /, delete the / at the end of the URL and try again. Regardless of what the servers like, MSIE tries to keep life simple and tends to work better without extra forward slashes hanging around.

You will frequently see an http:// type of URL without a file name at the end (as with our http://www.msn.com example). By default, most servers are configured to look for a file named "index.html" (or "index.htm") when no file name is specified. A URL that only specifies the protocol and server name will normally take you to the site's main page, called the *home page*.

The protocol designation and the URL's domain name are not case-sensitive. However, path and file names *are* case-sensitive if the target resides on a Unix-based machine (and the majority of sites and servers reside on Unix machines). When copying a URL, it is best to enter the URL exactly as you see it in the original.

Common Protocol Designations

As I mentioned earlier, a number of different protocols exist. Following is a short discussion about some of the more common protocols you will encounter during your MSIE explorations.

HTTP

The most common of all protocols is HTTP, which, as I just mentioned, stands for Hypertext Transport Protocol (you may also see HTTP referred to as *Hypertext Transfer Protocol*). HTTP is used to transfer documents written in Hypertext Markup Language (HTML). HTTP servers are popular because they can distribute hypermedia information quickly and efficiently, as well as deliver hypertext documents containing embedded links.

The general form of an HTTP URL is:

http://host[:port][/path-name][/file-name]

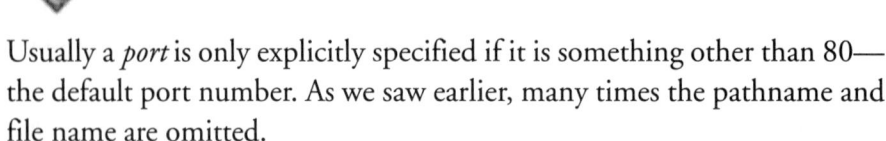

Usually a *port* is only explicitly specified if it is something other than 80—the default port number. As we saw earlier, many times the pathname and file name are omitted.

If no path is specified, the server looks for the default path. As stated previously, if a file is not specified, the server initially looks for a file named "index.html" to serve as the specified, or default, path name. The advantage of unspecified path and file names is that the location of the start-up file, and subsequently read files, may be moved to another location without having to change the URL used by clients.

Another URL variation is that sometimes the www portion of a server name may be omitted, such as the following:

http://microsoft.com

The www is implied in this instance. Entering **http://microsoft.com** in your Address box would take you to the same site as entering **www.microsoft.com**. You can't always count on the www portion of a URL to be implied, so I recommend you don't make a habit of deleting this part of a URL.

HTTPS

The HTTPS protocol is the same as the HTTP protocol, except that a level of security has been added to the protocol. The "S" stands for *Secure*. HTTPS is a unique protocol that includes a Secure Sockets Layer (SSL) protocol between the HTTP protocol and a connection protocol such as TCP/IP. I'll talk more about Internet security in Chapters 3 and 4. HTTPS URLs appear the same as HTTP URLs, except for the added S in the protocol prefix, as shown here:

https://host[:port][/path-name][/file-name]

In this protocol, the default port number is 443, and it does not have to be explicitly specified unless it is something other than 443.

FTP

FTP stands for File Transfer Protocol. FTP is a client/server protocol that allows a user on one computer to transfer files to and from another computer.

In other words, FTP supports uploading and downloading files. FTP is kind of like email, except that you transfer entire files from one machine to another instead of relatively unformatted messages. I use FTP quite regularly; as I finish each chapter of this book, I transfer it using FTP to a directory on my publisher's computer in Scottsdale, Arizona. Then, all my editor has to do is open the directory and download the chapter file. As of this writing, MSIE only supports downloading files, but it is expected to support both uploading and downloading in the near future. The general form of an FTP URL is:

ftp://[userid[:password]@]host[:port]/path-name][/file-name]

The default port for FTPing is 21, which does not have to be explicitly specified unless it is something other than 21.

Entering an FTP URL without a trailing file name causes the path's directory contents to be displayed. This may be a big help if you know the directory, but you aren't sure of the name of the latest version of the desired file.

You may have already used FTP to get a file or program from a distant site (FTP, in one form or another, has been around almost as long as the Internet). If you haven't FTPed anything yet, don't worry. You can use MSIE to retrieve files from FTP servers, even if you don't know a thing about FTPing. (That's one of the seriously cool things about MSIE. You may not even realize you are accessing an FTP site if MSIE entered the FTP prefix in the Address box for you.) You can learn more about FTP and downloading from Chapter 13.

GOPHER

Gopher is a text search and retrieval system named after the mascot of the University of Minnesota, where Gopher was created. A Gopher server treats the hierarchy of Internet databases, directories, and files as a series of menus, which you can browse through to find specific information. Of course, the easiest way to access Gopher sites is by using a Gopher URL. The general form of a Gopher URL is:

gopher://host[:port]/document-type[/path-name][/file-name]

Gopher's default port is 70 and it does not have to be explicitly specified, unless it is something other than 70. The *document type* tells the Gopher server what file type is expected by the client. As an example, a document type of "1" represents a top-level menu. Once you get below a top-level menu, the Gopher URL will have a file name and most likely a path name. The URL for the top-level menu at the University of Minnesota is:

gopher://gopher.micro.umn.edu/1

Figure 2.12 displays the top-level Gopher menu page.

About four years ago (the Mesozoic Age in Internet terms), two ambitious attempts to organize Internet information were independently initiated. One, called Gopher, began its life at the University of Minnesota. The second, called the World Wide Web (or simply the Web), emerged from the European Laboratory for Particle Physics (CERN, the French acronym) in Geneva, Switzerland.

Both Gopher and the Web (in fact, most Internet services of any kind) are *client/server* systems requiring a client program on the user side and a server

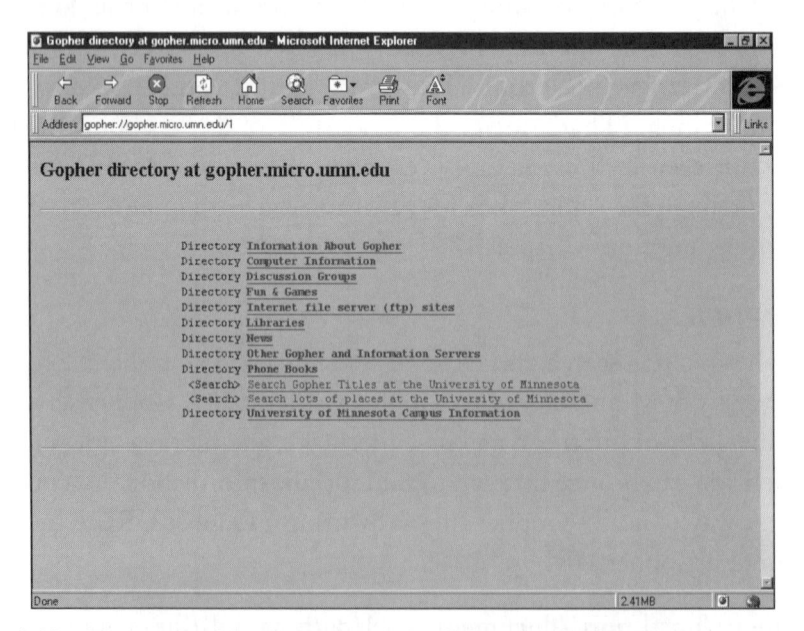

Figure 2.12   The top-level Gopher menu at the University of Minnesota.

program on the "big" system side where the "served" information resides. Gopher is a hierarchical, menu-structured, organizational technique defined in a set of protocols for client and server software. Cooperating Gopher sites organize their information in the format defined by the Gopher protocols and supported by Gopher server software. The result is an interface that yields as much information and detail as the organizers desire. The first Gopher site was brought online in 1992.

TELNET (AND ARCHIE)

Telnet is a remote logon protocol enabling users to work on one computer system via another system. In other words, Telnet allows you to use your computer to make "live" connections to other networks and computers. An account on a remote system, accompanied by a password, is typically required. When you Telnet to a remote system, your initial login sequence looks similar to the login sequence you use to open your own system. Telnet is more powerful than FTP because it lets you do more than just download files. With Telnet, you can actually log into a network or system and run programs and other services available on the network. Unfortunately, Telnet is text-based, so it might seem a little in need of a graphical facelift—especially after using Web and hypermedia documents. The general form of a Telnet URL is:

telnet://[host[:port]

Telnet's default port is 23 and need not be explicitly specified.

A common use of Telnet is to do an Archie search for a file name that exists somewhere out there in cyberspace. Archie was the first major attempt to organize Internet information that was otherwise scattered with no apparent pattern. If there was an organizational model for storing FTP-accessible files, it certainly escaped most mortals. A group of dedicated people at McGill University in Canada designed Archie, and the transition from Internet chaos to organization was launched. You can Telnet to an Archie client program and then query the Archie database about a particular file.

While Archie was a big step forward, it didn't fully solve the Internet organization problem. If you knew the name of the file, you were home free. If you didn't know a file's name, you were out of luck, because Archie doesn't know about file contents, only file *names*.

Anyway, enough of the Archie explanation, let's get back to Telnet. Let me show you how to Telnet to the Rutger's Archie server. Enter the following URL in your Address box, then press Enter:

telnet://archie.rutgers.edu

Log in as archie (no caps) when prompted for a login name. When you use the Telnet protocol, MSIE opens a Telnet window for you. The Rutgers Telnet site displays in the Telnet window shown in Figure 2.13.

USENET

If you've spent any time at all on the Internet, you've probably heard about Usenet newsgroups. Usenet is a massive networked collection of newsgroups, which are special-interest forums where Internet users get together to share common interests. Newsgroups are bulletin board systems where people can exchange ideas and read articles on related topics. In fact, newsgroups have sprung up for just about any subject area you can think, of from archery to Zen and the art of computer programming.

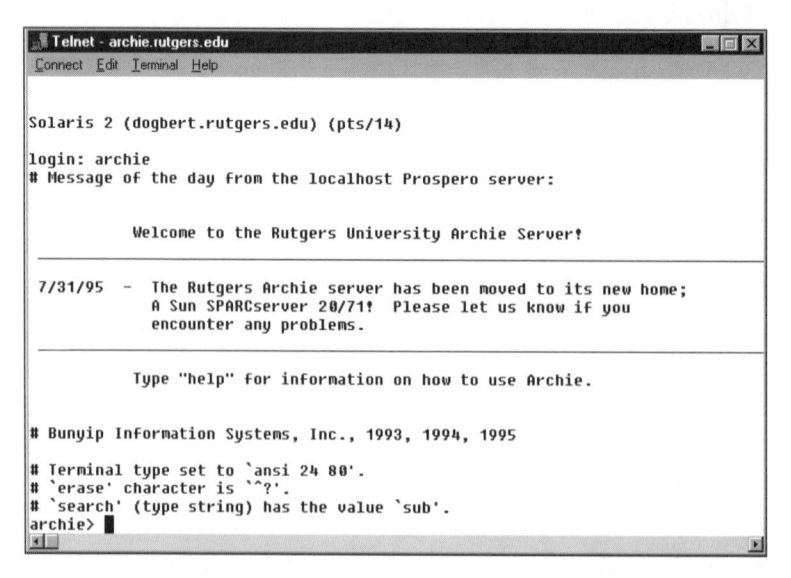

Figure 2.13   Using the Telnet protocol to access the Rutgers Archie search engine.

A word of caution: Be careful, because once you start using newsgroups, you might become hooked for life.

The URL format used to retrieve a Usenet newsgroup is different from those we have previously seen. To point to a newsgroup, use the following format:

news:group-name

As an example, the URL to retrieve the newsgroup comp.internet.net-happenings would be:

news:comp.internet.net-happenings

You'll need to perform some preliminary setup steps before you can access Internet News (and Internet Mail, for that matter) using the MSIE Address box. I'm not going to get into that here because Chapter 15 presents a detailed discussion on newsgroups.

Local File URLs

Finally, let's discuss local File URLs. Traditionally, the URL to access a local file appeared as:

file:///C:/Windows/Temporary Interent Files

There are several points worth noting in this example. There are truly three consecutive forward slash characters (/) following "file:"; it's not a misprint. Remember from our URL introduction that protocols are delineated by a colon followed by a "//", then the network host information. Three consecutive slashes indicate that the network host information is absent (or null, as computer techies like to say); therefore, the remainder of the path name must reside on the local computer, not on a remote host.

MSIE goes a few steps beyond and doesn't even request a file protocol. If you want to call up a local file, simply type a pathname, such as **c:\Windows\Temporary Internet Files**, and MSIE will know where to drop you off. Of course, if you prefer to be formal, you could access the same file by entering **file:///C:/Windows/Temporary Internet Files**.

Want to test out opening a local file? Ok, let's take a look at our Windows directory. Enter C:\Windows (capitals optional) in your Address box, then press Enter. Your display should appear similar to Figure 2.14.

You can open, delete, rename, move, and do anything else you want to do to your local files from within MSIE—it has the same effect as managing and accessing your files while in Windows Explorer. This feature is extremely useful and is specific to MSIE; no other browser offers complete file access and desktop management capabilites from within the Internet client.

Using Partial URLs

Once you have successfully retrieved a document located somewhere on the Web, you can get tricky and use a partial or relative URL to point to another file on the same site or in the same directory. To illustrate this idea, assume we have visited the Microsoft home page, having entered the URL:

http://home.microsoft.com

Let's say we now want to go to Microsoft's Internet Center page, all we would have to do is enter */internet* after the URL in the Address box, so that the URL would appear as:

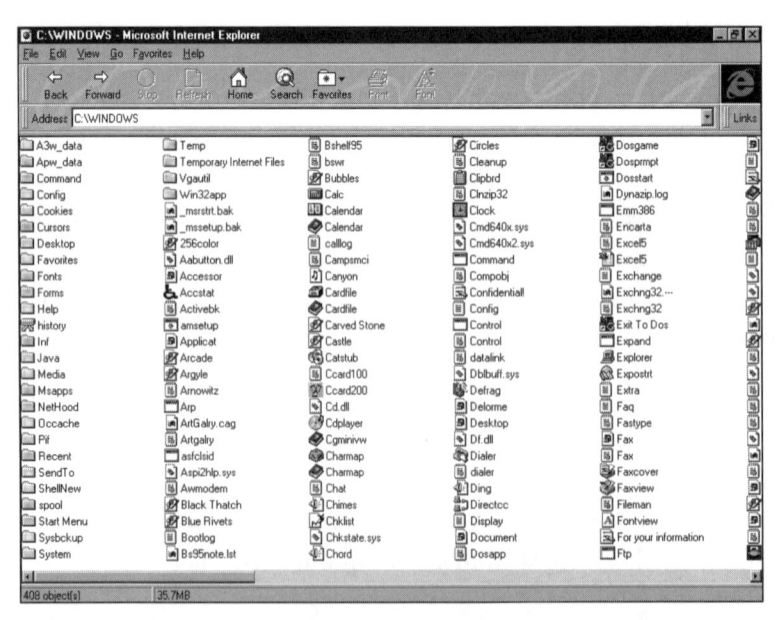

Figure 2.14   Displaying a local directory using MSIE.

http://www.microsoft.com/internet

You can also delete parts of URLs to move to other areas on a Web site. For example, let's say we were playing a game of Flip, located at **http://www.theglobe.com/fungames/flip/flip.html**.

Flip is a game using a Java applet (more about Java later). Playing Flip is similar to playing an animated version of Othello. If, after playing a couple games of Flip (which I highly recommend), you want to know what other games this site has to offer, you can visit a higher-level directory. To do this, click in MSIE's Address box, then delete the *flip/flip.html* portion of the URL. The Address box should now read **http://www.theglobe.com/fungames**. Pressing Enter will take you the The Globe's Fungames directory.

Pointing to a Site

By now, you know that you can type an Internet address, called a URL, in MSIE's Address box to point to a site on the Internet. MSIE provides a number of tools to help you point to sites quickly and efficiently. Later in this book, we'll talk about using shortcuts, Favorites, your History list, the History folder, and the Temporary Internet Files folder to access Internet documents. In the meantime, let's discuss the easiest way to surf from one Internet site to another—by clicking on hypertext links.

As mentioned earlier, the beauty of the Web is its capacity to transmit hypermedia documents. This means that pages can be designed using HTML coding that enables viewers to jump from one document to another with a single click of the mouse button. When you use the Web, you can travel around the world in a matter of seconds—without even realizing where you've been.

Hypertext links usually appear on Web pages (and Gopher pages) as underlined text displayed in a color different than the document text. Links contain Internet address information. When you click on a link, MSIE processes the address information contained in the link just as it would if you typed the address in the Address box. You can view the address of a link before you make the leap. Here, I'll show you. Go to your MSN start page, then move your cursor over the Contents link (don't click yet). When your cursor changes to a pointing hand, look in the status bar at the bottom of the MSIE window. It should display *Shortcut to roadmap.htm*. Now, if you click on the Contents link, you would "jump" to the MSN Sitemap page. (The Sitemap page used to be called the Roadmap page—hence the *Shortcut to roadmap.htm* message in your status bar.)

You can return to your start page by clicking on the Startpage link displayed on the Sitemap page. (You could also use your back arrow toolbar button, as we discussed earlier in this chapter).

See how easy surfing the Net is? No wonder it's all the rage. But, just so you don't think it's all roses out there, let me introduce you one of the Internet thorns—the error message.

Viewing an Error Message

There's no doubt that it won't be long before you fall prey to the error message. Error messages appear while surfing the Internet for a number of reasons. Some reasons for receiving an error message could be that a site is down, a link is miscoded, a Web page no longer exists, or you entered an address improperly. For example, let's say you wanted to visit Microsoft's Internet Center again, but by accident you typed the following URL in the Address box:

www.micrsft.com/internet

You should get the generic Microsoft Internet Explorer error message dialog box, as shown in Figure 2.15.

When you get this type of error message, simply click on the OK button, check your Address, and try again. In this example, you would correct the misspelling of Microsoft, then try accessing the page again.

Another type of error message appears when a site is down, missing, or too busy to accept your call. If you try to access a message with one of those criteria, you'll probably receive a default message page similar to the one shown in Figure 2.16.

Figure 2.15 Viewing an error message.

Figure 2.16 displays an HTTP/1.0 error message. HTTP/1.0 stands for Hypertext Transport Protocol version 1.0. Other down/missing/too-busy errors are displayed as DNS errors. DNS is an acronym for Domain Name System, which is the system used for naming Internet sites (recall in our discussion about the parts of a URL that a server name is also referred to as a *domain*).

A third type of error message you may encounter (which technically isn't an error message, but I'll mention it anyway) occurs when a site changes servers. If a site's manager is nice, you will see an error message with a link to a new site address when a site moves (otherwise, you'll get an error message similar

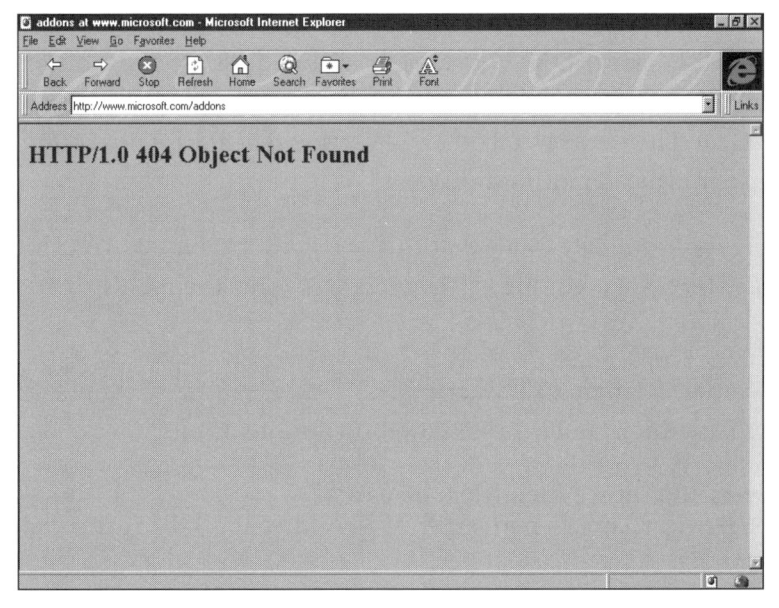

Figure 2.16 Viewing an error message when a site is down, missing, or too busy.

to the one shown in Figure 2.16. Site address change messages come in all shapes and sizes, but I'm confident you'll recognize one when you see one.

For the most part, you're going to surf the Net without too many hang-ups. When you do meet with an error message, don't give up on the first try. If the site is busy, you may get in within a matter of seconds (remember to click on your Refresh button so you don't continually call up the saved, error-message version of an address). If the server can't find the specified path, try connecting to the site's home page first, then add the directory and file extensions after you gain access to the site.

Chapter in Review

Congratulations. You made it through the laying-the-groundwork chapter. From here on out, this book only gets more fun. Well, after this Chapter in Review, of course (just a little more torture—I'll keep it short)!

MSIE comes chock full of features and options and emulates most Windows programs. This dramatically shortens the learning curve for most folks who are new to the Internet.

Behind the general usefulness of MSIE's features is the idea of the Universal Resource Locator (URL), a standardized addressing scheme used for all types of Internet data and services. Our discussion of URLs is by no means complete. There are several other URL types that are not used often enough to justify inclusion in this overview.

In the most unlikely event that this overview has piqued your interest in URLs, here are a couple URL references (and their URLs!) for you to check out:

A Beginner's Guide to URLs
http://www.ncsa.uiuc.edu/demoweb/url-primer.html

Universal Resource Identifiers in WWW
http://www.w3.org/hypertext/WWW/Addressing/URL/uri-spec.html

MSIE Extras

3

Success is the exception, not the rule. In Internet circles, MSIE rises as the exception. It's smaller, easier, quicker, and more intuitive than any other Internet browser around.

A browser is a browser is a browser. But then again, maybe not. Granted, the Microsoft Internet Explorer has all the features found in traditional browsers, but take a closer look. MSIE goes far beyond the call of duty when it comes to Internet exploration. Microsoft is loaded with extras that other browsers just don't offer. For you and me, that means MSIE improves the way pages look and work, adds tools for protecting children from adult content, handles international languages, and more. That's what this chapter is all about—MSIE's extras, the treasures found in MSIE that you may not find anywhere else.

Taking Advantage of Windows Compatibility

It comes as no surprise that Microsoft was thinking way ahead of the game when developing the Microsoft Internet Explorer. Many people figured that Bill Gates missed the boat on the Internet. That is, until Mr. Gates and Microsoft launched MSIE into the Internet scene with the usual Microsoft flourish. Microsoft shifted the emphasis away from the currently popular Internet-centered browser to an all-purpose browser that integrates Internet and operating system functions. This approach is a major advantage. MSIE implements and integrates many Windows features, making MSIE especially intuitive. Many user interface improvements and system services introduced with Windows 95 appear in MSIE. Familiar Windows technology, such as context menus, shortcuts, and drag-and-drop capabilities, is prepared to serve you in MSIE, just as it has in Windows.

Throughout this book, you will see features that feel familiar to you from your Windows experience. For example, organizing your list of Favorite sites on the Internet is similar to using Windows Explorer (see Chapter 11). You can right-click to your heart's content or you can use keyboard commands for quick access to MSIE features and options (see Chapter 12 for a discussion on right-click menus and keyboard commands). You can also customize your MSIE toolbars (as we discussed in Chapter 2).

Another Windows feature added to MSIE is called *Smooth Scrolling*. Smooth Scrolling helps you keep track of content while scrolling through a page packed with information. Pressing the Page Up or Page Down keys, or using the scrolling bars, scrolls the page without any jerky movements.

As you work your way through this book and as you gain experience using MSIE, you'll come to appreciate Microsoft's intuitive approach to computing. With MSIE, Microsoft takes a huge leap forward toward blending your desktop, local area network, and the Internet into one big, happy communication system.

Speeding Up Performance

All right, you say, so MSIE is a lot like Windows. But what about performance? What about speed? Obviously, quite a few people browsing the Web today are easily frustrated by the length of time it takes to download images, applications, and lengthy text, not to mention the wait experienced just to connect to different sites. Microsoft took the time to think about speed and came up with some solutions. MSIE supports several simple mechanisms to help quicken the pace of browsing:

- *ISDN Support*—MSIE enables you to connect to the Internet via an Integrated Services Digital Network (ISDN) line. An ISDN line is a high-speed digital telephone line that enables the transmission of Internet information at much greater speeds than traditional analog lines. ISDN lines are more expensive than basic telephone lines, but if you are an Internet junky, an ISDN line might be for you.

Why Does My Modem Take So Long?

One of the major drawbacks of the Plain Old Telephone Service (POTS) is its analog nature. Analog is particularly problematic for transferring data applications. Currently, most computers are digital devices transmitting computer data over analog lines. A process called modulation takes the computer's binary ones and zeros and converts them to a series of analog tones. On the receiving end, a process called demodulation converts the tones back to the digital equivalents. From the modulation-demodulation process, we get the term modem (for MOdulate DEModulate). The modem process can be very inefficient. Tones can be corrupted by noise and the bandwidth is limited. Most people believe that the modern algorithms have pushed the bandwidth envelope, and modern modem speeds have pretty much topped out.

On the other hand, with ISDN lines, computers and network devices (such as routers and bridges) transmit digital signals directly without converting them to analog tones. End-to-end digital connectivity results in higher speed connections and significantly reduced error rates.

- *Smaller Memory Requirement*—The code for MSIE is small and efficient, increasing performance and requiring less memory on your hard drive than other browsers. MSIE can remain small as an application because it takes advantage of the new ActiveX technology. We'll discuss ActiveX more in this chapter, as well as in Chapter 16.

- *Quick Links*—As you saw in Chapter 2, MSIE comes preloaded with a Links toolbar offering links to useful and cool sites on the Web. The MSIE Links toolbar helps you get up and running on the Internet quickly. We'll discuss the MSIE Links in other chapters throughout this book, and you'll find a detailed chapter on both the Services Links button and the Today's Links button. Eventually, after you review the MSIE Links offerings, you might want to customize your Links buttons to take you to the Web pages of your choice.

Omitting Protocols in URLs

You can save time when entering URLs in the Address box by omitting the protocol. MSIE is pretty smart these days. In the old days, you had to enter complete URLs; nowadays, MSIE will find a URL's protocol for you. For example, if you enter www.microsoft.com in the Address box, MSIE will add the http:// part for you.

- *Fastest Scripting*—MSIE provides faster scripting support for programming languages than all the other Internet browsers on the virtual market. In other words, MSIE can read and download applications from the Internet really fast. (Remember, your system capabilities come into play when downloading information, as well. If you have a 14.4 modem, MSIE will be faster than most browsers, but you are still going to experience periods of waiting.)

- *Smart Caching*—MSIE saves local copies of Internet pages, enabling you to access the page faster when you return to the site. We'll talk more about caching later in this chapter.

- *32-Bit Multithreading*—MSIE is a complete 32-bit application, meaning that MSIE can interleaf instructions and run a number of program executions at the same time. Multithreading helps MSIE provide excellent responsiveness to user commands. *32-bit* multithreading means that MSIE provides a high level of smooth multithreading and multitasking performance—a big advantage during lengthy downloads.

- *Progressive Rendering*—MSIE offers progressive rendering, which allows users to view low-resolution versions of complex graphics during download, eliminating the need to wait for the entire transfer before viewing the image. Progressive rendering support is included for both GIF and JPEG format images.

Giving Multitasking a Whole New Meaning

Multitasking doesn't necessarily mean using different applications concurrently. If you're loading a graphics-heavy page in MSIE, you can quickly open a second MSIE window and keep on surfing while you wait. Press Ctrl+N, or execute the File|New Window command. When you open a new window, your new window displays the same page your previous window displays. To verify that you have two MSIE windows open, look in your status bar, you should see two MSIE buttons. If you see two buttons—Congratulations! You're officially multitasking.

- *Fast Text Mode*—MSIE's Fast Text Mode allows you to display text and hyperlinks while you're waiting for large graphics to download. MSIE loads the text first and inserts placeholders for slower-loading images while they are downloading, enabling you to view important information and links much faster than other browsers. If you find that a site's text does not display, press any key and you will immediately see the text (a handy feature carried over from earlier MSIE releases). Once the text appears, you can scroll through the page to read the text without waiting for the graphics to appear.

- *Keep Alive Technology*—MSIE support for the HTTP Keep-Alive protocol provides fast access to complex pages, such as those containing many images, by maintaining a connection to a Web server until a Web page is fully loaded (most browsers use separate connections for each Web page element).

- *Fast, Integrated Java Support*— Performance tests show MSIE's "Just-In-Time" (JIT) Java compiler is up to 30 percent faster than Netscape Navigator's JIT compiler. And, as an added benefit, MSIE's Java support is built right in (no need for plug-ins or helper applications). We'll talk more about Java later in this book.

Introducing Added Interactivity with ActiveX, ActiveMovie, and More

MSIE supports most Windows 95 features, plus it's fast, so, what else? MSIE leads the browser pack as one of the best browsers for viewing all popular video, audio, and graphic formats on the Internet. To put it succinctly, MSIE presents the next generation of multimedia. MSIE brings rich content and fast multimedia performance to users and powerful multimedia services to developers and Webmasters. Web pages come to life with MSIE's integrated multimedia functionality (see Chapter 16 for more details on MSIE's multimedia capabilities). And, as if all that isn't enough to suit your multimedia fancy, MSIE simplifies users' lives by implementing a flexible architecture built from cutting-edge technologies like ActiveX and ActiveMovie (more on these two technologies in a moment). A flexible architecture means that when a new media format emerges, it can be supported by MSIE without having to download a new browser version or plug-in application.

Currently, MSIE supports all of Netscape's multimedia technologies, plus ActiveX, ActiveMovie, ActiveVRML (a proposal for running 3D virtual reality applications), Java, and TrueType fonts. Table 3.1 shows a quick summary of some of the multimedia formats supported by MSIE. For further details, see Chapter 16.

ActiveX

ActiveX is a term that describes Microsoft's family of technologies intended to help software developers create interactive Web pages. ActiveX enables developers to embed programs in Web pages that can interact with the user

Table 3.1 MSIE-supported multimedia formats

Multimedia Format	Supported FileTypes	Notes
Audio	RealAudio, WAV, MID, AU, and AIFF	RealAudio can now be played without a separate player.
Video and animation	AVI, QuickTime, MPEG (with audio), VDOLive, and Shockwave	ActiveMovie enables most video applications to play automatically when selected.
3D	VRML	This enables the virtual reality experience with interactive, realtime 3D graphics. VRML is brought to MSIE by Reality Labs' 3D engine.
Animated GIF	GIF and JPEG	MSIE progressively renders JPEG files, which means that JPEG images can now appear incrementally, the way interlaced GIFs appear.
Embedded programs		MSIE enables you to view and embed files and applets from any program within an HTML (Hypertext Markup Language) file using ActiveX technology.

or the user's system application resources. For example, you will be able to use MSIE to view a Word or Excel file placed directly in a Web page without the help of a plug-in application or having the parent application on your hard drive. We'll talk more about ActiveX in Chapter 16. For now, be aware that ActiveX technology enables new Web page design applications, such as:

- Dynamically updated Web page information, such as stock ticker data that refreshes every few minutes

- Animated sequences, such as pulsating buttons or rippling text

- Text displayed at various angles and different diminishing perspectives

- Applications integrated into Web pages, such as JAVA applets and spreadsheets

With ActiveX technologies, Web sites can come alive with the rich interactivity of action games, multimedia encyclopedias, and productivity applications—Web sites will only be limited by their author's imaginations.

For the user, ActiveX technologies make MSIE a powerful tool for accessing data in any location—whether it is on your hard drive, on another computer in your network, or on the Internet. Affordable, dedicated (full-time) connections to the Internet are edging closer to being realized. If you're connected full time, it makes sense to use the same tool to browse the Internet as well as your local resources.

All in all, ActiveX will prove one of the hottest MSIE features for Web developers and designers—not to mention one of MSIE's hottest advancements for users. A prime example of how ActiveX benefits users can be found in the following section about Microsoft's ActiveMovie.

For more information on ActiveX, visit the Internet Explorer site at **http://www.microsoft.com/ie/ie3**. Or, you can check out Microsoft's new Site Builder Workshop at **http://www.microsoft.com/workshop**.

ActiveMovie

Microsoft applied ActiveX technology to create a multimedia streaming format called ActiveMovie. ActiveMovie allows multiple data objects (for example, audio, video, images, events, URLs, HTML pages, and programs) to be combined and stored in a single synchronized multimedia stream. Having a single, synchronized multimedia stream means instantaneous playback of ActiveMovie files. ActiveMovie supports practically every audio and video format available on the Web. And, believe it or not, MSIE is designed to support future multimedia formats, as well.

With built-in support for Microsoft's next generation digital media technology—ActiveMovie—you won't have to wait to download a separate movie player or launch a separate helper application to see video or play audio over the Internet. MSIE gives you a break and does all the application work for you.

URLs: One Step at a Time

If you're having trouble connecting to a URL, and you suspect the link is slightly off, don't give up. Try again by first connecting to the site (the www.domain.com part of the URL). Once you have connected, enter the remaining directory names one by one. For example, if you were having problems accessing the Internet Explorer page, first connect to Microsoft by entering www.microsoft.com in the Address box. Once you're connected to the Microsoft site, enter the remainder of the URL in the box after the site name. In this example, you would enter ie/ after www.microsoft.com.

Communicating Online

In addition to enabling next-generation ActiveX Web content, MSIE provides users with a host of new features for easier-to-use and more personalized Internet communication. Communication plays a major role in the world according to the Internet. Therefore, Chapters 14 and 15 are dedicated to Internet Mail and Internet News, respectively. However, to give you an idea of how MSIE tools affect your Internet communication, I'll provide a brief introduction to them here.

Microsoft Internet Mail and News

Microsoft Internet Mail is a small, easy-to-use, lightweight email client targeted toward customers looking for a simple way to communicate using SMTP and/or POP email lines. Microsoft Internet Mail features include:

- A folder hierarchy setup for sorting mail and organizing messages
- Spell-checking (if MS Office spell-checking is installed)
- Remote usage and online usage
- A Preview pane for easy reading of messages
- Automatic signatures
- An address book to store commonly used email addresses
- Offline message composition

Microsoft Internet News

Microsoft Internet News shares all the same features as Microsoft Internet Mail, in addition to a few features unique to newsgroups, including the ability to:

- Subscribe to favorite newsgroups for easy access
- Display conversation threads
- Switch between newsgroups with a single mouse click
- Read news and post messages offline

Microsoft NetMeeting: Conferencing Software

Microsoft's NetMeeting offers advanced Internet communication and collaboration features. NetMeeting makes voice and data communication over the Internet as easy as a phone call, and realtime workgroup collaboration as effective as being in the same room. NetMeeting offers multiuser application sharing and whiteboard and chat capabilities. Because it supports international standards, two or more people can participate in realtime interactive conferences, even when separated by countries or continents. Eventually, MSIE will come equipped with NetMeeting automatically. For now, you have to download a free copy of NetMeeting from the MSIE download page (**www.microsoft.com/ie/download**).

Microsoft teamed up with Intel to implement MSIE's Internet conferencing software. This new software frees users to communicate and collaborate over the Internet in new ways, including attending classes via live audio and video interaction with course instructors, participating in realtime video teleconferencing with colleagues, and making long-distance video phone calls to friends and family members for the cost of local calls. The new communication tools will enable users to talk with each other and share applications in realtime for the first time.

MSIE's Internet conferencing supports the following features:

- *Application Sharing*—You can open an application on one computer and share it with all connected computers, even when the connected computers do not have the application installed. Application sharing enables two or more users to share virtually any existing Windows operating system-based application across the Internet or local area network, enabling business professionals and their clients around the world or within a local network to review and edit documents without leaving their office.

- *Whiteboard and Chat*—Users can display illustrations, text, and comments on a shared whiteboard or in a text window. Use the whiteboard and chat features to conduct meetings, create private chat rooms, brainstorm ideas, or sketch designs that can be viewed by all connected computers.

- *Multipoint Communications*—Multiple users can participate in realtime conversations and interactive conferences by making use of international standards. In the past, realtime conversation and interactivity was limited to two connecting systems at a time.

- *Internet Audio*—Internet audio enables point-to-point telephone conversations over a corporate intranet or the Internet.

For more information and NetMeeting product support, visit the NetMeeting home page at **http://www.microsoft.com/ie/ie3/netmtg.htm**.

MSIE Is Multilingual

If you speak a second language, then you'll be interested in the multilingual capabilities of MSIE. There are two ways to view different language options offered by MSIE: You can download a version of the browser in a different language and use the browser in a foreign language interface, or you can use International Extensions to view Web page contents written in a foreign language. Let's take a closer look at these two unique language options.

Foreign Language Versions of MSIE

Just as Windows 95 is available in a number of different languages, so is MSIE. In fact, Microsoft plans to offer the MSIE interface in over 23 languages. A foreign language interface means that all of the menus, controls, and documentation appear in the language of the corresponding operating system. *Do not install a foreign language version of MSIE on a computer running the English version of Windows 95.* Doing so will change the text appearing in parts of the Windows 95 interface to a foreign language. You can use International Extensions (we'll talk about those next) with any foreign language version of MSIE.

International Extensions

The difference between using a foreign language version of MSIE and using International Extensions is that using International Extensions does not change your browser's interface. International Extensions enable you to read Web pages authored in over 50 languages. The English version of MSIE shows the standard U.S. ASCII (American Standard Code for Information Interchange) character set in addition to non-English characters such as æ, ç, and é. This enables you to view Web pages authored in English, French, German, Spanish, and other Western European languages, with only a few character omissions.

However, when you try to view pages created with radically different character sets, such as Japanese, you'll see nonsensical text in MSIE's window. Let me show you what I mean. Figure 3.1 displays a Japanese character set as it would appear in MSIE using the default English setting.

Figure 3.1   Viewing a Japanese Web page without using International Extensions.

When you want to view a Web page with a non-English (non-ASCII) character set, you must choose the appropriate language character set by right-clicking on the small globe icon displayed in the right corner of your MSIE status bar. If the character set doesn't appear as a selection (such as Japanese or Chinese), you have to download the International Extensions from the Microsoft Internet download page (**http://www.microsoft.com/ ie/download**). Applying the appropriate international language extension allows Web pages authored in foreign languages to display using the appropriate character set. Figure 3.2 shows the previous Web page with the Japanese character set language extension applied.

Adding Multilanguage Support for Windows 95 and Foreign Language Versions of MSIE

If your version of Windows 95 does not have multilanguage support, you can use your Windows 95 CD-ROM to easily change the setting. Insert your CD-ROM into your drive, click on the Start button in the Windows toolbar, select Settings|Control Panel, and click on the Add/Remove Programs icon. When the Add/Remove Programs Properties dialog box appears, click on the Windows Setup tab. Check the Multilanguage Support option in the Components box, then click on OK. If you don't have the Windows 95 CD-ROM, you can download support for specific languages from the Microsoft Web site at http:// www.microsoft.com/windows/software/localize/localize.htm.

Rating the Sites

Netizens are becoming more and more concerned over users at home and in the workplace viewing inappropriate content on the Web. In response to this concern, MSIE became the first browser to support the Platform for Internet Content Selection (PICS) rating system, giving parents and supervisors control over which sites Internet users can access. (In Chapter 4, you'll see how to adjust your Rating settings.)

Rating settings enable you to control the types of content displayed by choosing levels of allowable language, nudity, sex, and violence on Web sites. Users can block sites that do not have a rating, as well as filter out

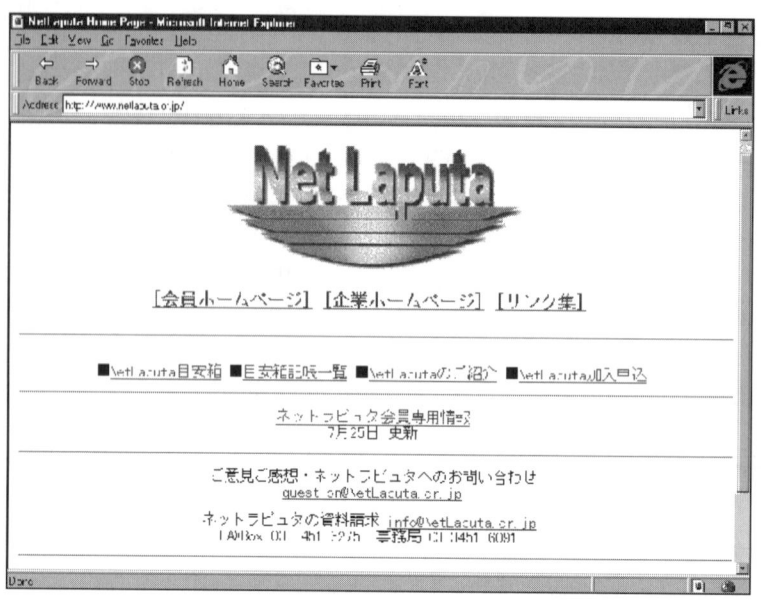

Figure 3.2 Viewing a Japanese Web page using the Japanese International Language Extension to display the page with the proper character set.

specific sites. MSIE's combination of rating options effectively blocks users from accessing objectionable material. Parents and supervisors set passwords that must be used before someone can change or override the Rating settings.

How Do Ratings Work?

Basically, MSIE reads special tags placed on Web pages by the Internet content providers or independent rating organizations. MSIE then determines whether a page meets the host's rating criteria. Web site authors can obtain a rating from the Recreational Software Advisory Council (RSAC)—the organization that created and now maintains the PICS ratings. RSAC distributes the PICS tags from their Web site at **http://www.rsac.org**.

The RSAC Web site contains more information on the rating system and information on obtaining a rating for a Web page. In a nutshell, RSAC created an algorithm-based rating system using a 0 to 4 scale, ranging from inoffensive to offensive. Ratings can be generated by Web site managers, as well as independent bureaus. Parents and supervisors can then choose which rating system best meets their needs. The ratings chart displayed on the RSAC page is shown in Figure 3.3.

MSIE Extras

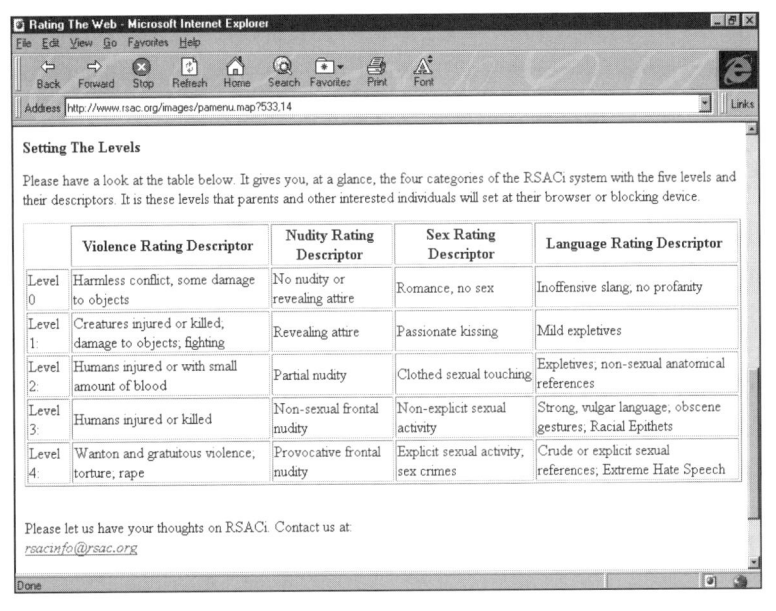

Figure 3.3 The RSAC rating levels.

Industry-imposed rating systems came about in response to the question of whether government should control what children see online. Before Congress could get into the business of inhibiting online speech, more than 30 online industry players organized PICS to develop standards for supporting a variety of rating plans and easy-to-use filtering software. MSIE's rating system fully complies with PICS standards.

For more info on MSIE's parental control software solutions, visit **http://www.microsoft.com/ie/ie3/ratings.htm**. To get more background on the PICS rating language, stop by the PICS Web site at **http://www.w3.org PICS**.

Browsing with Maximum Security

MSIE Security uses the Microsoft Internet Security Framework, enabling you to communicate privately, download code you can trust, and identify yourself to others across the Internet. MSIE's cutting-edge security comes in three forms: trusted code, secure channel protocols, and CryptoAPI.

While it is enough just knowing that MSIE is beefing up Internet security, we can still benefit by taking a brief look at each of MSIE's security categories.

Trusted Code

Trusted code assists users in safely downloading software and software components, such as ActiveX. MSIE is the first browser to support the safe downloading of code and controls by offering code signing, which provides accountability for software and software components found on the Internet. When you buy software at a retail outlet, you know what you're getting and who you are getting it from. On the other hand, software distributed on the Internet is largely anonymous. Users cannot be sure who published the software and whether it has been tampered with after being released by the software provider. MSIE helps users identify software publishers and check for tampering, before downloading the software. Figure 3.4 shows

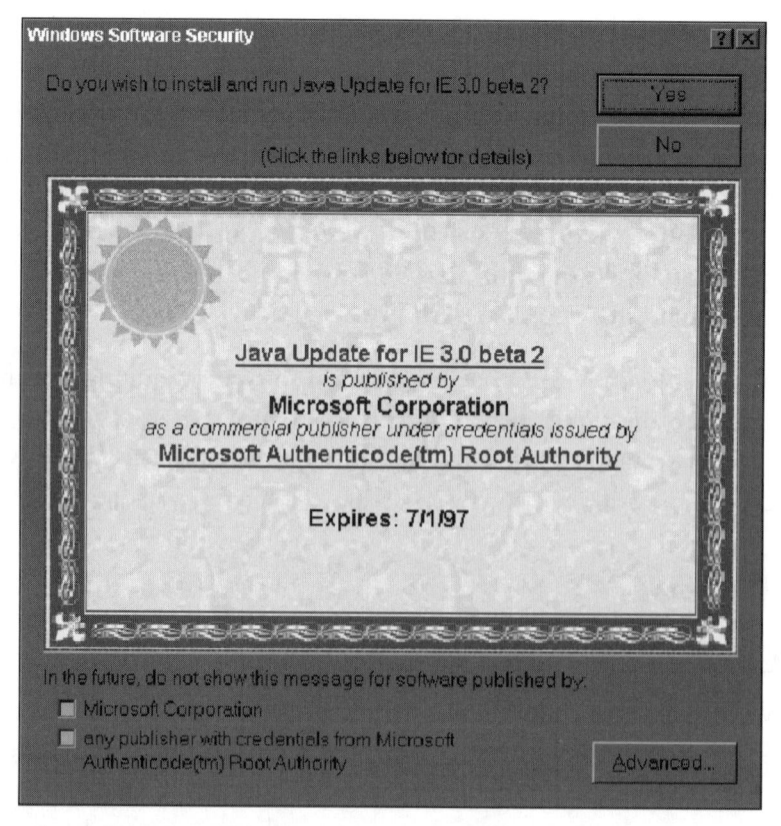

Figure 3.4 Software Code Certificates assure you that the software you're downloading is safe.

one of Microsoft's Software Code Certificates, similar to certificates that other publishers can use to sign their code.

Secure Channel Protocols

MSIE supports leading Internet security protocols such as Secure Sockets Layer 2.0/3.0 (SSL) and Private Communication Technology 1.0 (PCT). Secure channel protocols ensure that personal and business communications using the Internet and intranets are private. The SSL and PCT protocols create a secure channel, so no one can eavesdrop on Internet communication. As secure channel protocols evolve and become more and more secure (they are getting there), you will be able to send email, buy consumer goods, reserve airplane tickets, and conduct personal banking on the Internet without worrying that the information you're sending is not secure. The obvious drawback to secure channel protocols to date is that it usually is only a matter of time before hackers break through a secure channel—then vendors are forced to upgrade security. In this area, MSIE carries a strong advantage simply because it is backed by Microsoft. Microsoft has the resources and technology to keep abreast of security issues.

MSIE's secure channel protocol technology is rooted in client and server authentication. Client authentication means that you can present your digital identification or certificate when a Web server requests the information. MSIE stores certificates, or digital identification cards, similarly to the way a wallet stores IDs. For example, let's say you subscribe to an online entertainment service. The service asks you to enter your name and password. Support for digital identification would allow the entertainment service to request your certificate to validate your identity. Microsoft plans to extend the use of Microsoft Wallet to store a wider variety of personal information, such as credit card numbers, passwords, and keys. Conversely, server authentication ensures that you are communicating with your intended party. For example, if the entertainment online service sends you an email, you can verify that it is the service that actually sent the email (and you could identify whether someone intercepted it along the way).

Clearly, security is a global concern, so Microsoft is working with Netscape and others as part of the Internet Engineering Task Force (IETF) Transport

Layer Security working group to create a unified, standard secure channel protocol.

CryptoAPI

CryptoAPI is the cornerstone of MSIE's security framework. It provides programmers the ability to incorporate the Internet's underlying security services for secure channels and code signing. CryptoAPI delivers strong cryptography through MSIE.

While Internet security measures have increased dramatically, I don't want to give you the impression that complete security is a reality. You should continue to exercise caution when it comes to commerce on the Internet. Currently, security leads the Internet's hot-topic list, so it won't be long before we can feel more comfortable with Internet security. In the meantime, rest assured that Microsoft has the backing to continue to provide MSIE users with the latest and greatest in security technology.

Introducing Smart Caching

You've probably noticed that when you stop by a Web page you've visited before, the page comes up faster than it did the first time. Well, that's because when you visit a Web page, MSIE stores the content to a special directory on your hard disk, called a *cache file*. Calling a file up from your cache file is much quicker than downloading the file from the Internet. Caching makes redisplaying a Web page fast, because it won't be necessary to connect to the remote server the next time you request the document—your system will retrieve the cached copy of the page.

The main cache management feature of MSIE is the Temporary Internet Files folder. MSIE's Temporary Internet Files folder system makes it easy to read Web pages offline. You can view any cached document by clicking on the file saved in the Temporary Internet Files folder. Clicking on a file in the Temporary Internet Folder displays the selected Web page on your desktop, offline, with all the graphics intact. MSIE's easily accessible cache makes it possible to give demos without an Internet connection. You can even unplug your portable machine and take it on a plane or to a park—taking copies of Web pages with you. Of course, because you aren't online, hyperlinks won't work.

Before moving on, there are some caching issues that need to be addressed—specifically, when should a cached page be updated? And how can users manage the Temporary Internet Files folder? If you are browsing the Net and you go to a site you visited yesterday (for example), your system will access the cached page first. If you want to view the latest document version, you may need to click on your Refresh toolbar button. MSIE combats this problem in some ways by enabling you to choose to have MSIE check for updated versions of a document once every time you open your browser. To indicate how often you want MSIE to update cached files, simply execute the View|Options command, click on the Advanced card, and then click on the Temporary Internet Files Setting button. You can use the resulting dialog box to set your cache updating options, as well as empty your Temporary Internet Files folder. Chapter 4 discusses managing your MSIE cache in more detail. To assist you in cache management, Microsoft takes a self-proclaimed conservative approach to caching by checking the Last-Modified-Since and Expires attributes of every object on a Web page (Web designers can indicate modified and expire dates in their HTML coding). Other browsers only validate the page, without checking the content.

Using a Proxy Gateway? Not a Problem

A proxy gateway is used when a local network uses a proxy server (don't worry—it gets clearer than that!). A proxy gateway is a computer and its associated software that relays a request for a URL from a browser (client) to an outside server, then returns the result to the requesting computer. For example, let's say you are part of a local area network in your company. Your computer does not have an Internet connection, but it does have access to the company's proxy gateway. You can call up a Web site by opening MSIE and submitting the URL to the proxy gateway. In turn, the proxy gateway processes your request, downloads the Web page (if necessary), and sends the Web page to your system. Proxy gateways provide clients who are sealed off from the Internet a trusted agent that can access the Internet on the client's behalf. Often users are unaware that they are accessing a proxy and not the Internet directly. Figure 3.5 illustrates how a proxy gateway works.

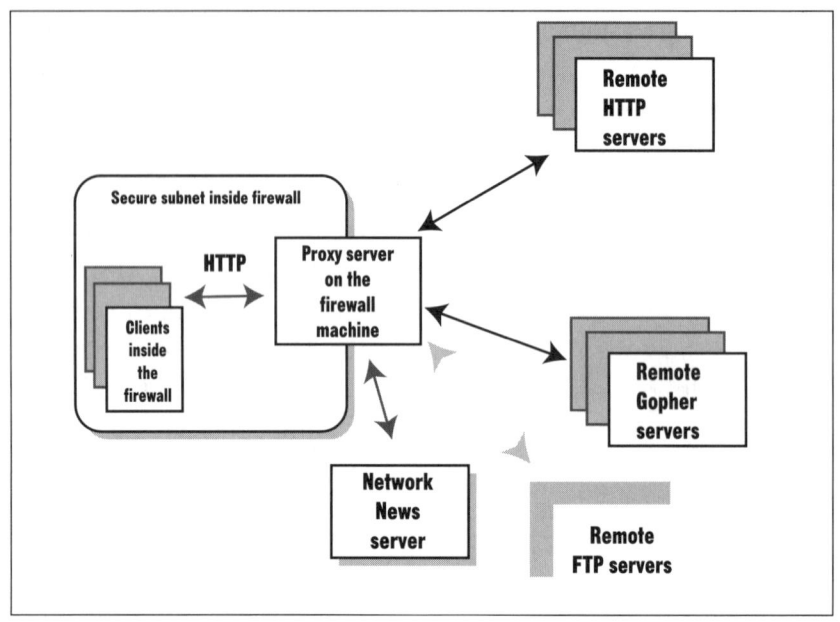

Figure 3.5 A proxy gateway allows networked users who aren't connected to the Internet to request Web pages from a proxy server.

A proxy gateway needs a proxy server to process the Internet access requests. The proxy server is a Web server that acts as both a server and a client. In its server capacity, a proxy server accepts URLs with a special prefix from local clients. When the request for a URL is received, the proxy server strips off the prefix and looks for the resulting URL in its local cache. If the URL is found, the cached document is returned to the client immediately. Otherwise, the proxy server puts on its client hat and requests the Internet document from a remote server. Once the file is found, the proxy server opens and saves a copy of the document in the cache memory and sends the document to the original requester. Usually, proxy gateways have a cache management algorithm which flushes documents out of the cache memory based on age, size, and access history. The proxy server process is illustrated in Figure 3.6.

MSIE works with a number of proxy servers and currently supports CERN-compliant proxies, SOCKS, TIS Gauntlet, WinGate, ANS, Catapult, and Netscape Proxies (including Secure SSL tunneling). Microsoft will continue to add support for proxy servers as the technology evolves.

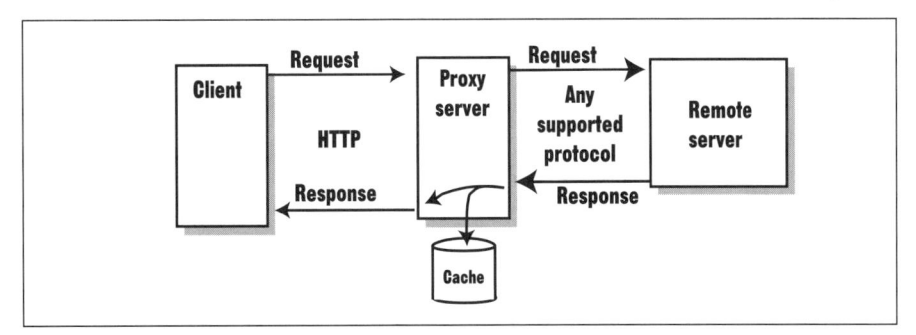

Figure 3.6 The proxy server acts as both client and server.

Tracing Your Travels

If you're getting hung up somewhere along the way, Windows has a handy way to trace the path you're following around the world. To see where a URL is taking you, open a DOS window, then enter tracer locationname. For example, the command "tracerttwww.microsoft.com" displays over 11 stops my system made on the way to the Microsoft site, as shown in Figure 3.7.

Chapter in Review

There are Internet browsers, and then there's MSIE. MSIE offers features beyond browsing the Internet. MSIE provides all the advantages of Windows applications without sacrificing any of the Internet multimedia capabilities available from leading browsers such as Netscape. To top it off, MSIE coats the entire technological package with a thick layer of ActiveX.

MSIE is faster and more interactive than browsers of the past—two features sure to sit well with netizens who have been craving to have their cake and eat it, too. Previously, speeding up Internet access meant reducing graphics. Incredibly, MSIE speeds up Internet access while *adding* multimedia components. ActiveX and ActiveMovie play a large role in MSIE's advanced multimedia offerings. As far as speeding things up, MSIE downloads Web pages faster using its 32-bit multithreaded user interface to perform more than one task simultaneously, such as scrolling through a Web page while it's downloading. Additionally, MSIE automatically establishes multiple connections with a Web server to increase responsiveness and speed up

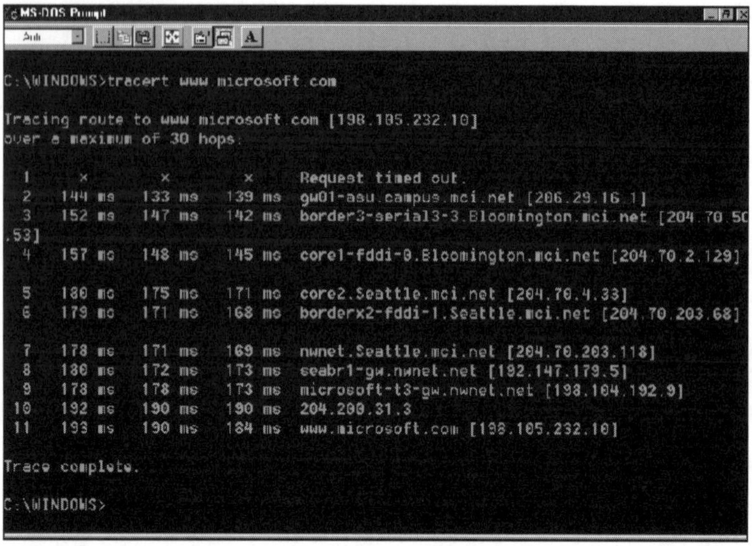

Figure 3.7 Tracing the route of your Internet connection.

downloading. Finally, MSIE displays Web page text immediately while rendering graphics progressively, enabling you to start reading a Web page before the graphics download completely.

MSIE comes equipped to work with the NetMeeting conferencing tool, expanding Internet communications beyond Internet Mail and News into the realm of realtime audio, and textual and graphical communication. In addition, the MSIE interface will soon be available in over 23 languages, and currently, Web pages can be viewed in over 50 languages through the use of language extensions (remember the difference?).

As the Internet expands, so does the need to control the kinds of sites kids and employees spend their time viewing. Parents and supervisors gain control by assigning rating settings. MSIE is the first browser to support the Platform for Internet Content Selection (PICS) rating system. MSIE also is the leader in offering Internet security features, memory caching, and proxy gateway adaptability.

Clearly, Microsoft has been focused on setting a new Internet standard with MSIE—something gives me the impression that we haven't seen the last MSIE trick to come out of Microsoft's bag.

Getting to Know the MSIE Options 4

Most people perform best when given the freedom of choice—MSIE comes loaded with user options.

*A*s you've probably discovered, flexibility is one of the strongest suits of MSIE. MSIE easily glides from local file manager to Web browser with the grace typical of Microsoft products. MSIE's layers of flexibility include a myriad of user options. For some people, too many options pose a larger obstacle than not enough options. MSIE combats this problem by providing simple-to-use option cards that people can use to customize their browser settings.

In this chapter, we'll take a look at the available browser option cards, and we'll take a quick peek at using MSIE as a local file manager. I've tried to make this chapter as straightforward as possible by giving each section the same name as the option card being discussed. With this arrangement, you can read about all the options, or you can pick and choose to read up on the options that interest you most.

You can view the MSIE property menu by right-clicking on your MSIE desktop icon or executing the View|Options command from within the MSIE browser. We'll start our discussion with the View|Options General

Options card, and then we'll work our way through the following options cards in order. Finally, before we leave this chapter, we'll call up our local hard drive, do a quick right-click, then look at the local hard drive property card using MSIE as a file manager. (If you are familiar with Windows 95, you'll feel comfortable with MSIE's file management features.) OK, I've laid the appropriate groundwork, let's get started.

View|Options

I know I just said, "Let's get started," but there *is* one minor detail we need to take care of before we talk options. I'm about to tell you to execute the View|Options command using the MSIE toolbar. Now, maybe this command will work, and maybe it won't (herein lies that little detail I just mentioned). As you know, MSIE has a habit of displaying different menus depending on how you are using MSIE at the time. If you are using MSIE to view local files, MSIE provides you with one set of available menu options; if you are using MSIE to access the Internet, MSIE provides you with another set of menu options. If you don't believe me, type *C:* in the Address box at the top of the screen and press Enter. Click on the View|Options menu command. Notice that nothing happens. Now, type *www.msn.com* in the Address box and press Enter. Click on the View|Options menu command again. You now should be able to view the Options cards that we are about to discuss. This means that while MSIE's local file manager options overlap (or seamlessly integrate with) the MSIE Web browser options, there are decidedly different actions you can perform in each area. This is a big advantage, as you'll see later on. For most of this chapter, we'll be discussing the options available while MSIE is being used as an Internet client. At the end of this chapter, we'll take a quick look at our hard drives without leaving the MSIE interface.

OK, getting back on track. Verify that your copy of MSIE is pointing to a Web page, then execute the View|Options command. The cards available in this set of options include the General, Connection, Navigation, Programs, Security, and Advanced cards. To move from one card to another, simply click on the card tabs displayed under the title bar. By default, the General card displays on top when you execute the View|Options command—so, we'll start our discussion with the General card.

General Card

The General card, displayed in Figure 4.1, is a fairly simple card with some handy options.

The General card has four main option areas: Multimedia, Appearance, Toolbars, and Fonts. Let's discuss each area briefly.

Multimedia

You use the Multimedia options on the General card to specify whether you want to show pictures, play sounds, and show videos. The default selection is to display all pictures and videos, and to play sounds. To disable any of these options, simply click in the check box located to the left of the option. An option is disabled when a check mark does not appear in the check box. Disabling the pictures and videos options speeds up your Internet access, which you will find especially useful if you are surfing the Net during peak usage hours or if you are accessing an especially busy server. When you disable either options, you will see small image icons on the Web page in place of the actual graphics. Here are a few tricks you should be aware of when using the Multimedia options:

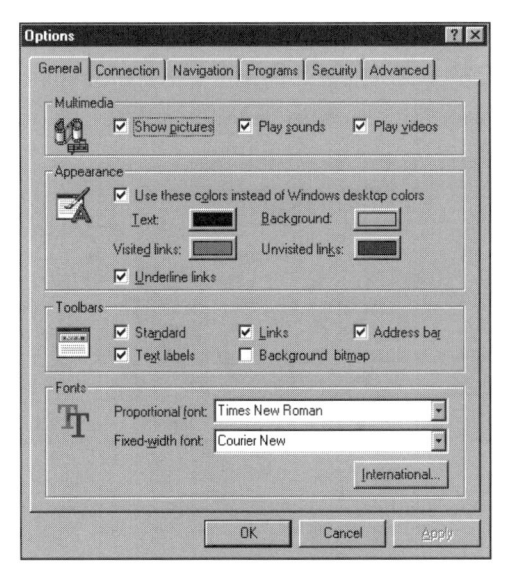

Figure 4.1 Options available on the General card.

- You can still display an individual picture or videos if your graphic options are disabled by right-clicking on the icon that represents the image and then selecting Show Picture.

- If pictures on the current page remain visible after you disable the Show Pictures option, you can hide the pictures by clicking on the Refresh button on the MSIE toolbar or executing View|Refresh from the menu bar.

- To interrupt sounds and animation while you are browsing, *without* turning off the options, press the Esc key or click the Stop button on the toolbar.

Appearance

The Appearance options on the General card provide you the opportunity to customize MSIE's colors and link attributes. First, let's look at customizing MSIE's color scheme. If you click on the "Use the colors instead of Windows desktop colors" check box, the option will show the text and background colors currently used by MSIE. To change either color setting, click on the color box to the right of the feature option. MSIE will then display a Color dialog box, as shown in Figure 4.2.

You can choose any color displayed on the color palette, or you can define custom colors. To choose a color from the Color dialog box, click on the color of your choice, click on the OK button, click on the Apply button,

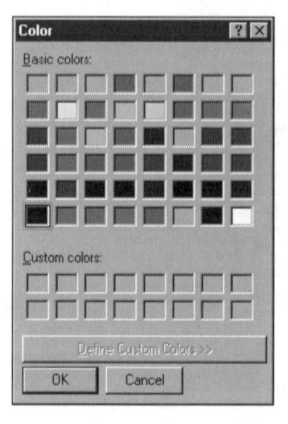

Figure 4.2   Customizing MSIE's colors in the Color dialog box.

and then click on the OK button. Your browser should now reflect your new color scheme. One word of caution: Changing your color preferences could result in instances where Web pages are difficult to read because your color settings clash with a Web page's assigned colors. Personally, I like to retain MSIE's default color preferences so I can view Web pages with the colors authors intended. I must admit, though, that there have been a few instances where changing the text or background color has assisted me in improving a site's readability (this is becoming more of a rarity as Web page designers are showing more Internet savvy). Keep in mind that new HTML coding techniques allow designers to indicate the color of a Web page's text; in those instances, your MSIE settings will have no effect on the Web page's display.

Below the MSIE color options are your link options. You can define the attributes of links on the Web pages you view. As we discussed earlier, a link is *hypertext* (don't let that term scare you), which allows you to jump from one Web page to another or from one spot on a page to another spot on the same page. Links usually appear underlined and in a color different from the body text color. Once you click on a link and visit the attached site, the link on the originating page displays in a different color. The color change helps you to easily recognize which links you have visited. The Appearance options allow you to change the colors of your Visited links and Unvisited links (see Figure 4.1). You specify link colors the same way you specify text and background colors: Click on the color box to the right of the option to display the Color dialog box, click on the color of your choice, click on the OK button, click on the Apply button, and then click on the OK button.

You can also determine whether you want links to appear underlined. Traditionally (keep in mind that "traditionally" in Internet terms means somewhere beyond one year ago), links appeared as blue text with an underline. MSIE gives you the option to keep the underline or discard it. This is one setting where I don't really have an opinion one way or the other. I tend to keep my links underlined because it makes them readily apparent. To turn off link underlines, click in the check box to the left of the Underline links option, then click on the Apply button. Remember, an option is enabled when a check mark appears in the check box.

Toolbars

In Chapter 2, we played around with rearranging the MSIE toolbars. We experimented by dragging the Address box and MSIE Links toolbar to different positions in the MSIE window. The General card provides more toolbar customization options. The Toolbars area of the General Options card enables you to turn off standard toolbar features using selection boxes. You can choose to turn off the Standard toolbar, the Standard toolbar's text labels (this is a nice feature because it reduces the size of the Standard toolbar—increasing your window browsing area), Links toolbar, Address bar, and Background bitmap. By default, MSIE displays all the available toolbar options except the Background bitmap. Background Bitmap isn't selected because it doesn't work yet. I have a hunch that eventually the Background Bitmap option will toggle the swirly graphic design underlying your MSIE toolbar. You can deselect any options you do not want to display on your desktop. Remember to click the Apply button before moving on if you make any Toolbar preference changes.

Fonts

Below the Toolbars option, there are a couple of font options. This area is used to choose text families for fonts appearing on your browser. Notice there are two types of fonts to assign: Proportional and Fixed-width. Most body text on Web pages is proportional font, therefore, the font family assigned as the proportional font will be the font you view most often (the text in this book is a proportional font, where each letter gets a space relative to its size). The default proportional font is Times New Roman. Fixed-width fonts are most often found on Gopher sites, FAQ (Frequently Asked Questions) pages, and FTP sites. (Fixed-width type is similar to old-fashioned typewritten text, where each letter gets an equal amount of space regardless of the letter's size.) The default fixed-width font family is Courier New. To change either the Proportional or Fixed-width font setting, click on the drop-down list arrow next to the appropriate setting and choose a font from the selection list. Here again, I like to stick with the default settings in an attempt to stay true to Web page designers' preferences.

You may be wondering what that International button at the bottom of the General card is all about. You can set the proportional and fixed-width font selections for foreign language text as well as English text. As you may recall from Chapter 3, you can use MSIE to view Web pages designed in foreign languages. MSIE provides the same font options for foreign languages as it does for English.

We've completed our review of the General Options card. Let's not waste any time and move on to the Connection card.

Connection Card

The Connection card is fairly self-explanatory: You use this card to specify how you want MSIE to connect to the Internet. Figure 4.3 displays the options available on the Connection card.

Dialing

The first option area on the Connection card is the Dialing section. The top feature in the Dialing section is used to indicate whether or not you want MSIE to automatically dial up your Internet service provider (ISP) when you double-click on your MSIE desktop icon. If you opt to bypass the "Connect to the Internet as needed" option, you must connect to your

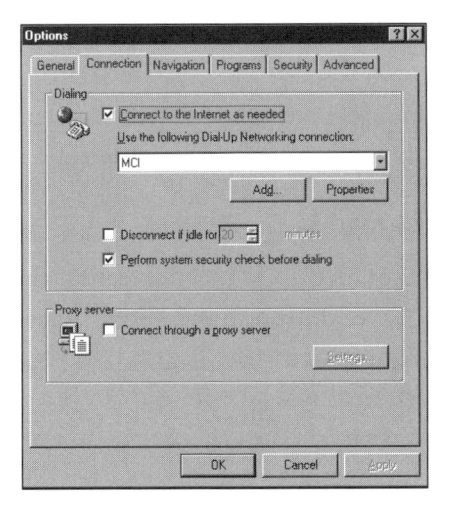

Figure 4.3 Options available on the Connection card.

ISP before opening MSIE. There are benefits to both scenarios. If you use your Internet connection almost exclusively to browse the Web, it is probably in your interest to have MSIE automatically dial up your ISP. It will save you an extra step or two each time you connect to the Internet. On the other hand, if you use other applications in conjunction with your Internet service—such as Telnet, FTP, and email—then you might want to keep the connection to your Internet service separate from MSIE. To toggle the dialing feature on or off, click in the check box to the left of the "Connect to the Internet as needed" option, click on the Apply button, and then click on the OK button.

Below the automatic connect selection box, there are dialing settings giving you some Internet connection flexibility. If you have more than one Internet connection, you can select which setting to use as the default setting using the drop-down box. If you would like to add a second dial-up setting, click on the Add button and work your way through a short serious of dialog boxes similar to the Internet Connection Wizard boxes we saw in Chapter 2. The Properties button displays the General Properties card for the current ISP settings. You can also use the General Properties card to configure a new ISP connection using the Add button.

The last two selection boxes in the Dialing section of the Connection card enable you to set how long MSIE should wait before it times out due to inactivity (a nice feature that disconnects you from the Internet if you aren't using it) and an option to perform a system security check before dialing. All in all, the Dialing section, while appearing slightly complex, is fairly simple if you take the time to review its options.

Proxy Server

The second option area on the Connection card is the Proxy Server section. You use the Proxy Server option to indicate whether MSIE should access a proxy server. If your system uses a proxy server, you probably have a system administrator nearby who takes care of the details for you. Proxies are similar to gateways to the Internet for people working on an internal network. Most likely, you don't use a proxy server, which means you should leave the option disabled. If you want to know a little more about proxy servers, refer to Chapter 3, where there's a brief explanation of how proxy servers work.

Navigation Card

The third options card—the Navigation card—is a good card to know about after you've become comfortable surfing the Net. You can use this card to specify the location of your start page, search page, and each of the five MSIE Links buttons. You can also use this card to manage your History folder. The Navigation card is shown in Figure 4.4. There are two main sections on the Navigation card, the Customize and History sections.

Customize

The Customize options portion of the Navigation card enables you to set the location of your start page, search page, and Links buttons. You customize each of these elements in the same manner. Let's look at how we can change our start page.

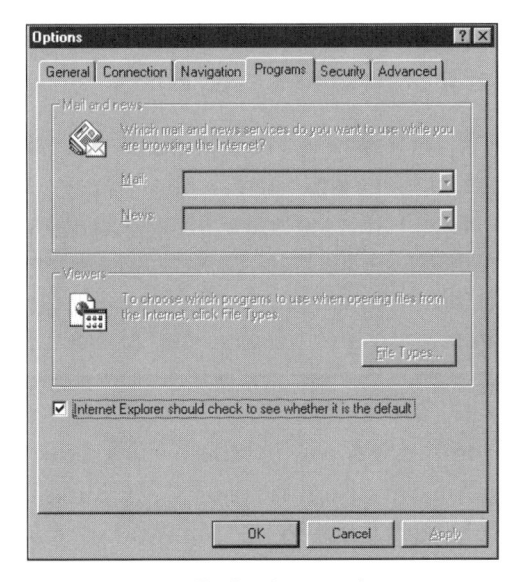

Figure 4.4 Options available on the Navigation card.

Basically, changing your start page option means you change the address of the initial page displayed on MSIE when you start your browser (or when you click on the Home button in the MSIE toolbar). There are three ways you can assign a page to a feature. First, you can enter the URL in the Address text box. Second, you can display the desired page in MSIE and then click on the Use Current button. And third, you can click on the Use Default button to revert to MSIE's original settings (in this case, clicking on the Use Default button would reset the start page to the MSN Welcome page). You can customize your search page in the same manner. The address you assign to the search page is the address you will access when you click on your MSIE toolbar search button. The only difference between assigning a new start page and assigning a new search page is that you have to select the Search Page option from the Page drop-down list.

Changing Your Start Page

To set your start page to a blank page, create a blank document in Notepad and save it as Homepage.htm. Then, open Homepage.htm from within MSIE. (Hint: by default Notepad saves files in your Windows folder.) Execute the View|Options command, click on the Start and Search Pages tab, click on the Use Current options button, and then click on the Apply button.

Later, in Chapter 17, we'll show you how to create your own home page. If you want, you can make this page into your default start page. If your page is stored on the hard drive, simply follow the instructions given above, inserting the name of your home page instead of the blank one. If you have placed your page on the Web, just enter its URL in the Address box on the Navigation Card. Now you can view you masterpiece every time you open your browser.

Notice that the drop-down list includes Quick Link #1 through Quick Link #5 options. You can customize your MSIE Links toolbar by assigning five Web pages of your choice to the Links buttons. After you assign an address to a Link button, don't forget to name your link using the Name text box. The text you type in the Name text box will appear on your MSIE Links toolbar.

Using SavvySearch as Your Default Search Page

As mentioned early in this book, SavvySearch is a great Internet search site. The site describes itself as an "experimental search system designed to query multiple Internet search engines simultaneously." You may want to try pointing your Search Page to this site. To do this, type the following URL in MSIE's Location textbox:http://guaraldi.cs.colostate.edu:2000/form. Once the SavvySearch page displays on your screen, execute the View|Options command, click on the Start and Search Pages tab, select Search Page from the drop-down list box, click on the Use Current options button, and then click on the Apply button.

Keep in mind that you can always revert to MSIE's default start page, search page, and Links settings by displaying the appropriate feature in the Page drop-down list and clicking on the Use Default button.

History

In Chapter 2, we touched briefly on the MSIE History folder. Later, in Chapter 12, we'll touch on it again. As you can see on the Navigation card, the History folder comes into play here, as well. The History folder maintains a list of links on your hard drive to Web pages you've visited. You can use the History options on the Navigation card to manage your History folder. More succinctly, you can perform three basic actions on your History folder. First, you can change the setting regarding the number of days MSIE holds a link in your History folder. The default setting is to keep each link for 14 days. You can increase or decrease the number of days by clicking on the up or down arrow.

Second, you can click on the View History button to peruse the links stored in your History folder. The links in your History folder are arranged in alphabetical order.

You can change the sort order by clicking on the column headings. Any link appearing in your History folder can take you to the Web site; all you have to do is double-click on the link.

The third action you can perform is emptying your History folder. To empty your History folder, click on the Clear History button. I recommend you click on this button fairly regularly. It doesn't take long to add up huge sums of links. If you have items in your History folder that you'd rather not delete, you can selectively delete links out of the View History window using basic Windows commands (highlight the links you want to delete, then select the Delete command). Regardless of *how* you delete links out of your History folder, ensure that you do it fairly regularly—too much junk on your system can slow it down unnecessarily.

Programs Card

The Program Card appears a little dim at the moment. That's because, as of this writing, Microsoft is diligently working to integrate Mail and News into MSIE. Also, there doesn't seem to be a driving need to assign viewers to document types, since ActiveX technology takes care of those details for you. Still, I would be remiss if I didn't show you this card (who knows, maybe the Mail and News features have been successfully integrated by the time you read this book). Besides, there is one small feature worth noting at the bottom of the Programs card, as shown in Figure 4.5.

Mail and News

As I noted above, Microsoft is currently working to integrate Mail and News into the MSIE interface. Most likely, by the time you read this book, Microsoft will have succeeded in this quest. Therefore, we've included a Mail chapter and a News chapter to help you use Microsoft's Mail and News applications.

Viewers

Presumably, the Viewers portion of the Programs card was the Registered File Types feature found in past versions of MSIE, as well as most Windows applications. Registering file types with applications is how Windows knows which application to open with which file. (For example, when you click

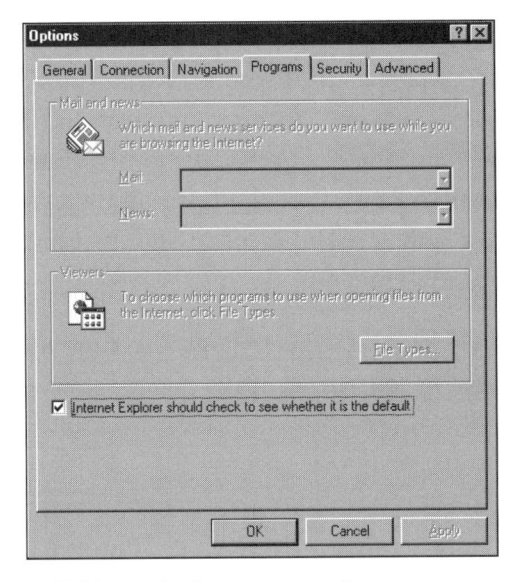

Figure 4.5 Options available on the Programs card.

on a file with a .doc extension, Windows knows it needs to open Microsoft Word before you can view the file contents.) ActiveX has eliminated the need for you to register file types with program applications because ActiveX manages those sorts of details for your. Your guess is as good as mine as to what will appear on the Programs Card in the future. Quite possibly, your version has been updated since this book went to press.

Default Setting

Here's a quick and easy option. This option indicates to MSIE whether it should open when you click on an HTML document on your desktop or from a disk drive. If you have more than one browser on your desktop, you need to indicate which browser should open automatically when you open a hypertext document (you have to view HTML documents in a viewer/browser to see the effects the hypertext markup language). MSIE sets itself as the default. I suggest that you retain MSIE as your default viewer.

Security Card

As we discussed in Chapter 3, information security is one of the hottest topics on the Internet today. The Internet populace is racing to ensure security, and major Internet clients, such as MSIE and Netscape, are working together to create a high level of security for business and private use. If security is mastered, business and communication on the Internet will boom—even more than it has up to this point! Presently, the Net does provide *some* security to businesses and private users. MSIE allows you to set the highest available levels of security options using the Security card, which is displayed in Figure 4.6.

The Security card offers security settings affecting your privacy, security certificates, and active content security.

Privacy

The Privacy option area of the Security card addresses whether you want to be warned before sending or receiving data over the Internet that is not secure. (In other words, if you are sending or receiving data over an open communications line without security features or encryption, then anyone who intercepts the information will be able to read the text.) If you choose to receive warnings, you can then specify how often you want to be warned: Only when you are sending more than one line of text, or always. You can also receive warnings when you are crossing zones, receiving an invalid site certificate, or accepting "cookies." Cookies are data containers

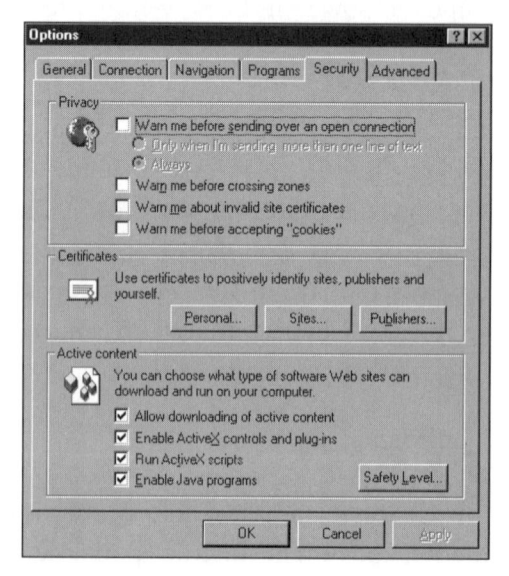

Figure 4.6 Beefing up security with the Security card options.

that enable your browser to retain information from one page to the next. MSN uses cookies when you customize your MSN start page.

Certificates

Certificates are going to become more popular as security issues force netizens to become more cautious. Certificates enable software publishers and other companies to identify themselves as official sites. The Personal option is still under construction, but the Sites and Publishers Certificate buttons work. You use the Sites and Publishers buttons to identify which certificate providers you will accept when viewing Web sites. Clicking on the Sites button in the Certificates area of the Security card displays as shown in Figure 4.7.

Active Content

The final section of the Security card is the Active Content area. You use this area to specify how you want MSIE to handle active content such as

Figure 4.7 Viewing officially recognized site certificates.

animation, multimedia, scrolling marquees, and more. I highly recommend that you accept MSIE's default settings and retain the ability to view active content on the Net automatically. If you click on the Safety Level button, you will see that MSIE sets the default safety level to Expert. The description states that Microsoft recommends this setting for developers. I suggest you leave the setting at the default Expert level. You may get a couple more warning messages than you would if you chose the Normal setting, but it only requires a click if you want to accept the active content after receiving a warning. In my mind's eye, if you're going to accept every active content component on the Net, you might as well balance things with a little caution elsewhere.

Advanced Card

Here it is, the last options card. This card, vaguely named the Advanced card, provides a mishmash of options. The Advanced card provides settings for rating Internet page content, managing your cached files (cleverly renamed the Temporary Internet Files), cryptography (which doesn't exactly work yet as of this writing), and Additional (even more vague than "Advanced"). The Advanced card appears as shown in Figure 4.8.

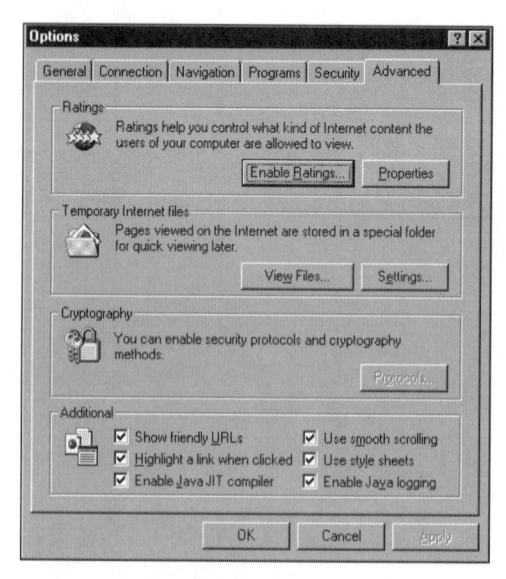

Figure 4.8 Options available on the Advanced card.

Ratings

From international security to home monitoring systems, MSIE spans all levels of Internet Web use. MSIE's Ratings area helps MSIE shift from global server to personal server by enabling you to control access to rated Web sites. There are two buttons included in the Ratings area: an Enable/Disable Ratings button, which toggles the rating settings on and off, and a Properties button used to configure your rating settings. You can control access to rated Web sites by setting your ratings properties, including acceptable levels of strong language, nudity, sex, and violence. Basically, the ratings options enable you to block users from accessing objectionable material on the Internet. To set your rating criteria, click on the Properties button, which displays a password dialog box. If no password has been set, type a new password, verify the password, then click on the OK button. You will be required to use the same password to enable and disable your rating settings until you change your password. Once your password is accepted, you should see the Content Advisor Cards as shown in Figure 4.9.

As you can see, three option cards are available in the Content Advisor dialog box—the Ratings, General, and Advanced cards. The Internet Ratings card displays on top by default. You use the Internet Ratings card to set the

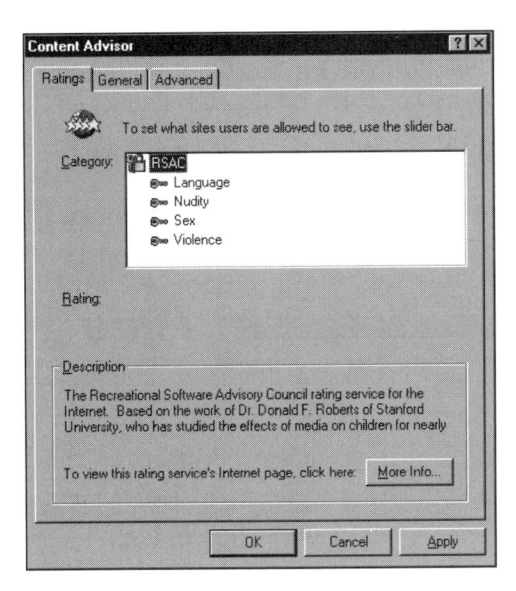

Figure 4.9 **Viewing the Content Advisor dialog box.**

rating level for the Language, Nudity, Sex, and Violence categories. To set a rating level, click on a category, then move the rating button to the right until you reach an appropriate rating level. A description of what users are allowed to see appears in the Description text box at the bottom of the Internet Ratings card.

The General card provides three main options. First, you use the General card to determine if users can see unrated sites. Not all Web sites carry a rating; this option determines whether unrated sites should be considered across the board as acceptable or unacceptable viewing. The second option on the General card allows you to choose which rating systems you would like to use by clicking on the Ratings Systems button. Finally, the third option on the General card enables you to change the supervisor password. You must know the current supervisor password before you can create a new one.

The third and final card in the Content Advisor card is the Advanced card, which enables you to add rating systems and rating bureaus to help you filter acceptable Web sites.

When you've completed setting your rating options, click on the Advanced card. Whenever you want to turn your rating settings on or off, you need only click on the Enable/Disable Ratings button found on the Advanced Options card (not the Advanced card in the Content Advisor dialog box). When you first click on the Enable/Disable Ratings button, you will be asked to enter your password. Then, depending on the status of the Enable/Disable Ratings button, you should see a message box.

OK, enough about ratings. Return to the Advanced Options cards, and we'll discuss the Temporary Internet Files options.

Temporary Internet Files

As we discussed in Chapter 3, MSIE's management feature uses the Temporary Internet Files folder. You use the folder to perform cache management processes. There are two buttons in the Temporary Internet Files options area of the Advanced card to assist you in cache management. One button enables you to view the files in your Temporary Internet Files folder. The other button enables you to manage the folder's settings. The first button is self-explanatory, so let's focus on the Settings button.

Clicking on the Settings button displays a dialog box used to specify when to update cached Web pages saved in your Internet Files Folder, how much space your folder should take up on your hard drive, and where to store the folder on your hard drive. Figure 4.10 displays the Settings dialog box.

The basic idea behind caching is simple: store Web page information in a local file, thereby making the information easier and quicker to retrieve the next time you request the information. Whenever you call up a Web page, your system saves the information in cache memory. If you link to another Web page and then return to the previous page, you will notice that the first page displays more rapidly on your screen the second time you access it. This is because your system opened the cached version of a Web page instead of downloading an Internet version. That's the good news; the bad news is that caching takes up some of your disk memory. Unlike your History folder which saves a link to each Web page you visit, your Temporary Internet Files folder stores an actual copy of each Web page that you visit, along with its components (remember, each component on a Web page has a separate URL, so every component will appear in your cache folder as a separate file). Fortunately, MSIE allows you to determine exactly how much of your system's memory can be dedicated to cache.

The first Cache Settings option available is the "Check for newer versions of pages" option. This option is used to specify whether you want MSIE to check if your cached files are the most up-to-date on Every visit to the

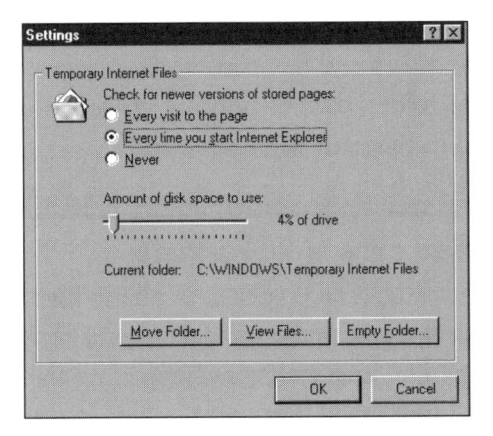

Figure 4.10 **Displaying the Temporary Internet Files Settings dialog box.**

page, Every time you start Internet Explorer, or Never. The default selection is to have MSIE check your cached files once per session. This is a good idea because Web pages change often and, for the most part, on no set schedule. MSIE checks for outdated Web page information in two ways. First, MSIE checks the Last-Modified-Since attribute for each cached Web page. Secondly, MSIE looks for Expire attributes (expiration dates assigned by the page designers) on every object within each Web page. Most browsers only check the Expire attributes.

You use the next option, the "Amount of disk space to use" option, to tell MSIE how much of your hard drive you want to dedicate to cached files. MSIE's default setting is 4%. I wouldn't go much higher than that unless you have quite a few sites that you visit on a regular basis. To set this option, click and hold on the arrow marker, and drag it left to decrease cache space or right to increase cache space. To assist you in selecting your cache size, the percentage number located to the right of the arrow selector changes as you drag the arrow.

The last couple of cache options deal with moving, viewing, and clearing your cache file. Notice the Folder section above the buttons indicating where your cached files are currently being stored. By default, MSIE stores disk cached files in your hard drive's Windows directory in the Temporary Internet Files folder (C:\Windows\Temporary Internet Files). You can change this setting by clicking on the Move Folder button and indicating the path of your choice.

To assign a new path, double click on the drive icon, then double click on the appropriate directory and file icons until you've delineated the path for your cache storage folder, then click on the OK button. Your cached files will now be saved in the path you indicated.

Accessing Cached Files of All Formats

You can listen to sounds, view graphics, and open files stored in your cache folder by opening your cache folder and double clicking on a file. If you choose to listen to a sound file, your system will open a sound application, such as Media Player, when you double click on the file. To view a picture file, your system will open an image program such as Paint Shop Pro, then display the graphic. If you double click on an HTML file, your system will open MSIE (if it is designated as your default browser) and display the file as a Web page. You can also copy or move files (including graphic and sound files) out of your cache folder to save them for other uses.

The middle button, the View Files button, is the same button appearing on the face of the Advanced card. Finally, the third button on the Settings card is the Empty Folder button. You click on the Empty Folder button to clear your cache folder (the Temporary Internet Files folder), which will delete all the Files stored there.

Emptying your disk cache folder deletes the files stored in your cache. I recommend you clear your cache folder on an even more regular basis than you empty your History folder. Keep in mind, if you want to save any cached files, copy or move the files out of the Temporary Internet Files folder before emptying your cache. An added benefit of deleting cached files is that it results in automatically updating the Web pages you regularly visit because MSIE will be forced to download the latest version of the Web page the next time you access the URL (as opposed to calling up the cached version). In addition, clearing your cache helps you get rid of Web page information stored on your hard drive that you are no longer interested in viewing. You may feel a little timid about deleting an entire folder of information, but don't worry—everything in your cache folder appears on the Internet; if you really need to get it back, it's still out there.

Cryptography

As of this writing, the Cryptography option on the Advanced card appears disabled. MSIE is currently working on this feature, and it may not appear disabled in your version of MSIE. It appears that this area of the Advanced card is going to be used to define the cryptography protocols you will use. Of course, this is speculation. If your feature is activated, I suggest you search your Help files or the Microsoft Web site for more information.

Additional

The final section of the Advanced card appears as a series of selection boxes. Basically, you can read through the options and select your preferences. Here's a quick run down of the available Additional options:

- *Show friendly URLS*—Displays friendly, summary URLs in your status bar as opposed to a full URL. Oftentimes, friendly URLs are more helpful than full URLs because the shortened address version is more descriptive.

- *Use smooth scrolling*—Turning on smooth scrolling enables you to flow throw a page without the jerky motion associated with scrolling in the past.

- *Highlight a link when clicked*—This options is responsible for the thin, single pixel boxes that appear around selected links.

- *Use style sheets*—This options enables MSIE to read and interpret HTML style sheets used on Web sites.

- *Enable Java JIT compiler*—Enables MSIE to run all Java programs automatically using MSIE's built-in "Just In Time" compiler. MSIE's Java compiler brings you Java applications automatically and 30% faster than other browser compilers.

- *Enable Java logging*—Turning this feature on specifies the MSIE can create a log of all Java program activity.

By now, you should be experiencing some feelings of control over MSIE as your Internet client. At least I hope so, because this concludes our MSIE-as-Internet-client options discussion (now that's a mouthful!). Don't take a break yet, though—we aren't finished with this chapter. I promised in the beginning of this chapter that I would do a quick briefing to show you how you can access the property sheets of local files without leaving your browser. As I mentioned earlier, one of MSIE's biggest advantages is its ability to easily swap hats between local file manager and Internet client.

Local File Properties

Up to this point in the chapter, we've been discussing the options available in MSIE when it is acting as an Internet client. For this section, type *C:* in the Address box and press Enter. Your MSIE interface should display the contents of your hard drive, and your screen should look similar to the one shown in Figure 4.11.

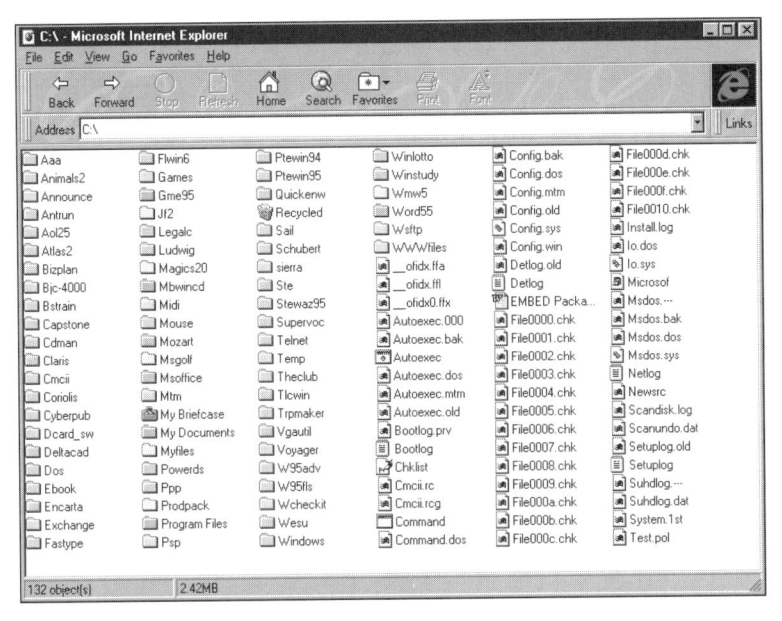

Figure 4.11 Accessing your hard drive.

Before going any further, click on the Go menu command. You should see the familiar commands we discussed in Chapter 2. This is one of those "overlapping" features I was talking about when I mentioned that some of MSIE's Internet features overlap with MSIE's local file management features.

If you are comfortable using Windows Explorer to manipulate and browse through files on your hard drive, you will feel right at home accessing your hard drive using MSIE. You can cut, copy, paste, move, and open folders and files in MSIE just as you can in Windows. You can perform most file management activities using your MSIE browser. For example, right-click in the MSIE window, then select the Properties command. Your Hard Disk Properties dialog box should appear, similar to the dialog box shown in Figure 4.12

The Hard Drive Properties dialog box you see using MSIE is the same Hard Drive Properties dialog box you can see using Windows Explorer. You can call up property boxes on each of the files and folders found on your hard drive. In later chapters, you will discover more about MSIE's ability to integrate local file manager and Internet browser functions and preferences.

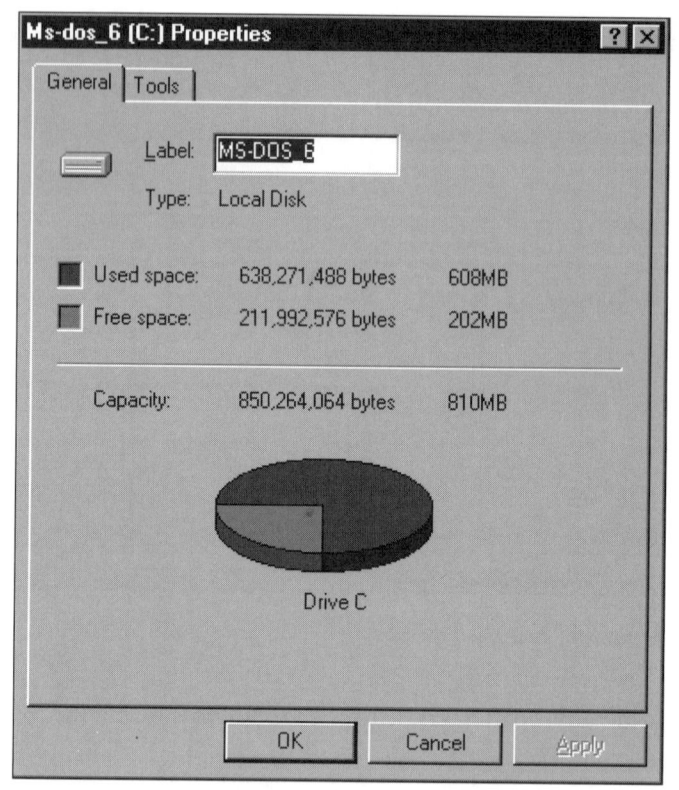

Figure 4.12 Hard Drive Properties dialog box.

Chapter in Review

In this chapter, we've been working on getting comfortable with MSIE's Internet client options. Instead of restating what you've just read, I'm going to give you a chance to practice and show yourself how much you now know about setting MSIE's options. Try to accomplish each of the following tasks without referring to the chapter. If you really get stuck (and I mean *really* get stuck—none of that laziness, please), then go ahead and refer back to the chapter sections until you find the card that accomplishes the desired task. Good luck, but most of all, have fun—I'll see you in the next chapter.

1. Direct MSIE to never empty your cache and set aside 25% of your hard disk space for cached files, then manually empty your cache folder. Reset your options to their original settings.

2. Change your Unviewed links to appear green without underlines (hint: take note of the original colors so you can revert back to them at the end of this exercise). Change your Viewed links to red. Change your screen background color to yellow and text color to blue. Reset your options to their original settings.

3. Verify that your MSIE connects to the Internet automatically as needed and that your option to use a proxy is turned off.

4. View the properties of your hard disk using MSIE as a file manager.

5. Set your browser to display a Normal level of security when you are opening files with active content. Reset your options to their original settings.

6. Set your start page to **http://newslinx.com**. View the change (and play with some of the links!), then reset your start page to MSIE's default.

Customizing Your MSN Start Page 5

Why surf all day long for basic information when your MSN start page can put most of the answers right at your fingertips?

*A*common complaint among new Internet users is that they can never find anything *useful*. As a Net veteran, I *know* the great stuff is out there, but finding it can be somewhat arduous. Lucky for us, Microsoft—in its infinite wisdom—provides a way for us to get all the information we need without doing a lot of running around. Microsoft gives us the MSN customizable home page. Customizing the MSN home page as your start page allows you to move quickly from top news stories to cutting edge computer reports, weather statistics, stock quotes, movie information, sports statistics, and even daily cartoons. It's all out there waiting for you, so make it easy on yourself—customize your MSN start page.

Customizing Your Start Page Links

The best argument for customizing your MSN start page is that the people at MSN will do a lot of your Internet leg work for you if you let them. All you have to do is select and display available options; the MSNers will link you to the appropriate Internet sites. You pick and choose which links you would like to display on your start page by using the Custom Options pages. Keep in mind that you are going to be customizing your *start* page, not creating a *home* page. A start page is a page viewed only by you, a home page is an HTML document accessed by the Web that can be viewed by others. We'll talk more about designing Web pages and home pages in Chapter 17. For now, make yourself comfortable—it's time to customize your start page and simplify your life in one fell swoop. Well, OK, maybe not your *life*, but at least we'll simplify how you access the Internet information you want and need.

Welcome to the MSN Start Page

By now, you've probably done some surfing on the Internet using MSIE. If so, you're familiar with the MSIE default start page, as shown in Figure 5.1.

The MSIE default start page (the page you access when you open MSIE or click on the Home button in your MSIE toolbar) is the MSN Start page. Figure 5.1 represents the Welcome page to the MSN Start page. We are going to customize the MSN Welcome page to display Internet features that interest you. The first step toward a custom start page is to click on the

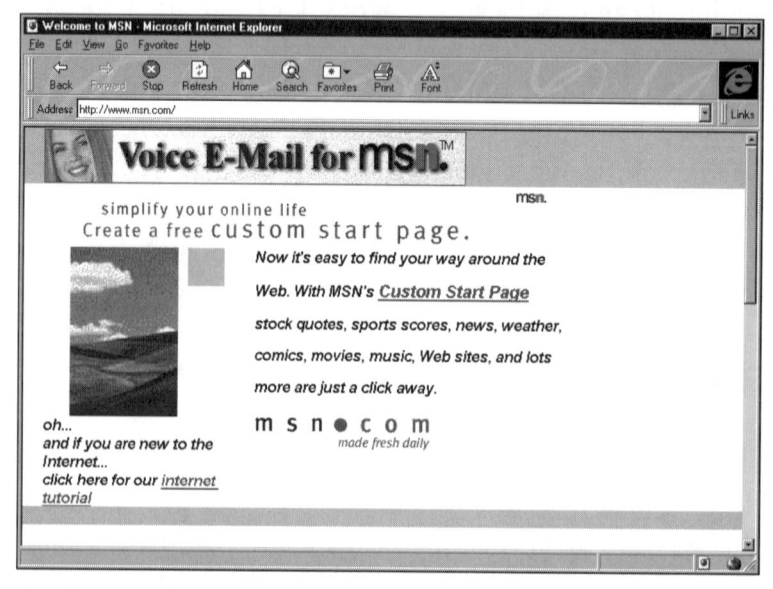

Figure 5.1   Viewing the default MSIE start page.

Custom Start Page link (imagine that!). Go ahead and click. You should see the MSN Customs Start Options page.

The MSN Custom Start Options page reviews the setup of your customized start page. Basically, you can select the links you want to appear in four main category sections on your start page. The four category sections are: Personal Preferences, Services, News & Entertainment, and Internet Searches. If you scroll down the Custom Start Options page, you will see two buttons at the bottom of the page, as shown in Figure 5.2.

The top button is the one we'll use in this chapter—the Click here button below the words, "Let's get customized". If you don't want to customize your start page now, you can click on the lower button and MSN will create a generic start page for you (but you'll be faced with the MSN Welcome page the next time you open MSIE—so you might as well customize your page now). Clicking on the "Let's get customized!" button will take you through four pages of Custom Start Options. Let's review each options page to see what can be included on your Custom Start page. Just to let you know, I'm going to choose every option MSN has to offer for illustrative purposes, but please feel free to choose only the options

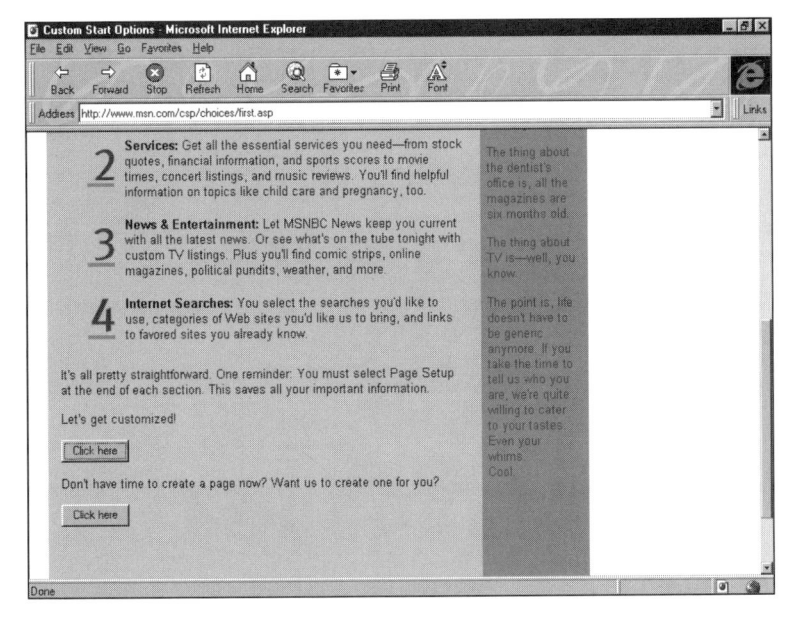

Figure 5.2 **Choosing to customize your start page.**

that interest you. Don't worry if you find you went overboard (or underboard) by the time we reach the end of this chapter—you can always revise your start page options.

Personal Preferences Options—Page 1

Clicking on the "Let's get customized!" button presents you with Page 1 of the MSN Custom Start Options Pages. Figure 5.3 displays the Personal Preferences Options page.

The Personal Preferences Options page consists of three sections: Who Are You?, Special Place for the Kids, and Music to Surf by.

Who Are You?

The Who Are You section is just that—you telling MSN who you are, where you live, and what your email address is (if you want). Don't worry about giving MSN your personal information, this section is merely used to provide you autoinformation down the road. For example, if you later choose to have your start page display you your local weather forecast, MSN needs to know

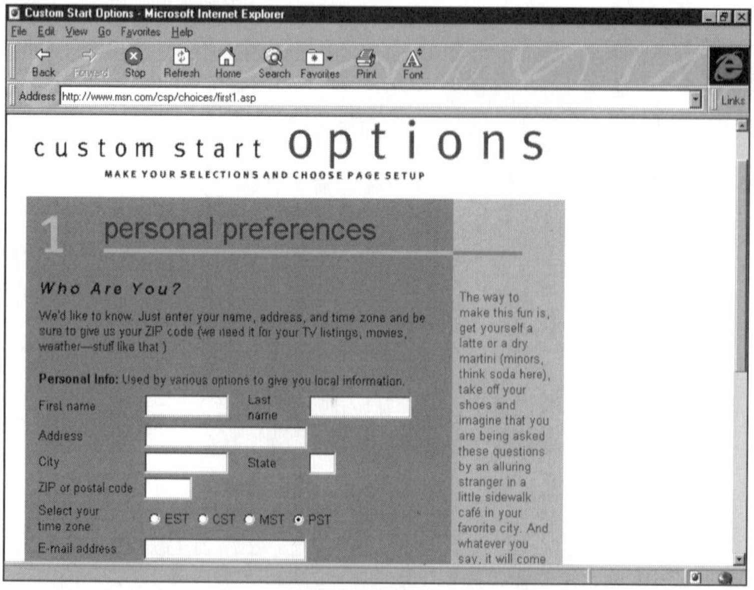

Figure 5.3 Entering your personal preferences.

where you live. If you filled in the personal preferences for your start page, MSN will download the appropriate weather forecast for your area at your request. There are other options that refer to your personal preferences. I'll point out those options as we work our way through this chapter.

Special Place for the Kids

Do you have kids? If so, you should select this option. If not...then you should still select this option. Turn the Kids link option on by clicking in the selection box. You may be wondering why I'm telling everyone to select this option. Well, choosing to display this link doesn't take up much space on your start page, and it won't be long before you discover that many of the best Web sites are designed for kids. And, if you're lucky, you're still a kid somewhere in there, regardless of the date on your driver's license. Now, don't get me wrong. The MSN Kids' site isn't the *best* kids' site around, but it's a pretty good one, and it's new. I think it will be worthwhile to see what Microsoft does with this site.

Music to Surf By

The last of MSN's Personal Preferences options is the Music Clip option. This option offers MSIE users the opportunity to listen to music while opening and viewing the start page. The music background is kind of a novelty, and if you keep your speakers turned down low, it isn't too much of a distraction. You can choose from a variety of music styles (none of which are too wild—we're not talking Pearl Jam here, more like synthesized, muzak-inspired arrangements.)

To elect to have music play while visiting your start page, simply click on the appropriate radio button to the left of the Music Clip option. I've found it doesn't really matter which music style you select because all the options tend to sound the same (if anything, the default selection is probably the most tolerable). Of course this option is only available for MSIE users who have sound-enabled systems. You can adjust the volume of the music the same way you normally adjust your speakers—either using your speaker controls or your system sound controls (in most cases, you should be able to adjust your volume by clicking on the sound icon displaying next to the time on your Windows 95 task bar). Keep in mind that the music only plays while you are displaying your start page. Clicking on a link will take you to another Web site and discontinue your music selection. If you're planning on staying on your start page for a while, pushing the Esc button on your keyboard will stop the music from driving you nuts.

After you have made your music selection, click on the Set Up Page button. It's time to visit Page 2 to set up your Services Options.

Services Options—Page 2

Page 2 of the MSN Custom Start Options Pages is where you choose which investment, sports, movies, music, and parenting features you want to display on your start page. The first half of page 2 appears as shown in Figure 5.4.

We'll start at the top of the Services Options page with investments and work our way down to the parenting features section. Along the way we'll catch the latest sports statistics, see what's playing at the movies, and listen in on music industry news. But before we do all that playing, we should check out our money situation.

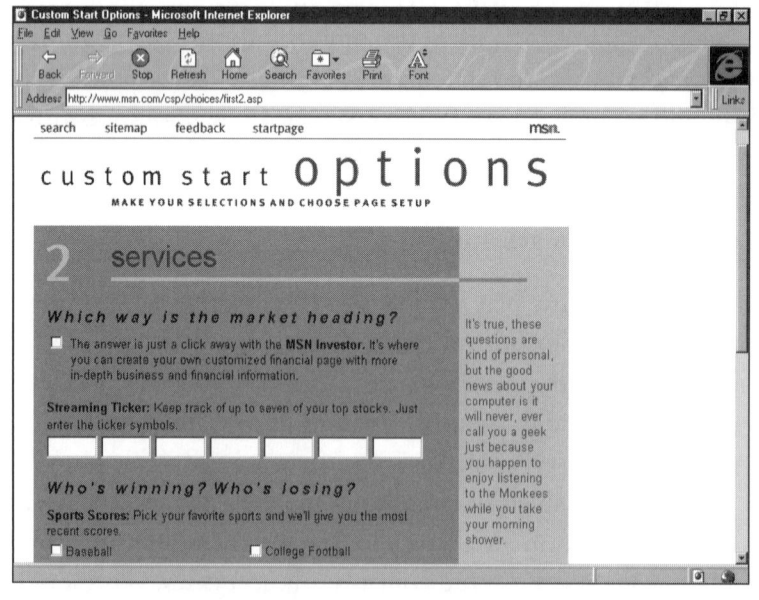

Figure 5.4 **Choosing to display investment, sports, movie, music, and parenting options on your start page.**

Investment Savvy

You have two options to choose from in the investment section of the Services Options page. You can opt to display a link to the MSN Investor home page (more about that in a second), and you can choose to display stock information on your start page for up to seven ticker symbols. Let's take a look at both options.

MSN Investor

The MSN Investor page is a new MSN feature, and it's quickly becoming very popular among investor-types. Turning on the MSN Investor option places a link to the MSN Investor page (shown in Figure 5.5) on your start page.

As you can see in Figure 5.5, the MSN Investor Page provides five main links, and a smaller link to MSNBC News. Each of the five links takes you to a different page on the MSN Investor site. You can view a quick market summary, check out today's top 10 stocks, review your personal portfolio, look up a quote, and access a comprehensive list of links to online investment resources. If you have any interest in investing, I suggest you elect to display the MSN Investor link on your start page. At least select it now, so you can view

Figure 5.5 Accessing the MSN Investor home page.

the site's offerings. If it turns out the link is useless to you, you can always return to the Services Options page and remove the link from your start page.

Finally, take a look at the MSNBC link located near the bottom of the MSN Investor page. You will find links to MSNBC throughout your start page. Depending on where you are in your start page, clicking on the link will take you to a relevant section of the MSNBC news site. For example, clicking on the MSNBC link found on the MSN Investor page takes you to the Commerce section of the MSNBC site. You'll have more chances to see how this ever-changing link works as we wind our way through the start page setup. For now, let's talk a little more about stocks.

Stock Market Update

The second custom option available in the investment area of your MSN start page is the Streaming Ticker option. This option enables you to continuously view stock prices for up to seven ticker symbols. Let's test the Streaming Ticker option. Notice there are seven text boxes. For demonstration purposes, let's choose seven random ticker symbols to enter into the ticker boxes. I'm going to enter the following ticker symbols: *for, scor, and, se, ven, rs, ago*. The easiest way to enter the symbols is to click in the first text box, type *for*, then press your Tab key to move your cursor to the next text box. Type *scor*, then press Tab again. Continue until you've entered all seven ticker symbols.

Figure 5.6 displays how your Streaming Ticker service will appear after you complete your start page customization. Notice the fine print beneath the Streaming Ticker indicating that the stock quote information updates every 20 minutes. If you desire a more detailed description about a particular stock, use the MSN Investor page.

Sports Scores and Statistics

Next option: Sports Scores. Some people may skip this option altogether, while others will check the Sports Scores links on a daily basis (or more). Customizing your start page to display links reporting the latest sports scores is very simple—click in the selection boxes to the left of the sport of your choice. You can display links to sites reporting scores for baseball, the NFL, the NHL, college football, college basketball, and the NBA. As usual, I'm going to select all the options for illustrative purposes (not because I

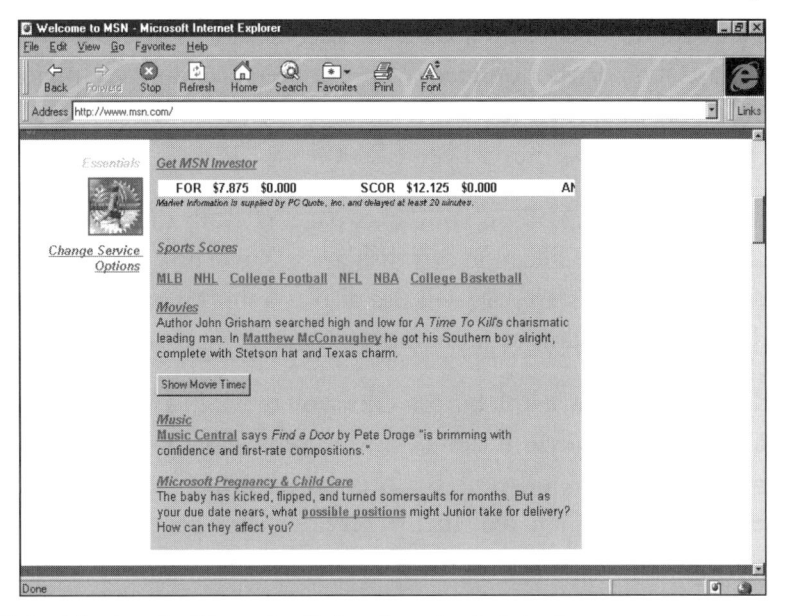

Figure 5.6 Viewing the Streaming Ticker for selected stock.

have latent Bob Costas tendencies). My sports links display as shown in Figure 5.6. Each link takes you to a Web page sponsored by ESPNet SportsZone, or to a page listing the latest sports scores followed by a link to the SportsZone Web site. The SportsZone Web pages offer much more than sports scores—each Sports Score link is more like a link to a sports magazine. Remember to click on your Refresh button in the MSIE toolbar each time you call up a Sports Score link. If you fail to refresh a page, you will most likely be viewing an old-news cached version of the sports page.

The World Wide Web of Sports
You can scout out more sports information at http://www.sl.com and http://www.sportsline.com. The first URL is the online version of Sports Illustrated (need I say more?), and the second URL is the SportsLine site with links to scores, play-by-plays, news, and live games (using Shockwave technology).

This Week at the Movies
Okay, it's Saturday night—you might as well find something to do besides surf the Web. Not only are your family and friends feeling neglected, but

the Net bogs down over the weekend as activity picks up between Internet enthusiasts, spiders (automated Web explorers), and server maintenance activities. So what do you say? Want to go to the movies? Planning your trip to the movies has never been easier.

To display a Movie link on your start page, click in the Movies selection box. Clicking in the selection box displays a Movie link and a Show Movie Times button. Your start page will also display a short movie-industry related blurb containing a link to more movie news.

Clicking on the Movie link button takes you to MSN's Cinamania Online, a site filled with movie reviews, local theater show times, and, in some instances, ticket box offices. (Be forewarned, when you purchase movie tickets over the Net, you may incur a service charge per ticket—you should be informed of the charge on the page, so read the fine print.) Clicking on the Show Movie Times button takes you directly to the MovieLink Web site, a site discussed in more detail in Chapter 8. When you click on the Show Movie Times button, you will see one instance where your personal information comes into play. The MovieLink site will ask you if you want to check out the movies in your city with your ZIP code. If you're looking for movie information in your neighborhood, you can move on to the movie information with a single click.

Music to Your Ears

Music lovers have made their presence known on the Internet. Opting to display the Music link on your start page gives you quick access to the MSN Music Central page. Music Central is a music-industry online zine-type site, with enough links to quench most people's musical thirsts. Chapter 8 discusses the Music Central page in more detail. If you have any interest in music, I suggest you add this link to your start page. To display a link to Music Central, as well as a teaser lead for one of the stories of the day on Music Central, turn on the Music link on the Services Options page.

Family Planning and Parenting

The last Services Option is what I refer to as the New Parent News option. When you elect to display this option, your start page displays a link to the Microsoft Pregnancy and Childcare Preview site, which overflows with information geared toward new moms, dads, and little ones. You can learn about everything from conception and pregnancy to at-home dads and childproofing your home (and everyone else's!). There's lots of good information here if you need it.

Well done! You've made it to the bottom of the Services Options page. After you've completed making your Service Options, click on the Setup This Page button to move on to Page 3 of the MSN Custom Start Options Pages.

News and Entertainment Options—Page 3

Is your house filled to the brim with old newspapers? Looking for a paperless alternative? MSN might have the answer. As you've probably begun to suspect, your start page can carry much of the same information as your daily newspaper. Figure 5.7 displays the top portion of the News and Entertainment Options page.

The News and Entertainment Options area of your start page continue in the start page/newspaper tradition by provide you with cutting edge news stories, Web picks, television schedules, comic strips, and more. Read on to find what options you can add to your start page to help you keep pace with today's news and entertainment developments.

Daily News with MSNBC

What's in the news? MSNBC is—Microsoft and NBC joined forces to bring you online, cutting edge Internet news and technology. While the cooperative effort alone is impressive, you'll also be glad to hear that you can get links to the top MSNBC news stories on your start page. You can choose to display news stories in six categories: World, Commerce, Sports, Science & Technology, Life, and Opinion. To select the news categories you want to display on your start page, click in the selection boxes that interest you. Once again, I'm going to select all categories to view the types of news each link provides

Displaying links to news stories really beefs up your start page. Each news category displayed on your start page provides a link to the subject page on

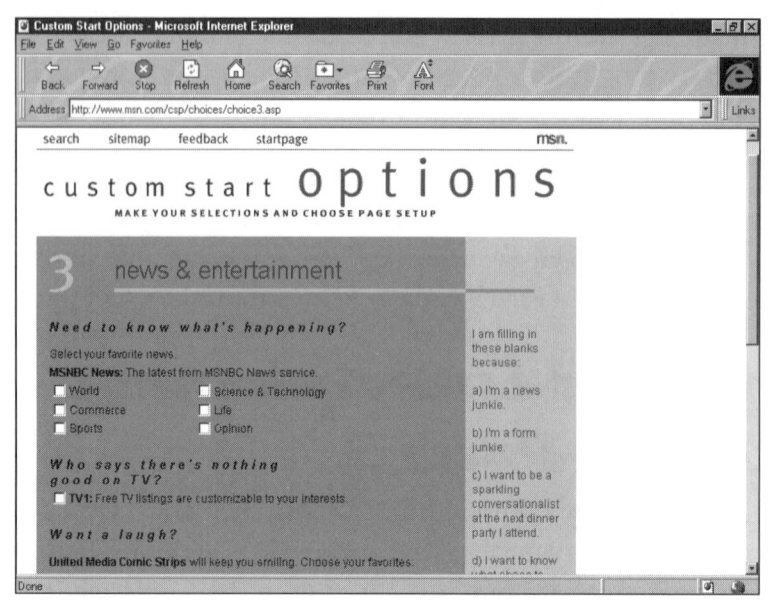

Figure 5.7 Setting your News and Entertainment Options.

the MSNBC site, as well as two or three short summaries of the top news stories in each selected category. To view a story, click on the MSNBC subject header link. Beware, though, when you click on a MSNBC link to read a story, the story will most likely contain more links—your news reading could last longer than you intended (mine did!). Figure 5.8 displays how links to MSNBC news stories appear on your start page.

Before we move on to the next Custom Option, I have one last news issue to address. After all my emphasis on refreshing your Web pages in this book, the MSNBC top stories links are one area where you don't have to worry about refreshment (unless you'd like to take a break for a glass of ice cold lemonade). MSN constantly refreshes your MSNBC news links for you. Your MSN start page updates every day when you open it. Then, MSN continues to update your start page throughout the day every time you return to the page, with one exception: at least one half hour must pass since you visited your start page before it will update itself automatically. Therefore, the news stories you read as you drink your morning coffee will probably be different than the stories you see at 5:00, which in turn could be different from the stories you see before tucking yourself in for the night.

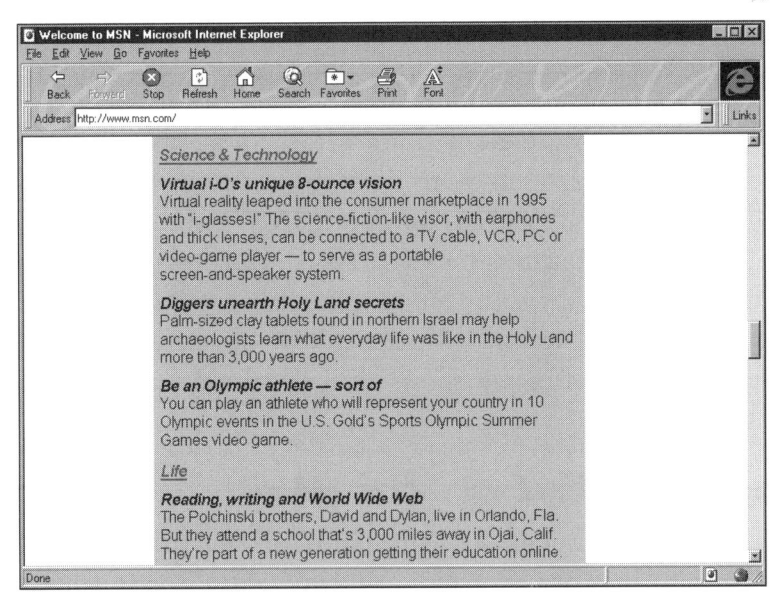

Figure 5.8 Viewing your start page links to MSNBC's top news stories.

Information Overload

For all you news junkies, you don't have to settle for the news stories on your start page. If you haven't quite satisfied your need, try clicking on the Today's Links button in the MSIE Links toolbar. (See Chapter 9 for more details on the Today's Links site.) Or, take a look at the online version of USA Today at http://www.usatoday.com.

Time for Television

If you still have time to watch television after reading all your start page news stories, stock quote statistics, and sports updates, then this is the link for you. TV1 is a television guide dream (or nightmare, depending on your point of view). The MSN News and Entertainment Options page concerns itself only with wanting to know if you want a link to TV1 or not. If you want a TV1 link to appear on your start page, click in the selection box next to the TV1 option (MSN will figure out your time zone and location from your personal preferences page).

The TV1 link displays on your start page at the bottom of the News and Entertainment section. The TV link consists of a Show Tonight's TV Listings button. Clicking on the button result in an online TV guide with networks, times, and program names appearing as links arranged in a grid format.

You can click on a program title to learn more about the program, customize your grid to show only those shows that interest you, and view television programs by network or topic. TV1 offers a free membership, so if you are interested in more features, such as receiving email reminders when your favorite shows are on, you should register with TV1. This site has many options—too many to cover here—but even the default grid display is helpful in that it shows all the network and cable programs airing throughout the day.

Comic Relief on the Web

Your next start page option, the United Media Comic Strips option, provides a break from the information overload that can easily occur while you surf the Net. To enter the cartoon zone, select any of the four available cartoon links by clicking in the selection boxes to the left of the cartoon names. I'm electing to display all four links; you can pick and choose at your discretion.

Once you have completed your start page customization, you will only be a click away from seeing a daily cartoon. The cartoon links are automatically refreshed daily, which means you won't ever have to worry about clicking on your Refresh button to view a new cartoon.

Expediting Downloads

If your system takes its time downloading graphics, minimize your MSIE browser window while the cartoons are downloading. You can open a second MSIE browser window by choosing File|New Window, enabling you to carry on doing other work on the Internet while your cartoons open.

Each cartoon link displays the daily cartoon plus links to all sorts of other fun places. For example, all the cartoon pages offer an archive of past cartoons, both the Peanuts and Rose is Rose pages offer links to the Sunday color comic of the week, and the Dilbert page offers one of my favorite links (this one takes a while, but you really should check this out)—the sock puppet link. If you scroll to the bottom of the Dilbert comic page, there is a small link embedded in the P.S. portion of a note from Scott Adams, the creator of Dilbert. The sock puppet link displays as the word *here*. Click on the link, then see what silly things people will do if given the opportunity.

Finally, you'll notice that on the bottom of each cartoon page there is a jump bar to UnitedMedia, The Comic Strip, and The Inkwell. All three of these links will provide you with links to more cartoon and cartoon-related sites than you'll ever need. Cartoon links are definitely a fun way to pass the time (why do you think it took me so long to write this short section?), and, besides, I'm sure your boss has heard that laughter is the best medicine.

Keeping Up on Computer Technology

Ok, enough frivolity. Do you want to read the latest computer industry news from *PC Week*, *Inter@ctive Week*, *MacWeek*, and *PC Magazine*? If the answer is yes, then click in the selection box next to the Ziff-Davis Computer News option on the News and Entertainment Options page. If your answer is no, then skip to the next section of this chapter. I'm going to select yes. If you do the same, your start page will add a Ziff-Davis Computer News section below your MSNBC top news stories.

The Ziff-Davis link provides three links to top computer news stories—unfortuantely, links are all you get. There are no link summaries as there are in the top news story section. On the other hand, once you click on a link, you can read the story, then click on a link to the story's originating magazine's home page or to ZDNet—the home page for Ziff-Davis. From there, the ball's in your court (or the disk is in your drive). You can read headline stories, search through magazine archives, or follow any number of other links.

Playing with Politics

As if you don't get enough of Bob Dole and Bill Clinton via the other news mediums, MSN will place a link on your start page to a Web page filled with the latest political gossip. As of this writing, this feature is named Decision '96, in honor of—you got it—the presidential election. The topic may have changed by the time you read this book, but I have a feeling the flavor will be the same: Politics.

Rain or Shine Weather Report

Just in case you've been spending too much time in front of your computer and you have no idea what's going on outside, MSN has provided you with an optional start page weather link. You can customize your start page to display links to local and national weather information and maps.

To display weather links, scroll down to the Weather Information section of the News and Entertainment Options page. As you can see, there are two selection topic areas. The first area addresses whether you want a national weather map, a link to a national weather map, or neither to appear on your start page. You can also elect to display the national weather map link for Canada. The second selection area allows you to choose a link to a local weather report to appear on your start page. Go ahead and decide, then click in the appropriate selection boxes. I, of course, am electing to display the national weather map and a local weather report link on my start page. The weather information displays above the TV1 link and below the comics, as in Figure 5.9.

Notice Figure 5.9 displays a Show Local Weather button and an NBC Intellicast weather map. Clicking on the Show Local Weather button takes you to the NetCast weather page. If you've set your personal

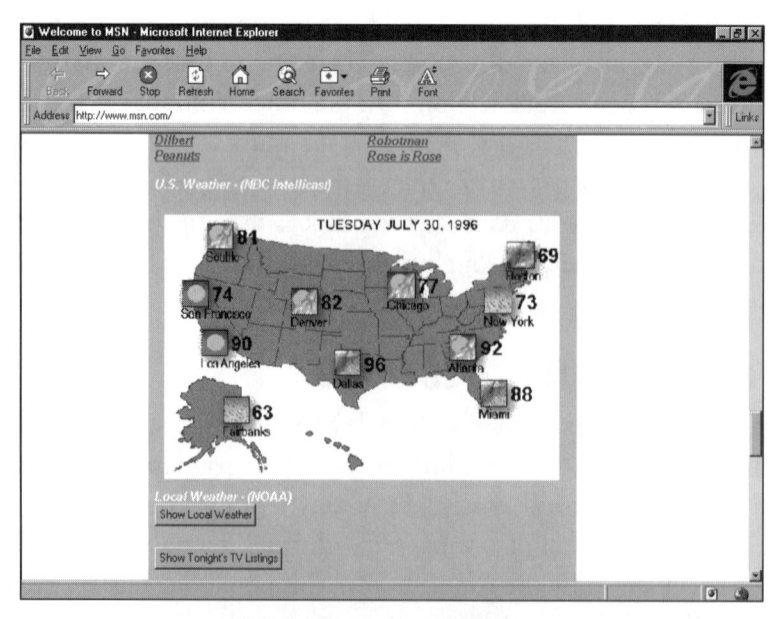

Figure 5.9 The lower portion of the News and Entertainment section.

preferences, your local area weather page (compliments of NetCast) will display automatically (if you haven't set your personal preferences, you'll have to give some information to NetCast before you can view your local weather report).

Clicking on the NBC Intellicast national weather map displays the MSNBC Weather page—a comprehensive weather site with enough information to help you weather any storm. All in all, both links are top-notch weather sites. If you are interested in more weather information on the Net, see Chapter 8.

Internet Searches Options— Page 4

The fourth and final custom options page is the Internet Searches Options page, as shown in Figure 5.10.

The Internet Searches page enables you to place links to Internet search engines directly on your start page. In Chapter 10, we'll discuss how to use Internet search engines to get the most out of the Web. The Internet Searches page also offers you links to Microsoft's daily and weekly Web picks. And,

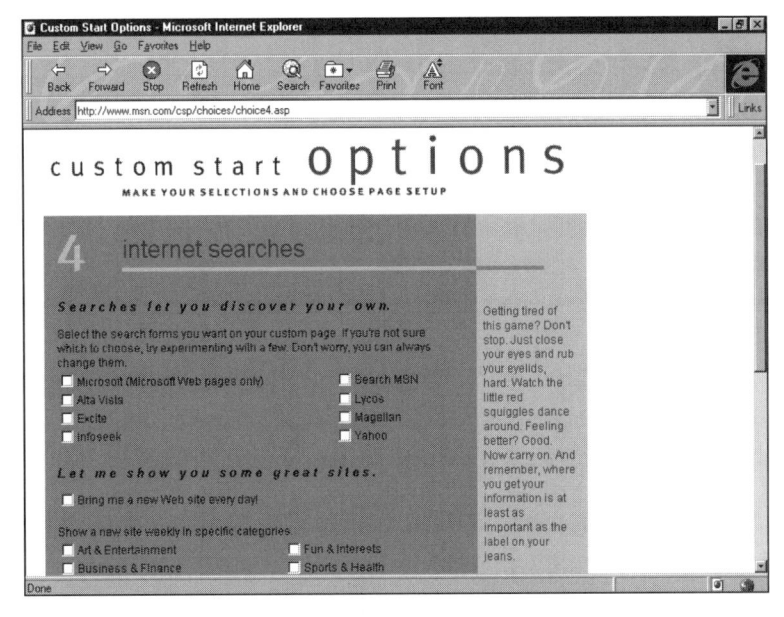

Figure 5.10 **Viewing the Internet Searches Options page.**

finally, Page 4 enables you to create and display links of your choice on your start page (a really handy feature).

Internet Searches

The first feature on the Internet Searches Option page is the search engines settings. Clicking in a specific search engine's selection box will display a keyword search text box on your start page for that search engine. You can select any or all of the search engines displayed: Microsoft, Alta Vista, Excite, Infoseek, Search MSN, Lycos, Magellan, and Yahoo. There are quite a few more search engines available on the Net, but these are eight of the more common ones. The Microsoft search engine searches for information on Microsoft Web pages only and the Search MSN searches MSN pages only; the other six search engines are discussed individually in Chapter 10. That chapter also presents an extensive discussion about how to use search engines, so I'm not going to get too specific here.

For illustrative purposes, I've selected all eight search engines. Unfortunately, the start page setup allows you to run only one search engine at a time. Chapter 10 tells you how to access the SavvySearch site, a site which allows you to access over 23 search services at once.

Stepping Up Your Searches with the Internet Sleuth

Another cool search site is the Internet Sleuth. You can use the Internet Sleuth to search for topics in over 1,000 databases of Web information. You can't display the Internet Sleuth in the Search Forms section of your start page, but you can add it as a link in your Favorite Links section. The URL for the Internet Sleuth is http://www.intbc.com/sleuth/.

It is up to you whether you want to display any or all of the eight search engines on your start page. Clicking on the search button in the MSIE toolbar provides you with the same search engine links.

The Ultimate Search Engine Site

For a comprehensive list of search engines, check out The Matrix of Internet Catalogs and Search Engines at http://www.si.umich.edu/~fprefect/matrix/

matrix.shtml. If you are using Windows 95, you can create a desktop shortcut to The Matrix. First, make sure you can see some part of your desktop, then display The Matrix Web page in your browser window. Click on the URL shown beneath The Matrix header (not the URL in the Address box), then drag the URL to your desktop.

Great Sites

According to WebCrawler, a Web indexer, the Web's size has increased sixfold—or 600 percent—over the past year. Prior to this last year, the Internet had been growing at a rate of 100 percent per year since 1988. According to Matrix News, as of March 1996, the core Internet consists of 16.9 million users of 7.7 million computers that can *distribute* information and 26.4 million users of 10.1 million computers that can *access* information. Obviously, the Internet's growth has been phenomenal. It is no wonder we can't keep up with all of the good sites out there. To help us out, MSN offers you the option to display a site-of-the-day link, as well as up to six site-of-the-week links on your start page. These selections differ from your top news stories links, because these links take you to interesting *sites*, while the top news stories links take you to interesting news *articles*.

To display a new Web site every day and new Web sites every week, click next to the "Bring me a new Web site every day" option. Below the daily site option is the "Show a new site weekly in specific categories" option, which includes six categories. I am selecting all six categories, as well as the option to display the daily site. Selecting daily and weekly Web sites will result in your start page appearing similar to Figure 5.11.

Hunting Down the Best Sites
Many Web sites display Sites-of-the-Week, Favorite Sites, or Site-Winners. Make sure you check out these sites whenever you have the chance. According to the FAS CyberStragey Project, 96 percent of Web users find Web sites through friends and other Web pages.

Once you indicate that you want the site-of-the-day and sites-of-the-week links displayed on your start page, you don't have to do anything but click

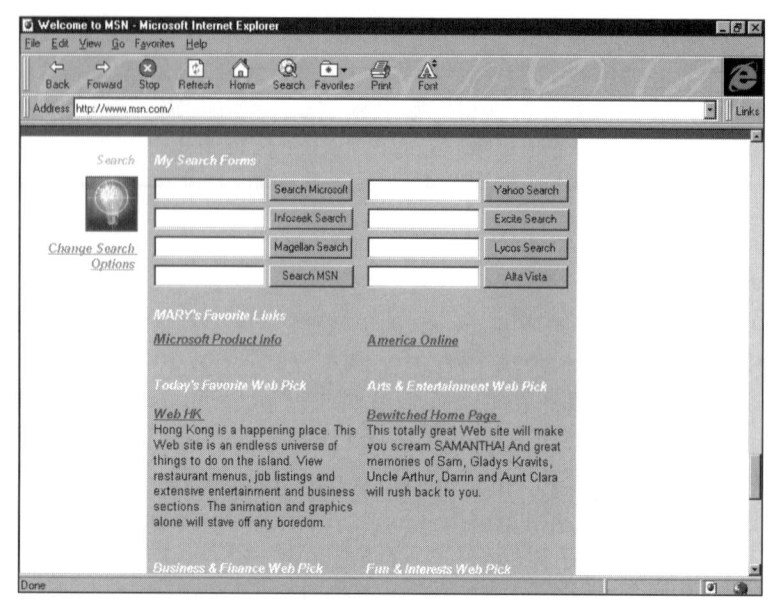

Figure 5.11 The bottom of your customized start page.

on the links. MSN will take care of updating your start page links for you. Also, when we discuss the MSIE Links toolbar, you will notice that the links on your start page are excerpted from the daily and weekly links found on the MSN Surf Stories page (the Surf Stories page is accessed by clicking on the Today's Links button in the MSIE Links toolbar).

Keep Track of Your Favorite Links

The final start page custom option enables you to add up to six Web page links to your start page. You can create and display up to six links to your favorite Web pages. This feature is great if you have a favorite page or two (or six) that you view often, because you can now place a link to the frequented page right on your start page. OK, that's the concept. Let's discuss the practicalities of how to create links on your start page.

Before you can create a link, you need to know the address of the Web page or site you want to associate with the link. Once you have identified an address, creating a link on your start page involves three steps. First you must indicate a protocol, next you must enter a URL, and finally, you have to name your link. Let's create a link on our start page to America Online's (AOL) home page (**http://www.aol.com**).

The first step in assigning a link to your start page is to tell MSIE what protocol to use to access the site. Remember from Chapter 1 that, in Internet terms, a *protocol* is a set of formal rules describing how to transmit data across a network. The Favorites Options link makes indicating a protocol easy by providing a drop-down list of six available protocols. The six protocols should sound familiar from our earlier discussions. They are: http, ftp, gopher, news, telnet, https, wais, and file. AOL's URL tells us that their home page transmits using http, the hypertext transfer protocol (http also tells us the file is an HTML document). Therefore, in the first field of the Favorite Links options section, retain the default protocol selection, http://.

The second step in creating a link on your start page is to enter a site's URL in the text box to the right of the protocol drop-down list box. In case you weren't paying attention earlier (although I'm sure you were), the URL for America Online's home page is *www.aol.com*. Other URLs are not so simple (as I'm sure you've noticed). One trick to ensure accuracy and save typing time is to copy a Web page's URL from the Address text box, then paste the URL into the text box on the Custom Options page. To accomplish this, follow these steps:

1. Display the desired Web page.
2. Highlight the URL in the Address box excluding the protocol information.
3. Copy the Address (if you are using Windows, type Ctrl+C).
4. Return to the Custom Options page.
5. Click in the Address text box to the right of the desired protocol list box.
6. Paste the URL into the Address box (if you are using Windows, type Ctrl+V).

The final step in creating a link is to name your link. Naming your link is extremely important. If you don't name your link, the link will not appear on your start page. You can name your links anything you want—you could call the AOL home page *The Star Spangled Banner*, and it wouldn't matter, the link would still take you to the AOL home page. Of course, I encourage you to give your links names that mean something to you. Let's be creative and name our link *America Online*.

You've filled the proper text boxes with the appropriate information, so you are ready to move on, right? Hold on just a minute—you aren't done yet. Don't forget to click on the Setup This Page button. Whenever you return to the Custom Options pages to make changes to your settings, you must click on the Setup This Page button to implement your most current settings.

Did you click on the Setup This Page button? If so, congratulations are in order—you've reached your customized start page! I want to talk a little about the overall page, but first let's check our America Online link. Scroll down your new start page until you see your America Online link in the Search section of your start page, as shown previously in Figure 5.11.

Click on your America Online link to verify that you entered the address information properly. The America Online home page should display. If you click on your link and get an error message stating that Microsoft Internet Explorer cannot open the Internet site, you may need to correct the address information on your Internet Searches Custom Options page. You can change your links and link information at any time by clicking on the Change Search Options link appearing to the left of your start page Search Options section. Remember, you must always click on the Setup This Page button after you edit any of your Custom Options pages to activate your changes.

Assigning a Start Page Link to a Folder

You can assign a start page Favorite Link to a folder (not a file) on your hard drive. For example, to create a link to the Games folder on your hard drive, select the file:// protocol from the drop-down list, enter c:\games in the address text box, then name the link Games. Click on the Set Up Page button to save, activate, and display your new start page link. Keep in mind, if you are going to be working locally for a while, you might want to disconnect your Internet connection.

Viewing Your MSN Start Page

Welcome to your customized start page. Now that you've completed your customized start page settings, the top of your start page should look similar to Figure 5.12.

This page will appear every time you open MSIE and every time you click on the Home button in your MSIE toolbar. As you can see, aside from all the lovely links we just discussed, MSN throws in a few standard links. The standard links appear at the top of your start page, as well as at the bottom of your start page as a text link footer. The standard links include:

- *Contents*—Takes you to the MSN Sitemap page, which shows a text only framework of the pages included in the MSN site. We'll talk more about the Sitemap in Chapter 9.

- *Try MSN*—Click on this link to see how you can win a free trial membership to MSN's commercial services.

- *Tutorial*—Yes, yet another way to get to Microsoft's lightweight Internet tutorial.

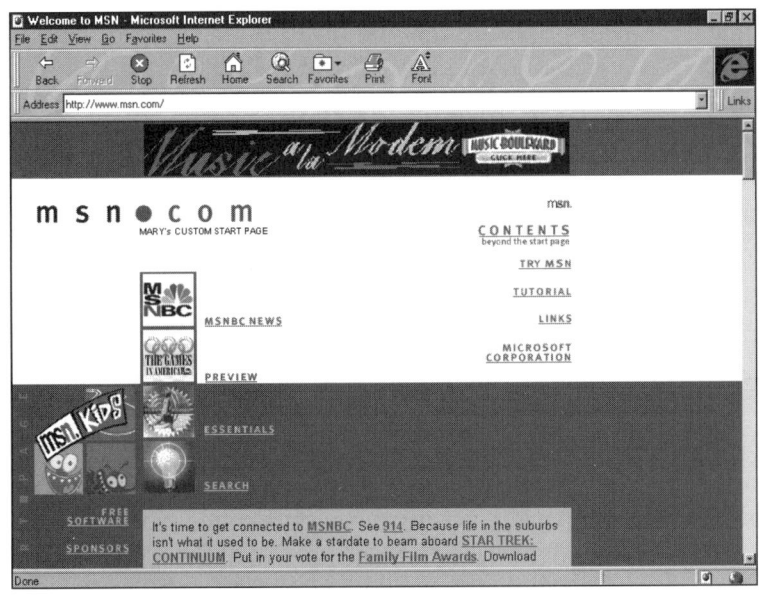

Figure 5.12 Viewing your customized MSN start page.

- *Links*—This standard MSN start page button takes you to the Surf Stories page (you can also get to the search stories page by clicking on the Today's Links button in the MSIE Links toolbar).

- *Microsoft Corporation*—Yet another way to find your way to Microsoft's home page.

- *MSNBC News*—Getting straight to the meat of the matter—this link takes you directly to the MSNBC home page.

- *Preview*—Introduces you to special features available to MSN customers.

- *Essentials*—A link to the Essentials Services directory. I'll go through the entire list of Essentials directory links later, in Chapter 8.

- *Search*—Clicking on this button opens the Microsoft Internet Searches page.

The remainder of your MSN start page should look familiar from our chapter discussion. It's now time for me to shut down this chapter and give you a chance to surf the Web and play with your new start page links. Remember, if you want to change your start page settings, click on the Change Personal Options link. Good luck!

Chapter in Review

This chapter has covered a lot of ground—from checking your stock quotes to looking up sports statistics to playing clips of music while you start your Internet "day." You'll probably find yourself tweaking your start page here and there until you create a comfortable zone for yourself. For example, your Favorite sites and news preferences will probably change over time. Of course, you are free to recustomize your start page at will, and I encourage you to do so (just don't forget about that Setup this page button).

Also, I should point out that there are many available start pages on the Web. Basically, *any* page can constitute a start page—your browser doesn't care, although you might. Later in this book you'll learn how you can create a blank start page. As you become more proficient on the Internet, you can create and design your own start page from scratch. In the meantime, enjoy your MSN start page. I think you'll find quite a bit of useful information—not only *out there*, but right in front of you.

MSIE and America Online 6

AOL's integrated package of proprietary software has merged with Explorer in a dynamite package that is extremely useful for Internet surfers.

When I think of America Online (AOL), I first think of the colorful graphics, the enormous amount of information I have access to, and the many online friends I've made there. My next thought is of the millions of disks that have been distributed in tidal waves for each successive AOL upgrade. AOL has had record membership increases in the past years, and now with version 3.0 recently released, more users than ever will be captivated by AOL's global community and Internet access.

AOL 3.0's improved technology allows users to get art faster, browse the Web with fewer hang-ups, and navigate the service easier and more efficiently. Features have been added to customize your mail, find out which of your friends are online, and update the AOL software automatically without reinstalling. And that's not all. In a celebrated agreement with Microsoft, AOL has included the Microsoft Internet Explorer in its software package (for Windows 95, Windows 3.1, and Macintosh), which means that you only have to launch AOL to access both AOL and the Internet.

AOL has also agreed to provide its customers with MSIE upgrades as soon as Microsoft makes them available.

Together, this dynamic duo provides you with the efficiency and organization of an online service bundled with a superior Internet browser. As you'll see as we work through this chapter, with this combination, you just can't lose.

So, no more dallying, let's get started.

Downloading AOL and Explorer

Of course, our first task is to get a copy of the AOL 3.0 for Windows 95 software and Microsoft Internet Explorer. With so many AOL startup disks floating around, you're sure to have picked up a copy somewhere—from your mailbox, from a computer magazine, or perhaps bundled with your modem. In that case, you can stop here and move on to the *Installing AOL 3.0* section. If you weren't fortunate enough to have AOL come knocking at your door, you'll have to download a copy. Depending on your membership status with AOL (current member looking to upgrade or new member), you can download your copy in one of two ways.

Navigating with Keywords

Each area on AOL has a keyword which can also be thought of as a "password" to navigate directly to the designated area. With consistent use, keywords become intuitive. You will find the hour's top news when you use the keyword News. AOL gently reminds users of keywords in small type at the bottom of each screen that is accessible by keywords. To access the keyword function, you can select Go To|Keyword from the Menu Bar, select the Keyword button from the Toolbar, or use Ctrl+K from the keyboard. A dialog box will appear, and then you can just type the keyword and click on the Go button. If you're not sure of the correct keyword, type the name of a concept or topic (example: politics) and then hit the Search button and all of the political areas will appear in a list for your selection.

For Current Members Only

If you have an AOL membership, sign on and select the Keyword button from the Toolbar (or Keyword from the Menu Bar, or press Ctrl+K), and then enter Upgrade. For the remainder of this chapter, the directions will be provided as if you are selecting the Keyword button from the Toolbar. At this point, you have the opportunity to review the features of the new software and choose to download now or later. Read carefully because some users will have one download and others will have two. Currently, if you already have Microsoft Internet Explorer, you will only need a copy of AOL 3.0 for Windows 95. Conversely, if you have neither, you will need both. When you select Download Now, the process is free of connect charges (and the time is not deducted from your monthly "free" minutes). However, you'll need to monitor the process and manually sign off when it is complete. If you elect to Download Later, the downloading time is *not* free, but you can tell AOL to sign off for you after downloading. Whether you choose to Download Now or Download Later, the file will be sent to your AOL Downloads folder, otherwise known as c:\aol25\download (where aol25 represents the version of the software used to download the upgrade).

You can expect the downloads to take anywhere from 20 minutes to 4.5 hours (yes, hours!), depending on your modem's baud rate. I strongly suggest that you upgrade late in the evening or early in the morning to avoid high traffic times. And keep an eye on your PC in the event the download crashes. It's rare, but it could happen.

Downloading from the AOL Web Page

Whether or not you are currently an AOL member, you can download a copy of the program by visiting the AOL home page at **http://www.aol.com** and selecting Download Our Software. Be prepared—the files take some time to download onto your system, and of course, that duration depends upon the speed of your Internet connection. The truly techno-savvy with a T1 or ISDN will find that their download takes only minutes, while someone with a slower modem may find that it takes up to 4 hours and possibly more, if Net traffic is heavy. Be sure to pay careful attention to your browser's actions to note or designate the download location.

If you prefer to avoid the download delay, you can have AOL send you their software and Explorer on CD-ROM. The email address (fulfill2@aol.com) and phone number (800-827-6364) posted on the AOL Web site allow you to specify such an order. You'll need to indicate your postal address, your platform (Windows 95), and the desired media type (CD-ROM).

Installing AOL 3.0 and Explorer

Before you can get online and practice your surfing techniques, you must first install the AOL program. It doesn't really matter which you install first, but I think it is better to install and test AOL before you add Explorer to the recipe. Because there are numerous ways to acquire AOL and Explorer, users will encounter several different setup and startup procedures. But you can be sure that with AOL's simplicity, any type of installation will be a snap. We'll cover the basics of each type of install in this section.

Installing AOL from CD-ROM

Current members and new members can elect to install from the CD-ROM. If you are a current member, the installer will check your current settings and use them as the basis for establishing AOL 3.0 on your system. The programming will not overwrite your original software (as had been the case with previous upgrades). Your old settings will not be changed and your new version will incorporate your established settings. You will have two copies of AOL on your PC, and after you become accustomed to the new version, you may decide to uninstall the prior version.

Select Start|Settings|Control Panel and then Add/Remove Programs. At the Install/Uninstall tab, select the Install button. Pop the CD into the drive and the installer will handle the installation for you. You will be prompted to sign on and AOL will connect to an 800 number to complete your membership, modem, and access information. Once that is complete, just click on the Sign On button to connect to AOL.

Installing AOL from the Downloaded Program

To install AOL, locate the setup.exe file you downloaded. Because this file can be in any number of places, I suggest that you use the Find File feature to locate it. To use Find, click on the Start button, select Find and choose "Files or Folders". Type the name of the file (setup.exe) and designate the drive (most likely, your hard drive). When you've located setup.exe, double click on the file, and then click on the Install button to install AOL 3.0 to a new folder.

If you are already an AOL member, the setup program will locate the prior version and use those settings for the new version. It won't overwrite any files in your AOL 2.5 folder. That means your screen names, modem settings, and other custom settings will be intact. When the installation is complete, an AOL program icon will be displayed in your AOL 3.0 folder.

If you are not an AOL member, the program will take you through the sign-up process at the conclusion of the installation. Within minutes, you'll be on AOL and accessing the Internet. Just as with the CD version, the installer will handle the installation for you. You will be prompted to sign on and AOL will connect to an 800 number to complete your membership, modem, and access information. Once that is complete, just click on the Sign On button to connect to AOL. Figure 6.1 shows AOL's famed Welcome screen. You'll know you've gone through the sign-up procedures correctly when you are welcomed.

Installing Explorer from CD

The directions for installing Explorer from CD are basically the same as for installing AOL from the CD. Select Start|Settings|Control Panel and then Add/Remove Programs. At the Install/Uninstall tab, select the Install button. Pop the CD into the drive and the installer will handle the installation of Explorer for you.

Installing Explorer from the Downloaded Program

To install Microsoft Internet Explorer 3.0, locate the MSIE30.EXE file you downloaded. Because this file can be in any number of places, I suggest

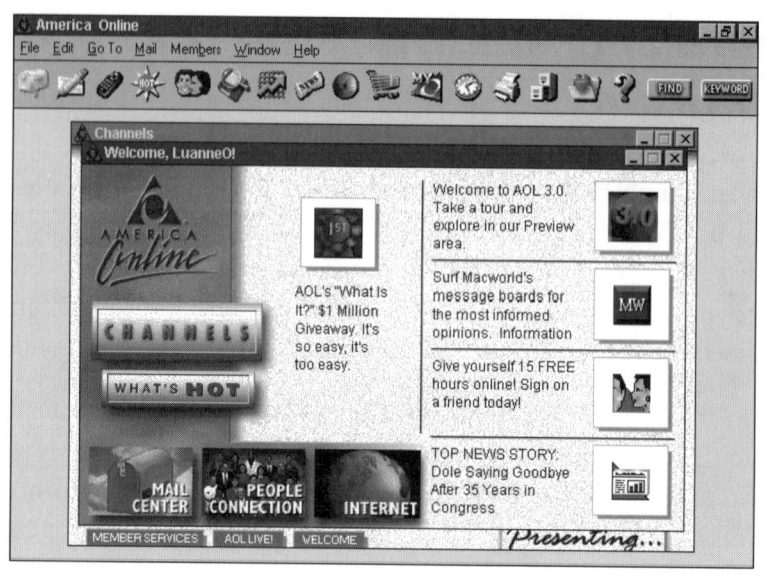

Figure 6.1 Welcome to the excitement of America Online.

that you use the Find File feature to locate it. To use Find, click on the Start button, select Find and choose "Files or Folders". Type the name of the file (MSIE30.EXE) and designate the drive. When you've located MSIE30.EXE, double click on the file. A dialog box will appear that says, "This will install Microsoft Internet Explorer 3.0. Do you wish to continue?" Select Yes and the Microsoft Internet Explorer License Agreement will be displayed. To continue with the installation, you must select "I Agree." This will install MSIE 3.0. A dialog box will appear that says, "You must restart your computer before the new settings will take effect. Do you want to restart your computer now?" Click Yes and when Windows 95 has restarted, move on to the next step.

The Windows 95 Difference

If you have a new PC with Windows 95 preinstalled, AOL is already waiting for you in an online services folder on the desktop—or through the Start|Programs menu—ready to launch. Explorer is waiting as well under the icon called The Internet. Pretty nifty, eh? And if you upgrade from Windows 3.1 to Windows 95, the program installer will guide you through the installation of AOL and Explorer.

If you have previously installed Windows 95, but have not yet installed AOL (from your Win95 disks or CD), you can use the Add/Remove Programs function to install the program as described previously.

With AOL and Windows 95, there are two options for PC users to access AOL. During the installation of Windows 95, you will encounter a dialog box offering the installation of MSN, AOL, and other online services. Once the installation is complete, you'll see AOL under the Start|Programs menu, and on the desktop there will be a folder that includes AOL's icon ready for you to launch.

Jumping Online

Now that you've got AOL installed (or upgraded), let's not waste any more time offline. The first thing you need to do (after starting your computer) is to launch the America Online software. I keep a shortcut icon on my desktop, and you may also wish to do so. That way, I just double-click on the desktop icon to start my way towards AOL.

There are other ways to get started as well. With Start|Programs you will find a selection for America Online. You may have to make one more selection, "online services," before selecting America Online. Depending on the original installation, you may also find AOL in a folder on the desktop.

No matter which way you choose to start AOL, all will bring you to the same Sign On screen. From there, select the Sign On button. Once you've signed on, we'll take a look at AOL's toolbar.

The AOL Toolbar

AOL's toolbar provides quick access to the more popular areas on the service. The toolbar icons, shown in Figure 6.2, represent the following functions: Read New Mail, Compose Mail, Channels (AOL content by category), What's Hot, People Connection, File Search, Stocks & Portfolios, Today's News, World Wide Web (which is also shared by the large Internet icon on the lower edge of the Welcome screen), Marketplace, My AOL (customize AOL to suit your needs), Online Clock (how long you've been connected),

Figure 6.2   The AOL 3.0 toolbar icons.

Print, Personal Filing Cabinet, Favorite Places, Member Services, Find, and Keyword. As you rest the cursor over each icon, a box will pop up with the description of each icon.

In this section, we're going to work with the World Wide Web, Favorite Places, and Find tools. Of the 18 icons and buttons on the toolbar, I've decided to discuss only these 3 tools, as they are the most pertinent to the AOL/Internet experience.

THE WORLD WIDE WEB ICON

The World Wide Web icon on the toolbar will take you directly to the Internet when you have Explorer installed. The browser will load your start page and begin your electronic journey. From there, everything is just as you would expect: enter Internet URLs in the Address box and surf away. So far, so good.

Quickly Accessing an Internet Site

You can use the keyword command to go straight to an Internet site. Simply select Keyword (or press Ctrl+K), enter the URL of the site you want to visit, and click on OK. I took the shortcut to the Los Angeles Times by pressing Ctrl+K and then entering http://www.latimes.com into the keyword text box.

Click on the Internet Globe now. Notice that when the browser opens, its window rests below the AOL toolbar and displays a row of tools, as well: Back, Reload, Forward, Search, Prefs, Home, Help, and Stop. On this first visit to the Internet, you might find it helpful to set a few personal preferences via the Prefs button. Selecting the Prefs button brings up the Windows 95-style properties card with six tabbed options. As shown in Figure 6.3, you can establish settings for graphics on the General card and select your preferred start page on the Navigation card. To select a new start page, simply enter the URL in the box provided.

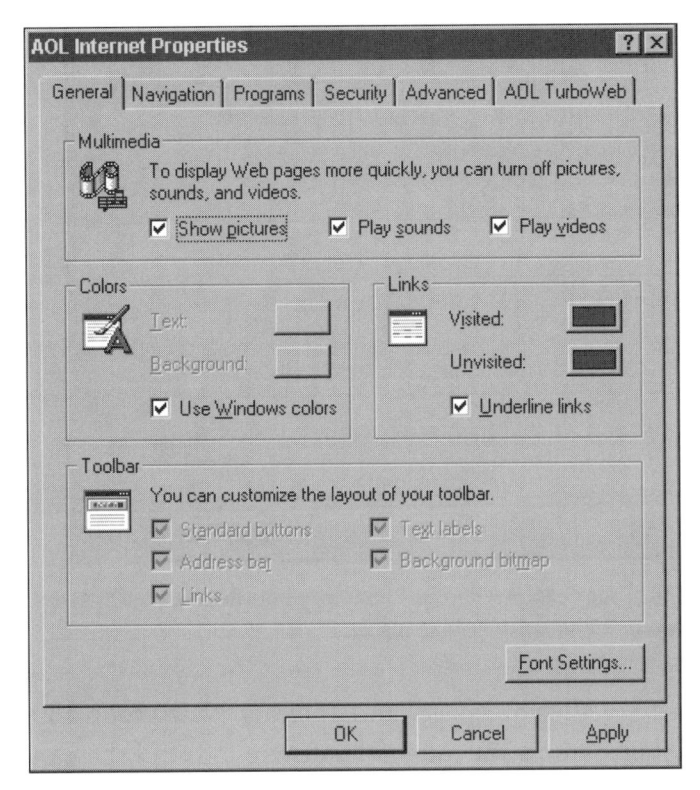

Figure 6.3 Set preferences for your browser with these clear choices.

The Advanced card provides access to preferences for setting and purging the cache, as shown in Figure 6.4. When troubleshooting any browser, purging the cache is an important first step. The cache stores a copy of all the sites you've visited, and sometimes the browser will call up an old page instead of a new one. Purging the cache of temporary Internet files will "clear the memory" for your browser and once again allow you to navigate freely through the Web. From the Advanced card, select Settings and Empty Folder to purge the cache.

THE FIND AND SEARCH BUTTONS

The Find button on AOL's toolbar is not the same as the Search button on the browser toolbar, although they are linked. The Find button carries you to a window known as both Find and Search, as shown in Figure 6.5. This AOL Search function is global. You can search by keyword, or browse through Places & Things, People, Events, AOL Access Numbers, AOL

Figure 6.4 Control your cache with the Temporary Internet files settings on the Advanced Web preferences card.

Classifieds, AOL Homepage, and Internet Newsgroups. One notable additional link covers searching for software. Most of these categories are self-evident, but let's take a look at searching by keyword, searching Internet Newsgroups, and searching for software.

Figure 6.5 AOL Find aids your searches on AOL and the Internet.

WebCrawler and Excite—as shown in Figure 6.6. WebCrawler, a product of AOL's Global Network Navigator, Inc., is AOL's primary search engine. However, Excite's editorial reviews and Web site rankings make it much easier for you to find the great content that's out on the Web, because you can tell in advance whether a site is worth your while.

Oops, I digressed. At this point, you've reached the same search page as the one you access through the Search button on the browser. There, type *federal and budget and congress* and select either search engine. My quick search with WebCrawler brought up 769 matches. (The same search without the "and" resulted in 37,873 matches.)

Accessing Excite and WebCrawler Directly

You can also use the keywords Excite and WebCrawler to access these search engines directly. Simply select Keyword, enter the appropriate keyword, and click on OK to launch the browser and the corresponding search engine.

You can begin your searches from this page or you can make additional selections for links to Alta Vista, Infoseek, Inktomi, Lycos, and Magellan.

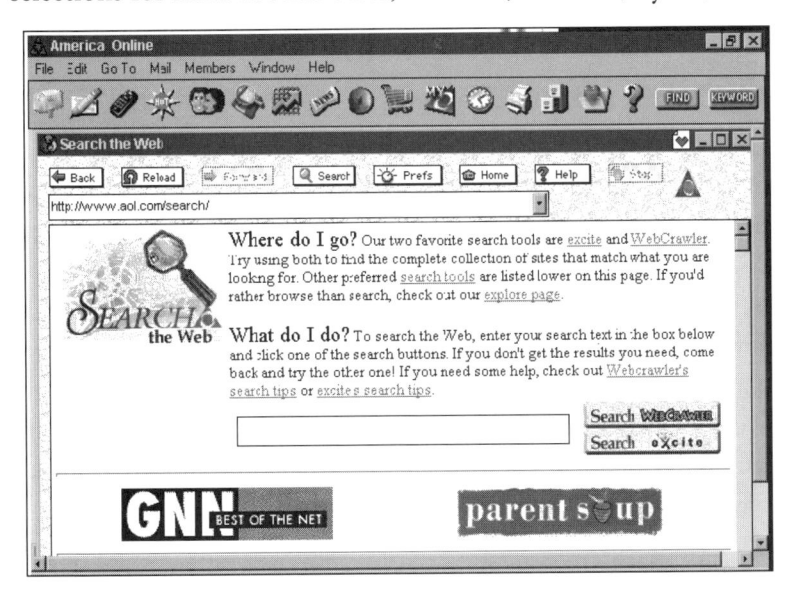

Figure 6.6 From the browser's Search button, you'll have immediate access to WebCrawler and Excite.

Of course, if you know the URL for another search engine, you can type it in the address line and then add it to your favorites by dragging the small heart icons to the Favorite Places folder icon. I'll cover more on adding to Favorite Places in a moment.

To search by newsgroups, select the Find button from the Toolbar, and double click to the Internet Newsgroups line. You will be conveyed to DejaNews on the Web, where you can search for newsgroups pertaining to your interests, work, or hobbies. Type *Sports* in the box and then select Search.

Find|Search for Software will bring up AOL's software search screen, allowing you to search among the tens of thousands of demos, shareware, and freeware programs on AOL.

Cases and Spaces

Many people get confused by capitalization and spacing in AOL's keywords and Screen Names (user IDs). As long as you stay within the realm of AOL, keywords and screen names are neither space sensitive nor case sensitive. However, for you to receive Internet mail, the sender must type your screen name without spaces.

Favorite Places

In Chapter 11, you'll learn about Explorer's Favorites, which entails setting bookmarks for the best Web sites. With AOL's Favorite Places, however, you can store sites on AOL, newsgroups, Web sites—anything delineated by the small heart icon. The small heart icon can be found in the title bar of most AOL screens (with the notable exception of message board screens). Whenever you find a feature or site sporting the heart icon that you would like to add to your Favorite Places, simply select the icon and drag it onto the Favorite Places button (the folder with the heart) on the AOL toolbar. You can also double click on the small heart icon to add that location to your Favorite Places.

If you want to add a site to your Favorite Places without actually being at the site, simply select Favorite Places|Add Favorite Place. A dialog box will appear and a description and Internet address must be entered manually. It sounds simple enough, but be careful. Manually entering Internet addresses can lead to typos. And typos lead nowhere.

Once you've added locations to your Favorite Places, you can quickly access them by clicking on the Favorite Places toolbar icon, and then double clicking on the desired icon in the Favorite Places window. Click on the X in the upper right of each screen to close all of the open windows and to navigate back to the Welcome screen. From there, we'll resume our tour of AOL and MSIE.

Testing the AOL/MSIE Integration

So far, we've seen how easy it is to access the Internet via AOL, but we haven't really seen the total integration that exists between AOL and MSIE. Instead of stumbling over some complex explanation of this integration, I'm going to show you how it works. Bear with me a moment while I set the stage.

For many of us, college was our first brush with independence—when good times and responsibility merged together to form a blissful union. Remember the football games, the all-night parties, and the late-night study sessions? If these memories come to you with some semblance of fondness, you might want to check in at your old alma mater and see how things are going. AOL makes this super easy with the Alumni Hall area—our first stop down memory lane.

Select Keyword, enter Alumni, and then click on OK to access the area. Your first step is to select the geographic location of your school. To keep things simple, follow along with me as I catch up on the latest news on the Fighting Irish. Select Midwest from the map, and then Indiana from the state list. In response, AOL displays a list of folders corresponding to all the universities and colleges in the area I specified. Now here's where that integration comes in: Among other things, the University of Notre Dame folder contains a Web link to Notre Dame's home page. Clicking on this link loads the browser and whisks you off to the home page featuring ND's Golden Dome, as seen in Figure 6.7. That's it. From AOL to the Web in a matter of seconds. To navigate back to AOL, you can pull down the Windows menu to return to an

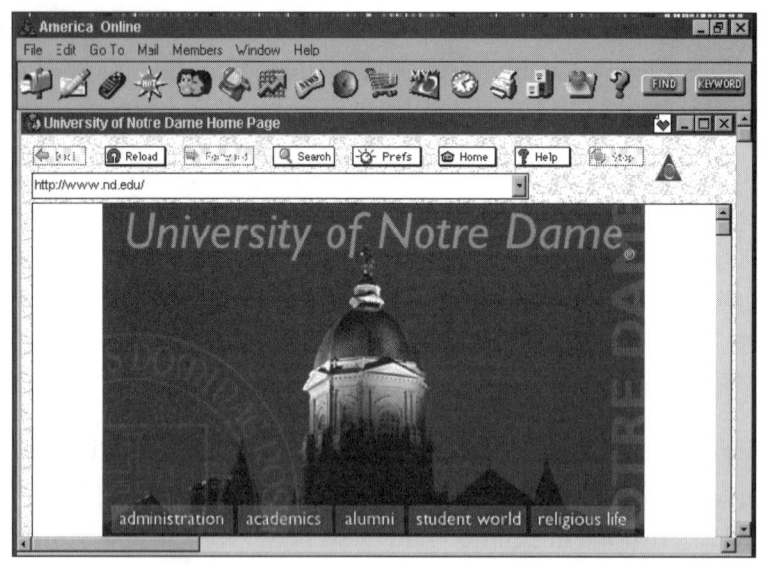

Figure 6.7 Thousands of Notre Dame alumni are comforted by the sight of their Golden Dome.

AOL screen, or you can click on the X on the top right of the title bar for the browser. That action will close the browser.

Web links are noted by a symbol that looks like a diamond-shaped graphic linked chain. The graphic representation leaves no doubt that these are Internet links and generally they are noted as Web sites. As an example, let's take a tour of AOL's Sports Channel and find the Web links to sports scores. Begin with Keyword: Sports. Select News & Scores, then Top Internet Sites. The next screen contains a scrollbox filled with sports links to the Web. Two of the most popular are ESPN SportsZone and USAToday Sports.

AOL has integrated the Web links so that the information you need is readily available, whether or not it resides on AOL's servers. You have the support and organization of an online service, together with the resources of the Internet in one neat package with AOL.

Multiple Access

Do you like to do two (or more) activities at once? With AOL and Explorer, you can have multiple browser screens simultaneously surfing the Web. As I write this, I have four browser windows loading my favorites pages. Each time you click on the World Wide Web globe icon, another browser window will open.

AOL's Internet Features

With Microsoft Explorer, Microsoft Internet Mail (covered in Chapter 14), and Microsoft Internet News (Chapter 15), you can do just about anything. However, if you have selected AOL as your primary source for Internet access, I strongly recommend that you continue to use AOL's proprietary software for Internet mail, newsgroups, Gopher, and FTP. While they may not have the individual features found in other programs, AOL's tools are dependable, consistent, and integrated.

Mail

Incoming and outgoing mail are always present on your toolbar. The Mailbox is highlighted when messages are waiting for you, and whenever you wish to compose a message, simply select the pencil and notepaper icon. Of course, you can compose your mail offline, which helps to save on connect charges. Use Mail|FlashSessions for a quick logon, exchange of mail, and automatic signoff. You'll find more on FlashSessions later in this section.

FTP

File Transfer Protocol, or FTP, is your key to the vast files resources of the Internet. FTP archives are maintained by various associations, non-profit organizations, and volunteers. To learn more about FTP and downloading directly from the Internet, see Chapter 13. You can access FTP sites via AOL through the Internet Connection (Keyword: Internet) or directly with Keyword: FTP. From the FTP screen, you can choose the Search for FTP Sites button to search for topics on all available sites, or you can choose the Go To FTP button when you know the address for a particular destination.

Gopher

Gopher servers contain simple lists (called menus) with easy-to-access, in-depth information on just about every subject. Use Keyword: Gopher to reach AOL's Gopher access, where you can learn a great deal about how to use Gopher and how to find files. Select Gopher Treasures from the middle of the screen to take a look at the broad range of resources, including the Congressional Record, Network Television News Archive, and the College Slang Dictionary.

If you know where you want to go, click the Quick Go button and type the URL in the space indicated. Someday you can use the Search function to locate a topic of interest to you. For now, let's navigate to the College Slang Dictionary found in Gopher Treasures. Select Gopher Treasures|College Slang Dictionary and then click on the image of the Gopher site. The browser screen will launch (with no wasted time) and the College Slang Dictionary will appear on your screen. You will have the opportunity to learn that the definition of *crash* differs at Berkeley from its meaning at the University of Kansas.

Another good choice is to select the Gopher Directory. Let's have some fun. With a double click, choose Rice University's Directory and then with a single click, choose Census and each successive Gopher selection. Let's take a look at 1990 Census Data from St. John's. If you choose California, the California portion of the census will appear, and you'll see that there are 10.4 million occupied housing units as well as a lot of other trivia.

As I mentioned before, to retrieve information from a Gopher server, all you have to do is click on a menu item and that item will be downloaded to your computer and displayed on your screen. Most often, Gopher files are text files, but you may also find collections of images. Gopher archives can contain files pertaining to government, science, cooking, sheet music, genealogy, and just about anything else you can think of.

Newsgroups

Newsgroups are one of the best features of the Internet. Newsgroups provide forums for discussion on particular topics. Whether you're interested in gourmet cooking, sailboarding, or the Grateful Dead, a newsgroup exists for you. AOL makes accessing newsgroups a snap.

READING NEWSGROUPS OFFLINE

Because reading and posting to newsgroups can be lengthy and expensive, AOL provides you with a way to read and respond to your newsgroups offline: FlashSessions (more on FlashSessions in the next section). From Keyword: Newsgroups, you can select which newsgroups you would like to read offline. Search all Newsgroups is the best place to start if you are new to newsgroups. I'm a coffee fanatic, so I typed *coffee* in the search phrase box. It brought up eight newsgroups relating to coffee. At this point, you can highlight each group and select View Description or Add. On AOL, Add means to add the newsgroup to your list of newsgroups. With other services and newsgroup clients, this process is referred to as *subscribing*. AOL also diverges from the norm as they do not adhere to the convention of listing each newsgroup according to its official name. Once you know newsgroup naming conventions, it's pretty easy to understand that alt.food.coffee is a newgroup. Another group on the list of eight is called "Discussions about Coffee." This makes it a bit more difficult to know which newsgroup to add if a friend has suggested one. When I viewed the description for this newsgroup, I found out that its official name is rec.food.drink.coffee.

This brings us to Expert Add. If you know the name of a newsgroup that you'd like to add to your list, select Expert Add from the Newsgroups screen, then just type the Internet name in the box provided. Typing rec.food.drink.coffee and selecting Add will place this coffee newsgroup on your list.

Once you have subscribed to a newsgroup, it will appear on the list when you select Read My Newsgroups. Newsgroups postings can really add up. The busiest newsgroups receive hundreds of messages each day. After you read your newsgroups, I highly recommend that you select "Mark All Newsgroups Read" before exiting, so they don't build up in the folder.

To read newsgroups offline, and save large sums of money, select Read Offline from the Newsgroups screen. A list of your subscribed newsgroups appears, and you can make your selection from that list. The newsgroups selected for offline reading will appear in the box on the right side of the screen. Click OK when the correct groups appear. Then, select Mail|Set Up FlashSession and select either the "Retrieve unread newsgroup messages" or "Send outgoing newsgroup messages." You can choose to activate a FlashSession just prior to signing off. With this option, you will be able to select "Sign off when finished," allowing you to walk away from the computer. Any time you are not online, you can choose to activate a FlashSession or run a FlashSession on a schedule that can be set at the Set Up FlashSessions screen. That's all. Quite simple and cost effective.

Getting Online Support

Members Helping Members (Keyword: MHM) is the #1 place for online support. All time spent in this area is free of connect time charges, making it the best, first place for problem solving and AOL tips. There you can search the database or participate on message boards.

The Internet Connection (Keyword: Internet) may seem to be an obvious place for help with all-things-Internet, but you just may be surprised at the depth of help to be found here. When you arrive, the first place to check is the Help folder, followed by the Internet Help Forum. There are multiple resources available to smooth the bumps on the Internet trail, including tutorials and message boards.

Indispensable Features

AOL 3.0 with Explorer has brought forth innovative tools to make the AOL experience everything you need and want it to be. Some of 3.0's hot tools were introduced prior to 3.0, but together with the new features, they add a lot to this dynamite package.

Hyperlinks

Woven throughout AOL, you'll now find Web links to additional resources that just happen to be located somewhere other than AOL's servers. With hyperlinks, you can send Favorite Places and URLs in email messages to friends—just drag-and-drop a Favorite Places heart icon from an AOL area or Web site into the body of your email, and it turns into a hyperlink. When your correspondent clicks on the hyperlink, they'll go right to the area or Web site you're referring to (currently, this doesn't work with all email programs); there's no need to type Internet URLs or keywords. You'll also encounter hyperlinks cropping up around AOL's content areas. In Figure 6.8, you'll see email with a hyperlink to newsgroups.

Buddy Lists

Buddy Lists are a new feature of AOL, and your list can help you track (or stalk!) other members. When you create a Buddy List (Keyword: Buddy), you'll be alerted the moment one of your friends or associates comes online. Think of it as online Caller ID. In the Buddy List window, you can review the options for Buddy Lists and blocking, in case you don't want everyone to know you're in AOL.

FlashSessions

As mentioned in the Newsgroups section, FlashSessions are a great tool that AOL has created to save you online time and money. With judicious use of FlashSessions, the cost of participating in newsgroups and email is minimized. FlashSessions let you compose, read, and reply to email messages offline. You can also use FlashSessions to download newsgroups, so that you can stay current on your favorite topics—and compose, read, and reply offline.

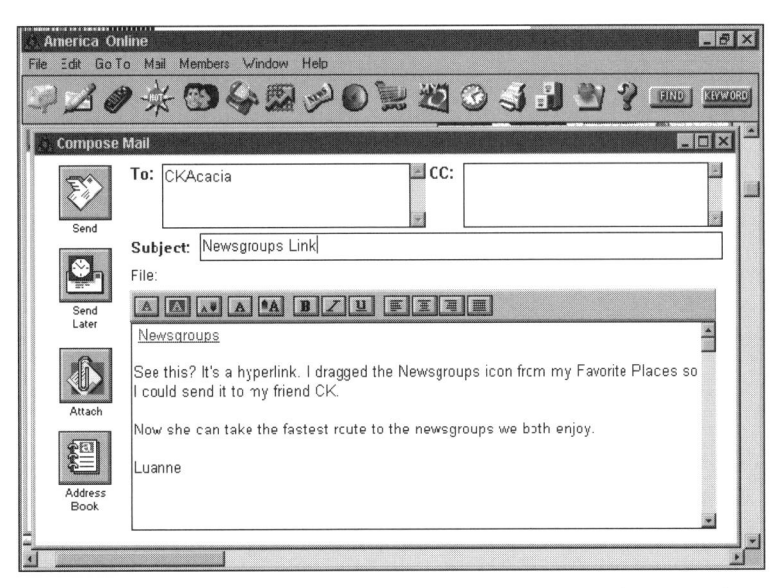

Figure 6.8 While touring the Internet, I help friends such as CK find the information they need.

With FlashSessions, you are charged only for the time it takes to transmit your messages. Just imagine what it costs users who are unaware of this feature. When you activate a FlashSession, you are charged for a minimum of one minute of connection time.

FlashSessions can be activated through the Mail menu and the setup can be done offline. Select Set Up Flash Session to establish your FlashSessions preferences. With checkboxes, you can select whether you wish to Retrieve unread mail (with or without attached files), Send outgoing mail, Download selected files, Retrieve unread newsgroup messages, or Send outgoing newsgroup messages.

From the Set Up Flash Session screen, you'll need to Select Names to designate the passwords for each screen name using FlashSessions. Simply check the appropriate name and type the password in the corresponding box. Select OK and you're set. Depending on who else has access to your computer, you may need to be wary about this feature. A coworker could select to run a Flashsession and then stay online running up your bill.

FlashSessions can be activated whenever you wish, or you can set your PC to conduct them at set intervals throughout the day. To set the time for a FlashSession, select Set Up Flash Session and then Schedule Flash Session. Check to Enable Scheduler, and then select the days of the week for your sessions. Sessions can be set as frequently as every half hour or as infrequently as once per day. A pull-down menu will allow you to make your selection. To minimize the load on AOL's servers, AOL has established preset times that have been randomized in the software. My software allows me to run FlashSessions at 14 and 44 minutes after the hour. Yours may allow 7 and 37 minutes after the hour, or one of 58 other combinations.

Mail|Activate FlashSession Now is the fastest way to start. (You can also select Mail|Set Up Flash Session|Activate Session Now, but that takes an extra step). If you wish to "Stay online when finished" check that box. Then, click Begin and you'll be in the express lane.

Parental Controls

The online world has good neighborhoods and dark alleys just as you'll find in the "real" world. AOL has taken the lead among the online services in providing safeguards parents can use to control their children's AOL and Internet wanderings. The master account holder, assumed to be a parent, can establish the parental controls options for the screen names under the main account. (Remember, AOL allows you to utilize up to five screen names for each account.) Parental Controls (Keyword: Parental Controls) offers several protective options for children. From the Parental Controls screen, you can select to "Block all But Kids Only" or choose Custom Controls to block chat and instant messages, downloading, or newsgroups. You'll need to prowl through each button to see the level of restriction available. AOL does not currently have a way to block Web access, but you should check the message boards in this area often for any software updates or third party applications that can be used to block Web access.

Free Areas

Have you ever been busy online only to be interrupted by a knock at the door, a crying child, or something else requiring your immediate attention? It's inconvenient to sign off and on throughout the day when such disturbances occur, but what can you do to avoid accruing charges without signing off? Luckily, AOL offers a little-known option to suspend charges when you're away from your computer: free areas. My favorite free area is Members Helping Members (Keyword: MHM), because I can get online technical support while I'm there. To enter this free area, simply select Keyword, enter *MHM*, and click on Go. Select Yes when the AOL screen asks if you wish to enter this free area. AOL will transport you from your present location to the MHM free area and will suspend your online fees. When you are ready to get back to work, simply exit the free area. When you are ready to leave the free area, you can select Go To|Exit Free Area or use a keyword. Exit Free Area will return you to the area that you were in before you jumped to the Free Area.

Free areas offer more than just a place to cool your heels. You can make changes to your preferences settings or My AOL, check your current and past billing patterns (Keyword: Billing), or set or review Parental Controls, among other things. If you are in the free area, you can use the keyword search function to find areas of interest, but you will be charged when you navigate to the featured areas. Take your time and explore your options. You may be surprised at the functions you find. Try the free area first. After all, it's free!

Chapter in Review

AOL's integrated package of proprietary software combined with Microsoft Internet Explorer provides you with all the tools you need to seek out the information you want. In this chapter, we barely scratched the surface of the enormous amount of information AOL brings you. However, using AOL's intuitive approach, you can access an abundance of software resources and figure things out on your own with a minimum of aggravation and adjustments.

Microsoft Internet Explorer and CompuServe 7

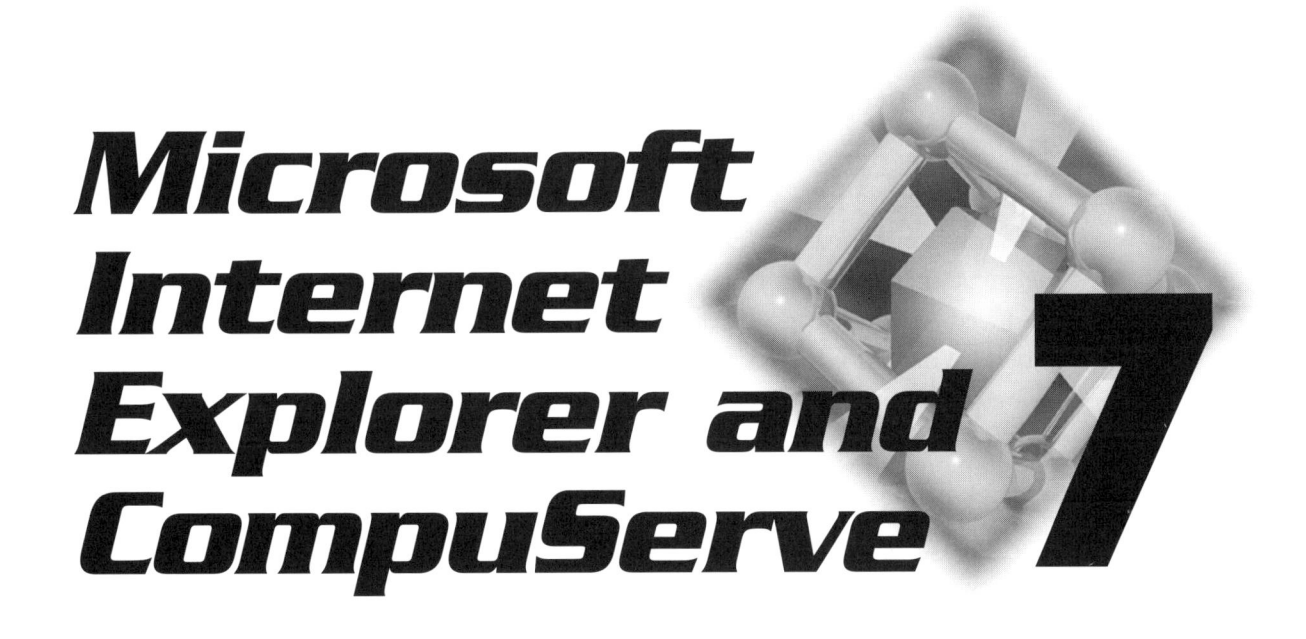

Explorer helps CompuServe users make the most of WinCIM and the Internet.

Microsoft's deals with CompuServe Information Systems (CIS) and America Online (AOL) signify the serious commitment Microsoft is making to capture the Internet. This commitment began with the development of Windows 95, which provides users with a major advantage when it comes to having the world of Internet communications at their fingertips. With the integration inherent in Microsoft's products, users can seamlessly connect and communicate on the Internet; and with Microsoft's market leadership, the Microsoft way becomes the most efficient way. With the new cooperative agreements between Microsoft and both CompuServe and America Online, access to those services comes with Windows 95. In response, those cooperative online services are supplying Microsoft's Explorer browser to their millions of users—to 5 million CompuServe subscribers, in particular.

Microsoft Internet Explorer will be the default Web browser distributed on the installation CDs for CIS 3.0 and WOW!, as well as in CompuServe's packaged software offerings. The CIS 3.0/Explorer integrated package, which will use desktop icons to connect users to CIS, will be distributed in the Fall of 1996.

The Parts

In this chapter's discussion of CIS, I worked with WinCIM version 2.0.1—the most current version of WinCIM at the time this book was being produced—because the next version, named CIS 3.0, was not yet available in beta. WinCIM is the most popular application for accessing CIS, and it seemed to be the most appropriate for use here.

The Explorer you'll be using is the same Explorer available to Microsoft Network (MSN) users and those who gain access through an Internet Service Provider (ISP). You'll want to read or skim most of this book to take advantage of Explorer's many features.

The setup for CIS and Explorer is a bit more difficult than setting up Explorer with your ISP account (which is fairly easy) or MSN (which is wonderfully simple), but I'll be walking you through the specifics to ease the pain. With the checklists in this chapter, you'll be steps ahead going online; plus, I'll include setup tips and techniques for CIS users, as well as the places to go for CIS for support. We've got a lot to cover, so let's get started.

Setting Up Explorer for CompuServe Users

Users who are new to Windows 95, or who obtain a new PC with Windows 95 installed, have the great advantage of having CIS preinstalled. If you are one of those lucky users, CIS will be accessible through the Start|Programs menu or through a folder on the desktop. In the Preparations section that follows, we'll review the installation process.

If you're like me, you may already have Explorer and CompuServe, but you haven't yet used them together to access the Internet. When you set up Explorer to work with CIS, it will continue to work with other access you've established (such as with MSN or an ISP). Due to programming differences, however, it will not work with America Online (AOL). If you are an AOL user, turn to Chapter 6 for specific information for that system. It's a bit more confusing to configure Explorer to work with several access providers, but once you have established the setup, you can count on Explorer to take you wherever you want to go, through the provider of your choice. This will get easier as soon as CompuServe distributes CIS 3.0, as that software will have one installer for both CompuServe and Explorer.

In the creation of this book, I worked with Explorer and Earthlink, Explorer and CIS, and the AOL/Explorer combo. My biggest fear was that once Explorer was compatible with one, it would suddenly be incompatible with another. Luckily, that fear was never realized, and once each was installed and set up, the changes to switch from one program to another were quite minor.

Preparations

The first step in setting up Explorer is to make sure that you have the most current versions of WinCIM and Explorer. Open WinCIM, select Continue (don't sign on), and select Help|About CIM. The next screen will show your current version of WinCIM. Connect to CompuServe and GO WINCIM to check for an updated version. If necessary, upgrade WinCIM. Download and install the upgrade. The interface for WinCIM 2.0.1 is shown in Figure 7.1.

To install or upgrade WinCIM from the downloaded version, locate the file WCINST.EXE, which should be in your CIS Download directory. Double click on the program icon and the installer will handle the installation for you. If you are currently running a version of WinCIM, the installer will use your existing settings for the new version.

If you obtain the disks or CD for WinCIM 2.0.1, just follow the installation instructions on the disk, or use Start|Settings|Control Panel and then Add/Remove Programs. At the Install/Uninstall tab, select the Install button. Pop the disk or CD into the drive and the installer will handle the installation or upgrade for you.

If you do upgrade the WinCIM software, I strongly advise you to test the connection to CompuServe before proceeding with Explorer, as shown in Figure 7.1. It seems wise to make sure that the connection operates correctly, rather than compounding errors with a premature install of Explorer. If

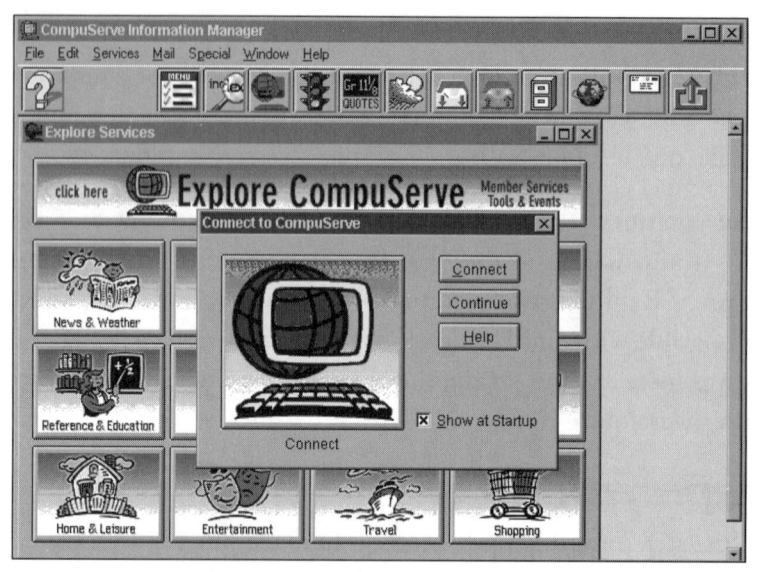

Figure 7.1 Test the connection with WinCIM before adding Explorer to the recipe.

you have problems with WinCIM, contact CIS Customer Service at 800-848-8990—I won't be providing troubleshooting techniques for WinCIM.

Next, make sure that you have Explorer 3.0. To check this, double click The Internet icon on your desktop, or use Start|Programs|Internet Explorer to bring up the initial screen (it is not necessary to sign on). Select Help|About Internet Explorer to check the version number for your copy of Explorer. If you don't have MSIE 3.0, follow the instructions in the *Microsoft Internet Explorer* section shown later in this chapter.

Going through the Motions

If you've been using CompuServe with Mosaic, or if you've been running Explorer through an ISP or another online service, you're going to have to make some changes in your setup. The instructions in this section cover the A to Z setup of MSIE with CIS. Review each instruction group before making any changes. The complete range of instructions may be overkill, but with multiple programs and versions for CIS access, coupled with the fact that you may have been using Explorer and CompuServe separately, I designed the instructions to accommodate all possibilities. You may not need to complete each set of steps.

Before we begin, you'll need to know your CIS access number, user ID, and password. To locate access numbers, GO PHONES. To install Microsoft Internet Explorer to use CIS as a gateway to the Internet, begin with the steps in the following sections.

TCP/IP

Your first task is to make sure that you have TCP/IP installed. Select Start|Settings|Control Panel|Network to verify that you have TCP/IP installed, as indicated in Figure 7.2.

DIAL-UP NETWORKING

Next, you must determine if Dial-Up Networking is present. If it is not present, you'll need to install it.

1. Open My Computer from the desktop and check for the Dial-Up Networking icon. If it is there, skip the remainder of this section and proceed with the Microsoft Internet Explorer section. If it is not there, continue with Step 2.

2. Select Start|Settings|Control Panel.

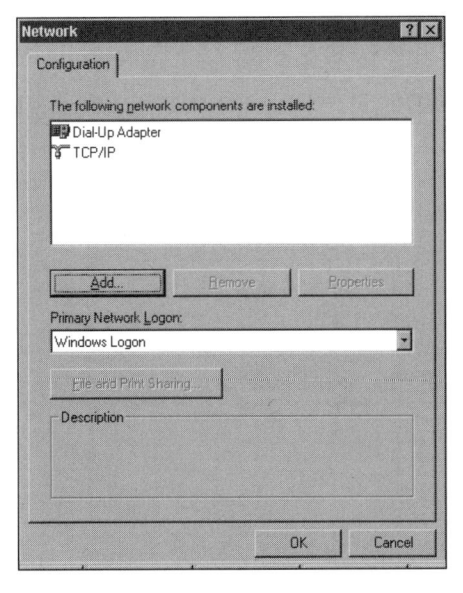

Figure 7.2 The TCP/IP network component has been installed on this system.

3. Open Add/Remove Programs.

4. Select Windows Setup and Communications.

5. Check Dial-Up Networking and click on OK.

6. Click on OK.

Dial-Up Networking should now appear as an icon in My Computer on the desktop, as shown in Figure 7.3.

MICROSOFT INTERNET EXPLORER

Earlier in the chapter, I had you check the version number of your installed copy of MSIE. If you did not check the version at that time, do so now by double clicking on The Internet icon to display the initial screen, and select Help|About Internet Explorer. If your version is any version prior to 3.0, it's time to update.

You can get an updated version of Explorer through a download from CompuServe. (If you have other online access methods, you can also obtain an update of Explorer through Microsoft's Web site or MSN.) Follow these steps to upgrade your copy of Explorer.

If you are installing the upgrade from a disk or CD-ROM:

- Select Start|Settings|Control Panel and then select Add/Remove Programs.

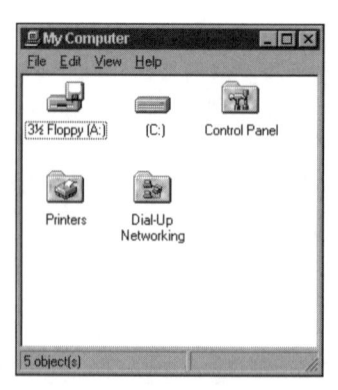

Figure 7.3 **Dial-Up Networking appears ready to go.**

Microsoft Internet Explorer and CompuServe 153

- Select the Install/Uninstall tab, click on the Install button, and insert the product's first installation disk or CD.

If you are downloading the upgrade from CompuServe:

- Sign on to CompuServe and GO INTEXPLORER. This will take you straight to a special screen featuring Explorer. Select "Download Internet Explorer, 32 bit version" and select Retrieve. Note the file name when it appears on the screen. As of this writing, it is MSIE30B1.EXE, but will change with each new upgrade.

- Sign off from CompuServe.

- Locate the EXE file and double click on it to begin the installation.

Throughout the installation, you'll be asked a series of questions. Here are the tips for filling in those blanks:

- Where it says "How to Connect", select "I already have an account..."

- Add "CompuServe" where it asks you to specify the "Name of Service Provider".

- Enter the CIS access number for your calling area.

- Make sure "Bring up terminal window ..." is not checked.

- Enter your CIS User Name and Password.

- Under IP Address, check "My Internet Service Provider automatically assigns me one".

- Under DNS Server Address, enter 149.174.211.5 in DNS Server (another DNS Server address is 149.174.213.5).

- Make sure Internet Mail is not checked.

- As you finish, the Wizard closes and suggests you double click on the new icon on your desktop. *Do not follow this direction.* Close the window, but don't double click on The Internet (Explorer) icon at this point. In order to use Explorer, you'll need to configure your newly created connection to CompuServe.

If you wish to set up connections from other cities, just repeat this setup for each city. You'll need to be prepared with the access numbers. For example, set up CompuServe-LA, CompuServe-NYC, CompuServe-Miami, and you'll be ready to hit the road.

The Cost of Access

Whether you are on CompuServe or the Internet through the CompuServe connection, you are accruing charges ranging from $2.00 to $2.95 per hour, depending the terms of your subscription.

Establishing a PPP Connection to CompuServe

In the previous section, we established the CompuServe software connection settings. In this section, we will establish Explorer's connection settings for access through CompuServe. The options you will be modifying are shown in Figure 7.4.

1. From the desktop, right click on The Internet icon and select Properties to display the Internet Properties window. (If the icon is not on your desktop, check for it in the My Computer|Control Panel area.)

2. In the Internet Properties window, select the Connection tab and the Add button.

3. Type the name for the connection (CompuServe) and click on the Next button.

4. Enter the local access phone number that you wish to use and click on the Next button.

5. Click on the Finish button.

6. Click on the Properties button.

7. Click on the Server Type button. Verify that the Type of Server option is set to "PPP: Windows 95, Windows NT 3.5, Internet".

Microsoft Internet Explorer and CompuServe 155

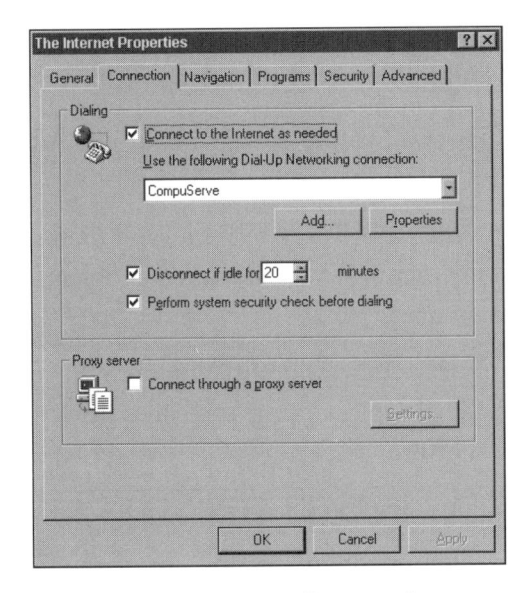

Figure 7.4 The Connection tab is your key to all connections.

8. Uncheck everything except TCP/IP (using data compression can cause problems, so you are advised to set up the connection without data compression), and then click on the TCP/IP Settings button.

9. Select "Server assigned IP Address" and then select "Specify name server addresses." Enter 149.174.211.5 as the Primary DNS and 149.174.213.5 as the Secondary DNS. Check both "Use IP header compression" and "Use default gateway on remote network." Click on OK to close the TCP/IP Settings window.

10. Click on OK to close the Server Types window, and again to close the Properties (CompuServe) window.

11. Finally, click on Apply and then on OK to close the Internet Properties window.

Installing and Configuring the Dial-Up Scripting Tool

To finish the setup, you will need to use the Dial-Up Scripting Tool, which should be located in the Start|Programs|Accessories folder.

If the Dial-Up Scripting Tool is not installed, you have a number of options. If you have the Windows 95 CD-ROM:

- Open the Windows Explorer and switch to the Admin|Apptools|Dscript folder.

- Right click on the RNAPLUS.INF file, and then select the Install option from the menu. If you encounter problems with this, follow the steps shown next.

- If you have the diskette version of Windows 95, you will need to download the Dial-Up Scripting Tools files from the Windows Connectivity Forum.

- Sign on to CompuServe and GO WINCON.

- In the Win95 Remote library section, locate the file DSCRPT.EXE. Download the file, placing it into an empty directory.

- Sign off from CompuServe and then go to the directory where you downloaded the scripting tools. Run the file to decompress it.

- Open the README.TXT file and follow the instructions to install the Dial-Up Scripting Tool. (Don't fret—this is a quick read and installation.)

In testing for this book, I downloaded the Dial-Up Scripting Tool files from both CompuServe and Microsoft. The version on the Microsoft site (**http://www.microsoft.com/windows/software/admintools.htm**) seemed more reliable. If the tool from the Windows Connectivity Forum does not work for you, download the file from Microsoft.

After successfully installing the Dial-Up Scripting Tool, you will want to continue the configuration of the Windows 95 Dialer:

1. Access the Dial-Up Scripting Tool through Start|Programs|Accessories.

2. Click on the Browse button.

3. Click on the CIS.SCP file and then click on the Open button.

4. Make sure that the "Step through script" option is not checked and that the "Start terminal screen minimized" option is checked, as shown

Microsoft Internet Explorer and CompuServe **157**

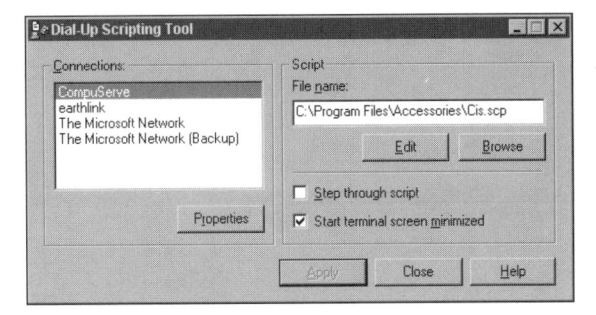

Figure 7.5 The Dial-Up Scripting Tool with the correct settings.

in Figure 7.5. Next, click on the Apply button and then click on the Close button.

That's all there is to it! You should now be able to select The Internet icon on your desktop to initiate the PPP connection to CompuServe, but be sure to review the following section on Winsocks before you get going.

Stuck? Start over!
If you get the error message that says "Dial-up Networking could not negotiate a compatible set of networking protocols you specified in the Server Type settings," reinstall the scripting tool.

Sorting Your Unmatched (Win) Socks

Before launching, from your Start menu run Find|Files or Folders and search for all occurrences of WINSOCK.DLL, as shown in Figure 7.6. There are two versions of interest: the Windows 95 version, which is 42 K, and the CIS/Spry version, which is 130 K. Make sure that the CIS/Spry version is not in either the \Windows or \Windows\System directories. If you find one in the wrong place, move it to \Cserve\Cid. You should also delete any WINSOCK.DLL files found in \Cserve\Wincim (and if you have CompuServe Navigator, \Cserve\Csnav). The Windows 95 version should appear in both the \Windows and \Windows\Sysbckup directories.

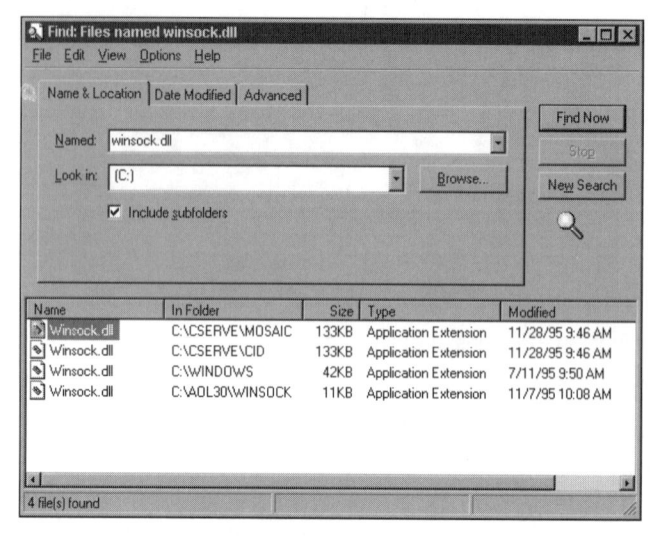

Figure 7.6 Use Find to locate all Winsocks.

Running Microsoft Internet Explorer

We're finally ready to test your setup (big sigh of relief).

- Right click on The Internet icon and select Properties to display the Internet Properties window. Select the Connection tab.

- Select the CIS connection you want to use from the settings list and click on OK.

- Double click on The Internet icon.

- When the dialer screen appears, your CIS account will appear and you will need to enter your password. Click Connect.

Depending on what version of Explorer you are using, you will be connected to either the CompuServe or MSN home page. The CompuServe home page is shown in Figure 7.7. As you can see, the Explorer interface is the same as the Explorer covered throughout this book (with the exception of the AOL chapter). To access CIS, make your selection through Start|Programs, and then select Continue. *Do not select Connect.* (If you were to select Connect, you would be activating the CIS dialer, which is in direct conflict with Windows 95's Dial-Up Networking.) A dialog box will pop up with the message "Logging into CompuServe," and then it will disappear. You will see the Connected time box activate when you are completely logged in.

Taking Your Browser out for a Test Drive

Now that you are up and running on Explorer with CIS, let's make a quick visit to a Web site. I've been frequenting *The Washington Post*'s Web site, and have been impressed by the content I find there. I'm hoping you will be equally impressed. Select Open and type **http://www.washington post.com** in the address window and click OK.

With the Post, you can get a daily dose of news from inside the beltway, including the antics of whatever First Family is residing at the White House. My Sunday favorite is the Style Invitational column found in the Style section. To find it, visit the site on a Sunday, select Style, and click on the GO button. At the bottom of the page, you'll find a link to all stories from "today's edition." Style Invitational brings a bizarre sense of humor to the

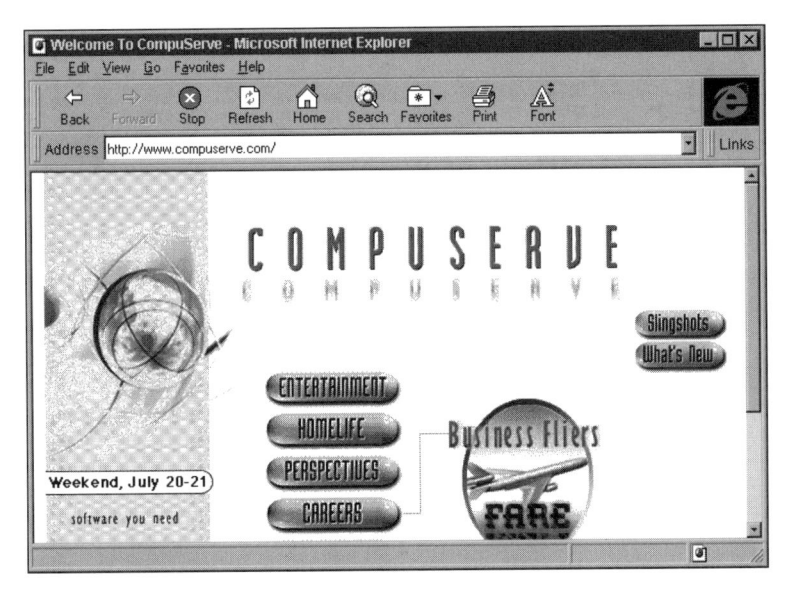

Figure 7.7 Your first connection may be to the CompuServe home page.

printed page—and now to the Internet as well. Humor cloaked in poetry and peculiar jokes provide irreverent reading to those staid beltway folks. Just to give you an idea of what you're in for, I've duplicated a selection from the Style Invitational in Figure 7.8.

Another terrific feature is Chapter One, where dozens of first chapters of current books are available for your perusal. It's a great place to spend an hour (time passes quickly!) in search of weekend reading material. When it is not featured on the home page, you'll always find Chapter One in the Style section.

Connection Tips

If you cancel a connection, you may need to close Explorer and then restart it in order to get the dialing script to start up again. If the line is busy, simply click on Connect to restart the dialing script.

Switching Providers

Once you've established the connection settings for CIS, you can easily switch among providers by changing the Connection Setting. Here's how:

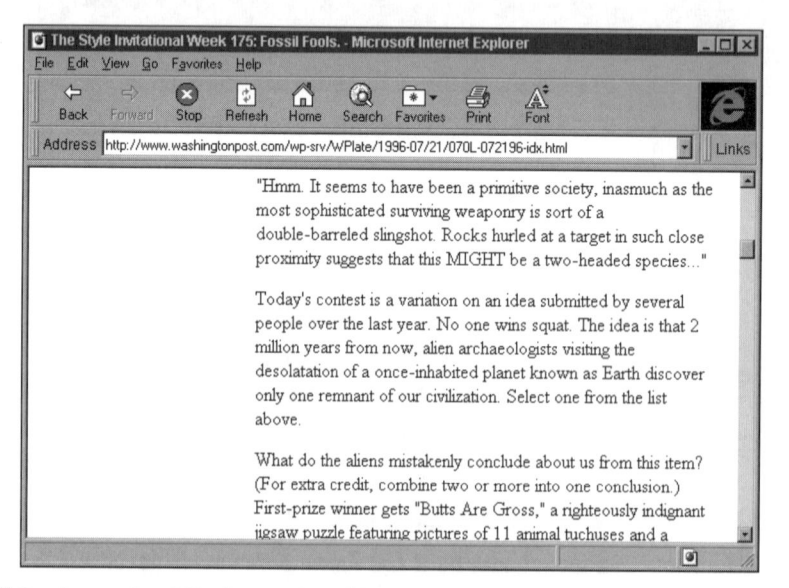

Figure 7.8 A sample of the humor found in the Style Invitational.

Microsoft Internet Explorer and CompuServe — 161

- From the desktop, right click on The Internet icon and select Properties to display the Internet Properties window.
- Click on Connections and select your preferred connection, as shown in Figure 7.9.
- Click on Apply and then on OK.

Troubleshooting Your Web Connection

When you're having trouble making the connection, make sure that "Connect through the Internet Proxy Server" is not checked. You can verify this by right clicking on the desktop's Internet icon and selecting the Connection tab.

Mail and News Features

As you spread your wings on the Internet, you can continue to use CompuServe's Mail and Newsgroup (GO USENET) functions, or you can configure Microsoft Internet Mail and News to work with the CompuServe connection. See Chapters 14 and 15 for information on these two programs.

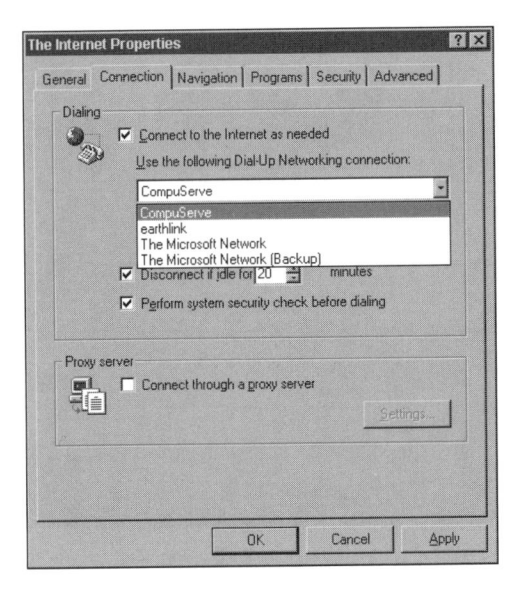

Figure 7.9 Make your connection selection here.

To configure Microsoft Internet Mail and Microsoft Internet News, the reset options are located under Mail|Options|Server and News|Options|Server. Change email address, POP3 account, and password to correspond to your CIS user ID. The server names are mail.compuserve.com and news.compuserve.com.

Getting Online Support

In this fast-paced, Internet-charged world, some things change faster than the printed page can reflect. Undoubtedly, Microsoft or CompuServe may tweak some setting, and as a result, your connection may have to be modified from what I have written here. If you encounter some strange goings on, don't hesitate to get help online. Begin your search for help by checking the *free* Member Support forums. GO WCIMTECH will take you to the WinCIM Technical Support forum, which is shown in Figure 7.10. GO WCIMGENERAL is the perfect place to ask general questions about the marriage of WinCim and Explorer.

If you don't find the answers you need in the free forums, then it is time to go to the not-so-free technical support forums for Windows 95 and Explorer

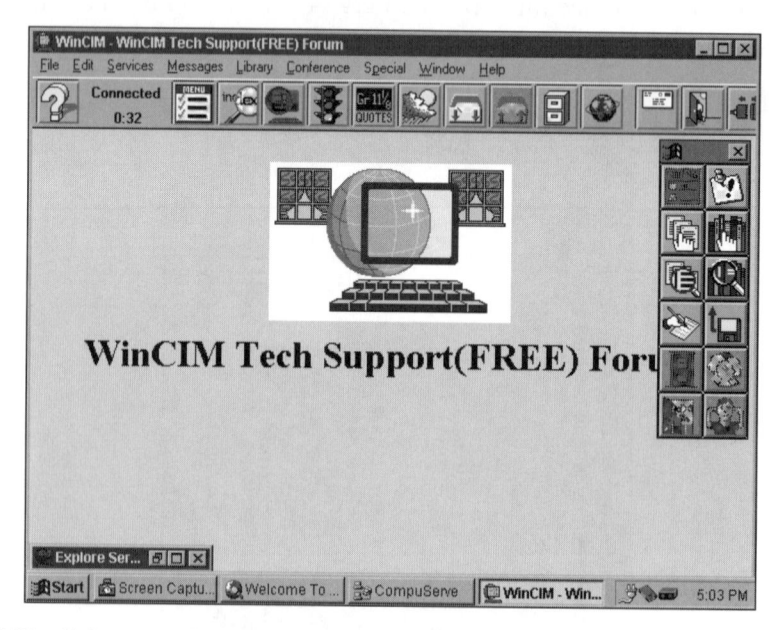

Figure 7.10   Help yourself to free advice in the WinCIM Support Forums.

(GO WINNEWS, WUGNET, MSWIN95, INTEXPLORER, and INETRESOURCE). Time spent in these forums is part of your monthly membership fee.

Signing Off

Let's assume you signed on with Microsoft's Dial-Up Networking and then accessed the CIS system with WinCIM. When it's time to sign off, make sure you sign off the same way you signed on: Use the Dialer. If you sign off from WinCIM's File|Disconnect command, your Internet connection will continue and you will be charged for the online time. Ouch!

Chapter in Review

In this chapter you found that whether you access Explorer via your ISP, through MSN, or with CompuServe, it's the same great browser—but with CompuServe as your home base, you reap a few added advantages.

We covered all the steps to make sure you have properly installed and configured the necessary components. If you have problems, be sure to check that you followed all the instructions correctly. With that taken care of, you are free to surf until you've ridden all the waves the Internet has to offer.

Microsoft's Essential Services Directory 8

Microsoft's Essentials Directory is your one stop information center. Read this chapter to discover some of the Internet services you ought to know about.

*N*o one has to tell you about the oceans of information facing the Internet surfer—you've heard it all before. Take heart, though, because there are secrets to filtering the sea of bytes to find the droplets of data you desire—and those secrets may *not* be something you've heard about before. In this chapter, and the next, we'll discuss some ways to find information you need without wasting hours of online time. (It is my theory that the faster you find information you *need* on the Internet, the sooner you get to *play* on the Internet!) In this chapter, we'll discuss the Essentials Directory, which you access by clicking on the Services button on MSIE's Links toolbar or clicking on the Essentials link on the Microsoft Network (MSN) home page. Either way, the Essentials Directory appears the same—a treasure chest of links.

Before we dive too deeply into this chapter, I have a quick disclaimer to share with you. Unfortunately, sites on the Internet come and go—regardless of how fantastic the site. Most of the sites discussed in this chapter appear to be rather stable, but you may find one or two sites that you won't be able to access. If that occurs, take note of the type of site being discussed. In Chapter 10, you'll see how you can conduct your own search to find a similar site.

As an added safety net, I've included the URL for each Microsoft link we discuss. That way, if clicking on the link doesn't work, or if the link has been removed from the Essentials Directory, you can try typing the URL in the Address box. Regardless of whether all the links work, this chapter should give you a good idea of some of the services provided on the Net, as well as a good starting point for some Net explorations.

Using the Essentials Directory

MSIE gives you the option to set any Web page as your default Start page. I recommend that you consider using the MSN home page (**http://www.msn.com**) as your Start page for a while. At least review the MSN offerings before setting your Start page elsewhere. You can change your Start page at any time (as we discussed in Chapter 4).

Even if you don't use MSN as your home page, Microsoft doesn't want you to miss out on the outstanding benefits offered by MSN; Therefore they've provided you with the Services link on the Links toolbar. Regardless of whether you access the MSN home page as a Start page, or you use the MSIE Links toolbar, the Essentials Directory is an excellent feature. The directory provides links to sites offering information such as health tips, movie reviews, flight schedules, stock quotes, and addresses. Dictionaries and magazine articles are at your fingertips via the Essentials Directory. To view the directory, click on the Services link in the Quick Link toolbar, or click on the Essentials hypertext link located on the MSN home page. The Essentials Directory should display as shown in Figure 8.1.

You should see eight Essential categories. At this writing, the categories include: Home Reference, Financial Information, Phone & Address Look-Up, Travel Tips, Writer's Reference, Publication Searches, Movies, and Music. You can scroll down the Essentials page to view the topics in each category. We'll discuss each category topic in the upcoming sections of this

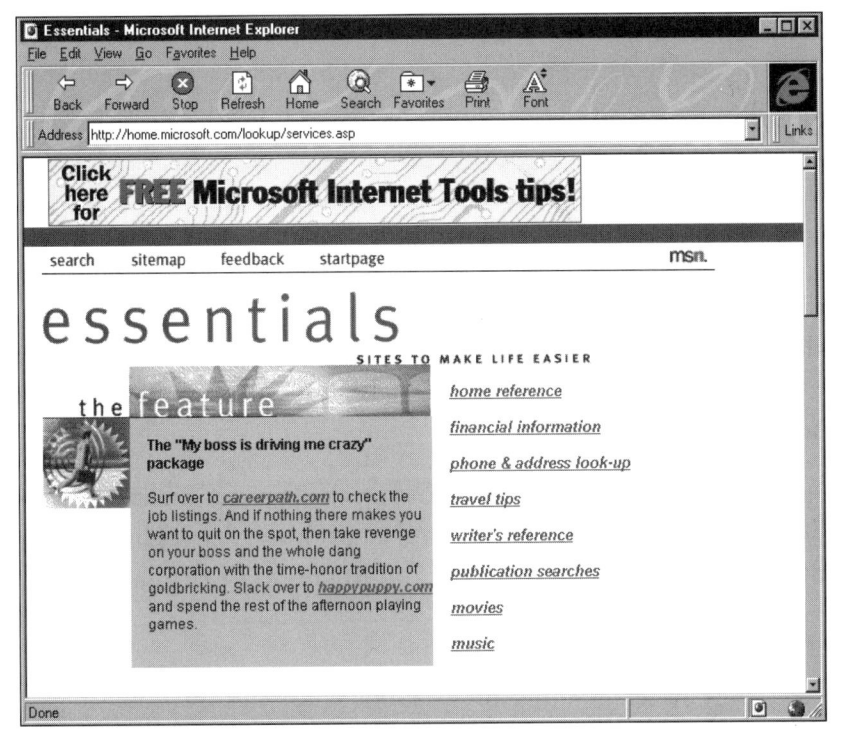

Figure 8.1 You can use Microsoft's Essentials Directory to find a wealth of information on a number of subjects.

chapter. Notice that both the category titles and the category topics appear as links on the Essentials page. You can click on either a category title or topic link to take you to the category page. If you click on a category title, you view the category page from the top of the page. If you click on a particular topic within a category on the Essentials page, the link takes you to the topic where it appears on the category page. You will still be able to scroll up or down to view the other topic options. As we discuss the following categories, I am going to assume you are clicking on the category title link. That way, we can start at the top of a category page and work our way down.

Finding the Extra Goods

Throughout Microsoft's Internet Essentials pages, you'll see embedded links in the text. Clicking on an embedded link usually brings you to a particular service's home page. In many instances, the home page offers other useful services in addition to the services highlighted by Microsoft.

Quickly, before we move on, I want to point out that Microsoft does not create the sites accessed by the Essentials Directory. Microsoft simply does some Internet leg work for you by creating a directory of helpful links to some of the better resources on the Net. The Microsoft links save you time because, as you probably know, sifting through the Net's gigabytes of information (and sometimes misinformation) can take you quite a while. Keep in mind, though, that the sites listed by Microsoft are not the only good ones. At the end of this chapter, you'll find a list of addresses to some other good sites relevant to the Internet services discussed in this chapter. In Chapter 10, you'll see how you can use Internet search engines to locate sites of particular interest to you.

Ok, let's get going. Have you clicked on the Services Links button or the Essentials hypertext link? If not, go ahead. Then let's start by taking a look at the Home Reference link offered on Microsoft's Essentials page.

Home Reference

The Home Reference link offers links to articles on home repair and maintenance, information on environmental agencies around the world, plant and garden information, medical documentation (described by the site designers as a Virtual Hospital), and a link to college home pages.

To view the Home Reference page, click on the Home Reference link on the Essentials page. Your display should show the top portion of the Microsoft Home Reference page, as shown in Figure 8.2.

Notice the product link (also known as an advertisement) at the top of the Home Reference page. In Figure 8.2, the product link displays as a link to the Ford Motor Company's home page. All of the Essentials pages display a product link at the top of the page. If any of the links look interesting as we work our way through the Essentials pages, feel free to click and wander off on your own. You can always use your back arrow key or click on the Services Links button to return to the Essentials Directory. One note of caution: while the Net is full of free goodies and information, it is also a medium for business (hence the advertisements—Microsoft has to be making money off of someone!). You'll probably want to stick to the free sites. Some sites end with a statement to the effect that you need to subscribe

Microsoft's Essential Services Directory **169**

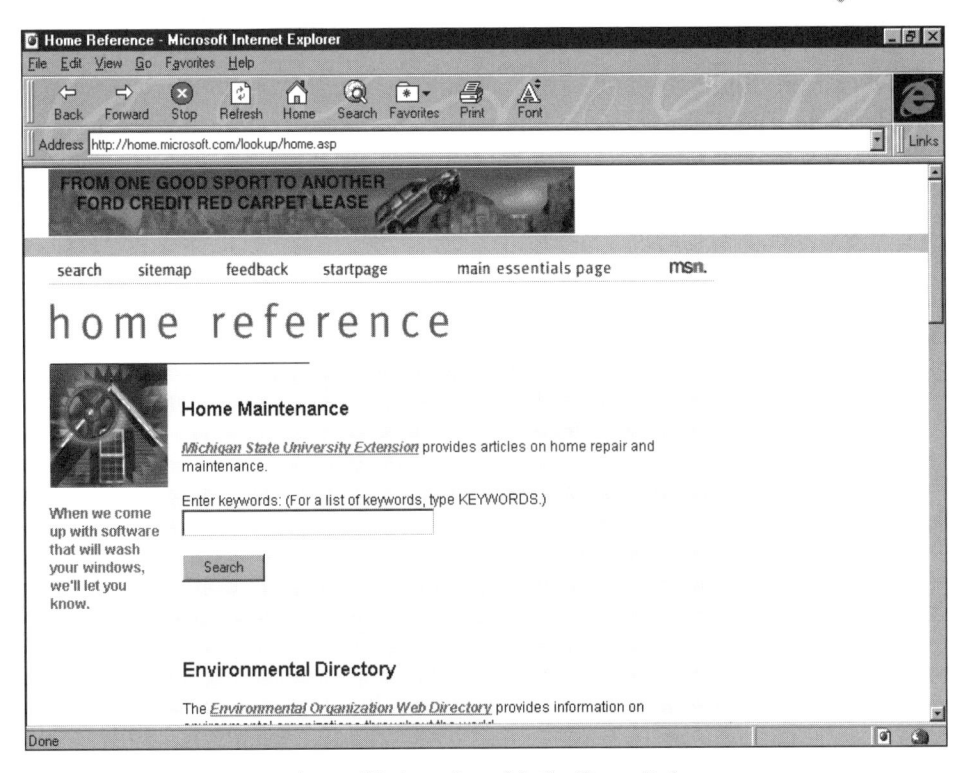

Figure 8.2 Keeping your home life in order with the Home Reference page.

and pay real money to take full advantage of the site's privileges. I suggest you don't pay for any services until you surf the Web for a while and decide what you can and can't get for free (there's an awful lot of free information out there). Enough of the "beware of advertisers" lecture. Let's talk Home Maintenance.

HOME MAINTENANCE
http://www.msue.msu.edu/msue/imp/mod02/master02.html

The Home Maintenance link provides informative essays and helpful hints about selected home maintenance topics. You can type a keyword in the search text box to look up a specific topic, or you can type the word *keywords* in the text box to view a list of available topics. Typing *keywords* results in an alphabetical, paragraph-style display of searchable keywords included in the site. It's rather intimidating at first, but it's very informative. I can almost guarantee that viewing the keyword list will result in your looking up more topics than you imagined you were interested in. You never know when you might need an article about thawing frozen pipes, checking a flood-damaged house, removing purple pen marks from your countertop, or repairing a lamp plug.

Take a minute to browse through the Home Maintenance database to become familiar with the informational topics included in this site. Remember, you can search for a specific topic or use the keywords list. I suggest browsing through the keywords list now for future reference. When you've finished browsing, return to the Home Reference page so we can continue our Essentials Directory exploration.

ENVIRONMENTAL DIRECTORY
http://www.webdirectory.com

We've just reviewed a site covering topics aimed at making our home a better place to live. Now, we'll look at a site aimed at making the world a better place to live. The Environmental Directory link appears directly below the Home Maintenance link on the Home Reference Essentials page.

Keep in mind that you can click on any links embedded in the text on any Essentials page. Clicking on a text link usually takes you to the home page of the creator of the link used by Microsoft on the Essentials Directory page. For example, clicking on the Environmental Organization Web Directory link takes you to **http://www.webdirectory.com**, as shown in Figure 8.3.

Using the Environmental Organization Web Directory home page might be more useful in some instances than accessing the simple word search provided on the Home Reference Essentials page. When you view the Web Directory, you can improve your search results by using available links and accessing major topic headings addressed by the organization.

OK, meet me back at the Home Reference page when you are finished saving the Earth so we can concentrate our efforts on our own backyard.

PLANT AND GARDEN INFORMATION
http://www.pathfinder.com/@@@Y*)u6Ck9gEAQC4Y/cgi-bin/VG/vg

The next section of the Home Reference page is the Plant and Garden Information section, which is shown in Figure 8.4.

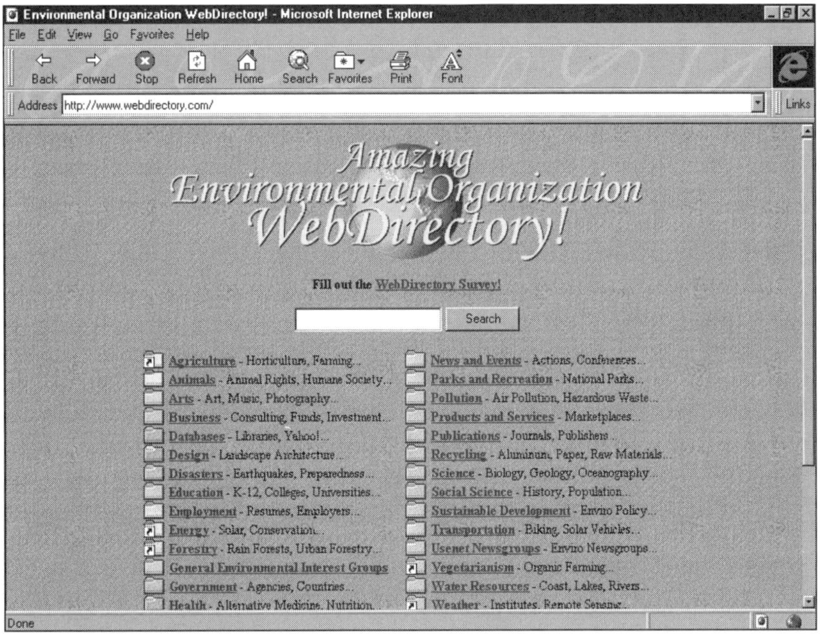

Microsoft's Essential Services Directory

Figure 8.3 Getting involved with the environment at the Amazing Environmental Organization Web Directory home page.

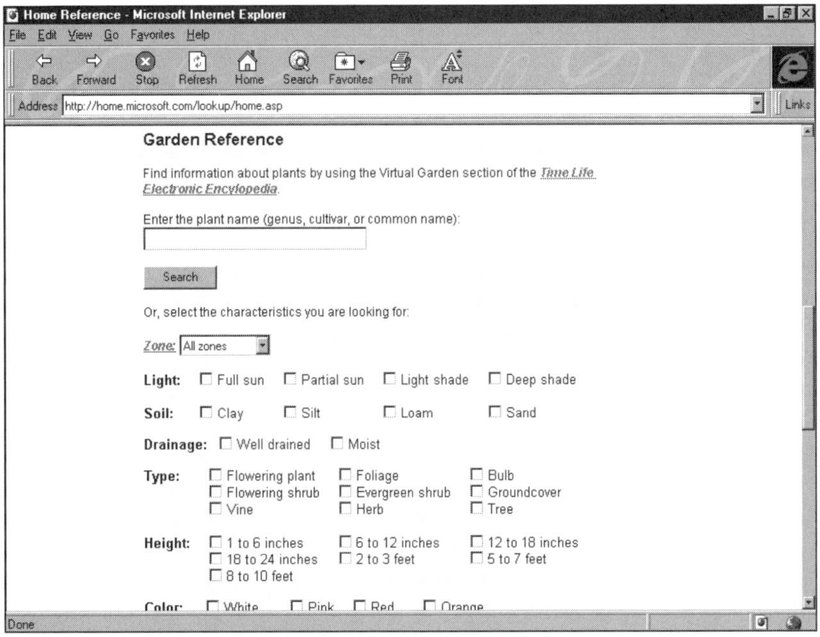

Figure 8.4 You can get great information on your garden using the Garden Information section of the Essentials Directory Home Reference page.

You can search for garden information in two ways: you can search for a particular plant type using the Enter the Plant Name text box along with the Search button, or you can search for plant information based on desired characteristics. Let's discuss both options.

Searching for a particular plant seems simple, but it can become complex (if you aren't aware that gardening is a science, this site will convince you beyond a doubt). I'm going to start our search with a simple keyword. Type *tomato* in the Enter the Plant Name text box, and click on the Search button. The search results should display a short list of available links. That doesn't seem so complicated, you say—well, scroll down a little and you'll see a list of about 10 other databases you can add to your search. Go ahead and select all of the databases, then click on the Search the Virtual Garden button. Your efforts should produce an extensive list of available links, ranked from 1 to 100 in order of relevance.

As I mentioned a moment ago, another way you can search for garden and plant information is by specifying plant characteristics as opposed to plant names. This section is fairly self-explanatory, so we won't spend an extensive amount of time with this search feature. One item in particular that I would like to point out is the Zone link.

The first specification to set in the search for plant characteristics section is the hardiness zone (not the time zone!). If you are like me, you don't have a clue as to which hardiness zone lies where. Fortunately, if you are living in the United States, you can easily find out which zone you live in by clicking on the Zone link. The Zone link displays a color-coded map of the United States hardiness zones, as shown in Figure 8.5.

Using the map, I see that I'm in the Southwest (I knew that part!) in zone number 9.

Return to the Home Reference Essentials page after you have completed investigating the Garden Reference link. Scroll down to view the next section of the Home Reference page. We're going to look up health information next.

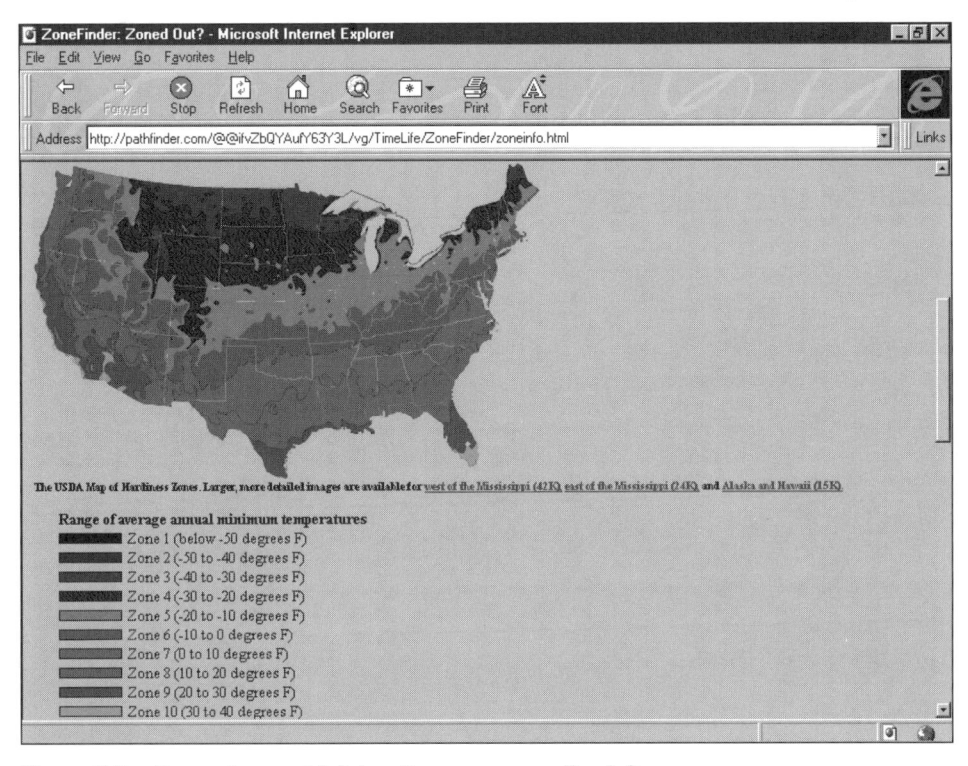

Figure 8.5 Do you know which hardiness zone you live in?

HEALTH INFORMATION

http://vh.radiology.uiowa.edu/Misc/Search.html

The lower section of the Home Reference page consists of the Health Information link and the Find a College link.

The Health Information page, also referred to as the Virtual Hospital, presents a one-stop shop for medical questions. You can pose search queries to the Virtual Hospital, ranging from common medical problems (such as bruising) to more ambiguous issues such as Prolonged QT Syndrome. You can search using layman's terms or medical jargon. Some results can be extremely complex, but other results are quite easily understood. Type *headache* in the Search text box, and then click on the Search button. Your results should look similar to those displayed in Figure 8.6.

Notice the word *headache* appears bold-faced within lines of text extracted from medical articles. You can click on any link above a text line that appears

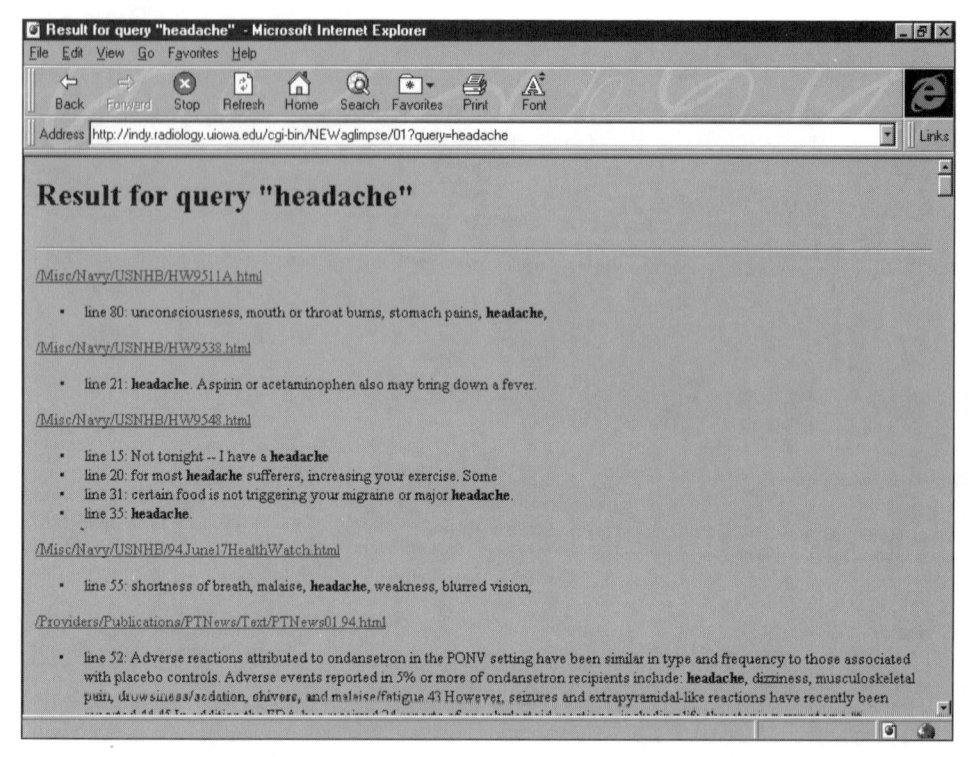

Figure 8.6 Headache search results.

relevant to your search. Some results may be complex, while others will be fairly simple. If there are a number of articles that interest you, you can return to the search result page by using your Back button or your History list. You can also click on the Services Quick Link button and return to the Health Information link to perform another search. After reviewing some of the medical articles, the next section we are about to discuss seems apropos—we're going to discuss how to look up a college (Med. School anyone?!).

FIND A COLLEGE

http://www.review.com/cgi-shl/waislook.exe

The final section of the Home Reference page is the Find a College link. You can use this link to search for a college by name, region, or state. For example, type *Notre Dame* in the Search Term text box, and then click on the Find College button. The Princeton Review will provide a list of articles and reviews related to Notre Dame. If you want to search for keywords other than college names, regions, or states, click on the Princeton Review link found in the Home Reference Look Up Colleges link area. The

Princeton Review home page offers a search option that allows limited topical keyword searches. Personally, I find the Princeton Review site a little clunky. If you are doing some serious college shopping, I suggest you look at the sites listed at the end of this chapter, and also conduct some of your own searches after reading Chapter 10.

Return to Microsoft's Essentials Directory page after you've reviewed the Look Up Colleges section of the Home Reference page. We're going to move on to the next directory section—the Financial Information category.

Financial Information

Microsoft's Financial Information link includes sections on stock quotes, IRS tax forms and information, business facts, and UPS and Federal Express package tracking. If you haven't done so already, return to the Essentials Directory page. Click on the Financial Information title link. You should see the top portion of the Financial Information page, as shown in Figure 8.7.

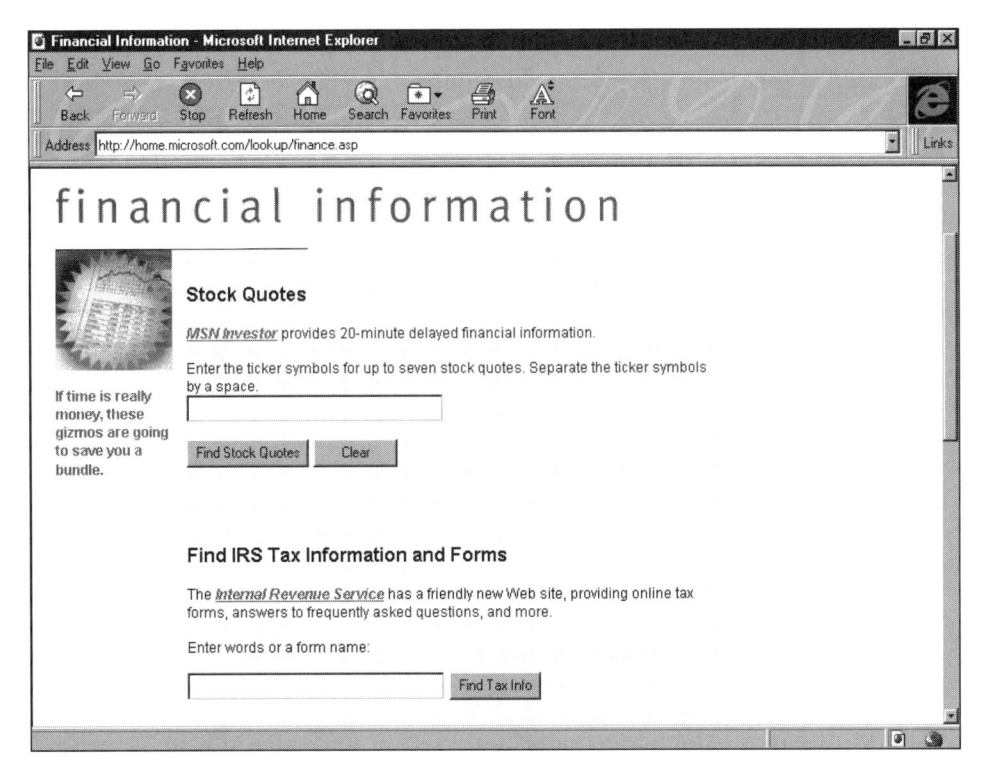

Figure 8.7 Keeping up with the times with the Financial Information page.

Let's start at the top and work our way down. The first link we'll test is the Stock Quotes link.

STOCK QUOTES

http://www.dbc.com

Do you own any stocks? Do you deal with stock quotes in your professional life? Do you just like to play on the Internet? Well, this site will satisfy all those needs. Microsoft has provided an easy (and I mean *easy*) way to quickly check stock market statistics by using stock ticker symbols. Ticker symbols are codes assigned to stock companies—for example, *hdi* is the ticker symbol for Harley Davidson. (Don't fret if you don't know a company's ticker symbol—I'll show you how to find a ticker symbol a littler later in the *Find Information About a Business* section.) After you conduct a search, you can see detailed statistics for each ticker symbol by clicking on the ticker symbol link that appears as part of your search results. Because the market changes so rapidly, all financial statistics are reported with a 20-minute delay.

I'm not going to get into the Financial details here, since this isn't a book about finances. You can access this information page as often as you desire, but you can't set the field to remember which ticker symbols you want to access. If you check some stocks on a regular basis, I recommend you use the MSN home page as your Start page—you can configure the MSN home page to post up-to-date stock quote information for certain ticker symbols each time you access your Start page.

There are many stock market sites on the Internet. You can get free information similar to the information provided by the Essentials Stock Quotes link, or you can use a paid service to obtain realtime stock statistics. For other interesting stock market sites, look at the short list I've compiled at the end of this chapter. When you are finished playing the stocks, click on the Services Links button, and then return to the Financial Information page so we can approach the IRS together.

FIND IRS TAX INFORMATION AND FORMS

http://www.irs.ustreas.gov/prod/cover.html

Ahh, the IRS—three letters that send a chill up your spine as you clutch your checkbook and wipe the sweat from your hard-working brow. Maybe that's a little too melodramatic if you've never been audited, but the IRS doesn't exactly bring visions of sugar plums dancing in the heads of any of us. This link shows a friendlier side of the IRS. The IRS now has a Web site providing online tax forms, answers to frequently asked questions, and tax news updates.

To access the IRS Web site, click in the text box under the Find IRS Tax Information and Forms header on the Financial Information page. You can type any subject, form name, form number, or other search topic in the text box. Let's look for information about the 1040EZ form. Type *1040EZ* in the text box, and then click on the Find Tax Info button. You should be rewarded with a list of articles that mention 1040EZ in their text, similar to the list shown in Figure 8.8.

At this point, you have a few options. You can click on the first link and read the article displayed, you can scroll down and view other related articles,

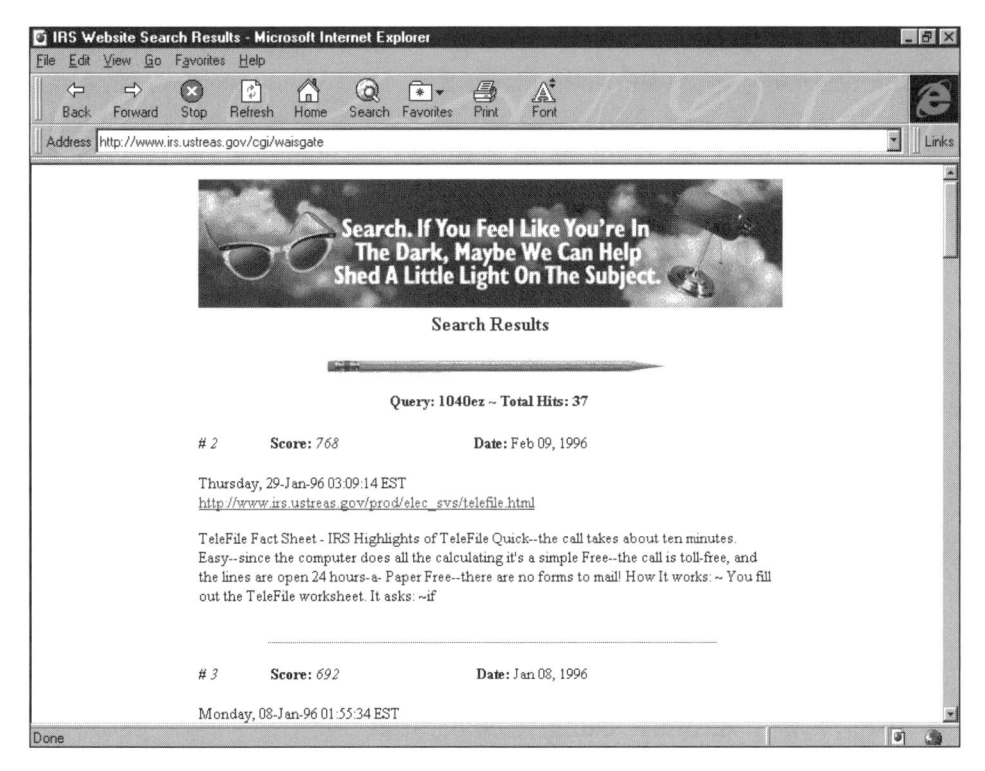

Figure 8.8 **The 1040EZ latest tax information provided by the IRS.**

or you can scroll to the bottom of the page and choose one of the option links at the bottom of the page. Let's say you want to download a 1040EZ form. If you scroll to the bottom of the current page, you'll see a group of links. One link is called Forms & Pubs. You can click on that link and gain access to all the available IRS forms by following the links to the Forms page (one word of caution, the Forms page counts down the days until the next April 15th!). If you're lucky, you might find another deduction or two. When you decide that you have spent enough time with the IRS, click on the Services Links button, return to the Financial Information Essentials page, and then we'll research some facts on a business or two.

Find Information About a Business

http://www.hoovers.com

Finding information about a business used to start with a trip to the library and a call to the Better Business Bureau. Now you can access information instantaneously via the Web and Microsoft's friendly Essentials Directory. The Find Information About a Business link is located on the Financial Information page, as shown in Figure 8.9.

As you can see, you can search for business information using a company's name or ticker symbol. If you search by company name, you can search by partial names as well as full names. For example, if you typed Marcus in the Search by Name text box, then clicked on the Search by Name button, you would receive results on the Marcus Cable Company L.P., The Marcus Corporation, and The Neiman Marcus Group, Inc.

Each business information listing includes address, phone, fax, Web site, and (remember I mentioned this earlier?) the ticker symbol. You can use the Look Up Business Information link to find the ticker symbol. Then you can use the ticker symbol to look up the stock prices in the Stock Quotes link. It's all very convenient.

Track a Package

http://www.fedex.com/track_it.html
http://www.ups.com/tracking/tracking.html

Some sites are obviously designed to make everyone's life easier—including customers and employees. The Microsoft Track a Package link is a link to a

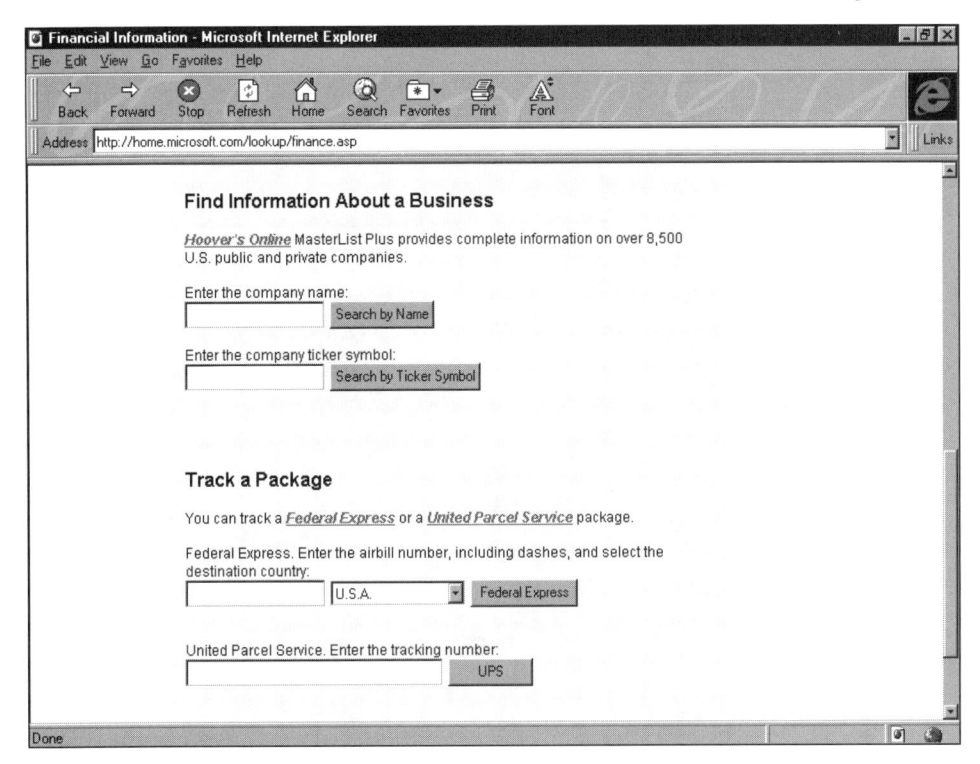

Figure 8.9 Lower half of the Microsoft Financial Information page.

couple of those let's-make-everyone's-life-easier sites. Notice that you can track packages delivered by Federal Express or UPS. Fortunately for us, a friend of mine recently received a Federal Express package from Boulder, Colorado. We can use the Federal Express tracking link to verify that he received his package. Type airbill number 3685271764 in the airbill number text box, leave the country setting at USA (the default selection), and then click on the Federal Express button. A status report should display as shown in Figure 8.10.

Notice my friend, C. Taylor, has already signed for the package and it has been delivered successfully. If you read through the comments on the status page, you can review every transaction the Federal Express package encountered along the way (information such as when and how the packaged was delivered from Boulder to Denver, to the Oakland Hub, and then finally to Tempe, AZ).

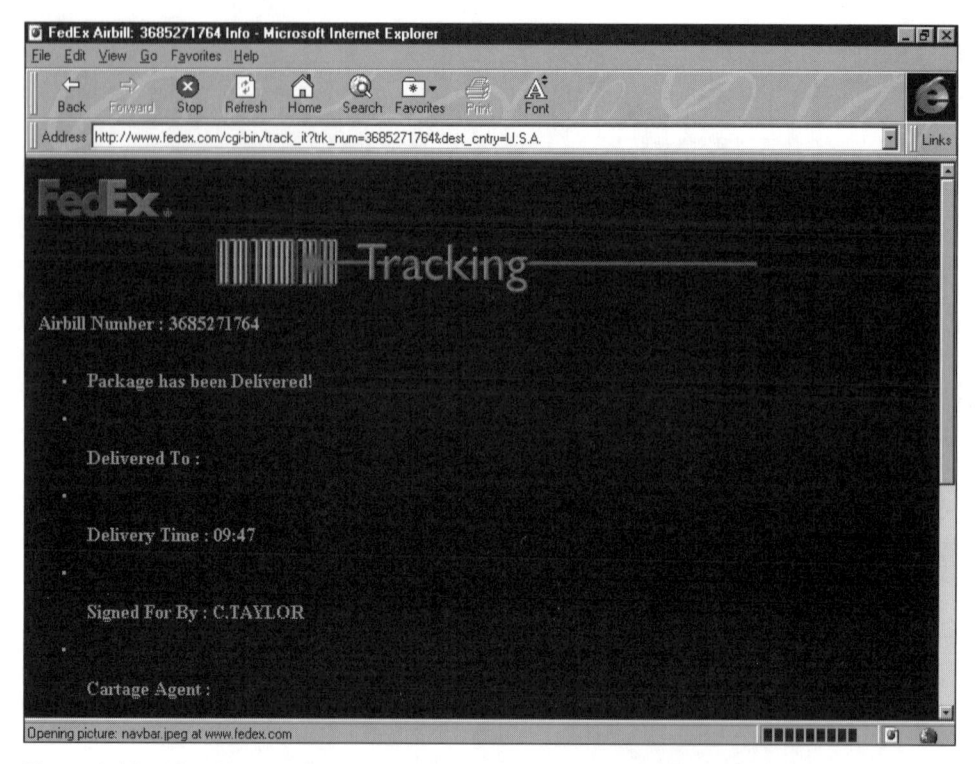

Figure 8.10 Tracking packages with the Federal Express Tracking Report page.

By now, you should feel comfortable with the Financial Information links offered on the Microsoft Essentials page. The sites are straightforward and easily accessible. Now that we've got our finances in order, we can call on some friends and look up some addresses.

Phone & Address Look-Up

We've been spending quite a bit of time submerged in electronic surfing (maybe submerged isn't the right word when you're surfing, but you know what I mean). Now it is time to think about some "old" technology—telephone calls and letters. Phone calls and letters may soon be replaced with NetMeetings, chat groups, and email, but for now, telephones and stamps are a big part of our lives. The Phone & Address Look-Up section of Microsoft's Essentials Directory helps make correspondence (of all sorts) easier. You can use this section of the directory to look up toll free (800) numbers, business numbers, area and country codes, ZIP codes, street addresses, and email addresses. Click on the Phone & Address Look-Up

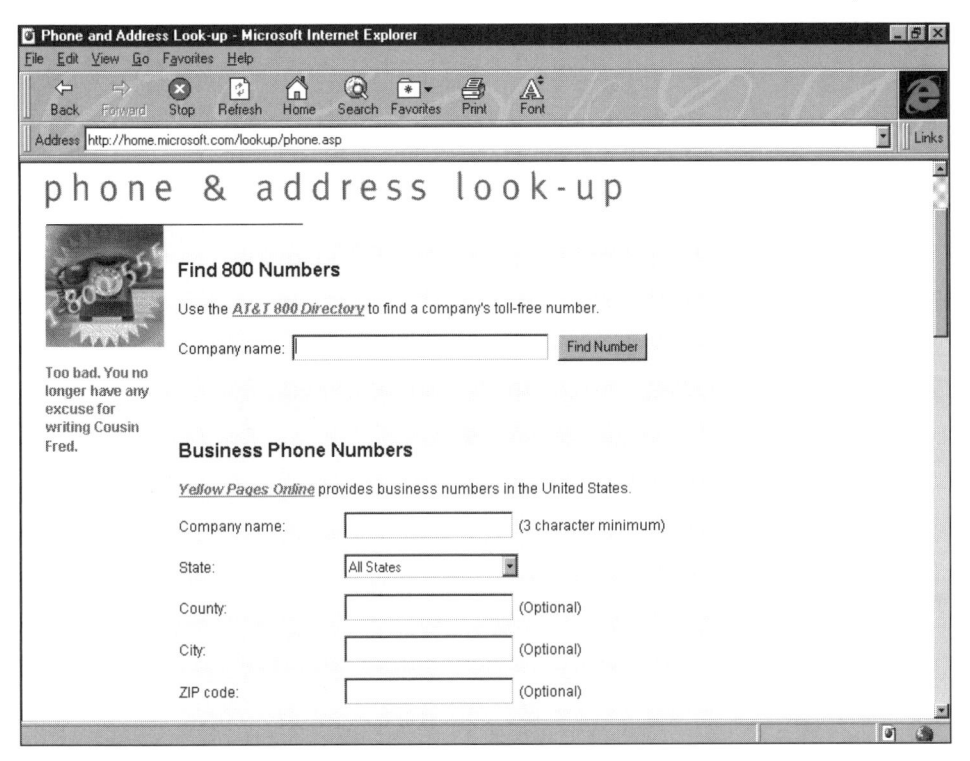

Figure 8.11 Looking-up address and phone information.

link to display the top portion of the Phone & Address Look-Up Services page, as shown in Figure 8.11.

The first link under the Phone & Address Look-Up Services category is the Find 800 Numbers link.

FIND 800 NUMBERS
http://www.tollfree.att.net/dir800

The 800 Numbers search feature allows you to access AT&T's online 800 Directory. To search for an 800 number, simply type the name of a company in the text box, and then click on the Find Number button. For example, if you typed Levi Strauss in the text box, then clicked on the Find Number button, you should get a result similar to the page shown in Figure 8.12.

The 800 numbers display to the left of each company's name. Notice the search results include links to the other businesses in the same category.

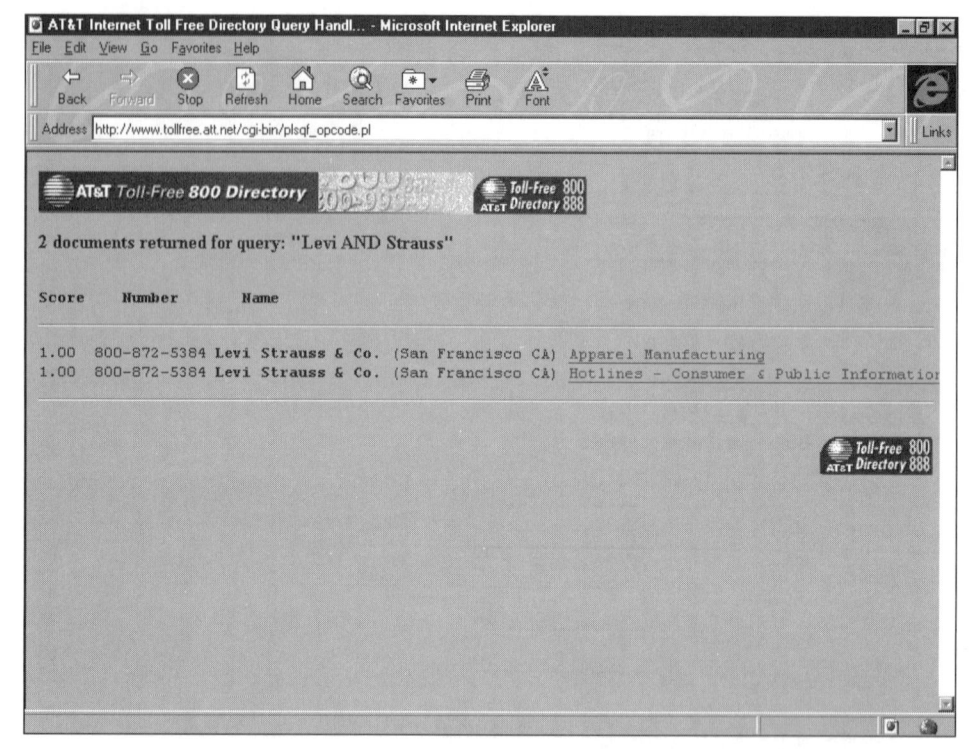

Figure 8.12 Searching for the Levi Strauss 800 number.

Referring to Figure 8.12, if you clicked on the Apparel Manufacturing link, you would get a list of 800 numbers for other companies in the apparel manufacturing category. Remember, not all companies have an 800 number for their customers. Therefore, Microsoft included the next services link—a link to business phone numbers. Return to the Phone & Address Look-Up page, and then we'll track down a business number.

BUSINESS PHONE NUMBERS

http://www.ypo.com

Who would argue with the idea of putting a phone book on the Internet? Not many. In fact, the people at Yellow Pages realized that many folks *want* online phone "books." Therefore, the Yellow Page people created the online Yellow Pages for business phone numbers. In turn, Microsoft teamed up with the Yellow Page people and added the Business Numbers link to the Essentials page.

I've found that the Business Numbers link works better if you keep it simple. There are a few optional search parameters that you can set, but for some reason, too many details bog down this search engine. The best way to use this link is to simply enter the company name in the company name text box and leave the State field set to All States. (The search separates the results alphabetically by state, so it won't be too hard to locate a particular company in a particular region later on.)

Feel free to play around in this area to get an idea of how it works. Remember to return to the Phone & Address Look-Up page when you are finished. Our next mission will be to determine area codes and country codes.

AREA AND COUNTRY CODES

http://www.xmission.com/~americom/aclookup.html

The middle section of the Phone & Address Look-Up page, shown in Figure 8.13, displays links to sites, helping you find area and country codes and ZIP code information.

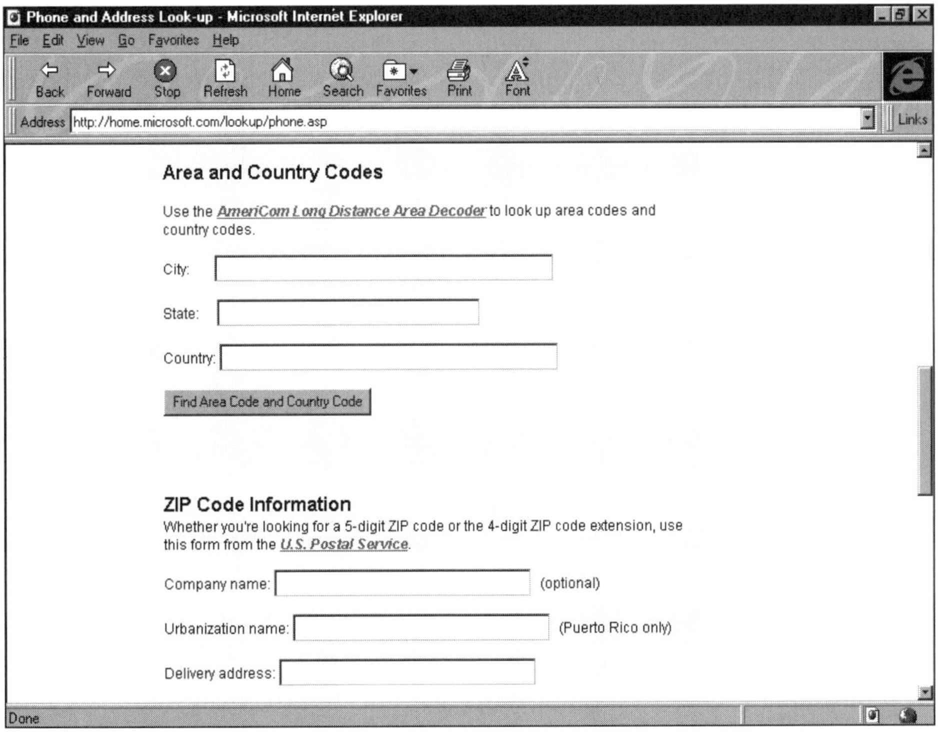

Figure 8.13 Finding country and ZIP code information from the Phone & Address Look-Up Services page.

The Area and Country Codes section is a straightforward search. Simply enter the city name, state name or abbreviation, and country name or abbreviation, and then click on the Find Area Code and Country Code button. For example, let's find the area and country code for Greenbelt, Maryland, USA. Enter the information into the form, and then click on the Find Area Code and Country Code button. Scroll down after you receive your results, and you will see that the area code for Greenbelt is 301 and the country code is 1. If you are searching for area and country codes outside of the U.S., leave the State text box empty.

For our next topic review, return to the Phone & Address Look-Up Essentials page and scroll down to the Zip Code Information area.

ZIP CODE INFORMATION

http://www.usps.gov/ncsc/lookups/lookup_zip+4.html

The Zip Code Information area of the Phone & Address Look-Up page is used to...you guessed it!...look up ZIP codes. This link is offered as part of the U.S. Postal Service's online resources. Notice there are four text boxes for information entry: the Company name, Urbanization name, Delivery address, and City, State, and/or ZIP code text boxes. Entering a company name is optional, and the Urbanization name text box is for searching for zip code information in Puerto Rico, only. The required fields are the Delivery address field and the City, State field (don't ask me why they put in the option to type in the ZIP code!).

This search link benefits those who know an address but not a ZIP code. You can use the next link, the Verify Addresses link, to verify addresses, look up ZIP codes, and print bar codes. Return to the Phone & Address Look-Up Essentials page when you are ready to do some address verification.

VERIFY ADDRESSES

http://www.cedar.buffalo.edu/adserv.html

The bottom portion of the Phone & Address Look-Up Essentials page consists of the Verify Addresses section and Find E-mail Addresses And Personal Web Pages section You can verify an address using the Center of Excellence for Document Analysis and Recognition link. To verify an address, type the address in the text box then click on the Process This

Address button. If you type an incorrect address, you will get an Address Rejected message.

When a correct address is verified, you have the option to postscript the address for printing along with its bar code, save the address as a GIF image, view a map from Yahoo, or, my favorite, view an InterActiveX map from MapQuest, shown in Figure 8.14. The InterActiveX Atlas at MapQuest is a fun, informative site. We'll be discussing maps in more detail later in this chapter, when we review the Travel Tips Essentials page. For now, when you've sated your current address and cartographic urges, return to the Phone & Address Look-Up page—next, we're going to see how we can ferret out email addresses and personal Web pages.

FINDING EMAIL ADDRESSES AND PERSONAL WEB PAGES
http://www.four11.com

The Find E-Mail Addresses And Personal Web Pages link becomes more and more useful as electronic mail becomes a major means of

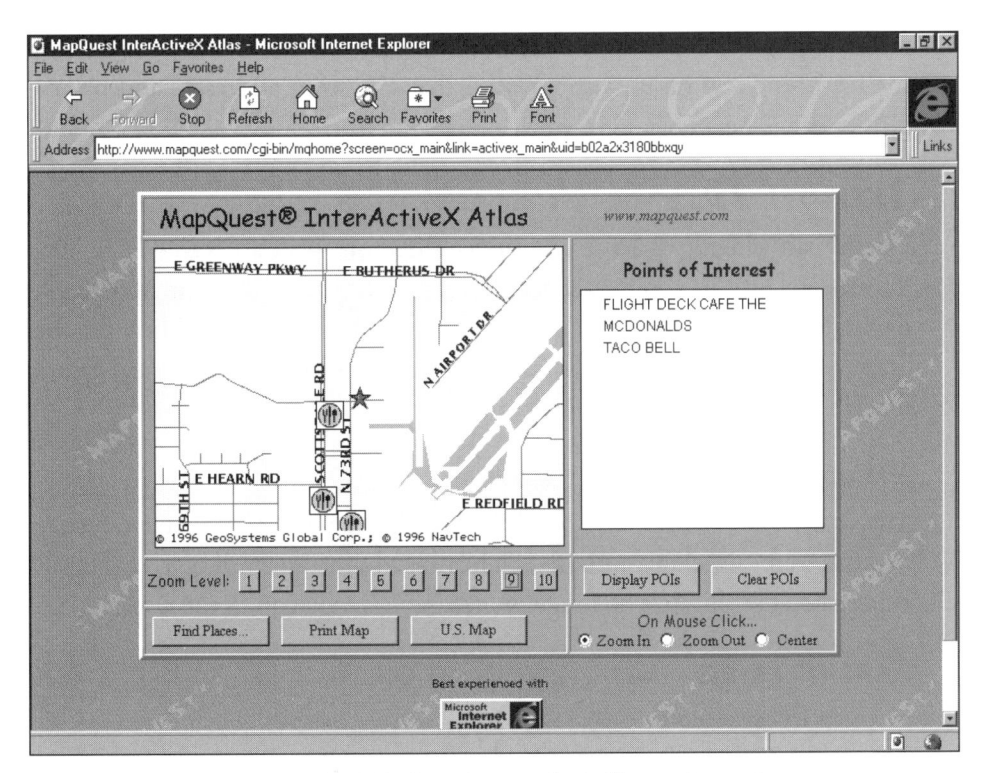

Figure 8.14 A map of The Coriolis Group's area, including restaurants.

communication. Microsoft provides the email directory link to assist us during this email explosion. The site provides a text box used to search the Four11 Whitepage directory. Recently, Four11 joined forces with LookUP (another large email directory service), becoming one gargantuan email directory.

To conduct an email address search, type a name in the text box, then click on the Search Four11 button. You should receive a list of names matching your search criteria. You can click on a name link to view the email address and interests (maybe) of the person you selected. MSIE automatically opens an addressed email window if you click on the linked email address below the name and address. If you would like to add your name to the Four11 directory, it's free and easy. All you need to do is click on the free listing hypertext link embedded in the text under the Finding Email Addresses And Personal Web Pages header.

This concludes our discussion of the Phone & Address Look-Up Essentials page. I hope you are feeling more comfortable about using the Internet to research phone numbers, addresses, and email addresses—once you use the features a few times, you'll realize that accessing addresses and phone numbers has never been easier.

Travel Tips

The fourth category on the Essentials Directory page is Travel Tips. The Travel Tips link provides sites to help you find a great vacation spot, look up flight times, view maps, and look at weather forecasts. Click on the Travel Information Services Directory category title, and then we'll figure out where we should go on vacation.

FINDING A VACATION SPOT

Microsoft's Find A Vacation Spot link consists of a series of search parameters that you set for searching purposes. Unfortunately, those parameters don't mean a thing because this link no longer works, so let's move on to the next site.

FLIGHT TIMES

http://www.sys1.com

The Flight Times link on the Travel Information Services page gives you a direct connection to the System One AMADEUS Computer Reservation

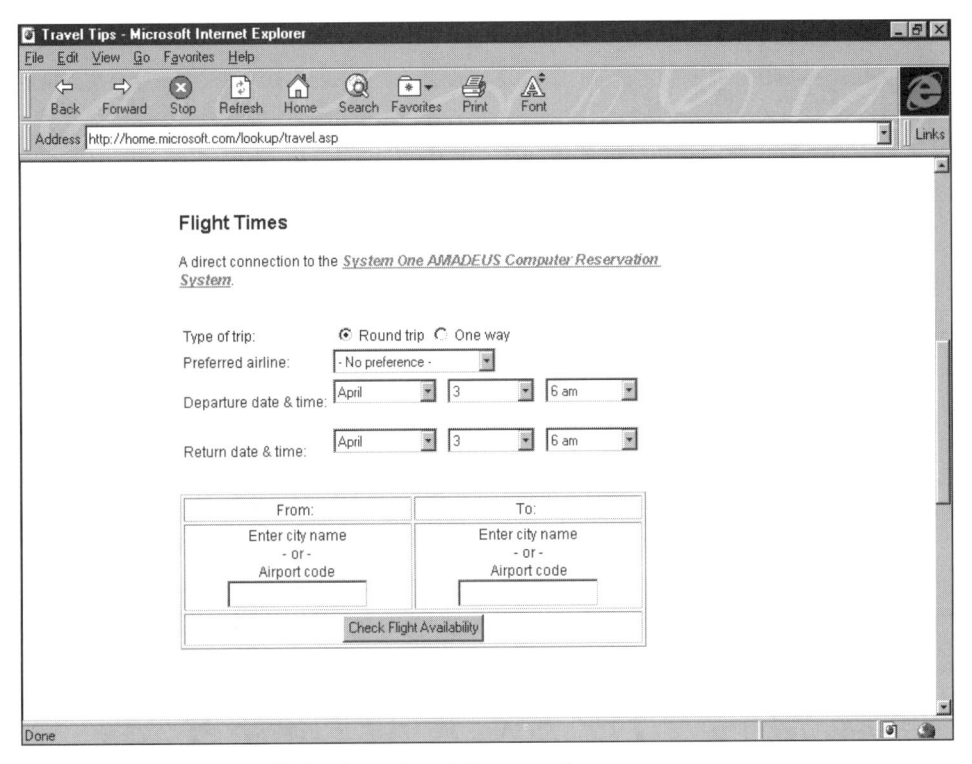

Figure 8.15 Checking flight times for airline travel.

System—the same system used by many travel agents. The Flight Times link, shown in Figure 8.15, requires detailed search criteria from you before you can view flight times.

Let's say you want to check flight times for a round trip flight from San Francisco to Chicago during the Thanksgiving holiday on all the available airlines. You could select the following information:

- *Type of trip:* Round trip
- *Preferred airline:* No preference (You may want to indicate an airline if you are a frequent flyer or if you are using coupons.)
- *Departure date & time:* November 26, 8:00 am (The selected time acts as a reference point and not a definitive time.)
- *Return date & time:* December 3, 8:00 am (Again, the time is just a reference point.)

- *From:* San Francisco
- *To:* Chicago

After entering the information, click on the Check Flight Availability button. Most likely, you'll receive a message page stating that your request couldn't be processed because you need to further indicate departure and arrival airports. Scroll down to view the From and To list boxes. Select *San Francisco Arpt, CA, US* in the From list box, and select *Ohare Arpt, Chicago, IL, US* in the To list box. Now, click on the Check Flight Availability button again.

The next step is to find the lowest fare on the most convenient flight. To do this, select departing and returning flights by clicking in the radio buttons next to your selections. Once you've selected a possible flight schedule, scroll down and click on the Lowest Fare button. At this point, you can try to find a cheaper flight by clicking on the Reselect Flights button to return to your flight selection list (actually it's quicker to use the MSIE back button), or you can book the ticket online by clicking on the Book It link.

VIEW MAPS OF LOCATIONS IN THE UNITED STATES
http://tiger.census.gov/cgi-bin/mapbrowse
http://venus.census.gov/cdrom/lookup

An ironic characteristic of the Internet is that even though you can easily get lost on the Net, it can help you keep track of things on land. The Map link on the Travel Information Services page can take you to quite a few map sites on the Net, some more complex than others.

The View Maps of Locations in the United States link consists of a simple search text box. To use the link, type the name of the city and state you are interested in viewing, then click on the Find Location on Map button. Instead of discussing the many options associated with this link, I encourage you to experiment on your own. Personally, I find this map site to be too complex for most of my needs and generally choose to use the MapQuest site we discussed earlier.

Return to the Travel Information Essentials page when you have completed your map survey. Our next adventure will be to check the weather—without holding our fingers to the wind or watching the nightly news.

LOCAL, STATE, OR ZONE WEATHER FORECAST

http://www.nnic.noaa.gov

The final Travel Information link, and one of the most important in my opinion, is the Weather Forecast link. This site is highly informative without being too complex. To display the weather forecast for a city or county, type the name in the first text box. Then display the remaining options by using the drop-down list arrows. For example, to see the weather forecast for beautiful Boulder, Colorado, type Boulder in the city or county text box, select Colorado in the state drop-down list box, and leave the area selection at the default Local option. Once your settings are in place, click on the Retrieve Forecast button. Your results should look similar to Figure 8.16.

Perusing this site is well worth your time. Take a moment to scroll through the page and view the available links (there are quite a few). Some are purely informative, such as the severe weather warnings links; others are fun, such as the Animate Image option.

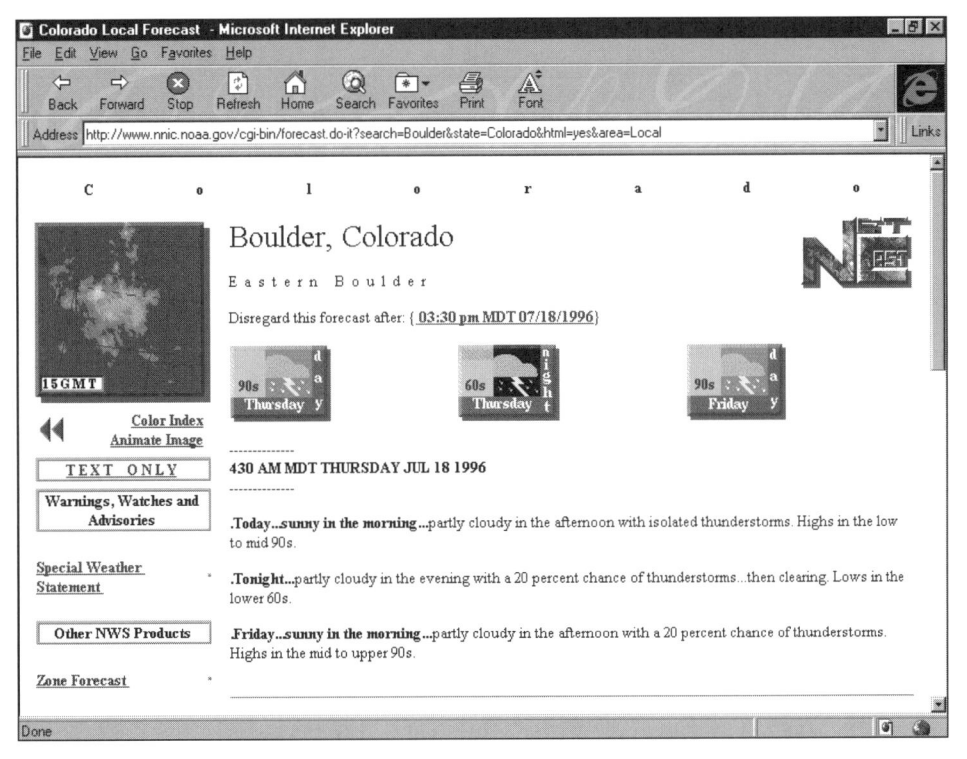

Figure 8.16 **Getting the weather forecast for Boulder, Colorado.**

After you finish checking the weather in your neighborhood, your mom's neighborhood, and your best friend's neighborhood, return to the Essentials Directory page. We've completed our review of the Travel Tips Essentials links; now, we are going to look at my favorite part of the Essentials Directory—the Writer's Reference page.

Writer's Reference

The Writer's Reference page consists of links to the books that sit on most people's bookshelves—a dictionary, a thesaurus, and an encyclopedia. Thrown in for good measure are three other reference resources: an acronyms link, *Bartlett's Quotations*, and the complete works of William Shakespeare (imagine the data entry involved). To display the Writer's Reference links, click on the Writer's Reference category title. The top portion of the Writer's Reference Essentials page should display as shown in Figure 8.17.

The first Writer's Reference section links you to an old friend, *Webster's Dictionary*. You'll have to excuse me if I get a little carried away here and

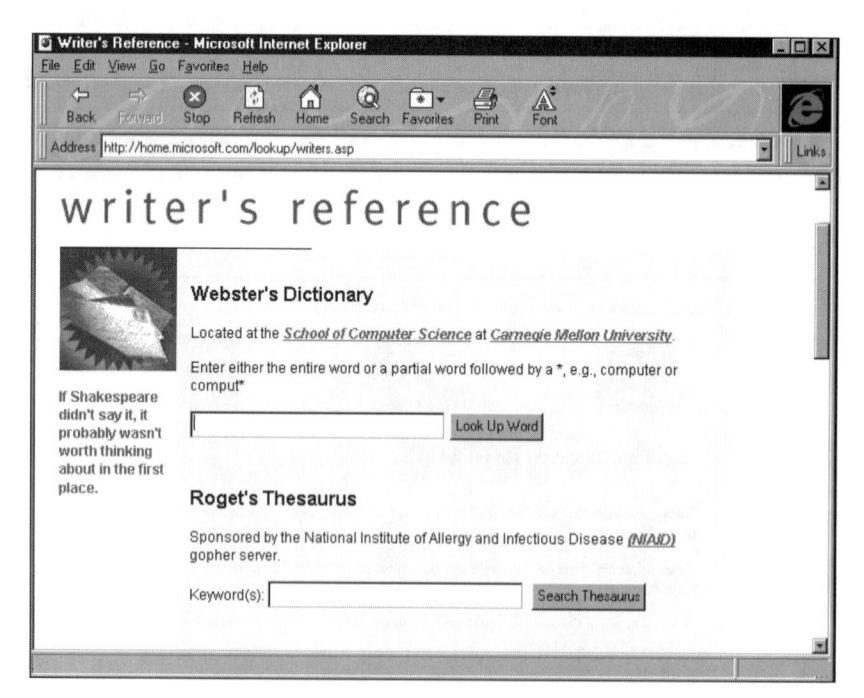

Figure 8.17 **The top portion of the Writer's Reference Services page.**

there throughout this section. As you can imagine, word play is one of my favorite pastimes. Enough about me, let's talk a little about *Webster*.

WEBSTER'S DICTIONARY

http://gs213.sp.cs.cmu.edu/prog/webster

First there were spell checkers, now there are online dictionaries—and lots of them. English, Japanese, French, German, and Spanish dictionaries; law, computer, slang, and medical dictionaries. Dictionaries are making their presence known on the Internet. Microsoft has provided a quick link to the dictionary most people probably access most often—*Webster's Dictionary*. To access *Webster's*, click on the Writer's Reference category link. The *Webster's* link should appear at the top of the Writer's Reference page.

The *Webster's* link provides a text box enabling you to search for a word or partial word (followed by an * to indicate missing text—for example, Micros*). Let's take *Webster's* for a spin. Suppose I said I just saw a camelopard walk past my window. Chances are, you're thinking I've been reading too many Dr. Seuss books. Just to make sure, though, type *camelopard* in the Look Up Word text box, and click on the Look Up Word button. You should arrive at the Hypertext Webster Interface, where you'll see that a camelopard is a giraffe. Notice that almost every word in the camelopard definition displays as a link. Each linked word takes you to the definition of the word. The word-link feature is especially useful for complex definitions.

One thing to keep in mind when you are using *Webster's Dictionary* is that the online version of *Webster's* is identical to the printed version. Recent terms, such as Internet and gigabyte, have not been added to either the hard copy or online version of the dictionary. Most linguists believe that words must stand the test of time before they can be added to the official word banks.

Techno-Jargon Takes Over

An estimated 10 percent of the American population logs on to the Internet or an online service at some point in their day. Many linguists believe this surge in wire-based communication is giving birth to an underground language—an offspring of computer techno-jargon and online shorthand (symbols, acronyms, etc.).

> In 1995, the *New World Dictionary* editorial board took a bold step, evidencing that the Internet is carving its niche in linguistic hearts. The board selected "World Wide Web" as its 1995 Word of the Year—an honor bestowed on a word that has attained the highest level of influence and cultural significance in a given year.
>
> Our spoken language is expected to change as a result of the Internet, as well. According to John Algeo, a University of Georgia professor and president of the Dictionary Society of North America, "The Internet is likely to change the way we talk more than the advent of television, radio, or the personal computer."

Feel free to visit *Webster's* for a while. I've also listed more links to online dictionaries at the end of this chapter (including my personal favorite time-thief, the *Oxford English Dictionary*, and *FOLDOC*, an especially useful online dictionary of computing terms). When you are ready, we'll leave dictionary land and head for Roget and his Thesaurus.

Roget's Thesaurus

gopher://odie.niaid.nih.gov/77/.thesaurus/index
http://www2.thesaurus.com/thesaurus

Most people who have ever used a thesaurus have probably used *Roget's Thesaurus*. Microsoft provides a link to an online version of *Roget's Thesaurus* on the Writer's Reference Services page. I haven't had much luck accessing Microsoft's Gopher link to *Roget's Thesaurus*, so I use the HTTP site address given above.

Using the *Roget's Thesaurus* site is as simple as typing a term in the Keyword(s) text box and clicking on the Search Thesaurus button. If you are having trouble accessing the thesaurus from the Services Directory page, display the HTTP site, and execute Favorites|Add to Favorites for easy access later. After adding the thesaurus site to your Favorites folder, return to the Writer's Reference Services page. The next link we'll be discussing is the Global Encyclopedia link.

Global Encyclopedia

The middle portion of the Writer's Reference Essentials page, shown in Figure 8.18, offers links to the Global Encyclopedia and the World Wide Web Acronyms and Abbreviations Server.

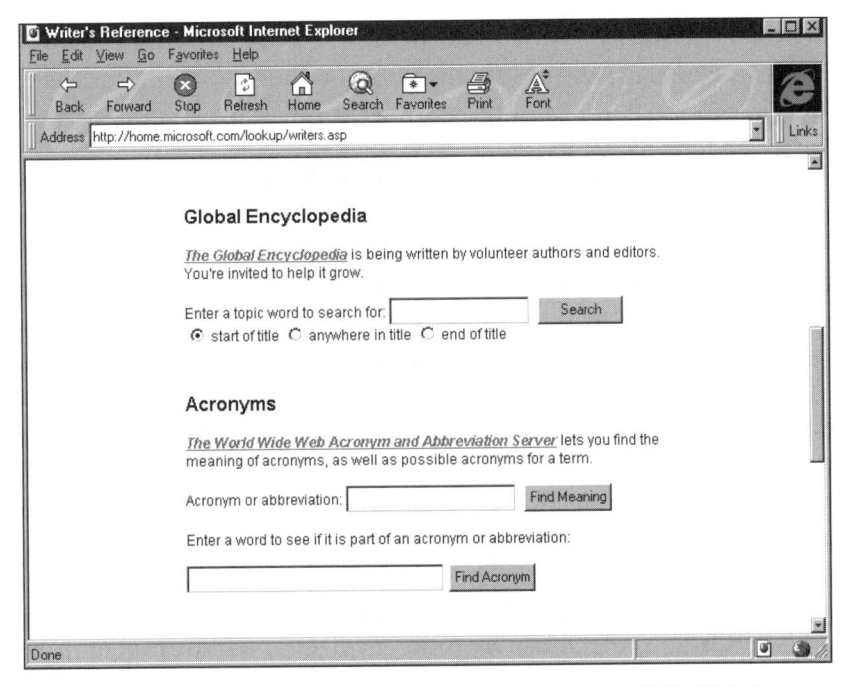

Figure 8.18 Accessing the Global Encyclopedia and the World Wide Web Acronyms and Abbreviations Server.

Unfortunately, I can't open the Global Encyclopedia Services Directory link. I tried accessing the encyclopedia through other channels, but without success, so go ahead and try some of the encyclopedia addresses listed at the end of this chapter. Online encyclopedias have a ways to go as far as maximizing the Internet's potential. If you are serious about using your computer to access an encyclopedia, I suggest you invest in a CD-ROM encyclopedia.

ACRONYMS

http://www.ucc.ie/info/net/acronyms/index.html

Toss up a dish of SLIP, PPP, W3, FTP, and HTTP. Add a scoop of FDA, NASA, OSHA, and NAFTA. Spice things up with a pinch of FOC, ABSOLOM, and SQUIRT, and what do you get? A mess of acronyms. It's no surprise that the acronym business is thriving these days. That's probably why Microsoft added the Acronym link to the Writer's Reference page.

There are two ways you can access an acronym definition. If you know the acronym, you can type the acronym in the Find Meaning text box, and then click on the Find Meaning button. Another way to use the Acronym link is to perform a key term search. Suppose you vaguely recall an organization that had something to do with sleeping. You could type the word *sleep* in the Find Acronym text box, and click on the Find Acronym button. Aha!—that's the acronym you were looking for (right?): SIESTA, the Society for the Introduction of Extra Sleeping Time in the Afternoon.

Notice there is a link to add acronyms to the database. You can add acronyms to the database by clicking on the New Entries link, or, if you are adding a new definition to an existing acronym, you can click on the acronym link to add your definition.

The Acronym link is quite handy—not only for Internet purposes, but for clarifying references in newspaper articles, government documents, magazine stories, labels, and other mediums of acronymania. Next, we're going to review the bottom portion of the Writer's Reference Services page, which consists of links to *Bartlett's Quotations* and the complete works of Shakespeare.

Bartlett's Quotations

http://www.cc.columbia.edu/acis/bartleby/bartlett
http://www.columbia.edu/acis/bartleby/search.html

The final section of the Writer's Reference Services page, shown in Figure 8.19, provides search capabilities for *Bartlett's Quotations* and *The Complete Works of William Shakespeare*.

The *Bartlett's Quotations* section on the Microsoft Writer's Reference links page is one of those sections where clicking on an embedded text link can be as informative as entering a search term in the Search text box. Clicking on the *Bartlett's Quotations* link takes you to an alphabetical list of all the authors included in the original 1901 version of *Bartlett's Quotations*. If you are looking for a quote by a particular author, take this route. The *Bartlett's Quotations* link also offers you the option to search for a keyword.

The second embedded text link is the Columbia University's Bartelby Library link. Clicking on this link takes you to the Bartelby Library home page—a site providing free, electronically published, original literary works

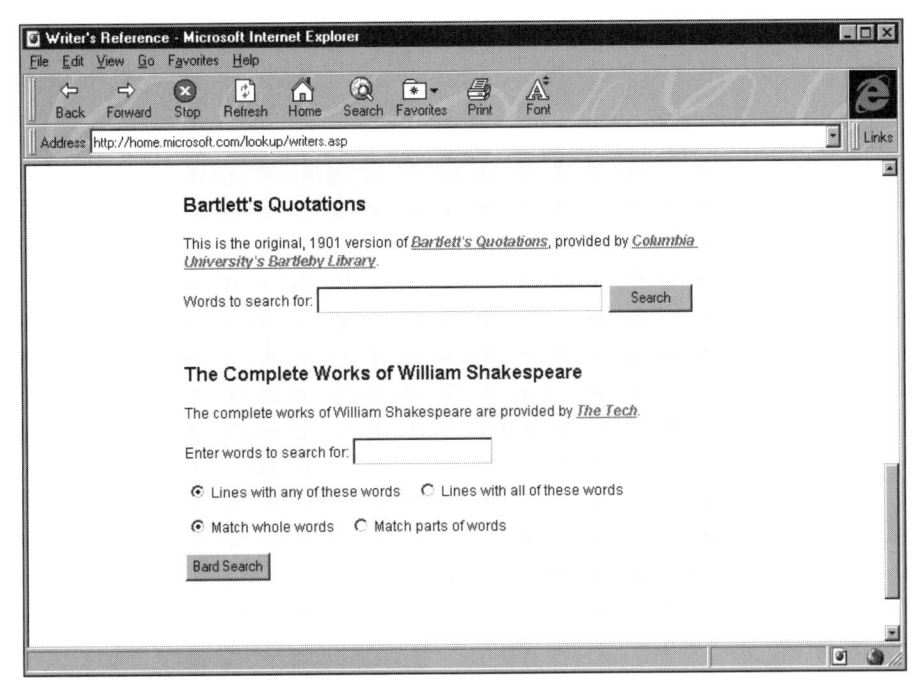

Figure 8.19 Polishing up on your flowery quotes with the help of Bartlett's Quotations and the Bard, himself!

with 100 percent accuracy. The Bartelby project is dedicated to a high standard of publishing literary works suitable for both pleasure reading and professional scholarship. Personally, all this literary scholarship talk is stirring up flashbacks of my college days, so I'm going to click on my Back button to return to the Microsoft Writer's Reference Essentials page. I'll meet you there when you're ready. Then we'll move along and see what Mr. Shakespeare has to say (and stir up yet more college flashbacks).

THE COMPLETE WORKS OF WILLIAM SHAKESPEARE
http://the-tech.mit.edu

William Shakespeare occupies the final section of the Writer's Reference page. You can search the complete works of Mr. Shakespeare using what The Tech refers to as a Bard search. I suggest we search for two Shakespearean themes that stand out in my mind: love and death. Type *love* and *death* in the text box, retain the default selection to search for lines with any of the keywords, turn on the option to match parts of the keywords, and click on the Bard Search button. Your results should display as shown in Figure 8.20.

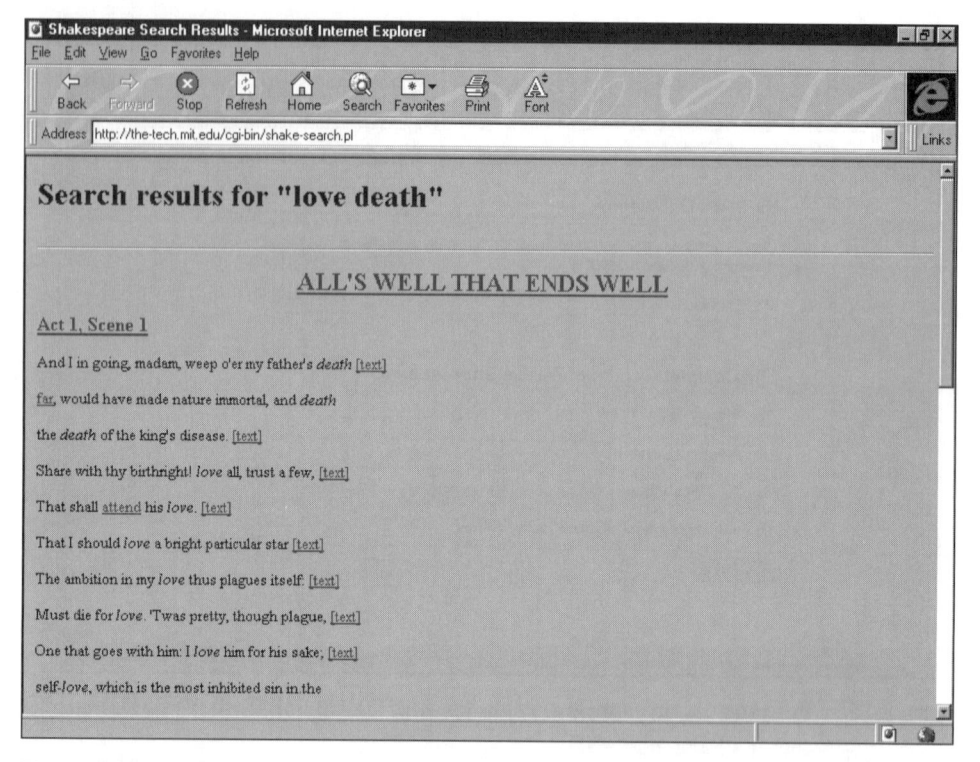

Figure 8.20 Bard Search's extensive results on love and death.

The results display in alphabetical order by the title of Shakespeare's plays. Within each play listing, the occurrences of the search terms are listed in order of appearance. You can display the context of extracted lines by clicking on the [text] link at the end of a line. The text link takes you to the page of the play where the text appears. The referenced line of text appears at the top of the page.

I'll leave the rest of your Bard musing up to you. I'm ready to jump back in the 20th century and see what's being published in today's magazines. When you are finished contemplating Shakespeare, return to the Essentials Directory page where we'll link up to some online magazines.

Publications Searches

Although we all know that magazines provide timely research information as well as leisure reading materials, researching this information often entails a few hours at the local library (or subscribing to many different magazines).

The Essentials page link to Publications Searches puts an end to tediously thumbing through magazines (and emptying your checking account on costly subscriptions), by conducting online searches of popular magazines. This section lists five sites with publication information. The first three sites are similar sites accessing different magazines. Since the search procedures for all three are so similar, I've lumped the databases together into a single discussion. The remaining two sections discuss the Art and Architecture link and the Government Publications link. Let's get started.

Magazine and Publication Searches: CMP Technology, Ziff-Davis, and Time Warner

http://techweb.cmp.com/techweb/programs/registered/search/cmp-wais-index.html

http://www.zdnet.com/plweb-cgi/topsearch/topsearch.pl

http://pathfinder.com/@@onENi5BZ4wEAQLTV/welcome

Information Week, *PC Week*, *Family PC*, *PC Magazine*, *Fortune*, *Money*, *People*, *Time*, and *Sports Illustrated*—you now have these and many other magazines at your fingertips, compliments of Microsoft's Essentials Directory. There are three magazine search engines provided on the Publications Search page: The CMP Technology Magazine Search, the Ziff-Davis Magazine Search, and the Time Warner Publication Search.

Each of the magazine search engines provides a keyword text box and a search button. To conduct a search, pick a magazine group that seems most relevant to your topic, type your keyword in the keyword text box, select which magazines you want to include in your search (CMP allows 1 click on the Search button.

Getting the Whole Story

The Publication Searches page provides you the opportunity to search by keywords through a number of magazines. After you conduct a search, you can click on a magazine's home page link for further reading. For example, if you enjoy sports, you could use the Time Warner link to search for Michael-Jordan (the hyphen indicates that the words are a phrase as opposed to two separate search terms). Undoubtedly, you would receive a link or two to a Sports

Illustrated article. After accessing the link and reading the article, you can click on the Back To Sports Illustrated Magazine button to view the online version of SI.

The magazine links are fun to view because, like magazines at your local newsstand, online magazines change on a regular basis.

ART AND ARCHITECTURE PUBLICATION SEARCH
http://www.ahip.getty.edu/ahip/index.html

Once again, I regret that I must report a nonworking Essentials link: the Art and Architecture Publication Search link. On the up side, you can access this sections referenced site, the Getty Information Institute site, by typing its new URL—**http://www.ahip.getty.edu/ahip/index.html**—in the Address text box.

The Getty Information Institute site provides a link to a searchable cultural information database. Clicking on the cultural information database link provides you with a couple links, including a link to the Art & Architecture Thesaurus. The Art & Architecture Thesaurus comes equipped with lots of instructions and easy-to-use search boxes, so I won't repeat those efforts here. Instead, review the database if you're interested. When you're ready, let's move on to the last link on the Publications Searches page—government publications.

GOVERNMENT PUBLICATION SEARCH
http://lib-www.ucr.edu/govpub

The final publications search displayed on the Publications Searches Essentials page is the Government Publication Search. We talked a little about IRS, tax, and government documents in the *Financial Information* section of this chapter, but this link provides broader access to government documents. The Government Publication Search provides access to documents beyond taxes and business information, and enters the realm of research grants, laws, water and land rights, military statistics, government agency data, and much more (this site is huge).

You use the Government Publications search engine in the same manner you use the other magazine search engines, by typing a keyword in the text box and clicking on the Search button. When you've finished being a legal beagle, return to the Essentials Directory page—after all this serious stuff, it's time for some entertainment.

Movies

With the rapid development of ActiveX technology, video streaming, and realtime audio on the Internet, links to movie pages are becoming more and more exciting. Many movie pages now sport video clips, animation, and sound bites. In addition to being fun, the Movie Essentials link takes you to sites where you can read movie reviews, view local show times, and even purchase tickets via the Internet. Microsoft provides some useful sites, and I've added more movie site URLs at the end of this chapter. After reviewing Chapter 10 on Searching the Internet, you'll be able to find a plethora of sites on your own.

The Movies Essentials link takes you to the Movies at MSN page, as shown in Figure 8.21. The Movies at MSN page provides two major movie links: Cinamania Online and Movie Link.

Are you ready to go? Click on the Movie link on the Essentials Directory page—it's show time!

CINEMANIA ONLINE

http://www.msn.com/cinemania

Cinemania Online is a weekly Internet zine (short for magazine) for film industry fanatics, as well as your average movie-goer (like me). You can access the zine by clicking on the Cinemania Online link. Cinemania Online dubs itself the "Internet guide to the film industry," bringing you weekly feature articles, movie reviews, film star biographies, video release information, and trivia contests. This is a must-see-site for movie buffs.

After getting the latest scoop on the film industry, let's see how we can find our way to the local theater.

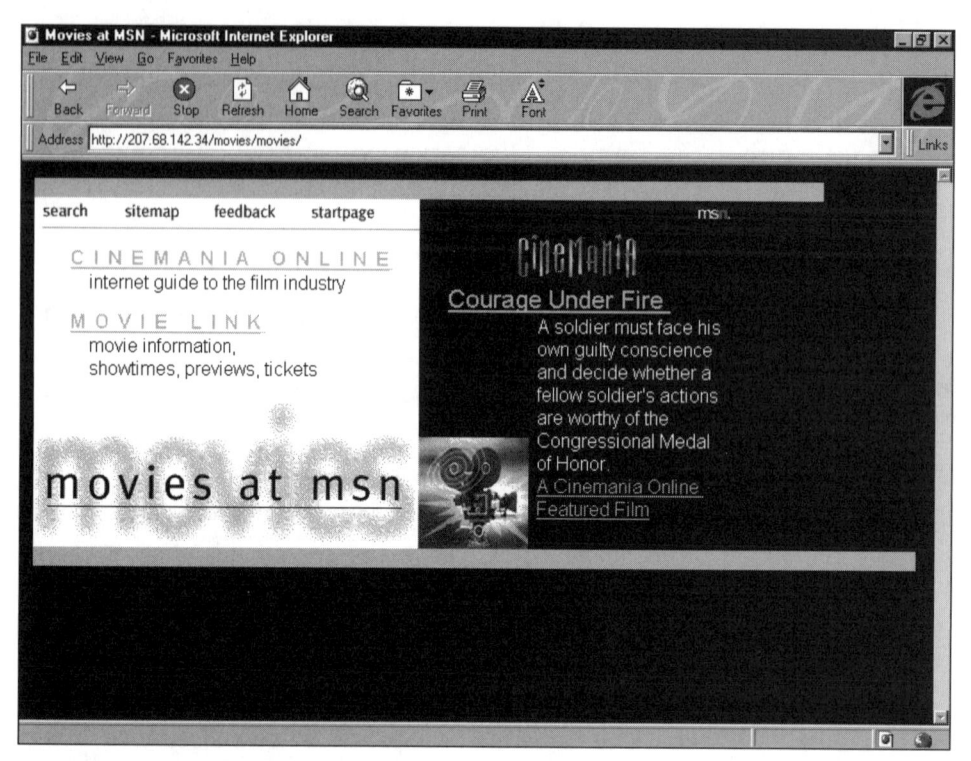

Figure 8.21 The links on the Movies at MSN page provide up-to-the-minute movie news and information.

MOVIE LINK

http://www.movielink.com

The second link on the Movies Essentials page leads to the Movie Link site, as shown in Figure 8.22. The Movie Link site provides what I think is a pretty cool feature—you can find out when and where a movie is playing in your neighborhood and, in some cases, you can purchase your ticket via the Internet.

To access the Movie Link site, click on the Movie Link hypertext link. Your screen should display a page with a featured movie graphic above three search option buttons (additionally, the featured movie graphic is a link to more movie information). The first time you click on a Search Option button, you will be asked to enter your ZIP code. Entering your ZIP code enables the site to pinpoint your area's movie information. Go ahead—enter your ZIP code. Then press the Enter button. The next time you access the Movie Link site, you'll proceed directly to the Movie Link database.

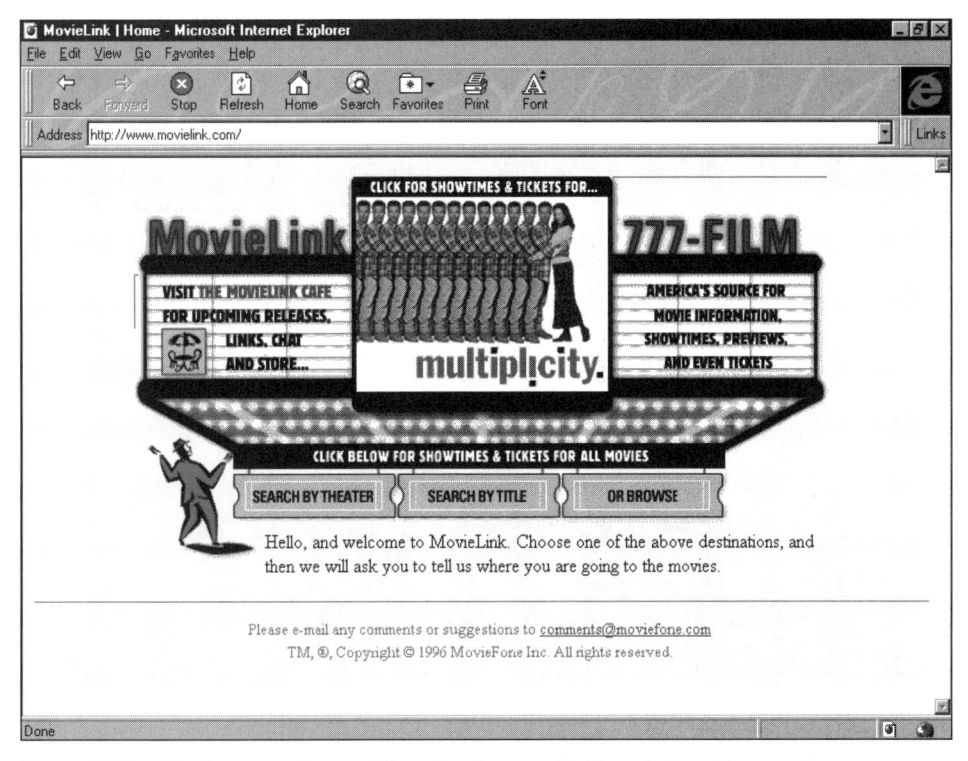

Figure 8.22   Don't waste time calling the theater, find local show times online.

You can use the Movie Link site to view the movies playing at a particular theater, search for a movie by title, and browse for movies by topic. As with the other Essentials site, this site is fairly self-explanatory. Feel free to explore the site and make your weekend movie arrangements. When you've finished browsing the theater offerings in your neighborhood, return to the Essentials page. Our next stop, and last stop, could bring music to your ears.

Music

As I mentioned in the introduction to the Movie link section, Internet advancements (such as ActiveX technology) have enabled Music Web sites to become more creative than ever. Music pages on the Internet abound. The Essentials page makes accessing some of the better Music sites easy. Click on the Music category link on the Essentials page. The Music at MSN page should display, as shown in Figure 8.23.

The Music at MSN page provides links to the Music Central, Pollstar, and Culturefinder sites. Let's take a brief look at each site.

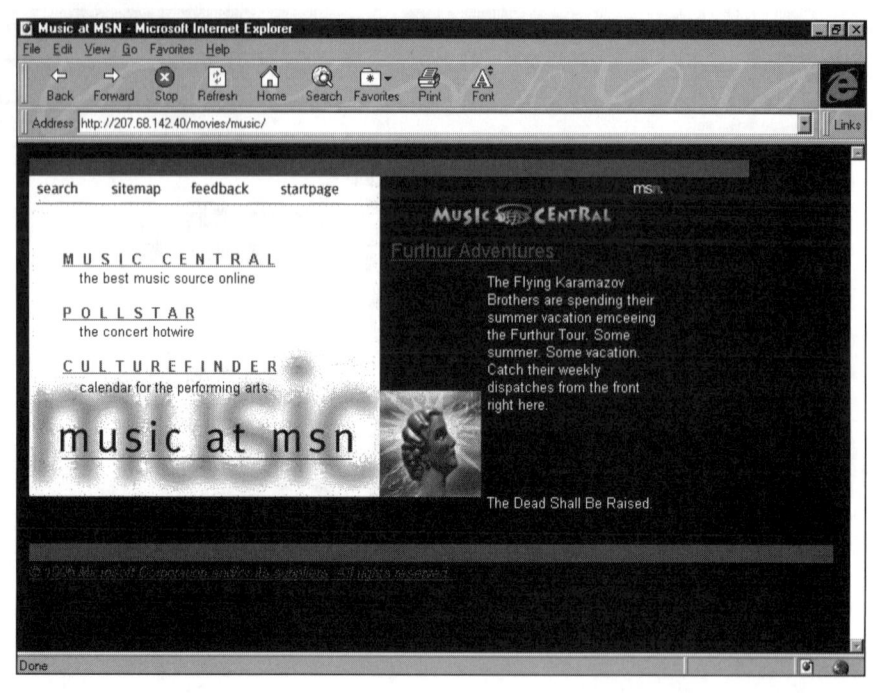

Figure 8.23 Let the Music at MSN page keep you abreast of cutting-edge music industry news and events.

Music Central

http://www.musiccentral.msn.com/default.htm

If you make it past this link, you're doing rather well. Music Central is the most comprehensive music site I've seen on the Net yet (and I have to admit that I've looked at quite a few music sites). Music Central is zine, search engine, newsstand, billboard, trivia game, and calendar all wrapped up into one. If you want to see a quick run down of the features found at Music Central, click on the Music Central link. Then click on the Table of Contents button. From there, the clicking choices are up to you.

Pollstar

http://www.pollstar.com

Anxious to find out where your favorite band is playing or what band is playing at your favorite club? If so, Pollstar's the place for you. The Pollstar home page, also referred to as "The Concert Hotwire," can be accessed by clicking on the Pollstar link on the Music at MSN page. Figure 8.24 displays the Pollstar home page.

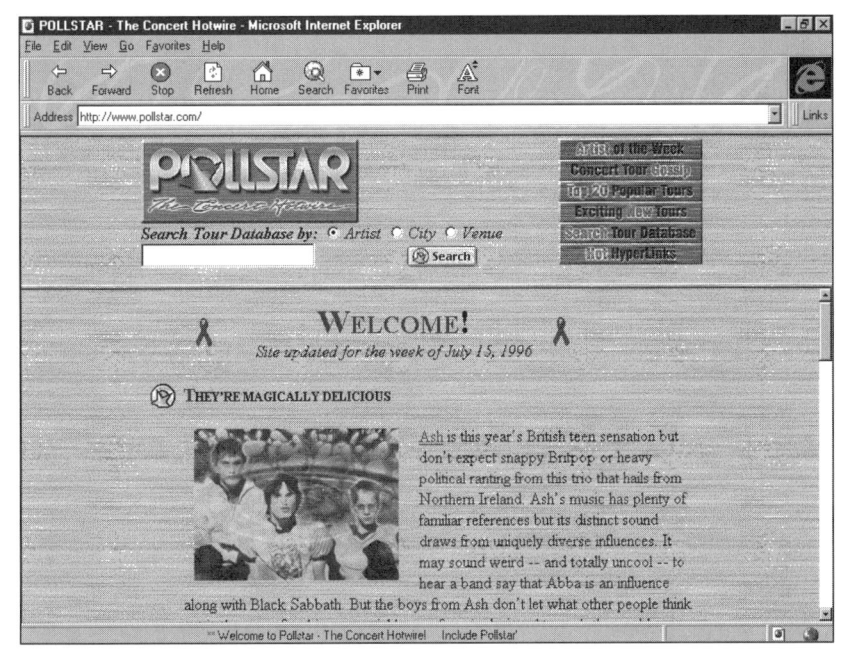

Figure 8.24 Find out what's going on in music circles that interest you using the Pollstar search engine.

The Pollstar site offers you the opportunity to search the touring database using Artist, City, or Venue keywords. Select a category, type a keyword, click on the search button, and you're off. One word of warning—Pollstar's Artist resources seem rather limited. I conducted a few searches, and Pollstar couldn't come up with any results. I had more luck searching in the Venue category. In addition to the touring database, Pollstar offers buttons to Artist profiles, concert tour gossip, top 20 pop tours, new tours, and other music links.

CULTUREFINDER

http://www.culturefinder.com

Ok, classical music lovers—just when you thought Microsoft forgot all about you, you're presented with the CultureFinder Web site. CultureFinder is the site for classical music, opera, dance, and theater lovers. You can access the CultureFinder home page, shown in Figure 8.25, by clicking on the CultureFinder link on the Music Essentials page.

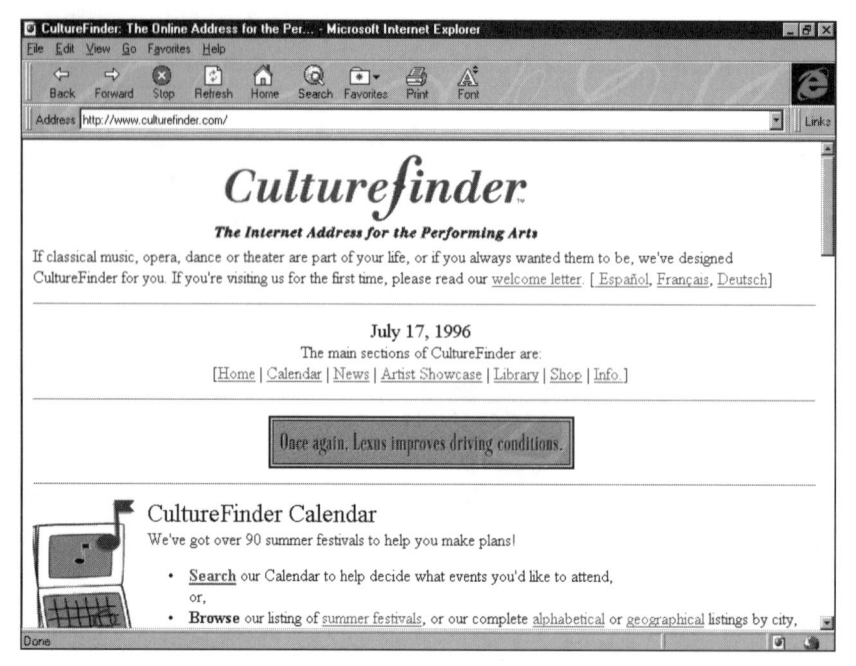

Figure 8.25 CultureFinder presents a comprehensive site for classical music, opera, dance, and theater enthusiasts.

The CultureFinder site provides schedules, interviews, cultural products, educational information, and performing arts news. I recommend that you read the Welcome letter when you first visit this site. The letter gives a clear, informative mission statement of the CultureFinder Web site.

Well—we've made it. Not only have we finished scaling the Net for musical information, but we've completed our tour of Microsoft's Essentials Directory. Following the short Chapter in Review are links (as promised) to more great sites on the Internet. I hope you don't have any big plans for the evening…

Chapter in Review

We've reached the end of our discussion about Microsoft's Essentials Directory links. I've enjoyed our tour, and I hope you have, too. Hopefully, this chapter has made you feel comfortable knowing what kinds of information you can access using the Services button on the MSIE Links toolbar. I've listed a few more sites related to the Essentials Directory. In addition, as I've mentioned a few times throughout this chapter, we'll discuss using Internet search engines in Chapter 10, so you can find sites that interest you on your own. Plus, in Chapter 11, we'll discuss how you can save and organize your favorite sites for quick and easy access. For now, enjoy some of the following Web sites. I've separated the URLs into categories similar to those covered in this chapter. Many of the following sites are lists of links—starting blocks for your own Internet explorations.

Home Reference

Home Maintenance

http://www.netzone.com/~stancorp
This home maintenance site is a fancier version (including ActiveX and background music features) of the site accessed using Microsoft's Essentials Directory.

http://www.teleport.com/~plans
This site focuses more on home improvements than on home maintenance.

Environmental Directory

http://www.yahoo.com/Environment_and_Nature
Here lies Yahoo's list of environmental links.

http://envirolink.org
EnviroLink is dedicated to providing the most comprehensive, up-to-date environmental resources available.

http://www.enn.com
Home page of the Evironmental News Network—a site filled with environmental news items, easily accessible by using the search feature.

Garden Reference

http://www.prairienet.org/garden-gate
The Garden Gate site is just that—a gateway to lots and lots and lots of gardening sites and information. This is a must visit site for gardeners.

http://www.gardenweb.com/spdrsweb
Links, links, and more links are listed here to garden resources on the Net.

HEALTH INFORMATION

http://www.bvrhc.org/findlay/bvhpha.htm
This site provides free patient information on any FDA approved prescription or over-the-counter medication.

http://www.2ask.com/is_a/fast_and/easy/way_to/surf_the/internet/direct.htm/Health
This site provides lots of medical sites within easy searching distance.

COLLEGES

http://www.jayi.com
Join Fishnet, a comprehensive guide for college students—it's free. The Fishnet site includes The College Guide, an online resource telling you how to get money and information from every college in the database.

http://www-net.com/univ
Let University Links help you find a school and keep you abreast of current college facts.

http://www.collegexpress.com
This is *the* Internet guide to private colleges and universities.

Financial Information

STOCK MARKET

http://www.secapl.com/cgi-bin/qs
This site is very similar to the site offered on the Microsoft Financial Information page. Added features on this site include a ticker symbol search feature, accessibility to online trading companies, and a realtime quote service for a fee.

http://www.quote.com
This service provides financial market data to Internet users, including current quotes on stocks, options, commodity futures, mutual funds, and bonds.

http://www.wallstreetweb.com
This site is called the Wall Street Interactive Page, and it offers realtime

information and stock-market tracking. This page will cost you a fee after the first free month.

http://networth.galt.com
NETworth: The Internet Investor Network is a 24-hour mutual fund marketplace, featuring in-depth information on more than 5,000 funds, absolutely *free* of charge. This site also provides free educational material to help individuals manage their money more effectively.

IRS AND TAX

http://www.ezone.com/taxman
Not only does this site provide you with new and out-of-date tax forms, but it offers the entire United States Tax Code online, complete with searching capabilities.

http://www.uni.edu/schmidt
Yahoo describes this sight as the directory of Internet tax and accounting resources for educators, students, and professionals. I call it a list of tax and accounting sites that will keep you so busy, you won't have time to file your taxes.

misc.taxes
misc.taxes.moderated
Here are two Usenet newsgroup sites you may want to check out if you want to talk to other netizens about tax issues. You can read more about newsgroups in Chapter 14.

BUSINESS INFORMATION

http://www.bbb.org
Business reliability reports, scam alerts, charity reports, and consumer buying guides are all a part of the Better Business Bureau site. You can even submit online reliability reports (formerly known as complaints) to the Bureau using the BBB's own Web page form.

MAIL SERVICES

http://www.usps.gov
Use this site to find out what's new at the United States Postal Service.

Phone & Address Look-Up

Phone Numbers & Addresses

http://www.switchboard.com
The Switchboard is a free nationwide residential and business directory from Coordinate.com.

http://www.princeton.edu
Enter the URL, click on the travel link, and scroll down the page to find a link to airline 800 numbers.

http://s11.bigyellow.com
Home of the Big Yellow yellow pages, which allows you to search as many state's yellow pages as you select.

http://ciccatii.attdocs.com
Click on this site's On-line Area Code Handbook link to access AT&T's easy-to-use area code locator.

Find Email Addresses and Personal Web Pages

http://www.worldemail.com/start2.shtml
This is a world-wide email directory to over 12 million email addresses and over 140 million business and phone addresses.

Travel Tips

General Travel Information

http://haas.berkeley.edu/~seidel/airline.html
Look here for links to every airline you've ever heard of and more! This site also includes airline and flight information links.

http://www.epicurious.com
The Conde Nast traveler link has joined forces with Epicurious to create a new Web site with many travel-related links and services.

http://www.hostels.com/hostels
This Internet guide to hostels hosts a database of over 3,000 hostels around the globe.

View Maps of Locations in the United States

http://map.bigbook.com/cgi-bin/navigator_map
You type in the address—this site displays a map. Here's a quick and easy map site that displays easy-to-read maps.

http://www.mapquest.com
This site provides access to maps anywhere in the continental U.S., city-to-city driving instructions, and customizable maps to mark your own points of interest. Definitely the site to visit before you hit the road.

http://www.bigbook.com
Travel the world or travel the U.S. using this comprehensive, easy-to-use map site.

http://www.avis.com/maps
Yet another site to visit for street maps and vicinity maps for U.S. cities.

Local, State, or Zone Weather Forecast

http://www.cnn.com/WEATHER
The CNN Weather page has as much class as its news channel and Web services page.

http://www.weather.com
This site is maintained by another cable channel—The Weather Channel. If you only look at one weather site, this should be the one.

Writer's Reference

Dictionaries

http://nimrod.mit.edu/depts/dewey/common/reference/oed.html
Home of the *Oxford English Dictionary*, as presented by MIT.

http://wombat.doc.ic.ac.uk
FOLDOC is the Free Online Dictionary of Computing that includes all those new words and acronyms not included in traditional dictionaries.

http://www.travlang.com/GermanEnglish
Schnitzel? Bier? Sauerkraut? I bet you know what these words are, but for a

bigger view of the German language, visit this site for a great English-German online dictionary.

http://humanities.uchicago.edu/forms_unrest/FR-ENG.html
I only know one French phrase, and I can't say it publicly! If you want to brush up on your French, check out this English-French online dictionary.

http://www.willamette.edu/~tjones/forms/italian.html
Traveling to Italy soon? Stop by this site for an English-Italian online dictionary before you leave.

Encyclopedias

http://www.cs.uh.edu/~clifton/encyclopedia.html
A pretty good online resource, considering there are no comprehensive encyclopedias currently online.

http://www.adventure.com/library/encyclopedia
This encyclopedia site is fun and interesting, but you never know what you're going to get when you search for a topic.

http://www.pantheon.org/myth
Here rests an encyclopedia on mythology, folklore, mysticism, and more.

http://www.eb.com
You can use this site to subscribe for seven free days to the *Encyclopedia Britannica*.

Publications Searches

http://www.worldwidenews.net/MAGAZINE/SUBJECT.HTM
This site provides links to more online magazines than you could possibly need (or read)!

http://www.trvltips.com
Check out this site—the home page of *TravelTips Magazine*—for all your travel needs.

http://www.latimes.com/HOME
http://www.usnews.com/usnews/main.htm
http://www.usatoday.com

Who needs a home-delivered newspaper when you can stop by the home pages of the *LA Times*, *US News and World Report*, and *USA Today* (among a growing list of others)?

http://www.newtimes.com
Speaking of newspapers—if there's a *New Times* in your neighborhood, forget picking it up at the local market, view the *New Times* news online.

Movies

http://us.imdb.com/search.html
Here's a link to the Internet Movie Database—a searchable database that includes 74,647 movie listings and 4,398 TV series titles. If you're a movie buff, be prepared to spend some serious surfing time here, as this site will create tangent after tangent for you.

http://www.cyber-cinema.com
Here lies the movie poster store and movie trivia page, with hundreds of links to movie-related Web pages.

http://www.worldwidenews.net/MEDIAAND/MOVIESSUBJECT.HTM
Still craving more movie news? This movie link page from World Wide News offers links to many, many more movie Web sites.

Music

http://www.worldwidenews.net/HUMANITI/MUSIC/SUBJECT.HTM
The World Wide News site provides links to more music sites than you'll know what to do with—try it and see!

http://www.bostonphoenix.com/alt1/standard/music/links.html
Hot links to music sites are listed here by Boston's Phoenix Media Corporation.

http://atn.addict.com/ATN
If you like alternative music, visit this site and scope out *Addicted to Noise* Magazine.

http://www.iuma.com
Follow this URL to experience the sights and sounds of IUMA—the Internet Underground Music Archive.

http://www.cdconnection.com
Visit the CD Connection to search and shop for CDs and CD information; you can even place an order or save items in your shopping basket when your shopping proves successful.

Today's Links to Microsoft's Best of the Web Picks

Save yourself some time. MSIE's Today's Links button shows you some of the cool links Microsoft has found.

*E*xploring the Internet is all about links. Clicking on links. Saving links. Following links. Sending links. You're surfing on sand if you don't use links, and if, perchance, you somehow make it to the water without using a link, you won't catch more than a single wave. The Today's Links button is all about staying in the water, catching wave after wave of Net information, and, best of all, doing it without the risk of coral reefs or sharks.

MSIE's Today's Links Button

As you saw in the Essentials Directory chapter, MSIE attempts to make finding and following links extremely convenient. Clicking on the Today's Links button in the MSIE Links toolbar provides yet another opportunity to follow links to noteworthy sites. The Today's Links button, the default setting for the left-most button on the Links toolbar (Quick Link #1), takes you to the MSN Surf Stories, Best of the Web page. (I'll refer to this page as the Surf Stories page throughout the rest of this chapter.)

The Surf Stories page is the home of MSN's daily and weekly Internet picks. If you've customized your MSN start page to display a site-of-the-day and sites-of-the-week, you should see similar sites on the Surf Stories site. In fact, the Today's Pick on the Surf Stories page is exactly the same as Today's Favorite Web Pick on the MSN start page. Daily and weekly sites are always in a state of flux, so we aren't going to concentrate too much on specific sites in this chapter. Instead, we are going to review the types of sites accessed using the Today's Links button, as well as look at the basic framework of the Surf Stories site. Go ahead and click on the Today's Links in the MSIE links toolbar or click on the Links hypertext link on your MSN start page. The Surf Stories page should display as shown in Figure 9.1.

The Surf Stories Page

The Surf Stories page consists of three main sections. First is the link to the pick of the day (*USENET Cookbook* in Figure 9.1), followed by a brief

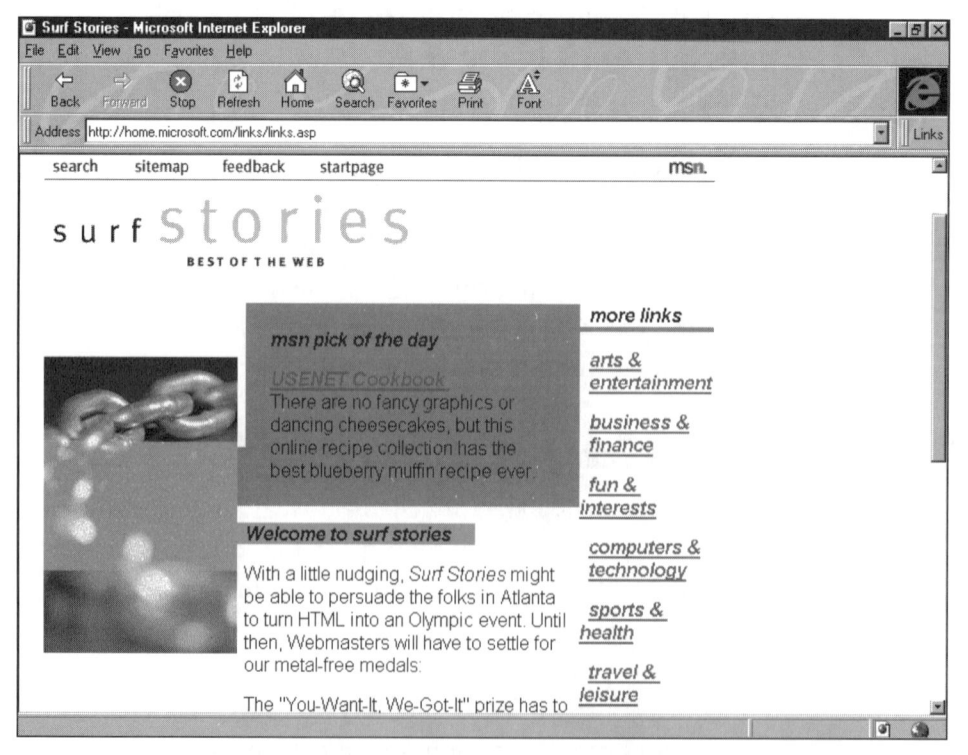

Figure 9.1 Viewing the MSN Surf Stories, Best of the Web page.

summary of the site. The summary information gives you an idea of what you'll be getting into when you click on the link. To view the current pick of the day, simply click on the link and follow your instincts. To return to the Surf Stories page after viewing the pick of the day (and possibly an assortment of tangential links), you can either click on your back arrow key until you return to the Surf Stories page, click on the Today's Links button in the MSIE Links toolbar, or execute the menu command Go|Today's Links.

The second portion of the Surf Stories page lies below the pick of the day. This portion appears as a short essay with related links interspersed throughout. For example, you can't really tell from Figure 9.1, but the short essay talks about the Olympics and includes three links: Atlanta Games, Women's Olympics, and Olympics Believe it or Not. You can read through the short essay and click on any links that interest you. This site updates on a weekly basis.

The third section of the Surf Stories page is the More Links section. The More Links section displays links to six topical pages, as well as links to previous picks and "stale surf." The More Links list makes up the bulk of the Surf Stories page, and its the place where you'll find Microsoft's weekly Web picks and Keeper sites (more about those in a minute).

Let's take a closer look at the Pick of the Day and the More Links sections on the Surf Stories page.

The Pick of the Day

I'm sure you've seen those once-per-day desk calendars proffering daily doses of witty quotes, sarcastic cartoons, catchy proverbs, short prayers, and even rude insults. MSN believes (and proves) that the daily message can go much, much further than the daily calendar rip-and-smirk routine, by offering a pick-of-the-day section on the Surf Stories page. Many other sites on the Web also like to direct you toward a noteworthy site-of-the-day (the folks at Cool Site of the Day lay claim to starting this tradition).

If you haven't been playing on the Web long, your first inclination might be to wonder how MSN, or any Web site for that matter, could come up with a cool pick *every day*. On the other hand, if you're a regular Internet junkie, you're more likely to wonder how any site could narrow the options down to a *single* cool site each day. Either way, don't worry, there are plenty of sites out there and the more help you have in finding the best sites, the better. You'll never find all the Web's cool sites on your own, so a little help here and there is a very good thing. Fortunately, the sheer enormity of the Internet, combined with the exponential growth of the number of Web sites, creates an overwhelming urge among netizens to point out cool sites to Internet compatriots—MSN is no exception.

More Links

In addition to choosing a site of the day, MSN pulls together a group of pages called *More Links* pages. More Links pages, arranged by topic, contain pick-of-the-week links and standby sites, dubbed *Keepers*. Keepers are cool links to informative sites that consistently appear on the More Links pages (unlike the daily and weekly picks that pile up in the previous picks files). More Links pages can be accessed by clicking on the category links displayed below the More Links heading on the Surf Stories page. There are six categories of weekly picks: Arts & Entertainment, Business & Finance, Fun & Interests, Computers & Technology, Sports & Health, and Travel & Leisure. Furthermore, two links display below the six weekly category page links: the Previous Picks and Stale Surf links. I'll introduce you to each linked page in just a moment; first I want to explain the basic setup of the More Links pages.

Basic Viewing Habits

Microsoft's More Links pages provide a number of links, including weekly picks, summaries for each pick, previous picks, and Keepers. Figure 9.2 displays the Arts & Entertainment More Links page.

On the average, MSN provides three weekly picks per More Links category page. You can visit any one of the featured sites by clicking on the embedded text link. Notice the disclaimer on the bottom of each More Links page. The disclaimer states that the links do not point to sites maintained by

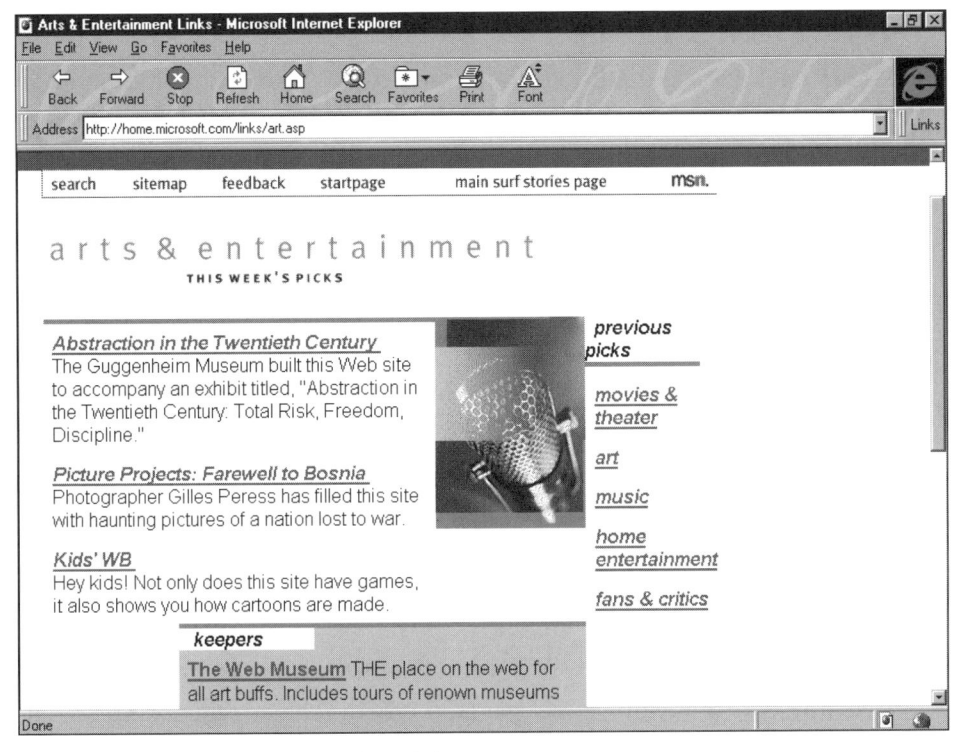

Figure 9.2 Viewing an MSN weekly picks page.

Microsoft servers; the links point to sites all over the world, so once you start clicking, you are on your own.

Each More Links page contains up to four components: a menu bar, This Week's Picks, Previous Picks, and Keepers. Here's a quick synopsis of each section.

MENU BAR

The menu bar appearing at the top of the More Links pages supplies you with some exploratory tools. First, the menu provides you a Search option so you can look for topics on the Internet. We'll talk more about searching for information on the Internet in Chapter 10 when we talk about using the MSIE Search feature. The remaining menu bar tools consist of MSN-friendly links, which are designed to help you tool around the MSN site. The menu bar includes links to the MSN Sitemap (we'll talk about the MSN Sitemap at the end of this chapter), a Feedback page, the Start page, the main Surf Stories page, and the MSN home page.

This Week's Picks

MSN's weekly picks are listed under the header *This Week's Picks* on each More Links category page. You can click on the embedded text links to take you directly to the featured site. If you've customized your MSN Start page to display a weekly pick, one of the sites on the More Links page may look familiar—the picks on your Start Page are excerpted from the picks on the More Links pages.

Previous Picks

The Previous Picks section maintains an archive of links featured as weekly picks. Previous Picks are organized by subject category. For example, Figure 9.2 shows that past weekly Arts & Entertainment picks are arranged in five subject categories: Movies & Theater, Art, Music, Home Entertainment, and Fans & Critics.

Keepers

Some sites recommended by MSN receive the distinction of appearing as fixed links on the More Links pages. These links are called *Keepers*. Of course, the information appearing in Keeper sites continually updates, even though the link remains the same.

Now that you have a grasp on the basic layout of the weekly picks pages, let's take a look at each More Links category page in order of appearance on the Surf Stories page. I'll provide the subject categories for each More Links page, describe the main thrust of the page in a quick sentence or two, and then list the Keeper URLs, followed by short summary statements of each Keeper site. This summary review of the More Links pages should give you a feel for what you can find on the Surf Stories site.

Arts & Entertainment

Subject categories: Movie & Theater, Art, Music, Home Entertainment, and Fans & Critics.

One click on an Arts & Entertainment link can take you to the Cannes music festival, while another click carries you off to a silly romp on the Saturday Night Live page. Visit the Guggenheim museum, or learn how to create cartoons. You can do all this and more by following the Arts & Entertainment links.

Keeper sites in the Arts and Entertainment category include:

http://sunsite.unc.edu/louvre/
The Web Museum is the place for art lovers to find online tours of world renowned art museums and updates on current exhibits.

http://www.unitedmedia.com
Check out UnitedMedia, home of the Dilbert and Peanuts pages. This link is also available when you customize your MSN start page cartoon link.

http://www.ticketmaster.com
TicketMaster Online, one of the nation's most popular ticketing agencies, now emerges as a major entertainment information source online. Check this site for performance information, ticketing services, cutting edge entertainment industry news, and more.

http://www.mrshowbiz.com
Stop by the Mr. Showbiz site for entertainment facts, figures, news, reviews, interviews, ratings, box office figures, and star bios, amidst loads of other industry-related features and links.

Business & Finance

Subject categories: Small Business, Markets, Personal Finance, Business News, Government Resources, and Doing Business on the Internet.

Cyber Atlas, Marketing on the Internet, stock market activity, career searches, and investment advice are commonplace topics on the Business & Finance More Links page. More comprehensive than any morning paper, the Business & Finance page links you to sites that could keep you busy well into the afternoon.

Keeper sites in the Business and Finance category include:

http://www.irs.ustreas.gov/prod/
The Internal Revenue Service wants to make sure you know where to find them. This is the same site accessed by the Essentials Services Directory link.

http://www.catalog.com/intersof/welcomec.html
FinanceHub's Web site provides links to banks, the stock market, venture capital firms, and commerce news. You can even enlist the folks at FinanceHub to create and maintain a home page for you.

http://www.sbaonline.sba.gov
This is the official page of the U.S. Small Business Administration.

http://www.msn.com/investor/content.asp
Microsoft's MSN Investor provides a site packed with investment information, including free stock quotes, a portfolio manager, market summaries, top 10 lists, and a comprehensive resource page with links to top investment Web sites.

Fun & Interests

Subject categories: Hobbies & Reading, Just for Fun, Food & Drink, Home & Holidays, and Kids.

From the Hungry Mind Review for books to the Internet Epicurean, this More Links page has links to send any fun-lover into a feeding frenzy. You can also look to this page to find sites such as the Kooks museum and the Lego Page, among other sites waiting for your attention (and your time).

Keeper sites in the Fun and Interests category include:

http://www.thespot.com
The Spot Web site carries on in the tradition of a television soap opera, offering a daily episodic Web drama dating back to June 1995.

http://www.cnet.com/Content/Reviews/Website/
C|Net provides links, links, and more links to Best of the Web sites. This site is extremely popular; you'll often see links to C|Net while surfing the Web.

Computers & Technology

Subject categories: Internet Tools, Development Tools, Games, News & Publications, Software, Products & Companies, Interest Groups, and Science.

Uploads, downloads, development tools, computer news—this site has all the nerdy computer facts that we want and need. Throw in some game sites and interest groups and most computer geeks (whom, I might add, are very much in vogue right now) won't leave this site for days.

Keeper sites in the Computers and Technology category include:

http://www.zdnet.com/home/filters/main.html
We mentioned ZDNet in the previous chapter. Not only is this site chock-full of computer-related links, but you can also browse through some of your favorite computer publications.

http://www.nasa.gov/NASA_homepage.html
NASA Information Services' Web site provides a way for you to contact the Office of Space Flight, view the NASA gallery, or follow recommended links to aeronautics research Web pages. You can also view the home pages of NASA field centers located around the country.

http://www.cnet.com
C|Net's online computer magazine includes links to cutting edge articles and feature stories.

Sports & Health

Subject categories: Spectator Sports, Outdoor Sports, Sports Servers, Health, Sports News, and Events.

The Sports and Health weekly pick page investigates the tranquillity of golfing, envisions the breathtaking beauty of rock climbing, and visits the roar of car racing. Add outdoor news, sports scores, and a link to the online version of *Sports Illustrated* and you have the making of a true sport's computer-chair potato (the couch is too far from the computer to be useful here).

For everything Sports, stop off at the following Keeper site:

http://www.sportsline.com
As the Sports & Health links page summary says, Sportsline USA provides "all the sports news you can use; all in one place."

Travel & Leisure

Subject categories: Destinations, Travel Servers & Searches, and News & Magazines.

Research your destination, print out maps, rent a car, and reserve your plane tickets without budging from your computer. The Travel and Leisure weekly picks can help you research ski trips, national park trips, and golf resort vacations. The site will even help keep you abreast of travel discounts available on the Web.

Got the itch to visit the great outdoors? Check out the following Keeper site before you make a move:

http://www.llbean.com/parksearch/

Looking for a park in particular? Or how about planning a camping trip? The Park Search link helps you find parks by name, attraction, and location.

Previous Picks

Below the six More Links category pages appears a link to the previous picks of the day. To access the previous picks list, click on the Previous Picks link—you should see a list of past links, similar to Figure 9.3.

You will probably want to spend some time catching up on missed sites of the day. A sampling of past links includes such sites as *The Billennium* (as of this writing, we have only 1.8 million minutes until the year 2000!), *Car Talk* (with links to the Shameless Commerce and Car Talk 101 pages), and *InterActivism* (providing links to activist groups by category, encompassing civil rights, environmental, and international links). After you've scanned the previous picks, return to the Surf Stories page, and we'll take a look at the Stale Surf link.

Biding Your Time with the Previous Picks of the Day List

Instead of spending the next 96 hours catching up on past Picks of the Day, try taking the following approach. On days when the current site of the day does not interest you (it could happen), click on the Previous Picks link and catch up on one or two past picks that look interesting. I say choose one or

two links because, as you're probably starting to realize, one link leads to another link, which leads to more links, which leads to entirely too many links to view in one day.

Stale Surf

Long ago, well, not that long ago, Microsoft included two additional categories among the Surf Stories page's More Links group (back then, the Surf Stories page was called Links Central). The two links included on Links Central, but dropped from the Surf Stories page, were links to an online news page and shopping page. The Stale Surf News page offers links to daily news sources, as well as magazines and news services. The Stale Surf Shopping page contains links to shopping malls, specialty shops, catalogs, and shopping search tools. You can click on the Stale Surf link to view what these two link pages were all about—past weekly links intact. Figure 9.4 shows MSN's explanation as to why they did away with the two category pages.

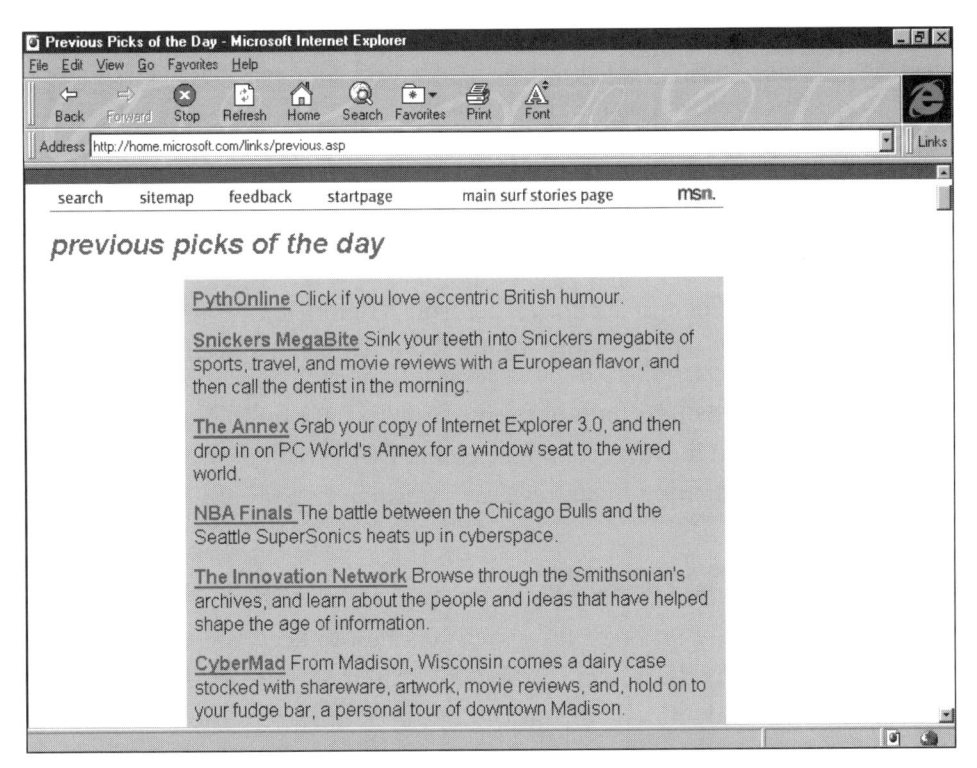

Figure 9.3 Catch up on the best sites by displaying the Previous Picks of the Day list.

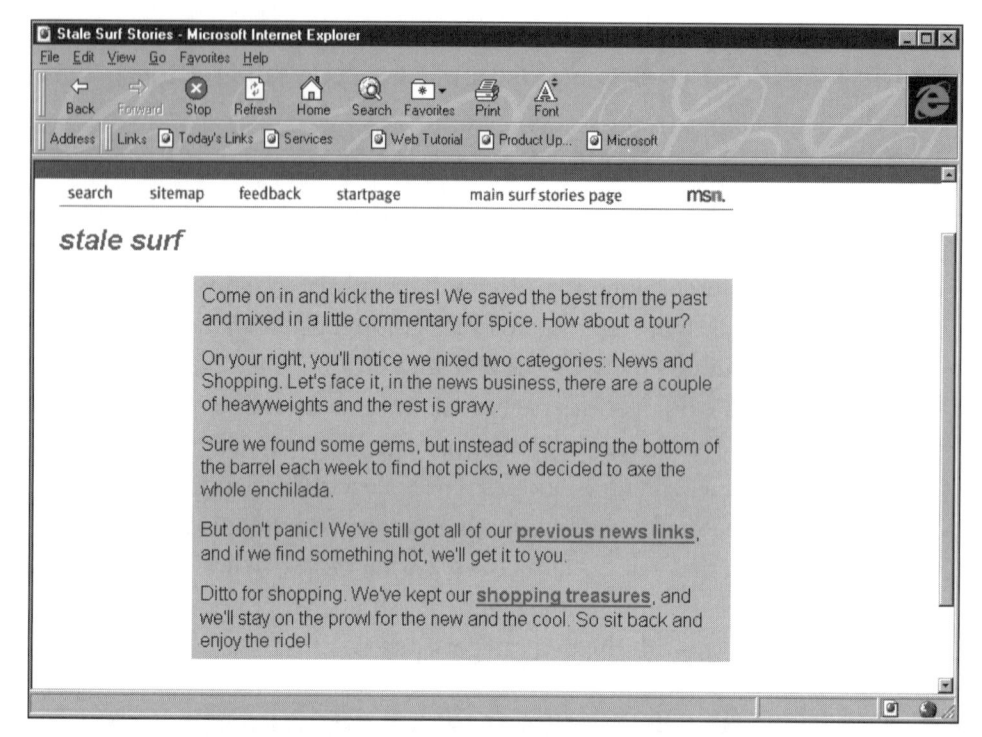

Figure 9.4 You can still use the links on the now-defunct News and Shopping category pages by clicking on the Stale Surf link.

Microsoft has promised to keep us abreast of any cool sites that might have fallen into either category, so don't feel like you're being cheated by the disappearance of the News and Shopping weekly pick sites. Furthermore, as you'll see in the next section, Microsoft has added a news service called MSNBC, which will probably meet most of your news needs.

We've completed our rounds of the Surf Stories page links. Now let's retrace our steps back to the menu bar. Remember I said we'd take a look at MSN's Sitemap? Well, here's a quick review to this handy page of links.

MSN Sitemap

As if daily, weekly, and past links aren't enough to keep you busy, the Surf Stories page provides access to the MSN Sitemap. The Surf Stories page isn't the only link-crazed culprit, though. Not only does the Sitemap link appear in the Surf Stories page menu bar, but we saw the link in the previous chapter when we covered the Essentials Directory. We also saw the Sitemap link as we reviewed the MSN Start page options in Chapter 5. As far as this chapter, the Sitemap link has been following us around ever since we clicked on the Today's Links button in the MSIE Links toolbar. I guess it's about time we paid attention to the Sitemap link before it starts acting out from neglect (can a link do that?). If you've gone off to some totally unrelated site, return to a Surf Stories site. Any Surf Stories page will do, as long as the Sitemap link displays in the menu bar (you can also access the Sitemap by clicking on the Contents link on your MSN Start Page).

Once you arrive at the Surf Stories site, click on the Sitemap link in the menu bar. Voila! Yet another list of links (that's why we're discussing the Sitemap link in this chapter). Look closely, some of the links should look suspiciously familiar. I'll display Figure 9.5, the Sitemap page, while you study the links.

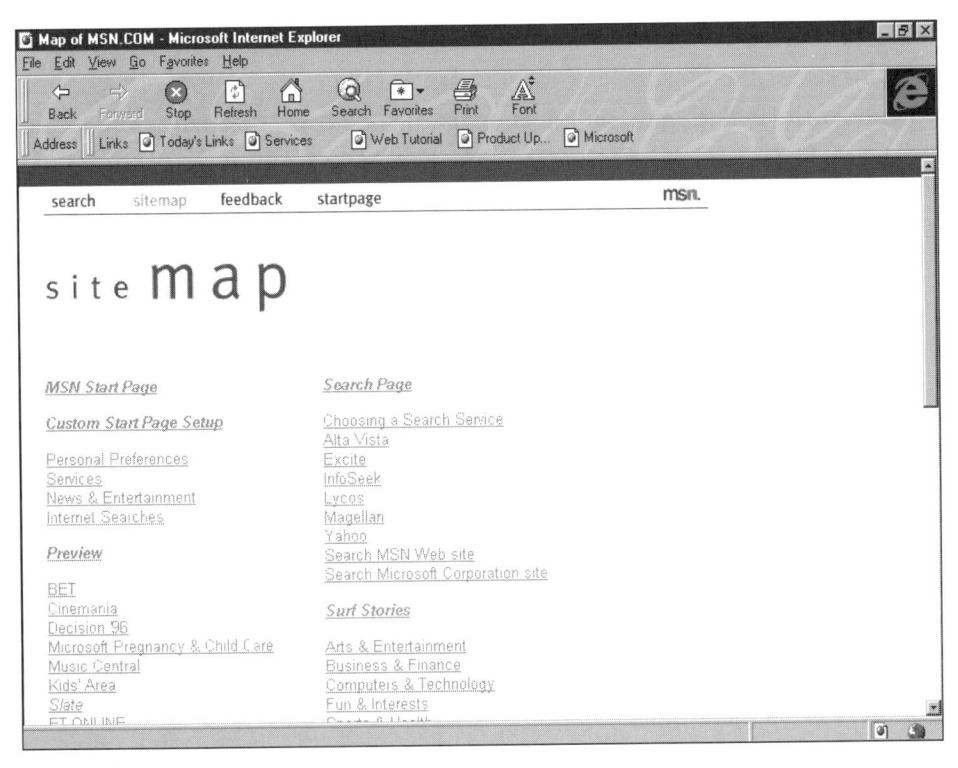

Figure 9.5 The MSN Sitemap page.

The links on the MSN Sitemap take you to many of the links accessed using the MSIE Links toolbar buttons or your MSN Start Page. Let's start from the top of the left column, work our way down, return to the top of the right column, then work our way down again.

MSN Start Page

Clicking on the first link on the Sitemap takes you to the MSN Start Page (whether you've customized it or not). Even if you've designated a different page as your start page, this link will take you to the MSN Start Page.

Custom Start Page Setup

Remember all those menus we plowed through as we set up our MSN Start pages? This link enables you to quickly access and modify your Personal Preferences, Services, News & Entertainment, and Internet Searches setup pages.

Preview

The Preview link shows you services available to MSN members. You can also access the Preview link from your MSN Start Page. Topic links listed under the Preview link on the Sitemap include BET, Pregnancy and Child Care, Kids' Area, ET Online, and the Star Trek: Continuum. You can use each link listed under the Preview section to access a limited amount of data; to get to the really good stuff you have to become an MSN member. MSN offers a free, one-month trial membership to people who live in the U.S. To find out how you can get your trial membership, click on the Try MSN link on the Sitemap page or access MSN's trial offer page at **http://www.msn.com/trymsn/trymsn1.asp**.

MSNBC News

MSNBC News, another link accessible from your MSN Start Page, is the new MSN service on the block. MSN teamed up with NBC to offer a top-notch 24-hour, multimedia news service. Click on some of the topical links on the Sitemap or go straight to the main MSNBC link—you're sure to find informative news features and up-to-the-minute details on breaking stories.

Try MSN

Click here to find out how you can try MSN free for one month. Follow the links to find out more about the MSN online services. (The Try MSN link appears on your MSN Start Page.)

InternetCenter

This page is a good page to look to for Internet information, but I recommend that you look at the Microsoft Internet Explorer home page as your primary Internet information source. Microsoft's Internet Explorer home page can be found at **http://www.microsoft.com/ie**.

Microsoft Corporation

This area provides quick link to the **http//www.microsoft.com** home page, as well as Microsoft's free software, product information, employment, and support pages. You can also access Microsoft's home page by clicking on Quick Link #5 in the toolbar (if it retains the default setting), clicking on the Microsoft Corporation link on your MSN Start Page, or executing Help|Microsoft on the Web|Microsoft Home Page.

Frequently Asked Questions

Do you have some questions about the Microsoft Network? If so, this link's for you. Click on the Frequently Asked Questions link on the Sitemap to see if someone's already thought of an answer for your query.

Sponsors' Index

This may sound like a link to a big commercial area, and it is—but it isn't. You can click on this site to find some great offerings on the Web. For example, you can find out how to get information on over 180,000 tuition scholarships, access the Time magazine site, visit an electronic library, tour the Kennedy Space Center, or get help finding a place to rent. All of the sites here also appear on the MSN pages as advertisements (remember we looked at the advertisements displaying at the top of the Essentials pages?). Since sponsor ads come and go, the Sponsors' Index assists you when you want to return to a featured site that may not be displaying at the moment. Figure 9.6 shows the Site Seeing Guide to the MSN sponsor pages.

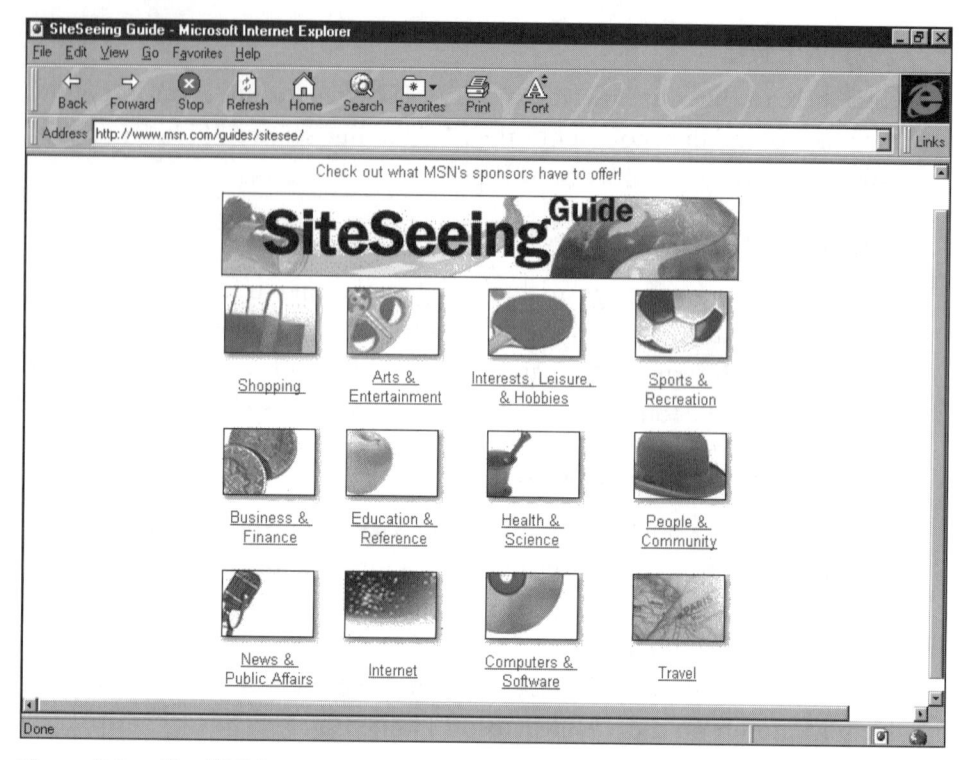

Figure 9.6 The MSN Sponsors' Index stores site information for sites advertised on Microsoft's Web pages.

DISCLAIMER

Clicking on the Sitemap Disclaimer link takes you to the same message as the disclaimer link found on the More Links pages. Basically, Microsoft informs you that many links on MSN pages take you away from the Microsoft site. Microsoft does not assume responsibility for Internet documents residing outside of the Microsoft site.

SEARCH PAGE

You can click on the Search Page link to take you to Microsoft's search page, or you can click on any link below the Search Page heading to go to a specific search engine. Clicking on the Search Page link is essentially the same as clicking on the Search button in the MSIE toolbar, clicking on the Search button on your MSN Start Page, or executing the Go|Search the Web menu command. You'll learn many of the ins and outs of searching in the next chapter.

Surf Stories

Okay, so you have a good idea what this link is all about! If you've forgotten—reread the beginning portion of this chapter. You can use the links on the Sitemap page to jump directly to a More Links page without visiting the Surf Stories main page.

Essentials

We shared a detailed discussion about the Essentials Directory in Chapter 8. The Essentials Sitemap link can take you directly to any Essentials services page (as can the Essentials button on your MSN Start Page). Microsoft pulled a fast one here, though, because the Sitemap slips in an extra Essentials topic called the MSN Investor. The MSN Investor page (also a Keeper found on the Business & Finance More Links page) provides investment facts and figures to add to your investment knowledge base. To view the MSN Investor page, click on the MSN Investor link under the Essentials Sitemap heading. The MSN Investor page should appear similar to Figure 9.7.

Figure 9.7 The MSN Investor Page provides free, up-to-date investment information.

MSN INTERNATIONAL

Want to view international versions of MSN pages? You can click on the MSN International links to view MSN information for Australia, France, Germany, and Japan. I'm sure this list will be growing as Microsoft continues to expand its international versions of MSIE.

Checking the Sitemap When You're Lost

Can't remember how to get to an MSN link? Was it part of the Essentials Directory? On the Search Page? Under the Today's Link button? Click on the Sitemap link for a quick glance and easy access to MSN's featured links.

As you can see, one of the primary purposes of the Sitemap is to provide a clear view of Microsoft's services. In addition, the Sitemap grants easy access to MSN links. If you know *what* you're looking for but not sure *where* you saw it, try clicking on the Sitemap—something is bound to ring a bell once you view the links.

Chapter in Review

In this chapter, you were introduced to more links and services found on the Internet. Some services are provided by Microsoft, other are independent sites. You can access quite a few useful sites by using the Today's links button, found in the MSIE Links toolbar. The Today's Links button takes you to the Surf Stories page, which contains a site of the day as well as six category links to top sites of the week. You can view current and past site selections at any time. Some sites, called *Keepers*, appear as ongoing links on the weekly category pages. You can gain an overall picture of Microsoft's links and offerings by clicking on the Sitemap link on the Surf Stories site pages or clicking on the Contents button on your MSN start page. Among other sites, the Sitemap provides links to the MSN start page, MSNBC, Microsoft's Sponsor Index, and MSN International pages.

Many large sites provide Sitemaps. You can use Sitemaps to view a site's features quickly. Knowing what a site offers helps you to streamline your Web surfing—saving you time and frustration.

Searching and Search Engines 10

Now that you know how to use Microsoft Internet Explorer, you need to know how to find what you're looking for. Start your search engines.

*L*earning what links are and how to use them is a very important part of navigating the Internet with Microsoft Internet Explorer. But what do you do if you want to find specific information on, say, a medical issue? Or what if you wanted to help your child do some research for a school project? MSIE has made it easy for you to find what you're looking for by providing you with a Search page that's linked to MSIE's default home page.

To get to MSIE's Search page, simply click on the word *Search* or the light bulb near the top of Explorer's home page. If you're not at Internet Explorer's Start page, click on the icon of the world with the magnifying glass on it at the top of the browser window. Either method will take you to **http://www.msn.com/access/allinone.asp**.

Understanding How Search Engines Work

When you arrive at MSIE's Internet Search page, you'll see nine different text boxes that represent eight different search engines and one Featured

Search of the Day, as shown in Figure 10.1. The Featured Search rotates between the eight engines on the page, with a different one appearing every day. A search engine is simply a program that allows you to find links to information on a particular subject. When the Internet first became popular, there were only a few search engines available to users, and finding what you were looking for could be a long and tedious process. Now that the Internet has exploded in popularity, there are dozens of search engines available. Each search engine uses different criteria to find what you're looking for; and each, of course, claims to search the most Web pages while doing it.

The search engines on the Internet Explorer Search page are some of the best on the Net. Only six of the eight engines actually search across the entire Internet, of the remaining two, one searches just Microsoft's site (which itself contains a great deal of useful information and is well worth using for technical and Microsoft-related questions), and the other searches

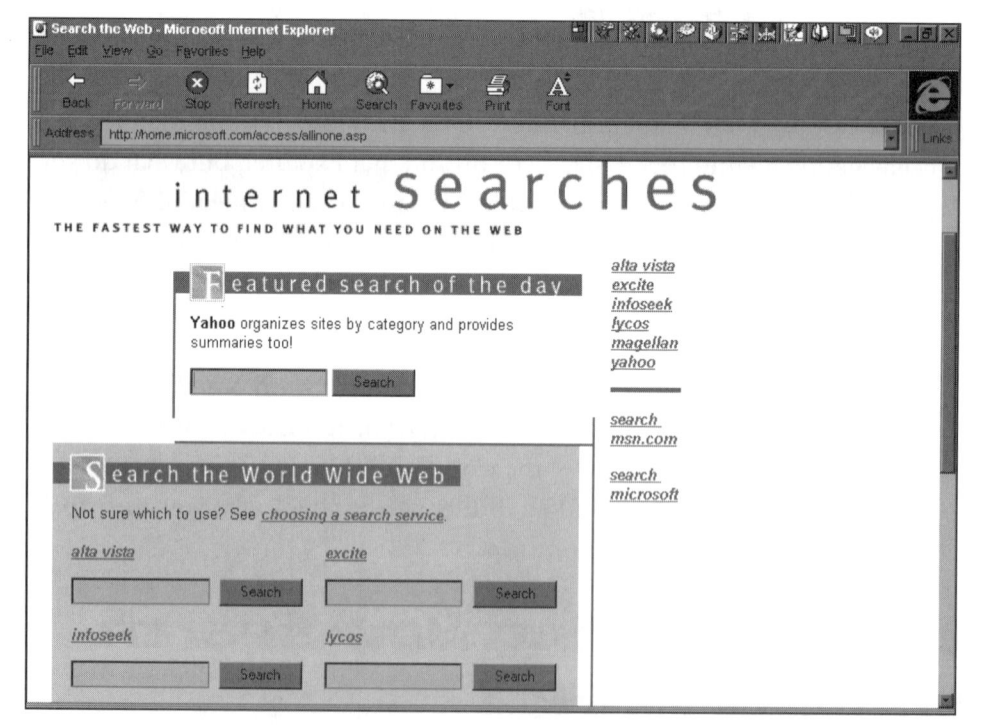

Figure 10.1 Microsoft Internet Explorer's Search page.

the Microsoft Network (which provides the start and search pages). In this chapter, I'll be concentrating on the six Internet search engines: Alta Vista, Excite, Infoseek, Lycos, Magellan, and Yahoo. I'll also take you outside of Explorer's Internet Search page and show you how to do a search on some engines that aren't included on Microsoft's short list. You'll be amazed at what you'll be able to find!

Keywords

Before we get into actual searches using the various engines, I thought it would be appropriate to give you some background on keywords, which are the fuel that run the engines. Keywords are nothing more than the words you enter into a search engine's text box to get your search rolling.

The trick to using keywords correctly is coming up with the right combination of words to find what you're looking for. When you look at the instructions for many search engines, you'll often see some mention of the word *boolean*. Don't let this scare you. Boolean simply means that you can use the words *and* and *or* in your keyword search.

Let's say you were looking for information on Hawaiian volcanoes for your daughter's science project. You would enter *Hawaii and volcanoes* into the text box. (Many times you don't even need to use the *and*, it's understood.) If you were looking for something different—let's say a poultry recipe—you could do a search for *chicken or turkey*.

Don't forget, though, that different words will produce different results. If you enter *Hawaiian* or *Oahu* instead of *Hawaii* (or even *volcano* instead of *volcanoes*), you could be given some completely different sites by the search engines. You'll certainly get a different result just by adding the word *recipe* to *chicken or turkey*. Each additional keyword will narrow your search even more. However, you have to be careful not to include too many keywords in your search, or you could confuse the engine into giving you no responses at all. For example, entering *extinct Hawaiian volcanoes on Oahu and Kauai* in the text box would probably confuse the search engine, and you might not get what you're looking for at all. Keep your keywords simple and to the point, and you should have no trouble finding what you're looking for.

The Big Six

The six text boxes that you see on the top of the Internet Search page represent each of the six search engines I mentioned earlier. You can only use one of the six at a time, however. Even if you try to use two search engines at one time, only the last Search button that you click will be considered valid. Later in this chapter, I'll introduce you to a separate search engine, called SavvySearch, that will actually use twelve search engines at the same time to give you the broadest response possible for your keyword search.

In this section, I'll provide you with an in-depth look at each of the search engines on MSIE's Internet Search page. Each of the six has its own strengths and weaknesses, and each can be a useful tool in its own right. Microsoft provides a page called "choosing a search service", which you can get to by clicking on the hyperlink near the top of the Search page, should you need help deciding which engine you should use.

Alta Vista

Alta Vista is one of the largest search engines on the Web; they claim to have over 30 million pages in their index. For a simple search, simply enter the keywords you're looking for into the Alta Vista text box and click on the Search button (or press Enter). Let's start off our search with something simple. My father's really likes to get out there and work in his garden, so let's find out about vegetable gardens. Simply enter *vegetable gardens* into the text box and click on Enter. The results should be similar to those shown in Figure 10.2.

Near the top of the page, Alta Vista tells us that it is displaying the first ten responses to our search, out of a total of about 60,000! That's a lot of vegetables! The good news is that Alta Vista displays the results in the order it thinks best matches your request, so the best matches should be near the beginning. It also says in small type that over 100,000 sites matched the word *vegetable*, and over 200,000 matched the word *garden*. There must be a lot of gardeners on the Web.

Each link will take us to a different page, totally unrelated to either Microsoft or Alta Vista. So we can be sure we're going to the right place, Alta Vista

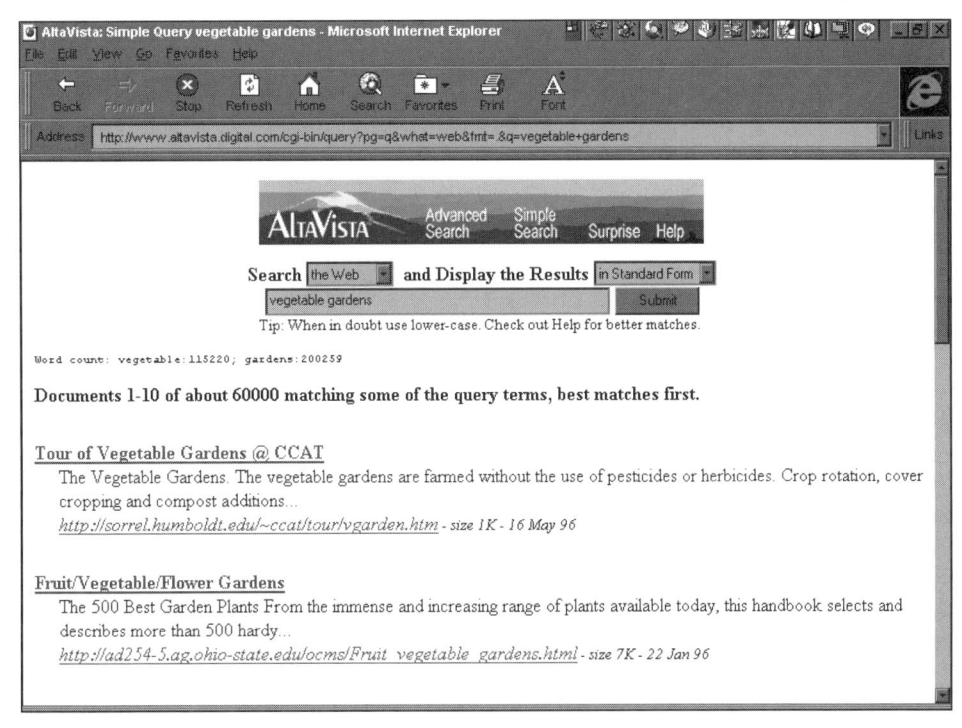

Figure 10.2 Planting the seeds for our search.

provides a brief description of each site below the link to the site, as well as listing that site's address.

What makes Alta Vista a little different from some other search engines is that it searches Usenet newsgroups. (For more on newsgroups, see Chapter 14.) If you're interested in hearing what a newsgroup has to say about vegetable gardening, simply go to the box at the top of the results screen (or go to Alta Vista's home page at **http://www.altavista.digital.com**) and enter *vegetable gardens* in the box. Then, in the pull-down box that says Web, click on the arrow and choose Usenet. The other pull-down box allows you to choose whether you want to have your results come back in Standard Form, in Compact Form, or in Detailed Form. Personally, I couldn't see any difference between Standard and Detailed. Compact simply gave you a more compact listing and a very short description. I'm going to stick to Standard on this one. Then all you have to do is click on Submit. The results are shown in Figure 10.3.

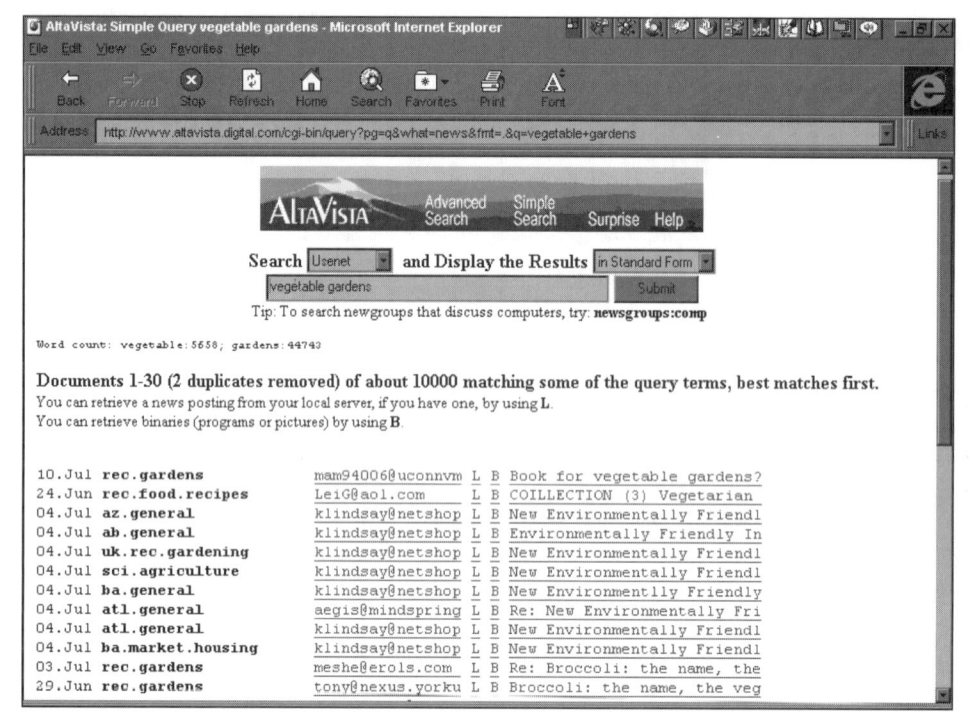

Figure 10.3 Searching newsgroups for veggie information.

The results look a little different, because they contain newsgroup addresses instead of URLs. Clicking on one of the links will take you to the newsgroup posting that matches the description to the right of the screen. Now, let's move on to a more "exciting" Internet search engine.

Excite

Excite, whose official search engine can be found at **http://www.excite.com**, is one of the newer kids on the search engine block. To search for a topic using Excite, simply enter keywords in the Excite text box and then click on the Search button to find what you're looking for. Let's do a quick search and see what we come up with. I mentioned looking for Hawaiian volcanoes before; that seems as good a place to start as any. Simply type *hawaiian volcanoes* into the Excite text box (most search engines aren't case sensitive) and click on the Search button.

Notice that after you click on the Search button, the status bar at the bottom of the screen indicates that we've been whisked away from the Microsoft

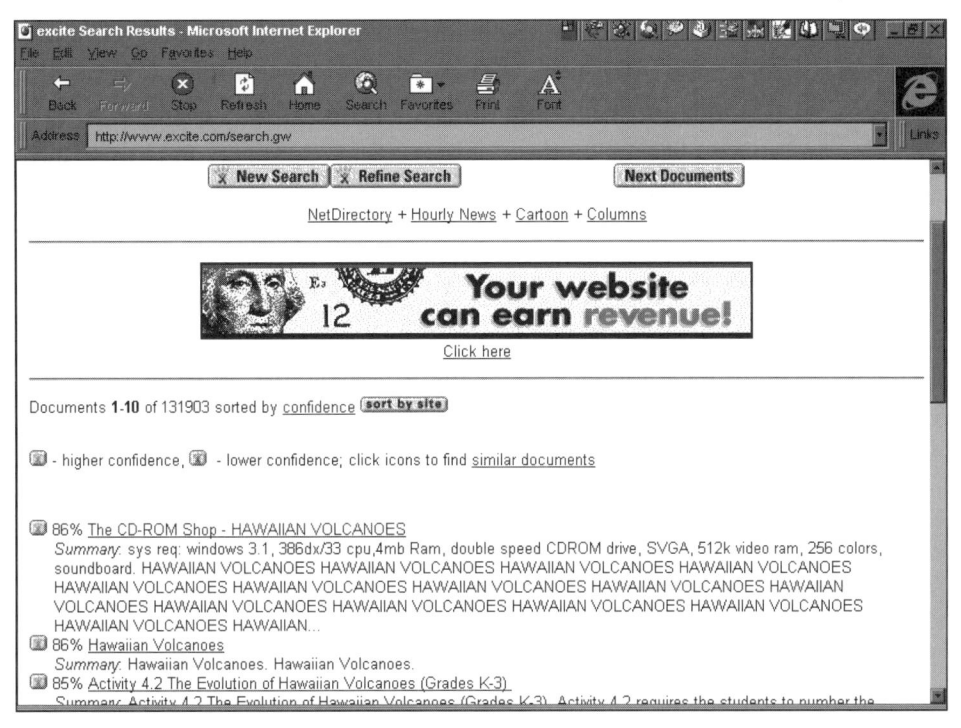

Figure 10.4 Just a few of the matches that Excite found on our search for Hawaiian volcanoes.

site to Excite's domain. After a few seconds, the results of the search will display on your screen. Figure 10.4 shows the top of Excite's Search Results page, as well as the first few responses to our search.

Notice at the top of Figure 10.4 that it says the results one through ten are organized by confidence. This means that Excite has given you the first ten results of its search, and they're ranked in order from most accurately fitting your request to least accurately. The red icons next to the results mean that Excite is very confident about this site matching your request, while the grey icons mean that Excite's not quite sure about the result's accuracy. And if that's not enough, Excite gives a percentage ranking to each response, again ranking its accuracy. To make sure it is actually what you're looking for, simply read the brief description of the site, which is taken from the first few lines of the actual site. Remember, Excite's results are computer generated, so its idea of a perfect match could be very different from yours.

The icons, however, are one of the features that make Excite different from other search engines. If you are particularly happy with one of the results that Excite found, and you'd like to see more sites that are similar to that one, you can simply click on the icon and it will reorganize an entirely new list of choices for you.

For example, let's say you want to see more sites related to Hawaii Volcanoes National Park, which is at the top of our results list. Simply click on the red icon next to the hyperlink, and Excite will provide a new page, again with Hawaii Volcanoes National Park at the top of the list. But this time, the other links are different; they're now closer to what we were looking for. Now, if you want to go to the National Park site, all you have to do is click on the hyperlink, and you're there.

If you're not happy with any of the results that you received, you can simply go to the top of the Search Results page and click on either New Search or Redefine Search. New Search lets you start all over again, while Redefine Search lets you play with keywords to narrow or broaden your original search.

When you click on New Search, you'll be taken to Excite's Search page (**http://www.excite.com**), shown in Figure 10.5, instead of back to Microsoft's page. Notice that Excite offers you more options for completing your search. Not only can you search the Web, which is where MSIE limits its searches to, but you can search reviews of sites that Excite has visited, or search Usenet newsgroups, or even search classifieds on the Internet! Not only that, you can search either by keyword or by concept. You already know about Keywords. Searching by concept is the other area in which Excite differs from other search engines. It will find what you mean, not just what you say.

Infoseek

It's time to move on to the third of the big six, Infoseek. Now that we've looked up information for your daughter's science project, let's look up something of more interest to us grownups. Adopting retired greyhounds is becoming more popular, and you've been thinking about getting a dog anyway. Let's see what kind of information Infoseek can dig up on the subject. Simply enter *greyhound adoption* into the Infoseek

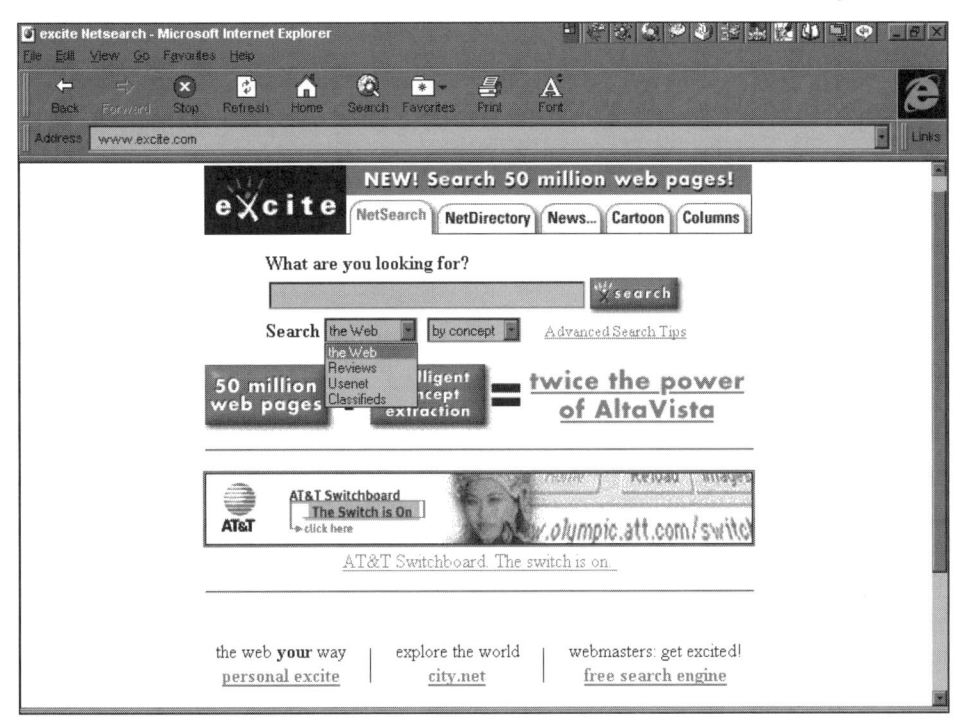

Figure 10.5 Excite's Search page.

text box and click on the Search button next to that box. Again, the status bar indicates that you're being taken to another Web location—Infoseek's Search Results page.

These results, shown in Figure 10.6, look different from Excite's. At the top of the page, it tells you that it is displaying the first ten of nearly seven thousand results that match greyhound adoption. With that many results, they can't all be accurate; and of course, they're not. Scroll down to the middle of the page, and you'll see one of the responses is for Greyhound Manor Crafts, not exactly what we're looking for.

Infoseek displays its results in order by accuracy. However, it doesn't have any of the nifty features that Excite has to help you to narrow your search. If you don't like the results you've been given, you must start all over again by clicking on the New Search button at the top of the screen, which takes you to Infoseek's Search page on the Microsoft Network. For a more complex search, you can go to Infoseek's own Search page

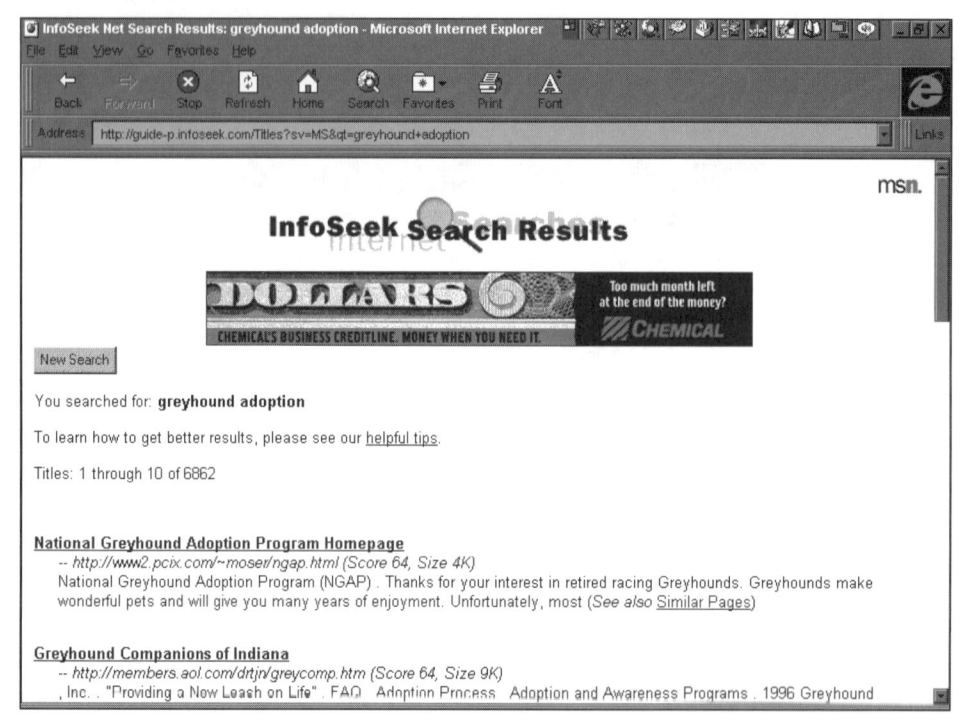

Figure 10.6 The results of our Infoseek search for greyhound adoption information.

(**http://www.infoseek.com**), shown in Figure 10.7. From there, you can simply enter your keywords and start again.

The advantage that Infoseek has over other search engines is that it searches entire Web pages, not just keywords. This can get you very accurate results, as shown in our greyhound example. Nine out of ten matches to a search is a pretty darn good result.

Lycos

Lycos, whose home page address is **http://www.lycos.com**, is one of the most popular and largest Web search engines available. Lycos also claims to be the biggest search engine, and it contains millions of URLs in its database, adding thousands each week. Let's see what kind of results it will give us (after hearing about its big reputation).

Now that we've helped your daughter out with her homework, and looked into getting you a greyhound, your son is jealous and wants help with his

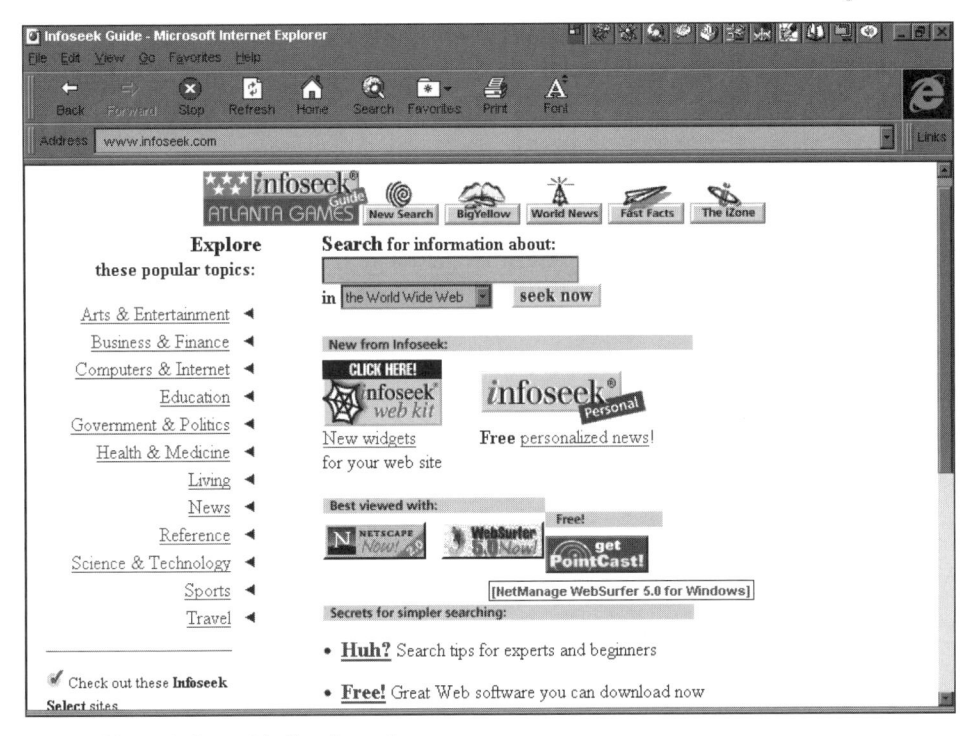

Figure 10.7 Infoseek's Net Search page.

Science Fair project on the Hubble Telescope. We can't play favorites, so enter *hubble telescope* into the Lycos text box and click on the Search button. The results are shown in Figure 10.8.

The top of the Search Results page says that Lycos has searched over 55 million URLs and returned over 19,000 responses that contained both *hubble* and *telescope*. That's a lot of pages to look at. Instead of overwhelming you with all those links at once, Lycos supplies you with the first ten, and if you want to see more, you can click on the hypertext at the bottom of the page that says Next 10 Hits. Also, if at this point you decide that you only want to look at sites containing the word *hubble*, you can click on that hypertext and Lycos will change the search results.

However, because we are interested in information on the Hubble Telescope, let's start looking at the search results. Lycos returns the results of its search in descending order from what it deems the best match to your keywords

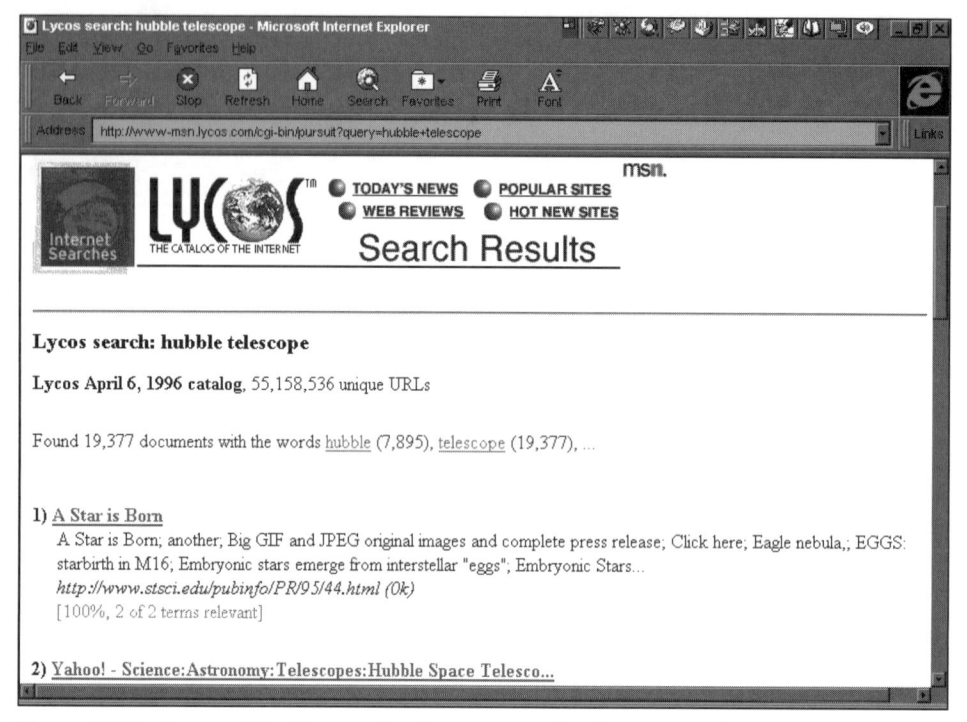

Figure 10.8 Some of the thousands of responses that Lycos gave for hubble telescope.

on down the line. This means that you should (hopefully) find what you're looking for in the first ten hits.

You'll notice that next to each hypertext link, there are a bunch of numbers. This tells you how Lycos ranked the sites it returned from its search, with 1.000 being the closest match. Again, this is a computer-generated search, so Lycos' idea of a perfect match may not even be close to what you're looking for. The results also tell you the number of terms that were found on each site—1 of 2 or 2 of 2.

The text below the hypertext link is an *abstract*, which is usually a list of terms that Lycos thinks will help you determine whether or not you want to go to a particular site. However, abstracts aren't the easiest thing to understand; you're not shown what exactly is on the site, only what keywords were found to match yours. However, some results supply the first few sentences of a site or a brief descriptive paragraph. These are especially helpful.

Once you've figure out which of these sites has what your son is looking for, you can simply click on the hypertext link and off you go. By the way, if you were wondering what Lycos means, it's the first five letters of the Latin term for Wolf Spider. Everybody's gotta have their little Web joke, I guess.

Magellan

It's time to do another search, this time using Magellan. Magellan reviews and rates Web sites, FTP and Gopher servers, newsgroups, and even Telnet sessions. Magellan is like an online guide to the Internet, which includes a directory of rated and reviewed Internet sites. Unlike other search engines, Magellan's sites have been reviewed by actual human beings. Because we're searching with an engine named Magellan (I'm sure you remember the Portuguese explorer Ferdinand Magellan from your many hours spent in History class), let's do a search on explorers. If you want to get fancy, Magellan lets you use a minus sign (-) to exclude certain terms. For instance, if you want to only know about explorers who weren't from Italy, you could enter *explorers -italy* into the Magellan text box. Italy won't be eliminated from the search, but it will be given a lesser value. For right now, though, we'll stick to the basics. Simply enter *explorers* into the Magellan text box and click on Search. The results are shown in Figure 10.9.

Notice that the top of the Results page looks very different from the previous three search engines that we've tried. Instead of just giving a list of sites to try, Magellan first supplies a list of Related Topics, which are the sites reviewed by Magellan's team of editors and writers. The sites are reviewed on a four-star system, awarding from one to ten points in three areas: depth, ease of exploration, and Net appeal. Simply click on the topic or subtopic that most closely meets your requirements; in this case, the subtopic History under the heading Humanities & Social Sciences is probably what we're looking for, so let's click on it.

The History subtopic has three sites under it that have been reviewed by Magellan's editors, and one of them matches what we're looking for, Voyages Around the World. Beneath the title is a brief synopsis of the review of the site. For the full review, simply click on the hypertext word *Review*, and you can read a full review of this two-star site. If you want to go directly to the site, simply click on the title and you'll be taken there.

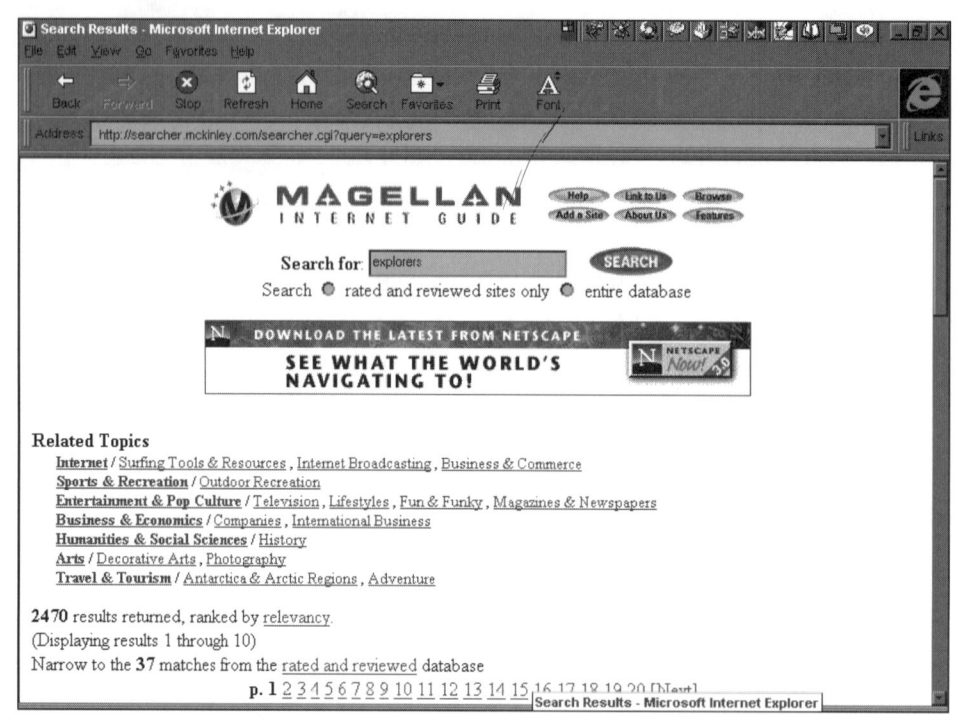

Figure 10.9 The results of our Magellan search for explorers.

Underneath these Related Topics are the results of our search for explorers. These results are again ranked by the search engine in order from most to least applicable to our request. Magellan supplies a brief summary of the site and a link to take you there. Our request for explorers returned a lot of Nordic Explorers links, as well as some sites that are totally unrelated to exploration. Unless you're looking for explorers from Norway, these results aren't going to help you very much. However, this doesn't mean Magellan isn't a good search engine; it simply means that your keyword was extremely vague, leaving a lot of room for interpretation by the engine.

Finding What You're Searching For

If you can't find what you're looking for in a specific search engine, you have two choices: try redefining your search with different keywords, or try a different search engine. Each engine will give you different sites—one's bound to have what you're looking for.

Magellan's home page, which you can get to by clicking on New Search, is organized in two parts. At the very top is a small text box, which is the search engine. The rest of the page is devoted to categories that contain sites reviewed by Magellan. This is really Magellan's strong point—site reviews. If you're interested in a certain subject and just want to know if there are any good sites devoted to it on the Net, Magellan is the place to look. Magellan's address is **http://www.mckinley.com**.

Yahoo

It's time for our final review of the search engines found on MSIE's Search page. Yahoo is another very popular search engine, and it has its own special twist, as we'll soon see. That last search for explorers has given me an urge to travel. Let's find out what information is available on a trip to the Bahamas. I think the keywords *bahamas travel* will give us the best results; we'll soon find out. Enter the keywords into the Yahoo text box and click on the Search button. The results are shown in Figure 10.10.

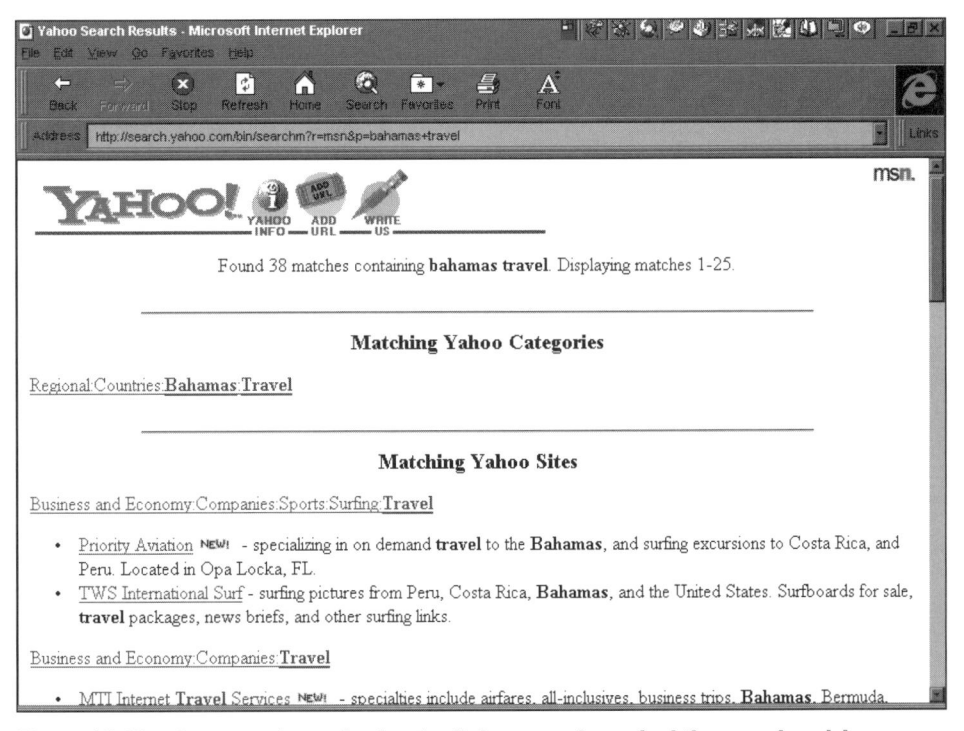

Figure 10.10 Our search results for the Bahamas—I can feel the sun already!

Yes! The keywords worked; Yahoo came back with results that matched exactly what I wanted. Notice in Figure 10.10 that the search results look a little different than they did in the other searches. That's because Yahoo is organized into lists that place each site into a different category. The first heading near the top of the page shows Yahoo categories that match our request. If we clicked on this link, we'd be taken to a page listing all of the sites in the category Regional, with the subcategories Countries, Bahamas, and Travel thrown into the mix.

Below the matching categories, Yahoo lists the sites that match our request. Each section of the results is headed by the Yahoo category list where each site can be found. These category lists are what make Yahoo unique, and can also be quite fun. Let's go to Yahoo's home page, and I'll show you what I mean. Just enter **http://www.yahoo.com** in the text box at the top of the MSIE page and press Enter.

As you can see from Figure 10.11, Yahoo's home page is divided into 14 categories. Underneath each of these categories are subcategories. Simply start with whichever category you're interested in, then keep clicking on

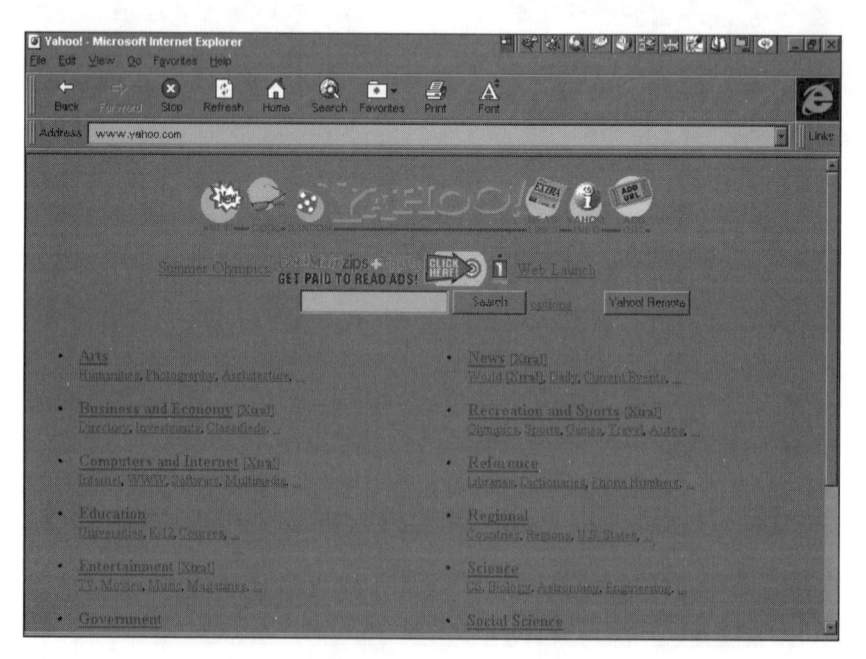

Figure 10.11 Yahoo's unique list-based search engine.

subcategories until you reach the sites that you're interested in. Yahoo is different from other search engines because it uses this list of linked categories. I suggest using these instead of just doing a search; if you're going to use Yahoo, you might as well take advantage of this unique linking feature.

Other Search Engines

The five search engines provided by MSIE are among the best on the Net, and they're worth using for most of your searches. But what if you want a variety of different results from your search, or if you want to find different types of shareware or freeware, or if you want to find out if your friend from high school has an email account. Well, you won't be able to find this information by using the search engines discussed previously, but there are other search engines out on the Web that *can* find what you're looking for.

SavvySearch

SavvySearch (**http://guaraldi.cs.colostate.edu:2000/form**) is one of the best search engines available. What's so special? Well, to start with, it searches using 12 of the most popular engines on the Net...at one time!

SavvySearch's home page, shown in Figure 10.12, doesn't seem any different from the average engine, it just appears to have a few more choices. You can choose what categories you think will give you the best results in your search, or you can just search the entire Web without choosing any subcategories, as I'm about to do. You can also choose the number of results you'll get (remember, more results takes longer), how verbose your results will be, and whether you want SavvySearch to find responses with all of your keywords, with your keywords exactly as written (a phrase), or just any of the keywords.

Earlier, I mentioned looking for chicken or turkey recipes, so let's look for a good recipe for chicken marsala. I'm just going to stay with SavvySearch's default settings, enter *chicken marsala* into the text box, and click on SavvySearch. The results are shown in Figure 10.13. The results list the top ten results from two different search engines. If you scroll to the very bottom of the Results page, shown in Figure 10.14, you'll see a table indicating which search engines were used. These engines are divided into groups of

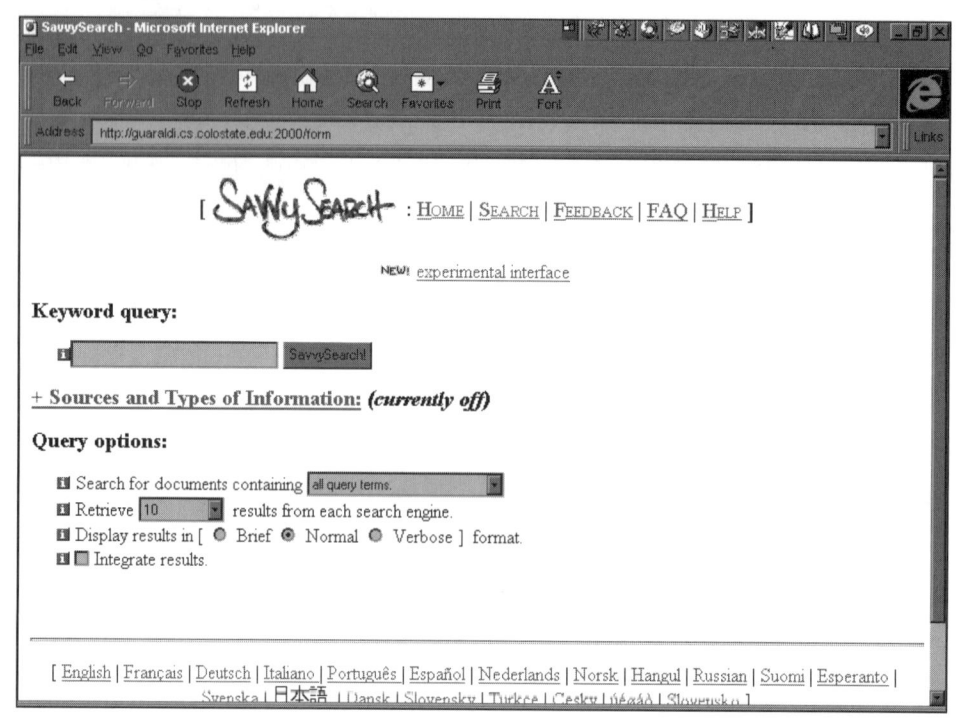

Figure 10.12 SavvySearch's home page.

two, and ranked from left to right in how applicable SavvySearch thinks the results from the individual search engines are to your search.

Of course, there are drawbacks to using something as all-encompassing as SavvySearch. When I did a second identical search for chicken marsala, two completely different search engines were chosen as the best matches. I'm not sure that SavvySearch's ranking system is very accurate, but the sheer size of the search and results more than makes up for any accuracy problems. If you can't find what you want in the first set of results, scroll down to the bottom of the page and choose another set of search engines.

Another drawback of SavvySearch is that it can be very slow; the engine must access multiple search engines, and then compile the results from the searches. And sometimes SavvySearch "times out" and doesn't allow you to complete your search. However, if you're looking for a lot of information regarding one subject, and you want as many choices as possible, SavvySearch is definitely for you.

Searching and Search Engines 249

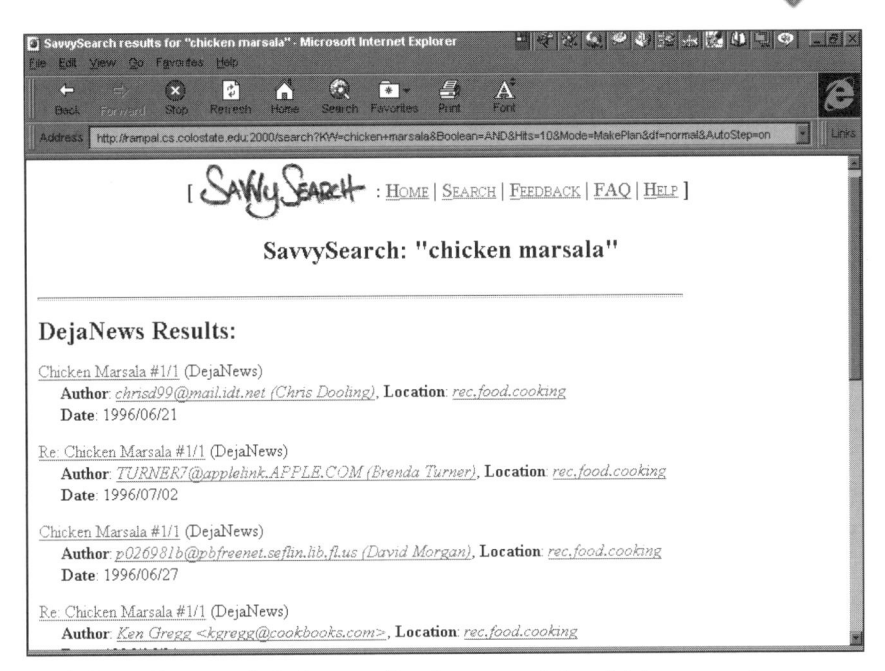

Figure 10.13 The overwhelming results of my search for chicken marsala.

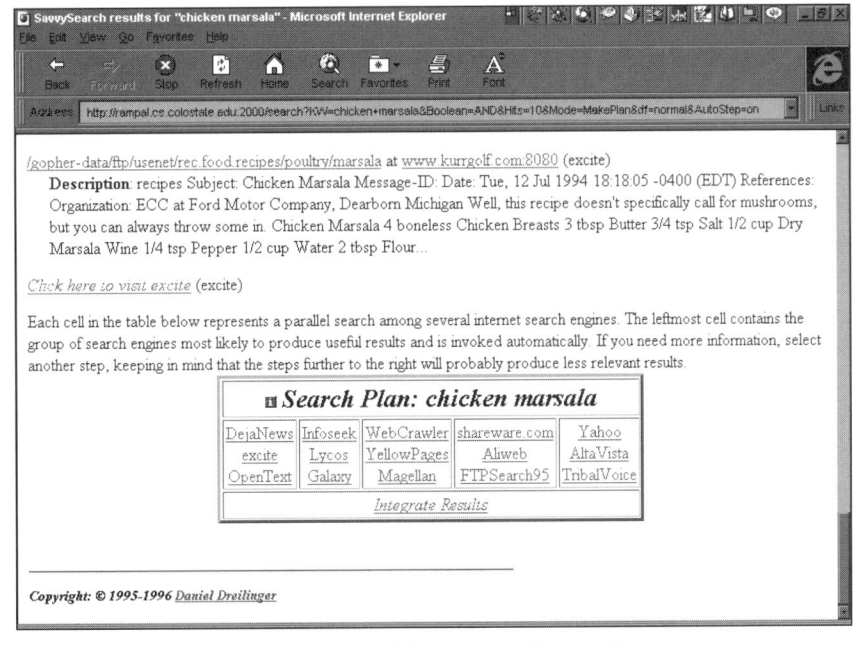

Figure 10.14 The table at the bottom of SavvySearch's results page.

search.com

If you still can't find a search engine to meet your every whim, then maybe you need to take a look at search.com (**http://www.search.com**). Shown in Figure 10.15, search.com is your one stop shop for search engines. search.com provides a hyperlinked list of over 250 search engines, five of which can be directly accessed from the search.com page—similar to the way we accessed engines from MSIE's Search page. What's different is that the engines are organized into 22 subject categories, including employment, science, health, news, sports, and entertainment. Each search engine listing has a brief description of what it does, along with some searching tips.

search.com even lets you create a personalized search engine page that will appear each time you use search.com. Simply pick the categories that interest you, choose up to 20 search engines within those categories, answer a few demographic questions, and you're set—your own personalized search engine page.

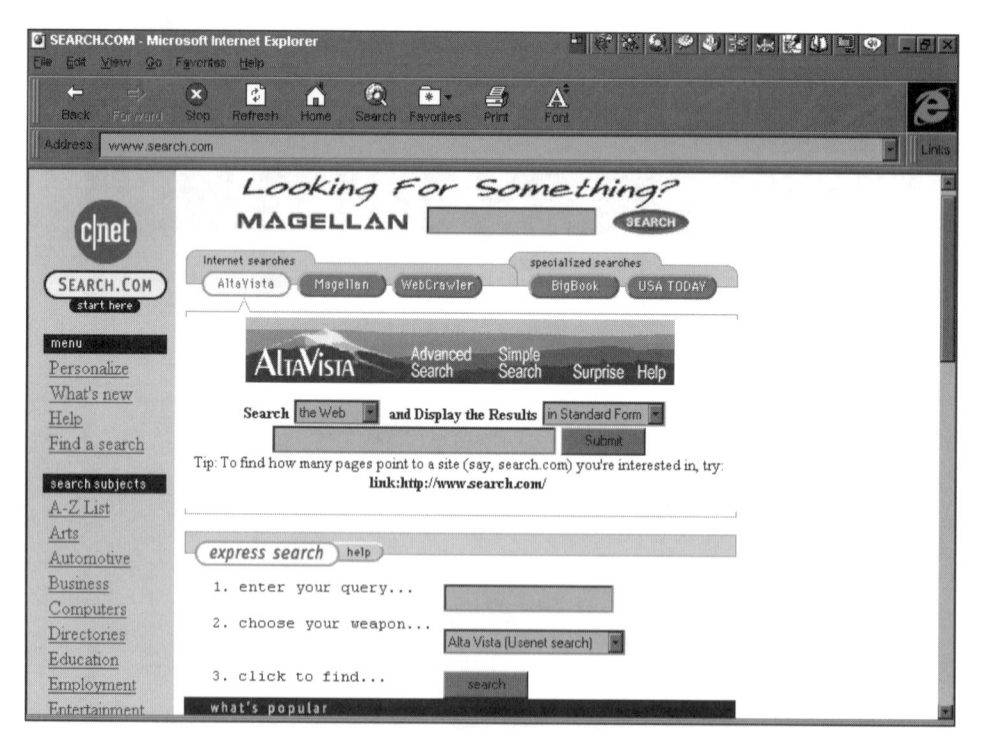

Figure 10.15 search.com's all-encompassing home page.

WhoWhere?

If you're trying to organize a high school reunion, that task would be a lot easier (and cheaper) if you knew everyone's email address. WhoWhere?, shown in Figure 10.16 and located at **http://www.whowhere.com**, can help you find that long lost buddy. WhoWhere? is a free service that helps locate people and institutions on the Internet. Simply enter the name of the person or organization you're looking for, and WhoWhere? will give you a list of relevant matches.

Don't expect WhoWhere? to find everyone you're looking for; it doesn't list everyone on the Internet, and some people just don't want to have their names and email addresses displayed by these types of search engines.

Chapter in Review

In this chapter, we've covered not only the search engines on MSIE's Internet Search page, but a number of other useful search engines, as well. You've

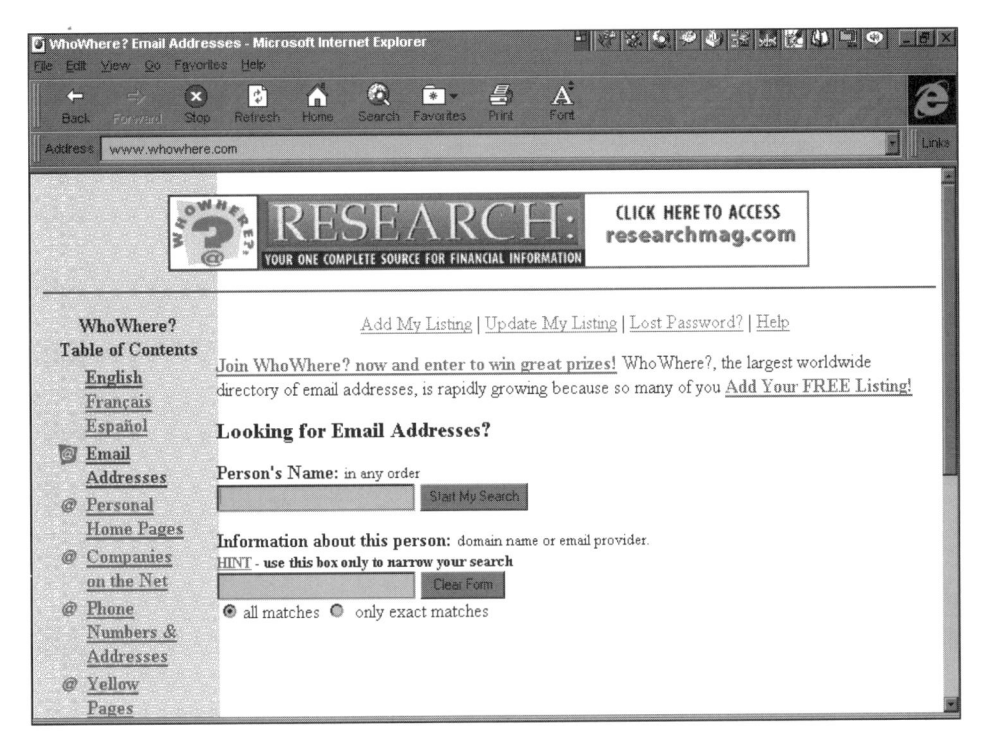

Figure 10.16   **WhoWhere? will tell you exactly what its name suggests.**

learned about keywords, which can make all the difference in your searching. When you're searching for something on the Web, don't forget that old adage: If at first you don't succeed, try try again. If your first keywords don't work, try other, similar words. If a particular search engine doesn't give you what you're looking for, don't hesitate in trying another. There are hundreds of search engines available on the Internet (you'll find that out if you do a search for search engines)....Now go find whatever it is you're looking for!

Your Favorites Folder and the History List 11

In 1492, Columbus sailed the ocean blue. But what about Magellan? No rhyming memory trick—no idea! Fortunately, as you circumnavigate the world via the Internet, MSIE has all kinds of memory tricks to help you log your travel history.

I have often wondered why people are so enthralled with explorers such as Christopher Columbus, Lewis and Clark, Ponce de Leon, and Chrissie Hynde (oops, she was a *Pretender*). Maybe it's because people like the idea that when explorers set out, they don't know where they're going or what they're in for—but they go anyway. Explorers force themselves to rely on a combination of wit and skill, challenging themselves to carve paths by mastering instruments, developing tools, honing skills, and charting courses.

As you set out to explore the Web with MSIE, you too will need to dust off your supply of wit and skill and challenge yourself to find the best of the Net. You'll need to hone your exploration skills—skills such as mastering your browser, creating links, perfecting your surfing abilities, and charting your courses. You'll need to analyze the Web terrain and chart landmarks for yourself. The more you know about using your History list and marking favorite sites, the better you'll be at exploring the Web. In this chapter, I'll introduce you to some of the basic MSIE exploration tools—namely, your Favorites folder and History list.

Your Favorites' Parts

Once Lewis and Clark blazed their trails, they became guides for others. Similarly, you can chart your paths across Webland and create guides for yourself—marking Web sites instead of landmarks and creating a Favorites folder instead of a map. MSIE provides all the tools you'll need for your Internet adventures. We have already seen how MSIE permits us to wander around the Internet by clicking on links or typing URLs in the Address box. Now it is time to venture further into the wilderness by finding, charting, and returning to favorite sites as if they were local hangouts or summer retreats.

Nature of a Favorite Link

Like any good explorer, I tend to veer off the beaten path with the hope of discovering obscure relics and out-of-the-way places. It's not surprising that I also tend to explore the Web in the same manner. MSIE can be extraordinarily helpful in this regard. With MSIE's linking and searching capabilities, you can easily link a trail of 15 or 20 URLs in less than an hour. MSIE is so helpful, in fact, that you may suddenly realize that you have no idea what path you've followed to get to that cool Web page displaying on your monitor. Fortunately, MSIE provides a handy feature called *Favorites*.

A Favorite, or Favorites link, is an electronic record that you make of a Web site address. It is very similar to a rolodex card, except that a Favorite stores Web site addresses as opposed to street addresses and phone numbers. Without Favorites, our computer work areas would probably be awash in a sea of yellow sticky notes containing all the great URLs we've heard about or discovered along our way.

A Favorite has two main components: a URL and a descriptive title. For example, when you surf to the Discovery Channel's home page, the URL **http://www.discovery.com** appears in the Address box. Recall that the URL is the Universal Resource Locator—a special Internet address assigned to every Web page. As we discussed earlier in this book, every Web resource, such as a document or graphic image, has its own unique URL. The descriptive title, *Discovery Channel Online* in this instance, displays in the top title bar, followed by the words *Microsoft Internet Explorer*. The Web page creator supplies the descriptive title.

Some Exploration Tools

MSIE provides a couple of exploration tools utilizing URLs and descriptive titles. First, MSIE automatically records a History list of any and all locations you visit during your current trip (notice I say, "during your *current* trip"—sites listed in a History list are temporary). The first two icons on the MSIE toolbar make use of the History list. The Back arrow button takes you back to the preceding site, provided you are not at the very first stop on your trek. The Forward arrow button takes you forward to the next site listed in the History list, provided you have backed up at least once.

Other exploratory tools reside under the Go option on the menu bar. Clicking on the Go option displays the Back, Forward, Start Page, Search the Web, and Today's Links commands; your History list; and an Open History Folder command. The Back, Forward, and Start Page commands are self-explanatory—they take you back one site, forward one site, or to your start page. The Search the Web link takes you to the MSIE Search page, as discussed in Chapter 10, and the Today's Links option takes you to the Surf Stories page, as discussed in Chapter 9. Beneath those five directional commands is your History list. Your History list consists of a list of sites you have recently visited, arranged in chronological order. The History list helps you avoid excessive clicking on your Back and Forward arrow buttons. Using the History list, you can leap over multiple URLs in a single bound (Superman never had it so easy). Finally, below the History list lies the Open History Folder command, which simulates a complete diary of links accessed beyond your latest Internet adventure. We'll talk more about the History folder in the next chapter. In this chapter, we're going to concentrate more on your History list and Favorites folder. To start, let's lay some basic groundwork.

Pointing Particulars

As you know, you can easily get to a particular Web site with MSIE once you know its URL. Let's visit Baltimore's Charm Net home page, which is located at **http://www.charm.net/**.

Note the "/" at the end of this URL. Technically speaking, the / is a required URL terminator. However, most browsers, including MSIE, allow you to specify a URL without using the / terminator. In fact, MSIE seems to work better *without* the terminal forward slash. Some browsers, on the other hand, require the terminator. As long as you're working with MSIE, I suggest that you make life easy on yourself and disregard the terminal slash mark.

Now, lets take a quick trip to Charm Net. You can click in the Address box or press Ctrl+O (hold down the Ctrl key while you press the O key) to access the Open Location dialog box. Enter Charm Net's URL in the Address box, then press enter to display Charm Net's home page, as shown in Figure 11.1.

Charm Net's opening display includes a giant emerald. The Charm Net "Emerald on the Matrix" symbolically represents the city of Baltimore. If

Figure 11.1 Charm Net provides you with tons of links to other cool places on the Web.

you like the Charm Net home page as much as I do (it has a fantastic collection of links to other places on the Web—its Internet Fun link is one of the best), you may want to ensure an easy return to the Charm Net site. MSIE makes return trips easy, and I'll show you how in just a moment.

Watch Your Case

Before we go any further, I have a few words of warning about URLs. As you know, a URL has several components. What you may not know is that entering the components can be a source of potential error. You are probably familiar with entering pathnames on your system to locate files and folders on your hard drive or disk drive. You know you can type directory and file names in either uppercase or lowercase without affecting your search. When you access URLs on the Internet, life is not so simple. All lowercase pathnames may not work on the Net if the server is running the Unix operating system (and most servers run Unix). Unlike DOS and Windows, Unix is case-sensitive. Take a look at the following URL:

```
http://www.microsoft.com/support
```

Unix will allow you to use uppercase or lowercase letters in domain names (such as www.microsoft.com in the above example) because domain names are not case sensitive. However, pathnames (support, in this example) must be entered exactly as they appear on the Web page. To a Unix-based server, "Support" and "support" are not the same thing. If you receive an error message after manually entering a URL, check your entered case very carefully.

Making History

Starting with the Charm Net home page, we're going to make a short History list for ourselves. To do this, let's click on The News Page anchor on the Charm Net home page. Scroll down until you see What's New Yahoo, then click on the Yahoo link. (As you saw in the previous chapter, Yahoo is an incredible site.) If you stopped and opened your Go menu at this point, it would appear as shown in Figure 11.2.

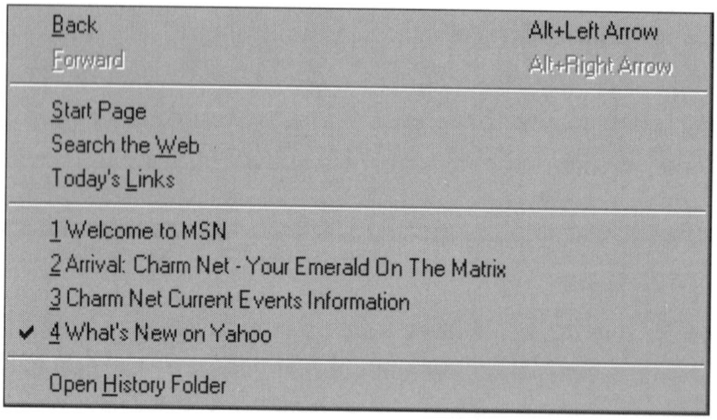

```
Back                          Alt+Left Arrow
Forward                       Alt+Right Arrow

Start Page
Search the Web
Today's Links

1 Welcome to MSN
2 Arrival: Charm Net - Your Emerald On The Matrix
3 Charm Net Current Events Information
✓ 4 What's New on Yahoo

Open History Folder
```

Figure 11.2   Viewing your History list.

The History list appearing on the Go menu displays your last few paths in chronological order. The most recently visited page, What's New on Yahoo in this case, is at the bottom of the list. The check mark to the left of the name indicates it's the currently displayed document. The Charm Net Current Events Information page is the Web page visited immediately before the current page. You can move to any page listed in the History list by using your toolbar arrow keys, clicking on the site's name, or typing the corresponding number to the left of a site's name. For example, if you press the Back arrow button on the MSIE toolbar, you would go to the Charm Net Current Events Information page. First on the list, the Welcome to MSN page, is where it all began. If you press 1, you'll return to your MSN Start Page.

You now know how to use your History list to jump around and return to sites previously visited during the current session. "Big deal," you might say, "how about tomorrow?" Enter your permanent Favorites folder.

Favorites: Extraordinary Tours de Force

Although serendipity may rule the day while exploring the Web, it can be difficult to make serendipity happen twice. When you find something really interesting on the Web, you certainly don't want to depend on your memory to find it in the future.

Exploring the Web feels almost like exploring the Milky Way. Among the zillions of stars out there, you are trying to pinpoint a particular one. To make matters worse, there are an infinite number of paths you can take to get to the star. Similarly, there are more Web pages out there than you can imagine, and getting to any one page in particular can happen (if you're lucky) in any number of convoluted, unintended ways. I don't know about you, but I have a hard time remembering where I put my sunglasses 15 minutes ago, much less where in the Web I found that great site to the nation's online newspapers (**http://www.infi.net/newsstand.html**). To be good Web explorers, we need to log our travels and chart our trails.

The MSIE History list charts your trails for you, but you are responsible for permanently logging your favorite Web pages. The MSIE Favorites folder allows you to store Web addresses made up of URLs and description titles. The Favorites folder also maintains the date a Favorite link was added to the folder and the most recent date the page was visited (we'll talk more about the Favorites folder properties in a minute). The Favorites folder may contain subfolders and links. Functionally, the Favorites folder organization simulates the Windows Explorer hierarchy system used in the Windows 95 operating system. Currently, our Favorites folder is empty. Let's add a Favorite link.

You can add new links to the Favorites folder at any time, but the easiest way to add a Favorite link is while you are viewing the actual Web page. Let's view the CNN Interactive Web page; I think you'll agree that it's a good page to keep handy. We'll add the CNN Interactive Web page link to our Favorites folder. To display the CNN Interactive page, enter **http://cnn.com** in the Address box, and then press Enter.

Cool page, eh? Before you start clicking on the CNN links, let's add this site to our Favorites folder. To do this, click on the Favorites command on the menu bar. Notice that the Favorites drop-down menu has only two items: Add To Favorites and Organize Favorites. To add the CNN page to your Favorites folder, click on the Add To Favorites command. MSIE displays the Add to Favorites dialog box, as shown in Figure 11.3.

The Add to Favorites dialog box is somewhat similar to the Windows Save As dialog box. You use the Add to Favorites dialog box to designate where

Figure 11.3 The Add to Favorites dialog box.

you want to save the Favorite link, what to name the link, and ultimately, to add the link to your Favorites folder. The Add to Favorites dialog box displays a default name for the link. You can rename the link by entering a new name in the Name text box. Due to screen limitations, I recommend that you try to limit your Favorite link names to fewer than 30 characters for best viewing results. Clicking on the Create in button enables you to designate where in the Favorites folder you would like to store the current link. Clicking on the OK button adds the CNN page as a top-level entry in your Favorites folder. As we add Web pages to our Favorites folder, our Favorite links will display in a list below the Add To Favorites menu command. Go ahead and click on the OK button. After you add the CNN link to your Favorites folder, display your Favorites list by clicking on the Favorites menu command. Your Favorites list should appear similar to the list shown in Figure 11.4.

You can now return to the CNN Interactive page at any time by displaying your Favorites list and clicking on the CNN Interactive link. Congratulations, you've just logged your first Favorites entry.

You can't just have one favorite link, though, so let's add another. Here's a useful site: **http://wombat.doc.ic.ac.uk/foldoc**. Entering this URL in your

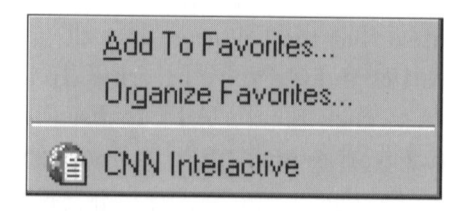

Figure 11.4 Displaying your CNN Interactive Favorite link.

Address box and pressing Enter will take you to the FOLDOC site. FOLDOC stands for Free On-Line Dictionary of Computing. This dictionary is great for keeping abreast of current Internet acronyms and words. Once the FOLDOC page displays, execute the sequence Favorites|Add To Favorites. When the Add to Favorites dialog box displays, click on the OK button. After you've added your second Favorite link, click on the Favorites menu command option to view your Favorites list.

You can now go to CNN Interactive or the Computing Dictionary site whenever you wish. You merely have to display your Favorites list and click on the link of your choice. When you exit MSIE, your Favorites list waits patiently until you return. You can continue adding links in this fashion, stocking up on interesting sites until your Favorites list fills your screen. Not surprisingly, most users blithely create monster lists before they're shocked into the realization that their Favorites list has grown out of control. The cure for an out-of-control monster list lies in a small dose of list management. I'm going to show you how to avoid the overflowing-Favorites-list syndrome before you have to face Godzilla on your own.

Viewing Your Favorites Folder

Speaking from experience, you need to organize your Favorite links before it becomes a major chore. MSIE makes viewing and managing your Favorites list easy by using file management tools such as folders. You can view, create, and manipulate your Favorites folder and Favorite links just as you create and manipulate folders and files in Windows Explorer (not to be confused with the Microsoft Internet Explorer). The default location for your Favorites folder is C:\WINDOWS\Favorites. You can open your Favorites folder within MSIE in three ways:

- Type C:\WINDOWS\Favorites in the Address box.
- Click on the Favorites|Organize Favorites menu option.
- Click on the Favorites button in the MSIE toolbar and select the Organize Favorites command.

Let's click on the Favorites button in the MSIE toolbar and click on the Organize Favorites command. Your Organize Favorites folder window should appear similar to the one shown in Figure 11.5.

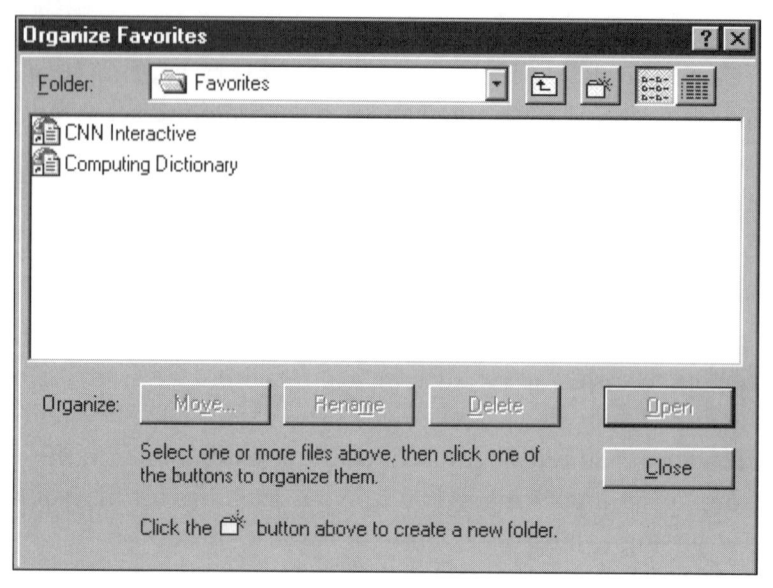

Figure 11.5 Displaying the contents of your Favorites folder.

Notice your two Favorite links display as shortcuts to the Internet. While your Favorites are simply URL place cards, you can manipulate your Favorite links as if they were files on your hard drive. You can even get property sheets on each link. For example, right-click on your CNN Interactive link. You should see a quick list menu like that shown in Figure 11.6.

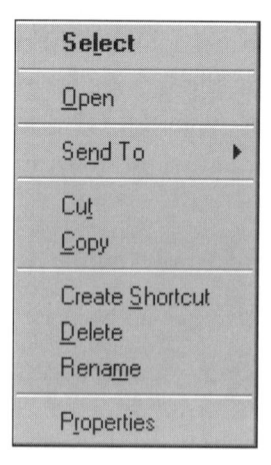

Figure 11.6 Right-clicking on a Favorite link displays a quick list menu.

You can use this menu to select, open, send, cut, copy, delete, and rename your Favorite link. You can also create a shortcut to your Favorite link using this menu—we'll talk more about shortcuts in the next chapter. Finally, you can use this menu to view the property sheet for the Favorite link. Let's view the property sheet for the CNN Interactive Favorite link. Right-click on your CNN link, then select Properties. The CNN Interactive link property sheet should appear similar to the one shown in Figure 11.7.

The property sheet for a Favorite link consists of two cards: the General card and the Internet Shortcut card. Figure 11.7 displays the General card. The General card gives you information such as the Favorite link's name, location, size, date created, date modified, and date accessed. The second card on the Favorites property sheet, the Internet Shortcut card, is displayed in Figure 11.8.

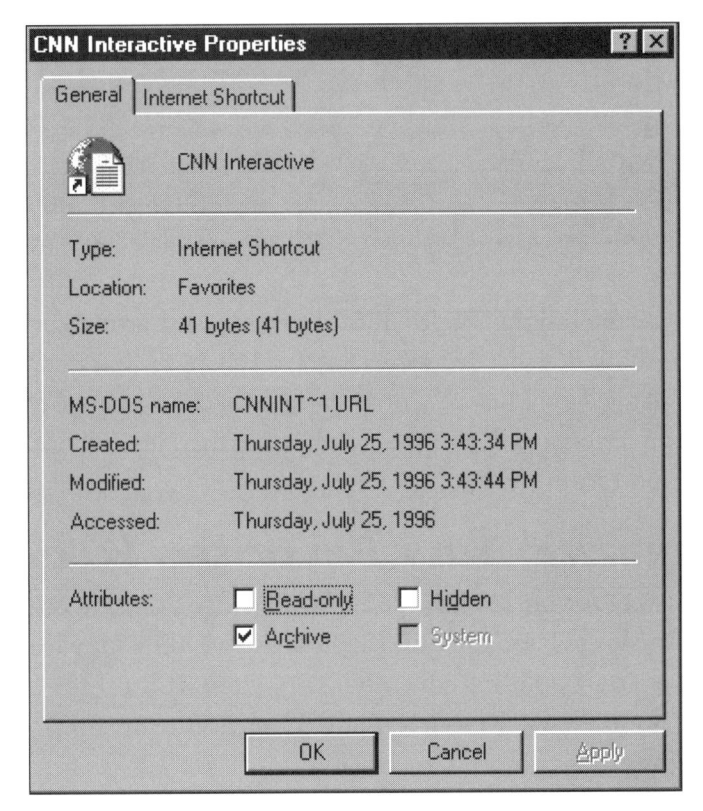

Figure 11.7 Displaying a Favorite link's property sheet—the General card.

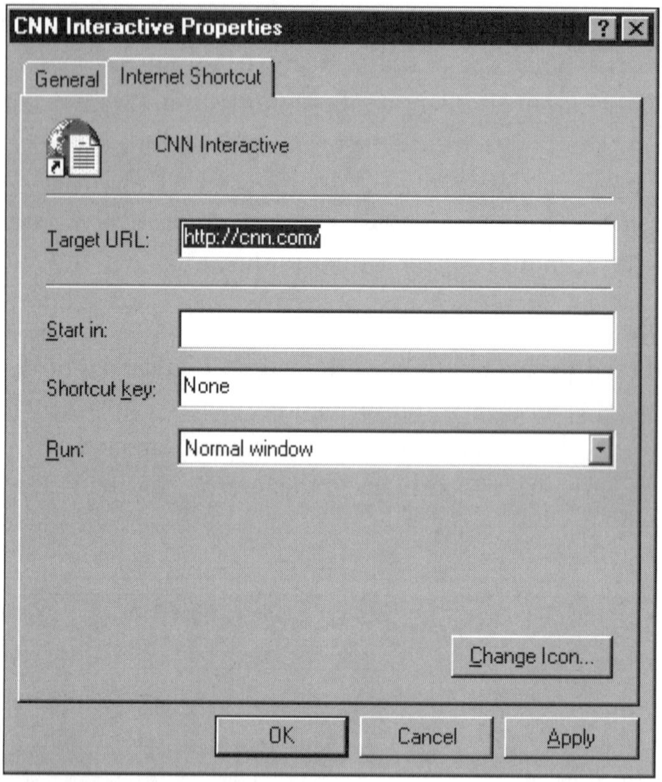

Figure 11.8 Displaying a Favorite link's property sheet—the Internet Shortcut card.

You can use the Internet Shortcut card to assign a shortcut key to a link or to change the icon associated with a link (you change a link's icon by clicking on the Change Icon button). For example, you could change the icon for a newsgroup Favorite link to appear as a newspaper, instead of the Explorer default world icon.

Organizing Your Favorites Folder

The best way for me to show you how Favorite links are organized and manipulated is to have you build a hierarchy within your MSIE Favorites folder. Let's start building a hierarchical system with a three-topic menu. We'll include News, Resources, and Entertainment as our three top-level items.

To start, if you've already closed your Organize Favorites folder, reopen it by clicking on the Favorites button in the MSIE toolbar and selecting the

Organize Favorites command (or execute the Favorites|Organize Favorites menu bar command). To create top-level directories in your Favorites hierarchy, you simply create folders in your Favorites folder. You can create folders in a couple of ways. An easy way to create a folder is by right-clicking in the Organize Favorites window and executing the New|Folder quick menu command. You should be rewarded with a folder titled *New Folder,* appearing under the Computing Dictionary Favorite link. Right-click on the New Folder, select the Rename command, and then type *News*.

A second, even easier, way to create a new folder is to click on the create a new folder icon. The create a new folder icon displays as a small folder with what looks like sun rays emanating from the upper right corner of the folder. Click on the icon, then rename the new folder *Resources*. Create a third folder using either method, and then name the folder *Entertainment*. Your Organize Favorites window should appear as shown in Figure 11.9.

Now, let's create some subdirectories beneath one of the directories. Entertainment seems like a particularly broad category (as well as the most fun topic of the three). Let's create the following three subdirectories under Entertainment: Music, Books, and Games.

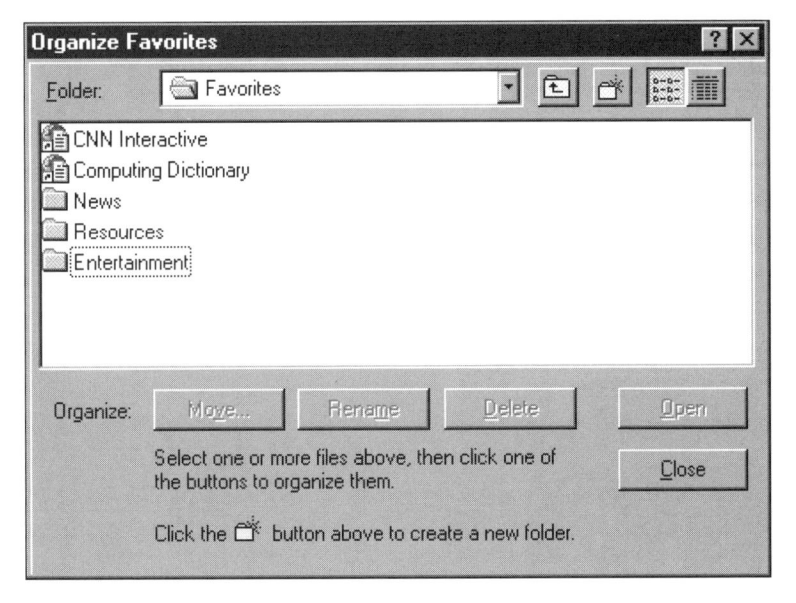

Figure 11.9 Creating top-level directories within your Favorites folder.

Creating subdirectories is very similar to creating directories. You can create and rename three folders in your Favorites folder window, as we just did, then drag the folders into the top-level directory. Or, you can open the top-level directory and create the folders from within the directory window. I'm going to double click on the Entertainment folder to open it, and then I am going to create three new folders within the Entertainment window by clicking on the create a new folder icon. Next, I'm going to right-click on the folders and rename them *Music*, *Books*, and *Games*. You can create your three subdirectories in whatever manner feels most comfortable to you. When you've finished creating the Entertainment subdirectories, open the Entertainment folder (if necessary). Your display should appear similar to the one shown in Figure 11.10.

You now have a decent start on an organized hierarchical structure for your Favorite links. Let's see how our newly created folders pan out when we view our Favorites list. Close your Organize Favorites window, then click on the Home button in your MSIE toolbar to display your start page. Once there, click on the Favorites menu option to display your Favorites list. Highlight your Entertainment folder to display the Books, Games, and Music subdirectories. Your cascading Favorites list should look similar to Figure 11.11.

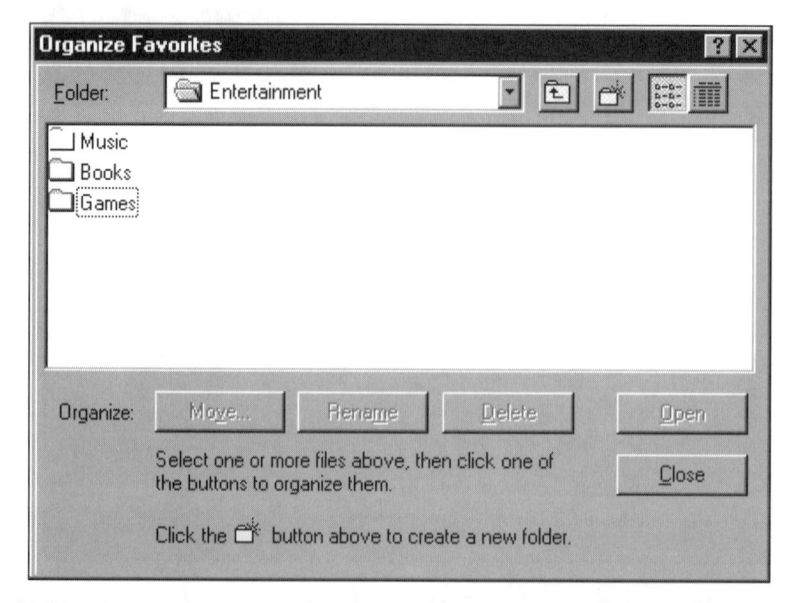

Figure 11.10   **Creating subdirectories within a top-level Favorites directory.**

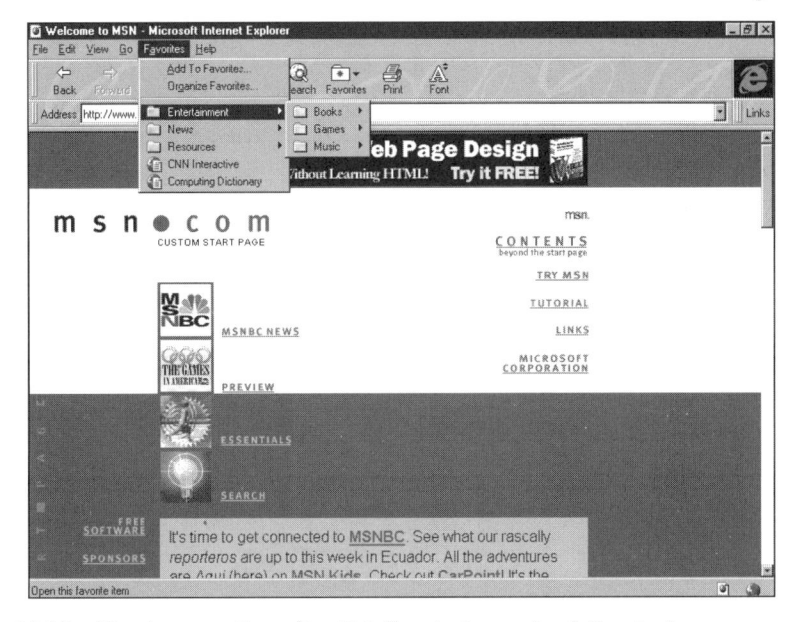

Figure 11.11 Viewing your Favorites list directories and subdirectories.

Notice MSIE has alphabetized both your directory-level and subdirectory-level entries. MSIE is good about alphabetizing your Favorites for you.

Okay, you say, so all these folders are neat, but what good is a menu hierarchy if the folders are empty?

Filling the Favorites Directories with URLs

The first task on our agenda is to do something with our two stray Favorite links. I think it would be handy to move the CNN Interactive link into the News directory and the Computing Dictionary link into the Resources directory (what a coincidence that it all comes together so easily!). To move the links, we need to return to the Organize Favorites window by executing the Favorites|Organize Favorites command. Once your Organize Favorites window displays, click on the CNN Interactive link and drag it into the News folder. You should see a dialog box indicating that the link is being moved into the News directory. Next, select the Computing Dictionary link and then click on the Move button; this will display the Browse for Folder window, as shown in Figure 11.12.

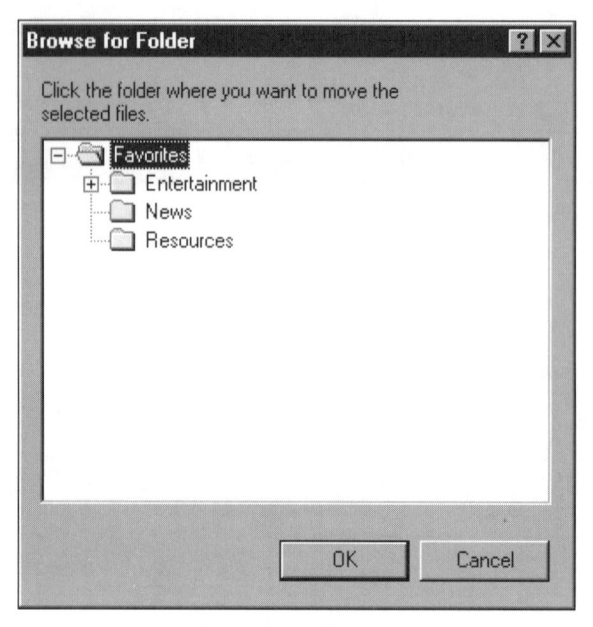

Figure 11.12 Using the Move button to organize Favorites links.

Click on the Resources folder in the Browse for Folder window (the Resources folder will display as an open folder after you click on it), then click on the OK button. The Move button is an especially handy organizational tool after you've created layers of subdirectories. Return to your start page, click on the Favorites menu command, and then highlight the Resources directory. Your Favorites list should now appear similar to the one shown in Figure 11.13.

Send Pointers, Not Documents!

An excellent way to share information with friends or colleagues is to send them one of your Favorite links or Favorites folder. Sending Favorite links is better than sending actual documents because a Favorite link contains pointers to documents, as opposed to actual documents. Sending a pointer ensures that the receiver will view the most current Web document when they call up the page. A mailed document may be older than the version of the document available on the server where it resides, and thus may be obsolete before the recipient even gets it. Finally, sending Favorite links instead of documents is a far more efficient use of network resources.

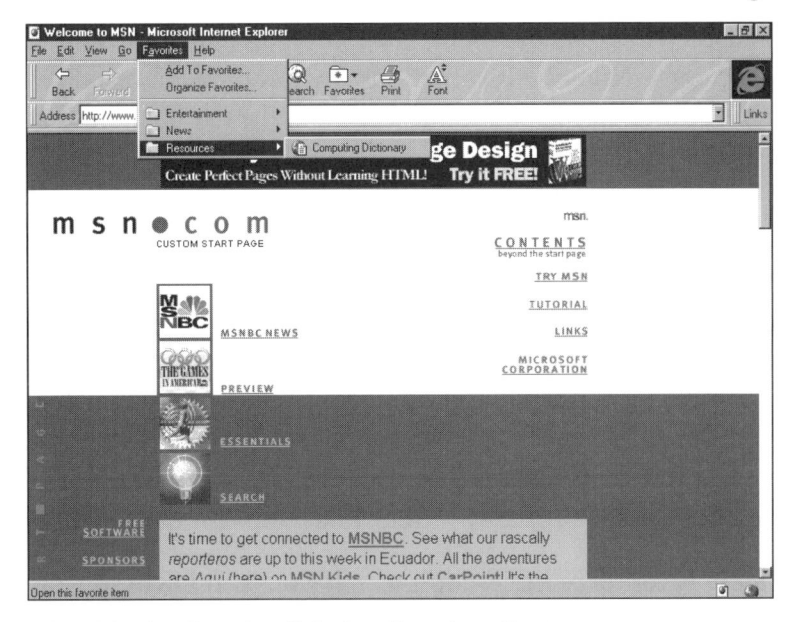

Figure 11.13 Viewing Favorites links in a Favorites directory.

Filling the Favorites Subdirectories with URLs

So far, you should have a URL in each of your News and Resources directories. You have subdirectories in your Entertainment folder, but no links to any Entertainment URLs. It's time we remedy that. I'm going to tell you about three sites that you can add to your Entertainment subdirectories. Don't worry, adding Favorite links to subdirectories is just as easy as adding links to directories.

A friend of mine just told me about a great Seattle-based Web bookstore. The bookstore boasts over a million available titles. They claim they can carry so many titles because they don't have the same overhead as traditional come-on-in-and-look-around bookstores. To get to this virtual bookstore, enter **http://www.amazon.com** in your Address box, and then press Enter. Amazon.com Books gets its name from the fact that the Earth's biggest river—the Amazon river—surges with 10 times the volume of the next mightiest river. In turn, Amazon.com Books offers more than five times as many titles as you'll find at even the largest Barnes & Noble, Borders, or other chain superstores. Believe me, you'll probably want to mark this site.

To add the Amazon.com Books link to your Favorites Entertainment subdirectory, execute the Favorites|Add To Favorites command. When the Add to Favorites dialog box appears, click on the Create in button, double click on the Entertainment folder, and finally, double click on the Books folder. Your Books folder is currently empty, so don't be alarmed at that empty window. Okay, check the destination: Does the Books Folder icon appear opened? Good. Now, check the Name text box. Hmm, the default descriptive title of the Web page is *Amazon.com Books! Earth's Biggest Bookstore*. If you ask me, that name seems kind of long. Let's rename the link *Amazon Books*. To change the descriptive title, click in the Name text box, highlight the text, and then type the new name. After you are satisfied with your link's settings, click on the OK button. Congratulations, you've just added a Favorites link to the Books subdirectory in your Entertainment directory.

For more Favorites practice, add the following two URLs to your Games and Music folders using the process we just discussed (both of the URLs will take you to cool sites, so this isn't just an empty practice in redundancy):

- http://www.fn.net/~jmayans/lemonade/
- http://www.nerdworld.com/cgi-bin/page.cgi?MUSIC/60

The first URL takes you straight to the Lemonade Stand game page. Play the game a few times, then check out the games page link for a big list of links to all sorts of games. The second URL takes you to the Nerd World Music page. The topic list is kind of hard to read on this page, but it is worth your while to search through the links. This site is *full* of music-related pages and links. For starters, take a look at the link to Musician Home Pages.

Nerd World Offers More Than Just Music

After you add the Nerd World Music page to your Music subdirectory, look at the Nerd World home page. To view the home page from the Music page, click in the Address box, then delete all the URL information except www.nerdworld.com. Nerd World contains over 60,429 links and serves over 1,000,000 viewers per month. The Index is updated several times weekly using a Web robot to bring in new resources, so the index is always current. Maybe you should add a link to the Nerd World home page in your Resources subdirectory.

You can create directories, subdirectories, and sub-subdirectories (ad infinitum) whenever and wherever you want. You can also place commonly used links directly under your top-level directories in your Favorites list. For example, remember our review of the Savvy Search site in Chapter 10? You might want to add Savvy Search as a top-level Favorites link. To add a Favorites link as a top-level link, simply execute the Favorites|Add To Favorites command, without changing the destination folder (as we did in the beginning of this chapter when we added the CNN Interactive and Computing Dictionary links). As you saw, MSIE adds Favorite links to the Favorites main directory by default.

Deleting Favorites Links

Web surfers are fickle by nature. What may have captivated you today may not be so exciting tomorrow. You don't need to keep former Favorites around cluttering up your Favorites folder; you can delete Favorite links and directories as quickly and easily as you can create them. Let's delete the CNN Interactive link for illustrative purposes. Open your Organize Favorites window by clicking on the Favorites toolbar button and selecting the Organize Favorites command. Open your News folder and select the CNN Interactive link. The selection buttons at the bottom of the Organize Favorites window should appear active. At this point, you can move, rename, and delete the selected link (or folder). Click on the Delete button, then click on the Yes button when you get the Confirm File Delete dialog box. Your CNN Interactive Favorites link should disappear. If you'd like to reinstate your CNN Interactive link, right-click in the Organize Favorites window and select the Undo Delete command. Your CNN Interactive link will reappear.

Another way to delete Favorite links and files is to organize your Favorites folder locally, using your Windows Explorer. As I mentioned earlier, you can manipulate Favorites folders and links whether you are currently connected to the Internet or not.

Keep in mind that when you delete a directory or subdirectory, you are deleting all the Favorite links (and subdirectories) contained in the folder. If you want to save selected records, move the Favorite links out of a folder before deleting. All in all, it is usually safer to delete links instead of folders.

Remember, you can always rename a folder if the internal links seem to be taking on a different flavor than your initial intention.

Shifting Your Favorites Directories

There may be times when you would like a subdirectory or link to become a temporary top-level item. Maybe you are going to do some serious topical research and need excessive access to a particular Favorites item for a while. If you shift your Favorites files using your Window's Explorer (not MSIE), Microsoft's drag and drop feature makes shifting your links and subdirectories easy. If you want to rearrange your Favorites list from within MSIE, you have to display your Organize Favorites window, display the subdirectory or link in question, and then click on the Move button. After clicking on the Move button, you have to use the Browse for Folder window to indicate where you want to place the file or folder. After you finish rearranging your Favorites links and directories, make sure you click on your Favorites menu option to verify your changes.

Saving Links in a Different Folder

Another link management trick is to create a subject or specialty link list folder, which you can then save somewhere else on your hard drive (more about how to create a separate Favorites links folder in Chapter 12). You could keep your specialty link folder close to your chest, accessing it only by typing the local address in the Address box (this is the way to go if you're trying to keep your Favorites subject link list secret—for example, maybe you're researching a special gift for someone, or gathering a huge list of games that you don't want your systems administrator to see). Or, you can make accessing your Favorites subject link folder easy by displaying your links file in your MSIE window, then adding the page to your Favorites list by executing the Favorites|Add To Favorites command.

Importing Netscape Bookmarks

Some people using MSIE may come from the camp of dual-browser users or MSIE converts. If you use or have used Netscape, MSIE makes importing your Netscape bookmarks easy. In past versions of MSIE, users had to run a free, online Microsoft add-on program to import Netscape bookmarks.

a free, online Microsoft add-on program to import Netscape bookmarks. Now, beginning with the MSIE 3.0 beta 1 release, MSIE automatically imports your Netscape bookmarks when you install or upgrade your MSIE browser. Imported Netscape bookmarks appear in a folder titled *Imported Bookmarks* in the MSIE Favorites folder. You can manipulate the Imported Bookmarks folder, links, and subdirectories just as you manipulate folders, links, and sudirectories created within MSIE.

Chapter in Review

We covered a lot in this chapter, so let's do a short recap, beginning with the History list, to help you organize some of the concepts.

A sequence of site names displays in the History list during each MSIE Internet exploration. You can display the History list by clicking on the Go menu command or pressing Alt+G. To return to a previous sight, display your History list and click on the site name or type the number displayed to the left of the site name. A site name appearing with a check mark to its left indicates that the page is currently displaying in the browser.

An MSIE Favorites list is functionally a folder containing pointers to Web pages or other Internet services. Favorites lists are completely user configurable. The MSIE Favorites folder is stored in C:\WINDOWS\Favorites. Favorite links and directories can be created, deleted, copied, moved, and renamed, in the same manner most Windows files can be manipulated.

You can add the currently displayed Internet site to your Favorites list by either executing the sequence Favorites|Add To Favorites or using the shortcut Alt+A+A to take you directly to the Add to Favorites dialog box.

Shortcuts: Beyond the Favorites Folder 12

You've heard the cracks about today's quick-and-easy mentality. Attention spans embrace 20-second news bites, and Americans pace as the microwave counts down the long minute before dinner. Microsoft has heard the news, too, and serves up a great side dish of quick-and-easy shortcuts with your MSIE application.

*N*ot to be confused by the rapid advancement of technology, a *shortcut* is still the path cutting through a neighborhood yard, the side street used to outsmart rush-hour traffic (if there are any of those left), and the Boboli used for homemade pizza. Of course, a shortcut is only effective if used properly—you can't expect a shortcut to make life easier if you cut through Fang-the-pit-bull's yard, drive down a dead-end road, or burn the pizza!

In MSIE terms, if something makes your Web life easier or more organized, it's a shortcut. Shortcuts can be keyboard commands, mouse tricks (of the electronic sort), link archives, and Favorites (remember those from the last chapter?). Of course, the best shortcuts on the Internet are links to Web sites. Links to Web sites, including Favorites, are electronic records of a Web site's URL and descriptive title. Links can appear on your desktop or saved in documents, folders, and even in your Start menu, if you use Windows 95. This chapter covers two distinct types of shortcuts. First, we'll discuss shortcuts that help make MSIE browsing more fluid. Second, we'll maximize the use and organization of links to Web sites beyond the basic Favorites folder.

Surfing Fluidly Using MSIE Shortcuts

Admittedly, some shortcuts discussed here are also Windows 95 shortcuts. MSIE takes full advantage of Windows 95 technology. Feel free to implement some of your favorite Windows techniques when using MSIE, and in turn, apply some of the MSIE techniques you learn here when working in Windows. A major advantage of the MSIE browser over other browsers is its easy integration of desktop and Internet applications. But we're not here to compare, we're here to explore. Let's start our exploration by looking at MSIE's right-click quick menus.

The Right-Click Trick

Remember when your middle finger had only one purpose in life—and not an especially good one? Well, those days are gone. Now your middle finger can gain a new level of respect as it teams up with the mouse to access right-click quick menus. The right-click quick menu (try and say that three times!) has gained enormous popularity since the onslaught of Windows 95. You can virtually right-click anywhere on a page and get a quick menu.

Using the Right-Click Quick Menus

Using a right-click quick menu is simple, usually involving three steps. First, you move your cursor over a particular feature (link, text, graphic, etc.); next, you click on the right mouse button; and finally, you select an option (highlight and click on the option). Figure 12.1 displays the quick menu accessed when you right-click on the MSNBC graphic link on the MSN start page.

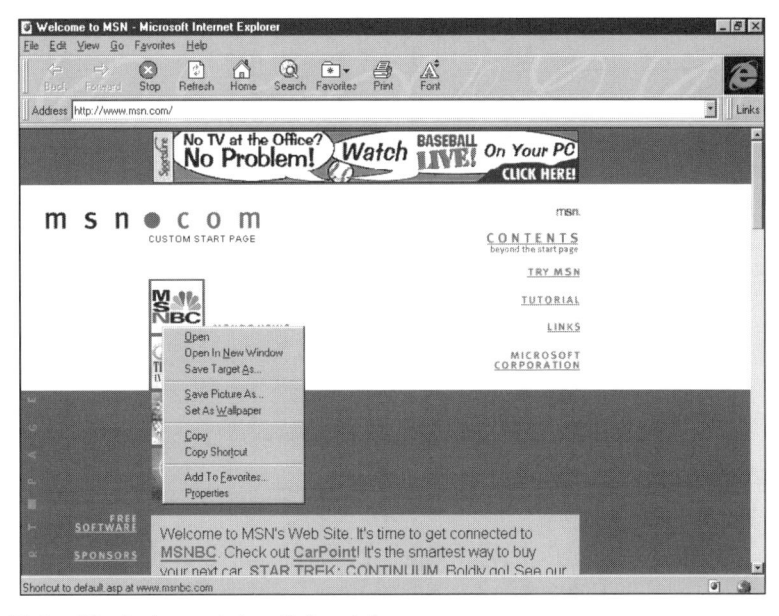

Figure 12.1 Displaying a right-click quick menu.

The quick menu displayed in Figure 12.1 is specific to right-clicking on a graphic link. There are six basic right-click menus used by MSIE. In MSIE, you can access quick menus by clicking on the title bar, Address box, standard text, hypertext links, graphics, and the Web page. Let's exercise our middle-finger rights and take a quick look at each of the right-click menus.

Accessing the Title Bar Quick Menu

Right-clicking on the MSIE title bar is similar to right-clicking on a Windows 95 title bar. The title bar quick menu assists you in manipulating your browser window. You can restore, move, size, minimize, maximize, and close your browser window by selecting the appropriate quick menu command. In addition to basic Windows features, you can use the title bar quick menu to toggle the display of your toolbar and status bar. You select the toolbar or status bar option to hide or display the feature. A check mark next to the option indicates that the feature displays in your browser window. Keep in mind that hiding your toolbar also hides the MSIE Quick Links toolbar and Address box. Figures 12.2 and 12.3 display the title bar right-click quick menus.

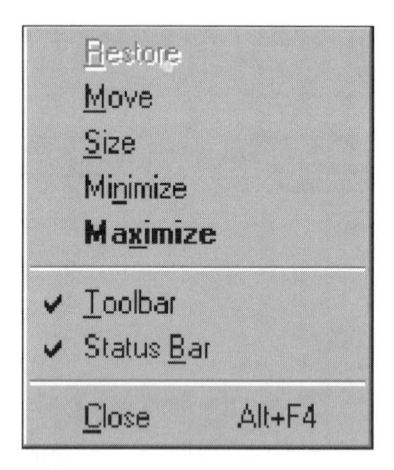

Figure 12.2 Displaying the title bar quick menu.

Notice a check mark displays to the left of the toolbar and status bar options, indicating that both features are displayed in the browser window. Unavailable quick menu options, such as the Restore option in Figure 12.2, appear dimmed.

Accessing the Address Box Quick Menu

The Address box displays as part of the MSIE toolbar beneath the title bar (remember, don't search too hard for the Address box if your toolbar is

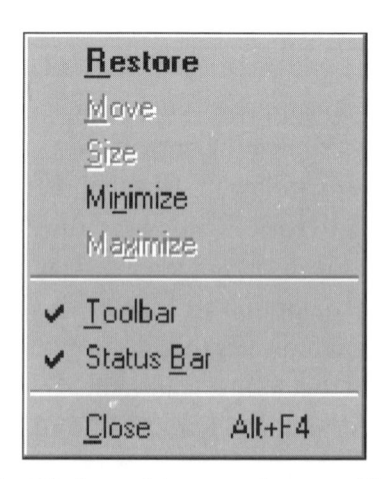

Figure 12.3 Displaying the title bar quick menu when your MSIE browser window is maximized.

Shortcuts: Beyond the Favorites Folder 279

hidden, because the Address box hides and displays in conjunction with the MSIE Toolbar). To display an Address box quick menu, right-click the Address box, and the URL is selected automatically. Figure 12.4 shows the Address box quick menu.

The Address box quick menu provides the following action choices: Undo, Cut, Copy, Paste, Delete, and Select All. Different options appear dimmed depending on the immediate situation (that is, you can't paste if you haven't copied). Most of the options in this quick menu should seem familiar to you from your Windows experience, so I won't go into much detail here. The Undo command undoes any typing you perform in the Address box. For example, if you mistype a URL, you can choose the Undo command to remove the entered text. The Cut, Copy, Paste, and Delete options are self-explanatory as long as you keep in mind that the commands apply *only* to the text in the Address box. The Select All command selects the text in the Address box. Among the six available options, you will probably use the Copy and Paste actions most often. You can copy and paste URLs to send to friends in email messages or to include as Web site addresses in documents (such as in this book). Or, if you are on the receiving end, you

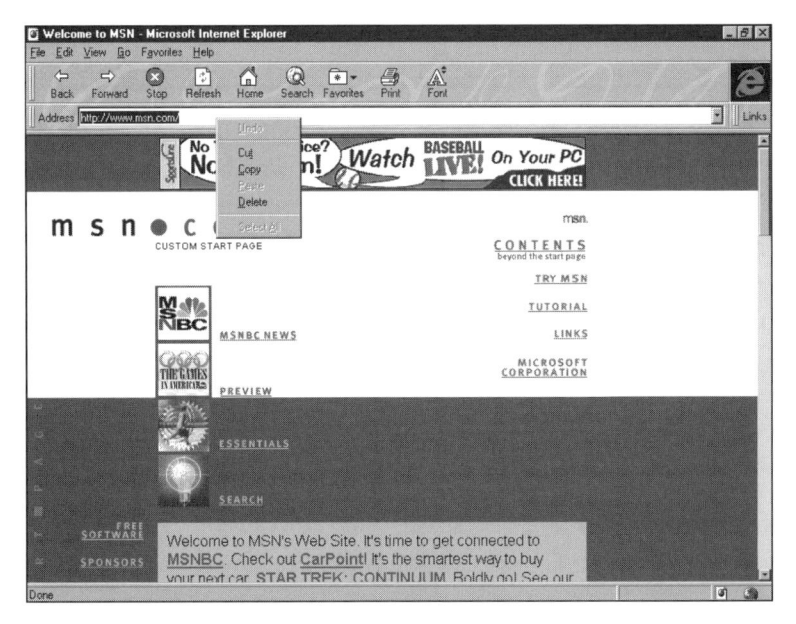

Figure 12.4 Displaying the Address box quick menu.

can copy and paste URLs into the Address box when someone sends you a hot URL to a great site or when you find a nonlinked URL on a Web page.

Avoiding Typos

When available, opt to copy and paste URLs as opposed to retyping them. Copying and pasting not only avoids excessive typing but prevents reproducing URLs incorrectly. Remember, URLs are path specific and, at times, case sensitive, so be sure to enter them carefully.

Accessing the Text Quick Menu

Our next right-click victim is basic text. To access a text quick menu, highlight some plain text (not linked text) on a Web page, then right-click. MSIE's two text menu options are short and simple: Copy and Select All. You can copy the highlighted text or select all of the text on the page (including hypertext links). Normally, you select text on a Web page because you want to copy it. As you'll see a little later in this chapter, you can copy selected Web Page text into documents using the drag-and-drop method.

An Easter Egg Surprise

Here's a fun right-click exercise. Many times, programmers hide mini-applets or other surprises in programs that the average user never knows about. These hidden tidbits are known as Easter Eggs. If you are running Windows 95, here's an Easter Egg you can find. Make sure you follow the directions closely and include the punctuation. Also, be sure you hit the Enter key each time after renaming the folder, then click on the desktop:

1. Right-click on your desktop, then execute New|Folder.

2. Name the folder "and now, the moment you've all been waiting for" (remember to press Enter after naming the folder, then click on your desktop).

3. Right-click the folder and rename it we "proudly present for your viewing pleasure" (press Enter, then click on your desktop).

4. **Right-click the folder and rename it "The Microsoft Windows 95 Product Team!" (press Enter, then click on your desktop).**

5. **Now, open the folder.**

ACCESSING THE HYPERTEXT LINK QUICK MENU

Naturally, right-clicking on a hypertext link results in a more Internet-specific quick menu. Let's view the options available in a hypertext link quick menu by right-clicking on the Microsoft link in the menu at the bottom of the MSN start page. The hypertext link quick menu should appear similar to the menu shown in Figure 12.5.

You can use the hypertext link quick menu to open, save, and copy a link. You can also use the menu to add the link to your Favorites folder and display the link's property sheet. Let's briefly discuss each of the options.

OPEN

Selecting the Open hypertext link quick menu option is the same as clicking on the link. If you ask me, it's more efficient to bypass this option and simply click on a link to open it.

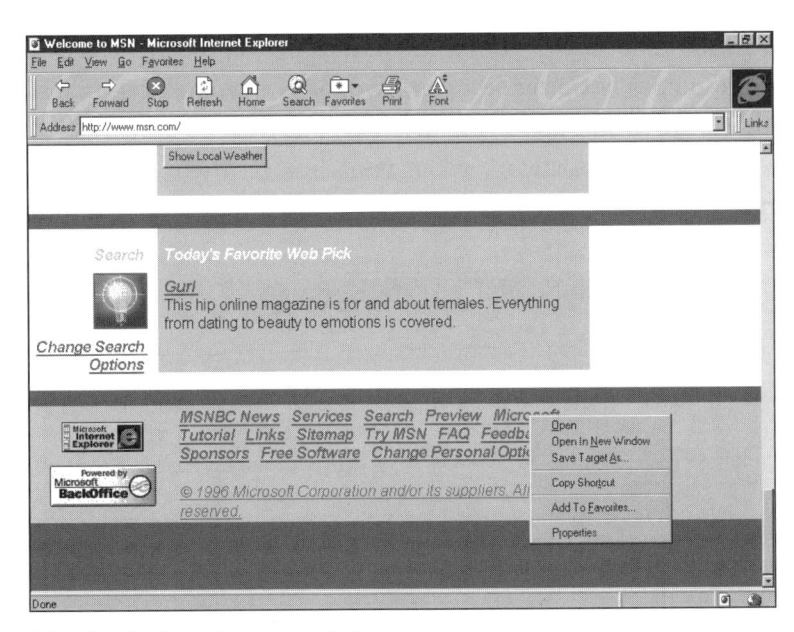

Figure 12.5   Displaying a hypertext link quick menu.

OPEN IN NEW WINDOW

This option opens the linked page in a separate MSIE window—a very handy feature. As we discussed earlier, you can have more than one window accessing the Internet at once. Opening a new window enables you to view a link without leaving the originating page. This option is especially useful when downloading information from another site (more about downloading in Chapter 13)—you can download in one window, while continuing your Net explorations in another. Now, before you get carried away and open six or seven windows to the Internet, keep in mind that the more windows you have accessing the Net, the slower your response time is going to be. Try to limit the number of MSIE windows to a maximum of two or three at a time for optimal speed.

SAVE TARGET AS

The Save Target As option allows you to save a link to disk. When you choose this option, you should see a window indicating that MSIE is opening the link, as shown in Figure 12.6.

After MSIE opens the link, a Save As dialog box displays. At that point, you can tell MSIE where you want to save a copy of the linked page. Keep in mind that using this option saves a *copy* of the linked page and its source code on your hard drive—not a link to the page on the Internet. Therefore, this option does not provide a page with active hypertext or graphic links. In other words, links appearing in a Web page saved using the Save Target As command will not work when you click on them. You use the Save Target As command when you want to view a page or a page's source code

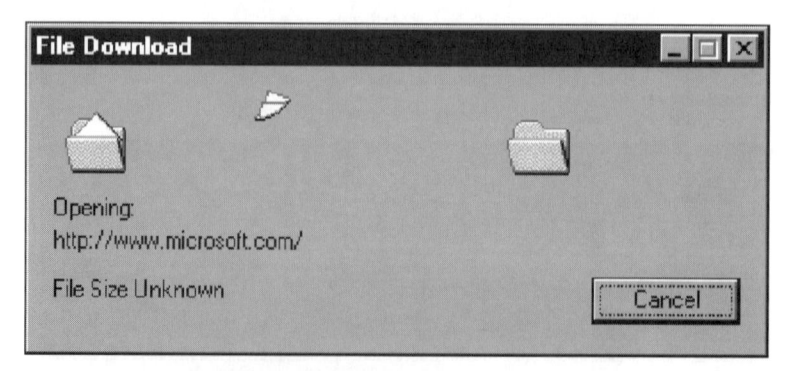

Figure 12.6 Opening a link before saving the link to disk.

without being online. If you want to save a local link to a Web page, use the Copy Shortcut command shown next.

HTML vs. Text

You can save a copy of a Web page as an HTML or text document. If you save a page as an HTML document, you must view the file using a browser (where you can also view the source code). If you save a document as a text file, you will save a text version of the Web page, and you must view the file using a text editor such as Word. MSIE's default setting is to save a Web page as an HTML document.

COPY SHORTCUT

Using the Copy Shortcut command is similar to creating a Favorite. Copying a shortcut is a great feature, but you should be aware of a couple quirks. When you select Copy Shortcut, you can paste a link onto your desktop. You can also paste the link into an email message if you are using Microsoft Mail. In most other applications, if you select the Paste command (most applications don't offer a Paste Shortcut command), you will only paste a copy of the link's URL. There is a workaround for this. If you copy a shortcut and then paste that shortcut onto your desktop, you can then drag the icon link into a document. To show you what I mean, right-click on the Microsoft link on the MSN start page, then select Copy Shortcut from the hypertext link quick menu. Figure 12.7 displays what would happen if you pasted the link directly into a Word document. Figure 12.8 displays what would happen if you pasted the link onto your desktop and then dragged the link into a document.

To use the link shown in Figure 12.7, you would have to copy the URL, then paste it into MSIE's Address box. To use the link shown in Figure 12.8, you would double click on the icon. Double clicking will automatically access MSIE.

ADD TO FAVORITES

Clicking on the Add To Favorites hypertext link quick menu option takes you directly to the Add To Favorites dialog box, shown in Figure 12.9.

Choosing the Add To Favorites hypertext link quick menu option adds a Favorite link to your Favorites folder just as if you executed the Favorites|Add

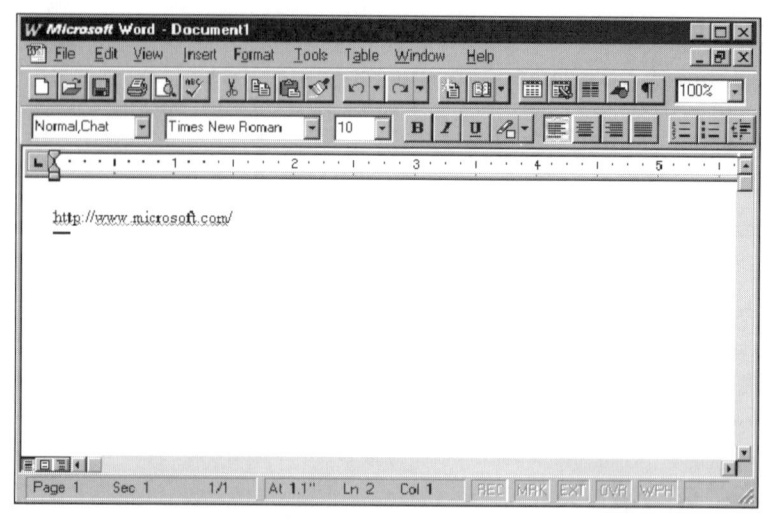

Figure 12.7 Selecting Copy Shortcut, then pasting into a document.

To Favorites command. For a more detailed discussion about adding Favorites to your Favorites folder, refer back to Chapter 11.

PROPERTIES

The final hypertext link quick menu option is the Properties option. Clicking on the properties option displays the link's property sheet. Figure 12.10 displays the property sheet for the Microsoft link on the MSN start page.

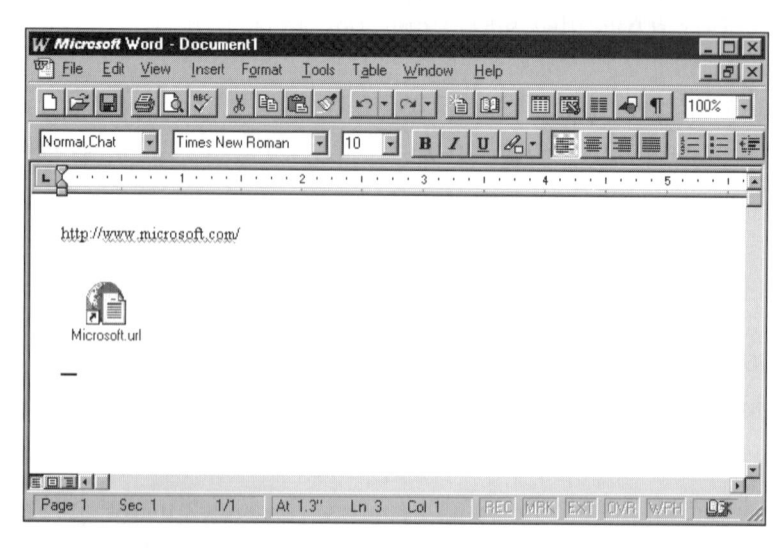

Figure 12.8 Selecting Copy Shortcut, pasting onto the desktop, then dragging the shortcut into a word document.

Figure 12.9 Clicking on the Add To Favorites hypertext link quick menu option.

The property sheet displays the link's name, protocol, file type, and URL used to access the linked Web page. Property sheets can also provide the size of the linked Web page and the dates when the Web page was created, modified, and updated. As you can see in Figure 12.10, not all hypertext links provide all the property sheet information.

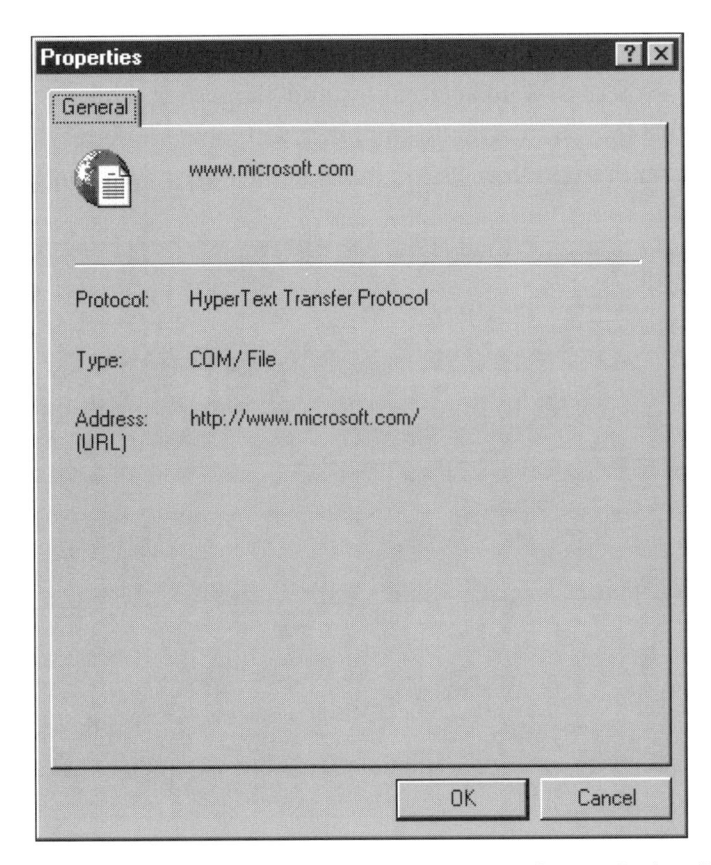

Figure 12.10 Displaying the property sheet for the Change Custom Options link.

Accessing the Graphic Quick Menus

The fifth basic quick menu is accessed by right-clicking on a graphic. My first word of warning is that there are two types of graphic images on the Web: plain (non-linked) images and graphical links. You need to be aware of which type of graphic you click on when you perform a right-click operation. If your cursor displays as an arrow when you point to a graphic, the graphic is a simple image. If your pointer changes to a hand, the graphic is a link. Let's view the Looney Tunes home page (**http://www.usyd.edu.au/~swishart/looney.html**) for a more graphic (pardon the pun) description.

Both linked and non-linked graphics are used on this page. The top graphic in the large frame—the graphic displaying the Looney Tunes title—is a non-linked graphic. Right-clicking on this graphic will display a quick menu, as shown in Figure 12.11.

Notice there are only four quick menu options available at this point: Save Picture As, Set As Wallpaper, Copy, and Properties. The Save Picture As option enables you to save the graphic as a graphic file somewhere on disk. Clicking on this option takes you to the familiar Save As dialog box. The Set

Figure 12.11   Right-clicking on a non-linked graphic.

As Wallpaper creates a wallpaper design on your desktop using the graphic. Go ahead and set the Looney Tunes graphic as wallpaper (I'll show you how to discard the wallpaper in a minute). Minimize your browser window. Your desktop should look similar to the desktop shown in Figure 12.12.

Admittedly, this particular graphic makes for a rather hideous desktop, but you get the idea. To revert back to your previous desktop settings, right-click anywhere on your desktop and select the Properties option. The Display Properties dialog box will appear on your screen with Internet Explorer Wallpaper highlighted, as shown in Figure 12.13.

Scroll to select the wallpaper of your choice, then click on the Apply button—your desktop should appear as good as new. Every time you set an Internet graphic as wallpaper, your system will save it as the Internet Explorer Wallpaper (overwriting existing Internet Explorer Wallpaper settings). If you want to save a particular wallpaper setting, you will have to rename the setting to avoid overwriting the pattern in the future.

The last two right-click menu options available on a non-linked graphic quick menu are Copy and Properties. Choosing the Copy command places

Figure 12.12 Setting a graphic as wallpaper.

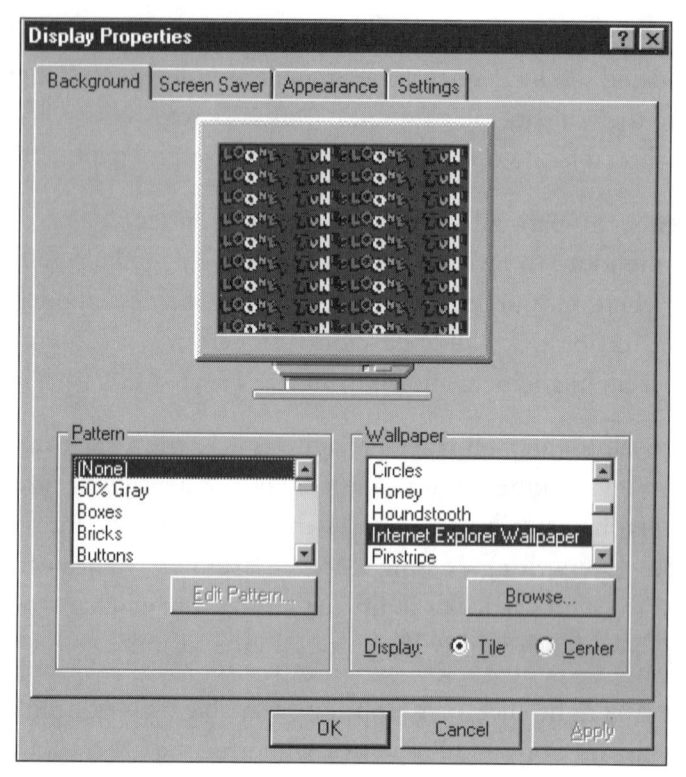

Figure 12.13 Reverting to previous desktop settings using the Display Properties dialog box.

the selected graphic in your clipboard. Once there, you can paste the graphic into another document in another application, such as Word or Photoshop. Remember, a copied item stays in the clipboard only until it is replaced by the next copied item. If you want to save a graphic for future use, I suggest you use the Save Picture As command. Finally, clicking on the last quick menu option for non-linked graphics, the Properties command, displays the same property sheet information available on hypertext link property sheets, as shown back in Figure 12.10. Unlike the Microsoft link property sheet we viewed earlier, the Looney Tunes graphic displays a property sheet with complete information, as shown in Figure 12.14.

Now let's move to the narrow frame on the left hand side of the Looney Tunes page. The graphics in this frame are graphical links. Let's right-click on Bugs Bunny's head. Your page should look similar to Figure 12.15.

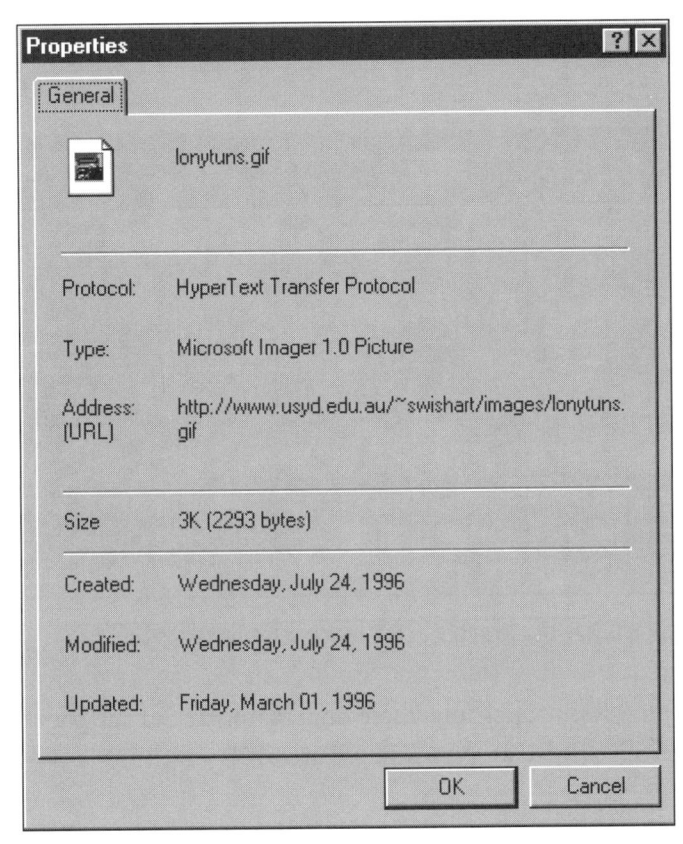

Figure 12.14 Displaying the Property Sheet for a non-linked graphic.

At this point, every option on the linked graphic quick menu should look familiar. We discussed the Open, Open in New Window, and Save Target As options under the hypertext link quick menu options (obviously, these are all link-related options). We just finished discussing the Save Picture As and Set As Wallpaper options (and just in case you're wondering, setting Bugs Bunny's head as your wallpaper is only a slight improvement over the first Looney Tunes graphic!). The remaining four options—Copy, Copy Shortcut, Add To Favorites, and Properties—are also familiar from our previous explorations of right-click menus.

Accessing Web Page Menus

Finally, the sixth basic quick menu appears when you right-click on a blank area of a Web page. Let's return to the Looney Tunes page to view this

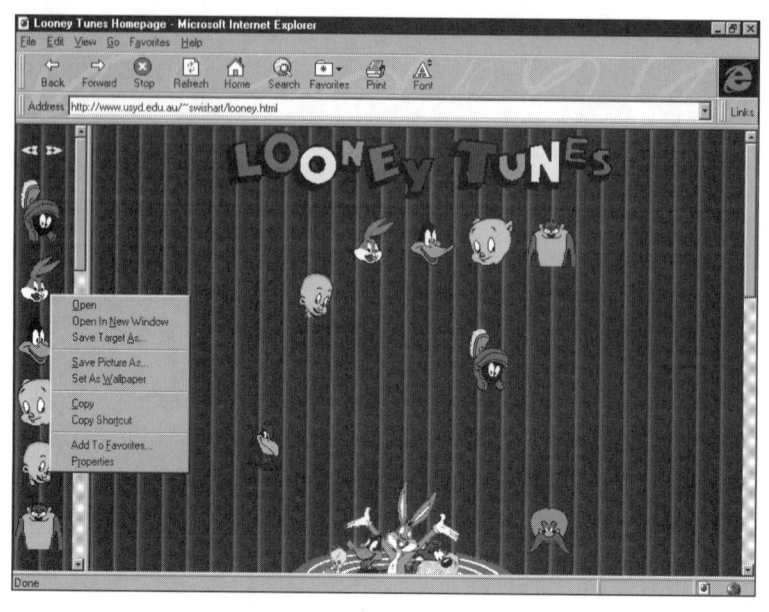

Figure 12.15 Displaying the graphic quick menu for a linked graphic.

quick menu. Right-click anywhere on a blank area of the page. Your quick menu should display as shown in Figure 12.16.

Figure 12.16 Displaying a right-click quick menu by clicking on the page.

Shortcuts: Beyond the Favorites Folder — 291

Some of the quick menu options shown in Figure 12.16 should look familiar. The first two options—Save Background As and Set As Wallpaper—perform the same functions as the graphic quick menu options. You can save the blue background on the Looney Tunes page as a file, or you can set the Looney Tunes background as your desktop design (which, I might add, is a far cry better than the Looney Tunes cartoon or Bugs Bunny head desktop designs!). The Copy Background option copies the blue background to your clipboard. Select All selects all your text (similar to the Select All option accessed when right-clicking on highlighted text). The Create Shortcut option, however, is new (in other menus, it appears as the Copy Shortcut command). Clicking on Create Shortcut creates a link on your desktop to the current page.

Continuing down the menu list, the Add To Favorites menu option should seem old hat by now, but View Source is new. Clicking on the View Source quick menu option is the same as executing View|Source from the menu bar. If you click on the View Source option from the quick menu on the Looney Tunes page, you will see a Notepad document with HTML coding, similar to the page shown in Figure 12.17.

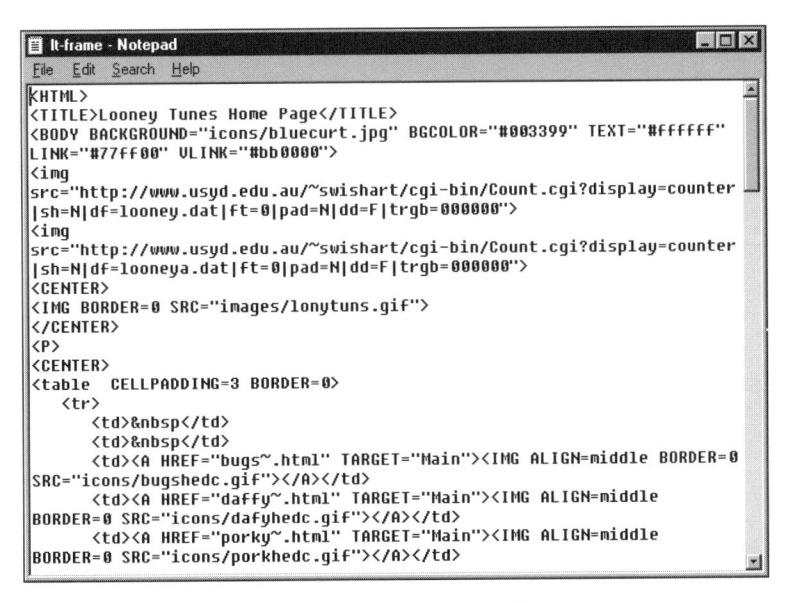

Figure 12.17 Viewing the source code for the Looney Tunes page.

The next menu item, Refresh, performs the same function as the Refresh toolbar button and View|Refresh menu bar command—it downloads a fresh version of the current page. Remember, you should refresh Web pages you access frequently to avoid viewing the out-dated versions of a page saved in your local cache folder. The last quick menu option available when clicking on the blank area of a Web page is the Properties command. Clicking on the Properties command displays two property sheets: the General property sheet, similar to the property sheets we saw earlier in the chapter, and the Security property sheet, which is shown in Figure 12.18.

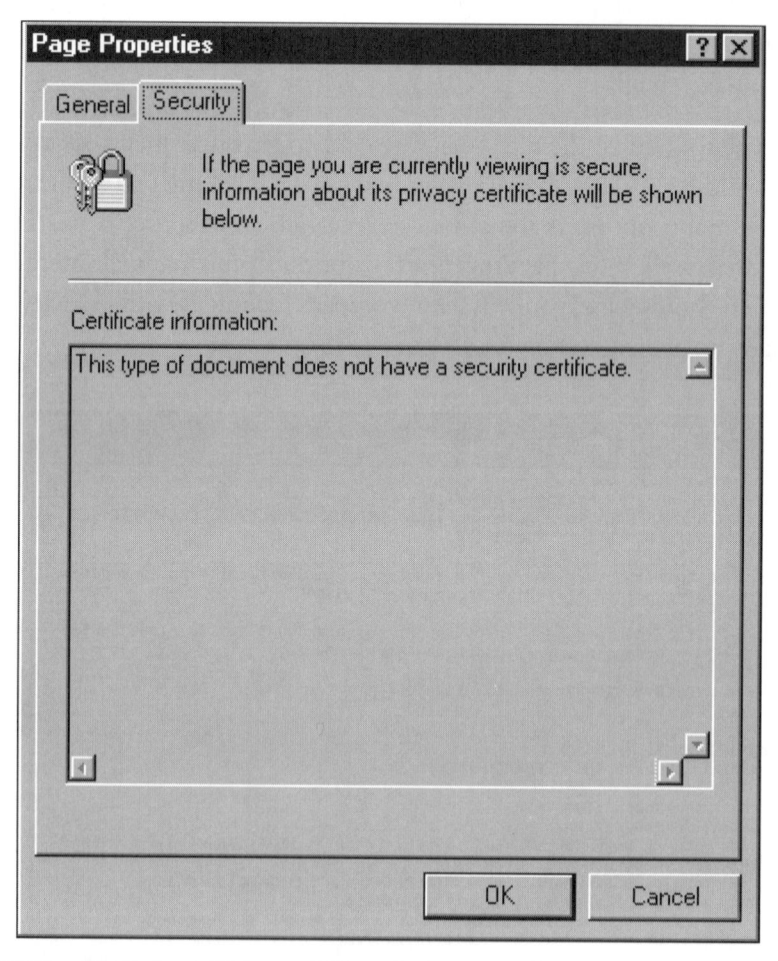

Figure 12.18 Displaying a Web page's Security property sheet.

If you are interested in knowing more about Internet security—a hot Net topic these days—check out Chapters 3 and 4, which delve into MSIE security features in a little more detail.

Well, we're finished with our discussion of the six main right-click quick menus available while browsing the Net with MSIE. As you've probably noticed, many of the right-click options are also available from the menu bar (which is good to know in case your middle finger isn't conditioned to all that right-clicking yet). Let's move on, give our mouse a rest, and see how we can use the keyboard to expedite Web exploration.

Keyboard Commands

We spend small fortunes on PCs that are so fast we have a hard time keeping up with them. If you want to access information in the fastest manner possible, you should learn keyboard commands. Keyboard commands save time because there's no fumbling for the mouse (plus you lessen your chances of getting carpal tunnel syndrome). Of course, the major drawback of using keyboard commands is having to learn the keystrokes. I read somewhere that if you are serious about learning keyboard commands, you should unplug your mouse for a month. Personally, I haven't had the courage to go cold turkey like that, but there are some favorite keyboard commands, that I use to make my life easier. If you are a Windows veteran (meaning you've used Windows for at least six months), most of the material in this section will seem familiar. Still, because you'll find some information on MSIE-specific keyboard commands, I suggest you scan through this section before moving on.

TABBING

MSIE proudly presents the first browser to provide tabbing capabilities. Much to the relief of your now-overworked middle finger, you can tab through a Web page's links using your Tab key. To see what I mean, display your MSN Start Page (you should have lots of links on that page), then hit your Tab key. Your first Tab hit should highlight the URL in the Address box. After highlighting the Address box URL, each succeeding Tab hit should move your cursor from one link to the next. In addition, tabbing stops on images and image map hotlinks along the way. MSIE indicates which link or graphic is selected by enclosing the object in a single pixel,

Table 12.1 Navigating the Web with Keyboard Commands

Key Command	Action
Alt+Left Arrow	Goes back to the previously displayed Web page.
Alt+Right Arrow	Moves forward to the next Web page (after moving back at least once).
Backspace	Goes back to the previously displayed Web page.
Shift+Backspace	Moves forward to the next Web page (after moving back at least once).
Ctrl+R or F5	Refreshes the page.
F1	Displays the Help Index.
Esc	Stops the downloading of a page, graphic, video, or sound clip.
Ctrl+O	Displays the Open dialog box, enabling you to go to a new location.
Ctrl+N	Displays the New dialog box, enabling you to open a new window.
Ctrl+P	Prints the current page.
Ctrl+A	Selects all the text on the current page (including hypertext text links).
Ctrl+F	Displays the Find dialog box, enabling you to search for text on the page.
Ctrl+Esc	Opens your Windows 95 Start menu.

dotted box. If you press your Tab key a second time while you are visiting your MSN Start Page, your selection box should encompass the sponsor graphic link found at the top of the page. You can tab your way through the remaining links on the page. If you want to move your selection box to a previous link, press Shift+Tab. To open a link, press the Enter key when the link-of-choice appears outlined. How about that! You can now explore a Web site and even jump to a different Web page without so much as glancing at your mouse.

More Keyboard Commands

Beyond tabbing through your links, you have many more keyboard commands at your disposal. Table 12.1 lists some of the more useful MSIE keyboard commands. In addition to the commands listed in the table, you can navigate the menus on the menu bar with key commands. You might already be aware of this technique, but bear with me. Look at your MSIE menu bar. Notice that each menu command displays an underlined letter. If you hold down the Alt key and press an underlined letter, such as Alt+F, the corresponding pull-down menu will display (in this instance, the File menu). To select an option on the pull-down menu, continue to hold down the Alt key and type the underlined letter found in the menu action command. For example, you could press P to print the page (Alt+F|Alt+P). Now, to further confuse matters, notice the Ctrl+P command listed next to the Print option in the File menu. MSIE provides Ctrl commands in addition to the Alt commands. Ctrl commands are quicker than Alt commands because they bypass drop-down menus completely. Ctrl commands move instantly from command to action. You'll have to memorize Ctrl commands to get the most out of them. Many of the Ctrl commands are listed on the menus, so until you memorize the Ctrl commands, you can always find a desired action using the Alt+ [underlined menu letter] sequence.

You will become more comfortable using keyboard commands the more you use MSIE. Don't feel obligated to use all the keyboard commands (or any of them, for that matter)—the key is creating a working style most comfortable for you.

Assigning Shortcut Keys

As you saw earlier in this book, you can assign keyboard commands, known as shortcut keys, to MSIE links. Assigning a shortcut key to a Web site link enables you to access a Web page by issuing a command. This feature is handy if you access a particular site frequently. You can assign shortcut keys to any links to Web pages that you've created, regardless of whether the links are stored on your desktop, in a folder, or as a Favorite link. Let's return to our Favorites folder, and I'll show you how to add a shortcut key to the CNN link we created in Chapter 11.

The first step in assigning a shortcut key requires accessing a link's property sheet. We can either open our Favorites folder in Windows (remember the default folder location is C:\WINDOWS\Favorites), or open our Favorites folder from within the MSIE browser by executing Favorites|Organize Favorites Folder (or typing Alt+A+G). Next, open your News subdirectory, then right-click on the CNN Interactive link. Click on the Properties option to display the Property dialog box. Click on the Internet Shortcut tab to display the Internet Shortcut card. Notice the Shortcut key text box halfway down the card. Click in the Shortcut key text box, then enter N (for News). The Shortcut key text box will display Ctrl+Alt+N as your new shortcut. Finally, click on the Apply button, then click on the OK button to accept the new shortcut key command, and then close the Organize Favorites window. After closing the window, test out your new shortcut key command. Press Ctrl+Alt+N—you should go directly to the CNN Interactive page, without passing Go! Pretty snazzy, eh?

Using the Drag-and-Drop Feature

As everyone knows, the point-and-click, drag-and-drop technology is the wave of today. Needless to say, MSIE takes full advantage of this capability. You can drag and drop hypertext links and graphic links from a Web page into an application or onto your desktop. Once you drag and drop objects onto your desktop, you are free to copy them into other documents or folders. You can also drag text off a Web page and drop it into a text editor (such as Word or WordPad).

Renaming Shortcut Links
You can rename your shortcuts after you drag them onto your desktop by right-clicking on the icon, then selecting the Rename command.

To drag text off a Web page, first open a Word document or some other text editor. Select the text on the Web page, left-click on the text, and continue to press your mouse button as you drag the text into your open document. To drag a link off a Web page, left-click on the link you want to save, and continue pressing your mouse button while you drag your cursor off the Web page and onto your desktop (of course, some portion of your desktop must be visible for this to work). You just learned two ways to create a link using the drag-and-drop technique.

You are probably asking yourself, "What in the world am I going to do with a desktop link?" Well, there are a couple of advantages to desktop links. First, if you want to open MSIE to the linked page, all you need to do is double click on your desktop link. If MSIE is already opened on your desktop, you can drag the link from your desktop into the MSIE window and the browser will open the page (without disrupting your desktop link). You can also copy desktop links into other documents, such as Word documents or email messages, with the new copy of the link retaining full-service linking capabilities. Imagine the possibilities: You could submit electronic reports created in Word that contain active Internet links; or, in place of a URL, you could email a shortcut—very suave (why offer a pansy when you can send a rose?).

With a little practice, you'll soon get used to MSIE's drag-and-drop technology, if you aren't already. In fact, dragging and dropping may become so easy that your desktop will soon be in dire need of some housecleaning. Now, I could care less if you washed the dishes, folded your laundry, made the bed, or balanced your checkbook, but working on a messy desktop is just too much—especially when the chore doesn't involve leaving your chair or straining your brain.

Storing and Finding Your Links

By this time, you have links on your desktop and links in your Favorites folder. Now, imagine that you have three or four windows open, and suddenly you want to access a link on your desktop. Or, you've filled up your Favorites folder, and you just don't have the desire to add one more level of subdirectories. You need to organize! I've found a couple of tricks to make your life even easier than MSIE has already made it.

Desktop Links

The next couple of tips probably fall under Windows 95 tricks, but I've found them very useful during my Internet explorations, so I'm passing them along to you.

EASY ACCESS TO DESKTOP LINKS

I've often discovered that I'll have three or four windows open at once, and suddenly I'll need to access an application or a link residing on my desktop. I used to have two choices: One, I could resize all my windows until I could see the application or link in question; or two, I could click on my start key and follow the flow of cascading menus to my Explorer option, and then proceed to open the application from there (I'm too lazy to explain that entire process, let alone do it!). So, I came up with this workaround: I created a link to my desktop as a top-level link in my Start menu, as shown in Figure 12.19.

Notice I also placed a link to MSIE in my Start menu. That was easy. I just dragged my desktop shortcut over my Start button and the link was added as a top-level Start menu item. Adding the desktop shortcut took a little more effort.

First, you have to create a shortcut to your desktop by following these steps:

1. Right-click anywhere on your desktop and execute the New|Shortcut command to display the Create Shortcut dialog box.

2. In the Command Line text box, type the path to your Windows Explorer (not MSIE), then add a space and type */root,* (the comma is required). Figure 12.20 shows how I would enter the information on my system.

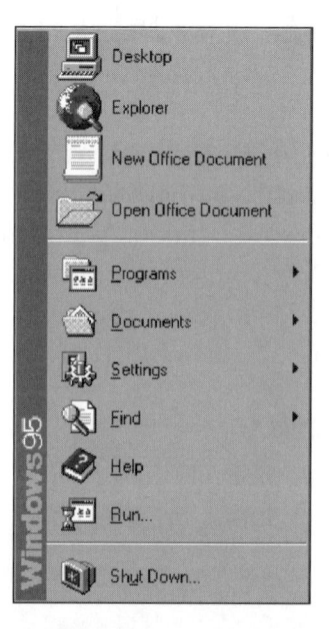

Figure 12.19 Displaying a link to your desktop in your Start menu.

Shortcuts: Beyond the Favorites Folder **299**

3. Click on the Next button.

4. In the Select a Title for the Program dialog box, enter Desktop in the Select a name for the shortcut text box.

5. Click on the Finish button.

You now have a shortcut link to your desktop sitting on your desktop. The next step is to move the shortcut link into your Start menu. Simply drag the desktop shortcut over the Start button in your Windows task bar.

Congratulations! You've just created a Start menu link to your desktop. Now that you've made accessing your desktop easy, it's time to do a little sweeping.

ORGANIZING YOUR DESKTOP LINKS

You can organize your desktop links by saving them in folders on your desktop. You can even move links in desktop folders into files (as long as you save the files as *text* files). It is up to you as to how elaborately you want to arrange your desktop links. To create a folder on your desktop,

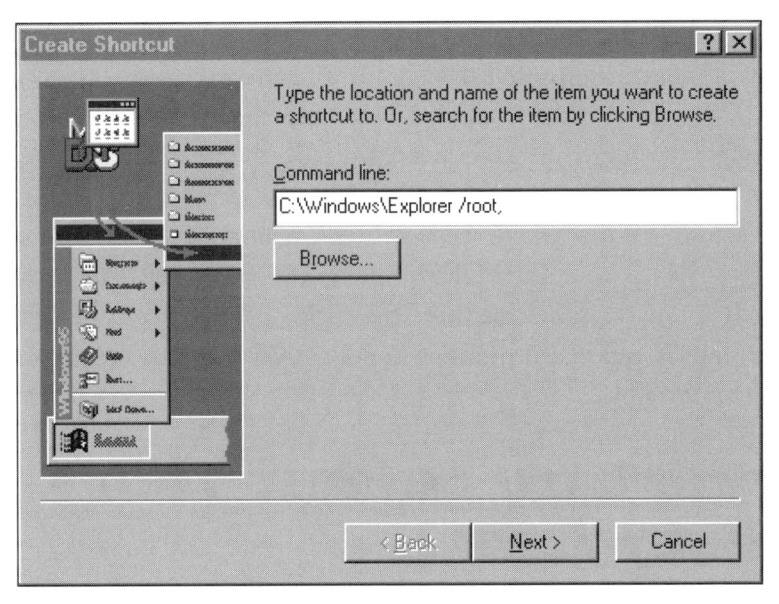

Figure 12.20 Creating a Shortcut to the desktop.

right-click on your desktop and select New|Folder. Name your folder, then drag your desktop icons into the folder.

More Favorites Folders

Having recently developed your Favorites folder, you are probably satisfied with the arrangement—and you should be. But there are other Favorites folder options that you might want to use in the future. For example, you can create any number of Favorites folders and name them whatever you want. Basically, a Favorites folder is a folder containing links to the Internet. As I mentioned earlier, the default path for your Favorites folder is C:\WINDOWS\Favorites—but the default folder doesn't have to be the only Favorites folder around. I recommend creating Favorites folders for any occasion, especially if you are doing research or if multiple people are using the same system.

Let's say you are doing some research on frogs. First, you would probably create a Frogs folder on your hard drive to hold your frog documents. While you're at it, create a Frog Jumps folder on your desktop or inside your Frogs folder. Now, when you're leaping from link to link on the Internet and you find the Froggy Web page (it's a real page, by the way: **http://www.cs.yale.edu/homes/sjl/froggy.html**), you can create a link to the page on your desktop, rename the link, and then drag the link into your Frog Jumps folder. You've just started a new Favorites folder where you can store all your relevant Frog research information. To access your Frog Jump links from within MSIE, execute the Favorites|Organize Favorites command and direct MSIE to your Frog Jumps folder. You will be able to click on the Frog links in the same manner you click on other Favorite links. This technique is especially useful whenever you want to create a specific collection of links.

The History Folder: Your Last 300 URLs

Remember when we were talking about your History list under the Go menu in Chapter 11? Below your Go menu History list, there is an option to open your History folder. Little did you know that while you were surfing the Web, your History folder was keeping track of your stops—up to 300 of them! Not only does this folder log your trail, but it enables you to revisit sites of your choice. To revisit a site listed in your History folder, simply open the folder and click on the history link. By default, your History folder is located in C:\WINDOWS\History. You can open your History folder locally, or you can execute MSIE's Go|Open History folder command. Once your History folder is open, you can double click on a link to visit a Web site, you can copy and move links out of the folder to create shortcut links and Favorites, or you can delete links to create more space on your hard drive. Currently, in the beta version I am running, there is no way to change the setting to log fewer than 300 sites. Rumor has it that you will be able to change your History folder setting in later versions of MSIE.

Keeping Up on Your History Folder

Microsoft is continuing to perfect MSIE's history management. In the meantime, check in on your History folder often. The first time I viewed my History folder's contents, I found over 2,000 stored links! Needless to say, I've been checking and emptying my History folder ever since.

Chapter in Review

MSIE gains much of its edge by integrating Windows features with browser capabilities. Shortcuts that feel comfortable in Windows 95 are welcomed with open arms in MSIE.

MSIE provides right-click menu opportunities at every turn and accepts keyboard commands with grace. MSIE also provides the innovative feature of link-to-link tabbing. And of course, nobody in software design circles omits the drag-and-drop feature anymore—MSIE feels a lot like Windows 95 in that respect.

Admittedly, finding, storing, and organizing links to Internet sites can be tricky, but with a little planning, your links can become extremely useful tools.

Finally, if you ever need to backtrack, don't forget about the links hiding in your History folder—300 links (give or take a few hundred). The list of past sites waits patiently to serve you if the occasion arises.

If you are interested in learning more about shortcuts, I suggest you turn to the Internet. Run a few searches on topics such as *shortcuts, Explorer hints, Windows tricks,* or…? (you decide). So far, many netizens benevolently pass along cool browser and Internet tricks as they discover them. Good luck, and, if you think of more cool tricks, feel free to pass them along.

Finding and Downloading Files 13

Microsoft Internet Explorer makes downloading incredible files from the Internet easy. Try it and see.

One of the best perks of being on the Internet is the ability to download and try thousands of programs for almost nothing. There are over 1,200 Internet sites that contain downloadable files for anyone who wants them, and new files are being placed into them every day. The process of downloading these files, which simply means transferring them from the Internet onto your computer's hard drive, is done by a process called File Transfer Protocol (FTP). This chapter is devoted to helping you find the files you're interested in downloading, and then use MSIE's downloading feature to store them in your computer. Once you realize how easy it is to get the programs you're interested in, you'll be hooked!

Before we jump feet first into the Internet FTP game, though, let's back up a minute so I can explain a few key aspects of what you'll need to have so you can FTP successfully, and what you should know about the types of files you'll be finding.

Zipping and Unzipping

No, I'm not talking about your clothes here, I'm referring to the files you'll find on the Internet. Many files are "zipped," which means that they are compressed. Basically, compression reduces a file's storage requirements, sometimes by as much as 80 percent. The benefits of file compression are twofold. First, it doesn't require as much storage space on the Net, which means there's room for more files. Second, a zipped file takes a lot less time to download, which means less time (and money) spent by you waiting for it to transfer from the Internet to your computer's hard drive.

But once you've downloaded a zipped file, you need to have a way to "unzip" it. That's where programs like WinZip come in. This shareware program (more on shareware in a moment) is a suite of utilities that both zips and unzips files. WinZip is one of the most popular utilities on the Internet (since you need it to take advantage of most of the other files out there), and we'll be downloading it later. But how do you unzip WinZip. Well, instead of making WinZip a zipped file, the creators of Winzip made it a *self-extracting* file, which means once it downloads, you simply have to double click on the file in Windows Explorer and it will open itself. The main user interface of WinZip is shown in Figure 13.1.

Public Domain, Shareware, and Freeware

Almost all of the files available for downloading on the Internet fall into one of three categories: *public domain*, *shareware*, and *freeware*. These terms basically concern the conditions of ownership of the program. For instance, there are no restrictions on the use or redistribution of public domain software. If you wanted to, you could even try to sell the software. However, public domain software is also the least common software found on the Internet, since it's obviously not a money-making venture. It's often government or university sponsored.

Shareware is similar to the commercial software that you're used to, but it's paid for on the honor system. Basically, you can download the software and try it out, pass it on to friends, or whatever you choose. The program

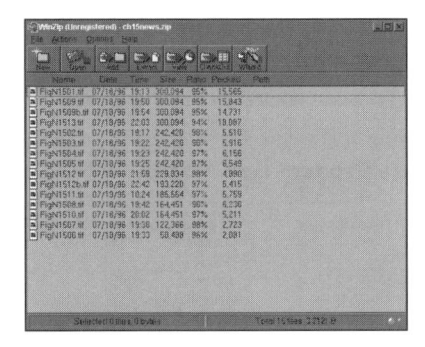

Figure 13.1 WinZip is one of the most useful tools a Web surfer can have.

is generally fully functional, so what you see is what you get. However, sometimes you get extra options from the creators if you register your copy. If you don't like the program and never use it, that's the end of it. However, if you use a shareware program on a regular basis, then you are legally and morally obligated to pay for it; it's only fair to the people who spent a lot of their own time developing this software that you think is so cool that you use it regularly. WinZip, which I mentioned earlier, is one of the most popular pieces of shareware around.

Freeware, as its name implies, is absolutely free (free is good!). The difference between freeware and public domain software is that the software is copyrighted, and therefore might have a number of conditions attached. For instance, it could be free for non-commercial use, but require a licensing fee for commercial use. Microsoft Internet Explorer falls into the freeware category—it's free, but you know Microsoft would come after you with an army of lawyers if you tried to modify it and sell it as your own!

Finding the Files You Want

The most obvious place to look for downloadable files is on your start page (if you use The Microsoft Network page as your start page, which we suggested earlier in this book). If you look at the page, you'll see the words "free software" on the left-hand side of the screen. Clicking on those words will bring you to Microsoft's Free Product Downloads page, shown in Figure 13.2.

Microsoft has a number of files related to their programs that you can download—including Microsoft Internet Explorer. Well, we already have

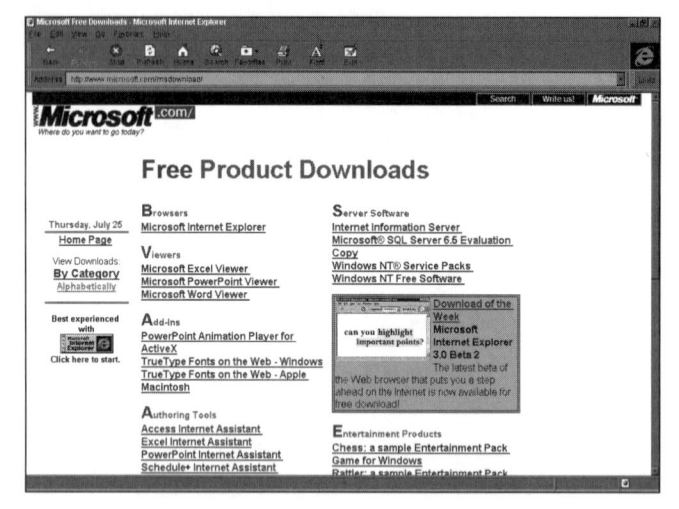

Figure 13.2 You can download lots of goodies from Microsoft's page.

that, so let's look for something else. Under the heading Entertainment Products is a program called Dangerous Creatures theme for Windows 95 that looks interesting. Someone I work with has it, and it makes a really neat desktop scene. Basically, it'll give your Windows 95 desktop a different background (a wildcat), some interesting-looking icons, and an undersea screensaver (complete with shark). Personally, I wouldn't mind having that on my computer, so let's make Dangerous Creatures our first downloading adventure.

Simply click on the hypertext Dangerous Creatures and you'll be taken to a screen touting the benefits of Microsoft Plus! (which contains the Dangerous Creatures theme), as well as instructions on how to download and then open Dangerous Creatures. After you've read these extremely simple instructions, click anywhere on the hypertext in Instruction 1.

When you click on this, or any download link, MSIE will display a dialog box, shown in Figure 13.3, warning you that some files can contain viruses, and to be sure that this file comes from a trustworthy source. Well, because Dangerous Creatures is from Microsoft, it is probably a safe file; however, this is a valid warning. Because some files can contain viruses, once you learn how to use FTP search engines later in this chapter, I recommend that you download a virus scanner as your first order of business.

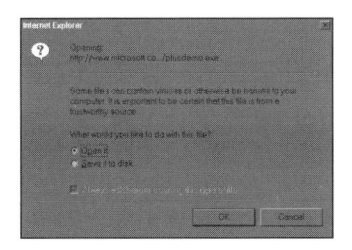

Figure 13.3 MSIE gives you the option of opening the file right away, or saving it.

Microsoft then offers you two options of what to do when the file downloads: open it or save it to disk. The default option is opening a file, which means that the file will run right after it downloads. Saving it to disk means that it will be saved on your hard drive (or on an actual disk, if you prefer and it fits) so that you can open it later at your leisure. I personally prefer to save it to disk, so I can open it after I've quit MSIE.

Finally, at the bottom of the dialog box is a check box asking if you want this box to always come up when you're downloading. I suggest keeping this box checked because it reminds you to think about what you're downloading and what you want to do with it.

After you choose to save the file to disk, you'll be presented with a Save As dialog box like the one shown in Figure 13.4. This is the same Save As dialog box that you'll find in most Windows applications. Simply navigate through the folders until you find the one you want to save the file in. In this case, the Microsoft site says to download the file into its own folder. Normally, I would place it into a temp (as in temporary) file, which you can create in Windows Explorer (the former File Manager). If you download your file into the temp file, and you like it, then you can put it into a

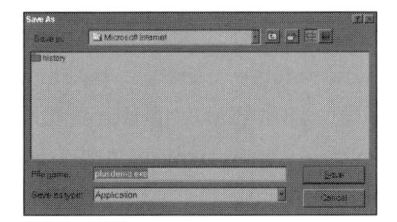

Figure 13.4 Microsoft's standard Save As dialog box.

different folder using Windows Explorer. However, if you don't like it, having it in one place makes it easy to delete.

After you click on the Save button, a final dialog box will appear, counting down the amount of time left (in seconds) until the file is finished downloading. A status bar also ticks across the screen as the file downloads, and a piece of paper flies from folder to folder at the top of the box, letting you know the download is taking place. These timers are rarely accurate, but the speed at which the time ticks down (or the status bar slides across the screen) will give you a good idea of how long the program will take to download.

When the file has finished downloading, simply navigate through the folder hierarchy to the temp directory, and then just follow the instructions on Microsoft's page—you'll soon be hearing animal noises coming from your computer. Figure 13.5 shows what your desktop will look like.

Opening Multiple Windows

Explorer allows you to open multiple browser windows to make the most of your online time. To open additional browser windows from the Windows 95 desktop, select File|Open and enter the appropriate URL. To open a window to one of your Internet favorites, select the Browse button and choose from your Favorites list.

If you're already downloading something in MSIE, simply select File|New Window to open additional Explorer windows. This can be a great time saver—you can download and surf at the same time!

Search Engines

There are currently a number of different search engines that are devoted solely to finding downloadable files. I'll be reviewing two of the most popular, shareware.com and Harvest Broker, for you in this chapter. However, if you simply want to browse through some software libraries, there are a number of enormous FTP sites you can look through. Some of the bigger ones are WinSite (**http://www.winsite.com**) and Garbo (**http://garbo.uwasa.fi**). I list several more sites at the end of this chapter.

Figure 13.5 The Dangerous Animals desktop scene.

We'll go visit WinSite later in this chapter. For now, let's try to find that WinZip program that I was telling you about earlier. Because it's so essential for opening compressed files, WinZip should be the first program we look for. Let's start our search using shareware.com.

SHAREWARE.COM

Located at **http://www.shareware.com**, shareware.com was created in 1995 from the Virtual Software Library. This search engine allows you to search over 190,000 software files. Its home page gives you the opportunity to perform a simple search, or look at some of the programs it has highlighted as worth downloading. The simple search form, shown in Figure 13.6, is extremely easy to use. There's only one choice you need to make—from a pull-down menu that offers a number of different platforms (Windows, DOS, MAC, etc.) to choose from.

Personally, I like to have a little more control in my searching, so let's take a look at the complete Quick Search form, shown in Figure 13.7. You can get to the complete form by clicking on the word Search in the shareware.com graphic at the top of each page.

There are four options on the Quick Search form that you can use to modify your search. The first, and most important, is the pull-down menu that

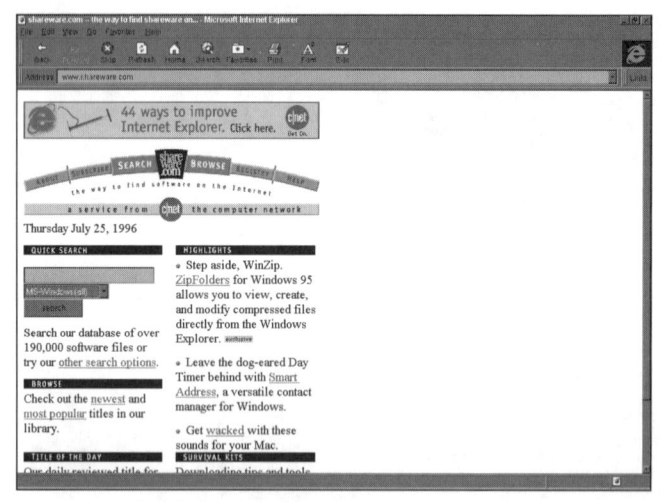

Figure 13.6 The shareware.com search form.

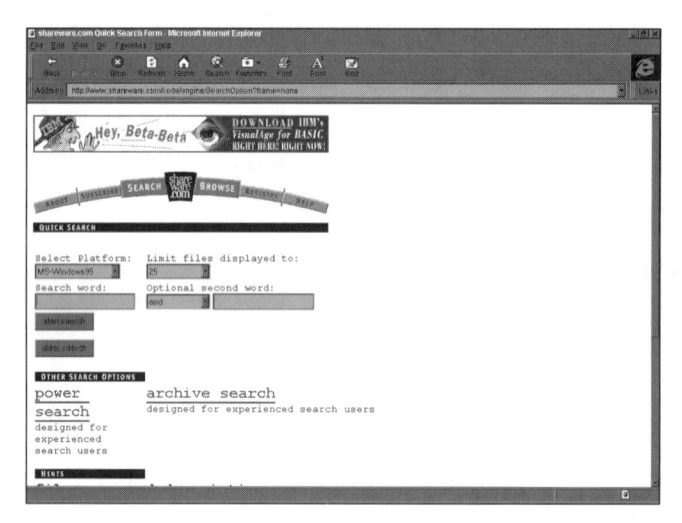

Figure 13.7 The Quick Search form available from shareware.com.

allows you to choose what platform you want the software to support. The second pull-down menu allows you to choose the number of responses you want returned. Remember, though, that bigger isn't always better. If you ask for shareware.com to return 50 different files that match your keywords, it'll take a lot longer than if you stick to 10 or 25. The third and fourth choices you'll have to make are what keywords you want to use. You can use one or two, to help narrow your search. The pull-down menu between the two keyword text boxes lets you choose *and* if you want both keywords included in what you're looking for, and *or* if you want either word, but not both, to figure into the search's response. (For more about keywords and searches, see Chapter 10.)

Let's start a search. Choose MS-Windows95 as your platform of choice, limit your search to 10 files (for a quick response time), and simply type *winzip* into the first text box. (Remember, most searches aren't case sensitive.) Then, click on the *start search* button. Figure 13.8 shows the first few results of our WinZip search.

shareware.com displays its results in order by what archive (the site that contains the files) the files are in. The name of the file is displayed in hypertext, with a brief description of the file beside it. In my search, my second result was named winzip95.exe, and the description said it was WinZip version 6.1 for Windows 95. Below this information is the date the file was placed in the archive and the size of the file. shareware.com has successfully found exactly what we were looking for!

To download this version of WinZip, simply click on the hypertext file name and you'll be taken to shareware.com's Download Options page, shown in Figure 13.9. This is one of the best features of shareware.com—

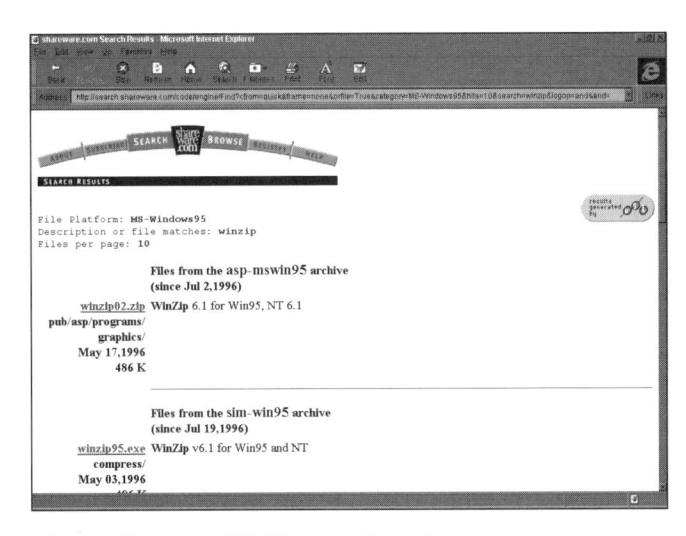

Figure 13.8 The results of our WinZip search on shareware.com.

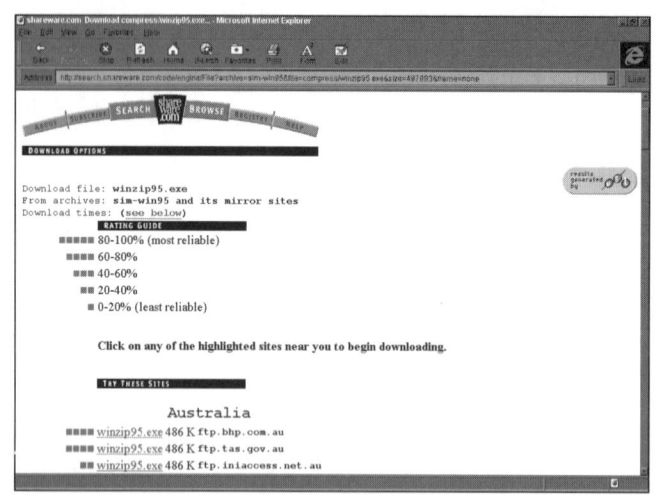

Figure 13.9 The Download Options page provides a lot of choices.

it gives you a list of sites that you can download the program from, and then rates those sites on their reliability. It first lists a number of sites in the United States you can try, and then lists other sites all over the world. That way, if one site doesn't respond or is too slow because a lot of people are using it, you can try another.

The hypertext files listed here are connected to the files in the archive listed to the right of the file name. When you click on one of these links, you will be traveling to that site, and MSIE's downloading process will automatically kick in. Because WinZip is a program you'll definitely want to keep, I suggest that you download it into a permanent *winzip* directory, so that you'll know where to find it later on.

If Quick Search hadn't brought back the files we wanted, we could have tried a Power Search as a follow-up (the form just has more pull-down menus so you can define your search more precisely). However, in most cases, a Quick Search will be all you need.

Also, if you're interested in just browsing, shareware.com has a list of the most popular and newest files available for downloading. Simply click on the word Browse in the menu at the top of all of shareware.com's pages, and you'll be taken to a page listing the most popular files, divided into different categories. Happy browsing!

Harvest Broker

If you aren't interested in paying someone for their program, then Harvest Broker is for you, because it only searches for freeware (remember, free is good!). It searches six of the largest and most popular FTP sites (one of which we'll be visiting on our own later on), which among them contain over 35,000 freeware programs. Let's take a look at Harvest Broker's search form, shown in Figure 13.10, which can be found at **http://www.town.hall.org/Harvest/brokers/pcindex/query.html**.

As you can see from Figure 13.10, Harvest Broker's search form is pretty simple. The form gives you one text box for entering keywords. There are also several check box options below the Submit button. The first two check boxes are checked by default. The first establishes whether or not to rank the results, and the second tells Harvest Broker whether or not to include a description of the files. The third check box allows Harvest Broker to create links to summaries of information about the files. (Personally, I found the summaries to be completely useless information; I'd just ignore that option.) Finally, the last option is a pull-down menu that allows you to limit the number of results that will be returned in your search.

Okay, let's face it, one of the best reasons (at least in my opinion) to download files is to get some really cool games. Let's do a search for poker, one of my

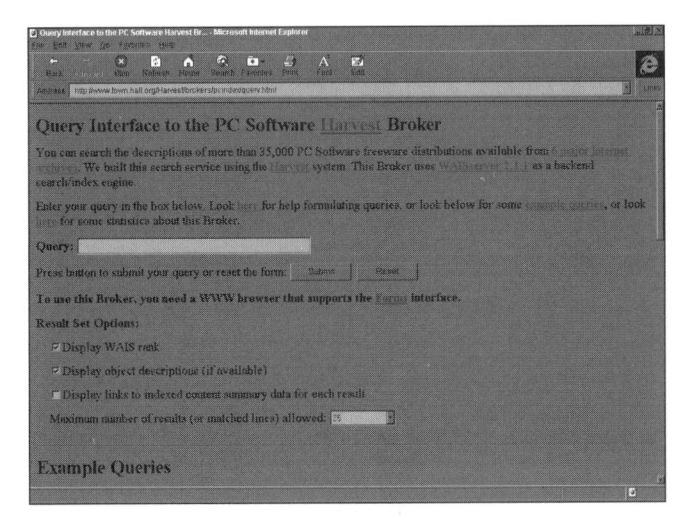

Figure 13.10   Get your free programs at Harvest Broker.

favorite card games. Simply type *poker* in the text box and click on the Submit button—remember, the two check boxes near the bottom of the page are checked by default, so we don't need to worry about them.

Figure 13.11 shows the results of our search. Harvest Broker found nine different poker programs. The results page gives you the name of each file, with a (very) brief description, and the URL of the archive where it can be found. Clicking on the hypertext name of the file will then download the file onto your computer, again setting MSIE's automatic downloading feature into action. And the best part is, because all these programs are free, you can keep and use as many as you like!

Doing It on Your Own

Search engines are great if you know what you're looking for, but a lot of times you just want to look around to see what's out there. There are hundreds of FTP sites out there for you to browse through, some containing thousands of files. Let's take a look at one of them.

WinSite

WinSite claims to be "The Planet's Largest Software Archive for Windows," so it seems like a great place to poke around for files. Type

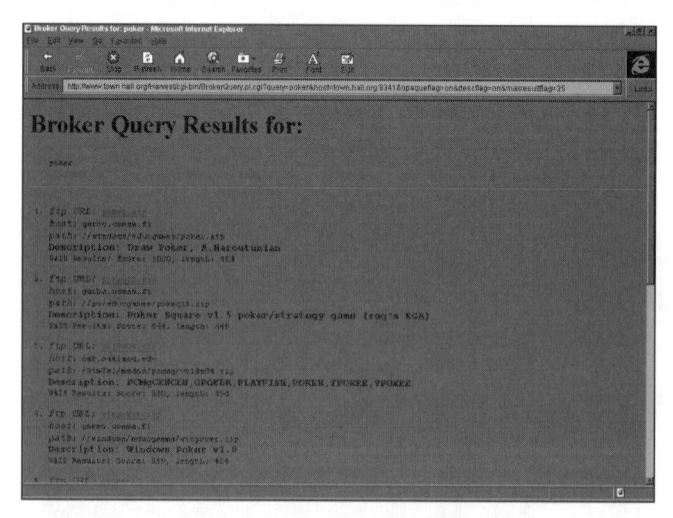

Figure 13.11   Deal me in for Harvest Broker's poker games.

http://www.winsite.com into the Address box at the top of the MSIE screen and press Enter. WinSite's home page is shown in Figure 13.12.

WinSite's home page has a number of options for us to choose from, including its own search engine. But like we said before, we're just browsing, so let's click on Browse Archive. (Normally, I'd go look in Hot Software, but for some reason, at WinSite, this area doesn't list the most popular files, just the most recent additions.) The next screen allows you to choose whether you're interested in software for Windows 3.1, Windows 95, or Windows NT. Let's look in Windows 95 and see what we can find.

Don't Just Look at Win95 Software

Just because you're using Windows 95, don't ignore software made for Windows 3.1. Most of the software will still work on your computer, just not in Windows 95 format. Many shareware, and especially freeware, developers just haven't jumped into Windows 95 yet. If you want to, you can even look into DOS software, it just won't be as simple as point and click. It's all worth looking into.

WinSite now presents you with another list to choose from; this time it's categories of software that you can look through to narrow down what

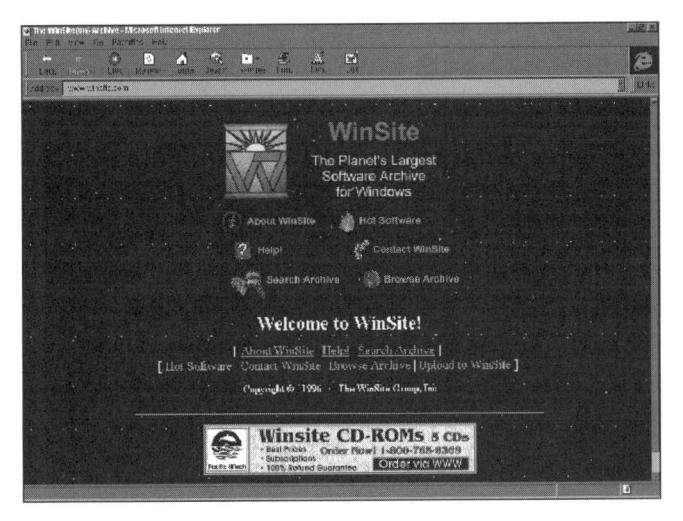

Figure 13.12 Browsing on our own for software at WinSite.

exactly it is you're looking for. The choices range from the very technical (programming files and Visual Basic function libraries) to the more low-key (games and Word for Windows files). Let's look somewhere in between. This book has shown me that I could use some help with scheduling and organization, so let's look in *pim*, which stands for Personal Information Management Systems.

We've finally gotten to the end of our browsing road—the software. WinSite lists all the applicable software in the personal management category, along with a brief one-line description and the size of the file. Don't ignore the size—if it's huge, it will take you a long time to download, and that free software won't seem so cheap when you get the bill from your Internet Service Provider.

Aha! What I'm looking for is right at the top of WinSite's list—a visual day planner for Windows 95. But wait, that's a huge file! It'll probably take me half an hour to download, at least. Let's see if we can find something a bit smaller. Further down the page is something called Organizer with Post-It note interface. That sounds interesting…and it's a heck of a lot smaller than the day planner, so let's try it. Now all I need to do to download it is click on the hypertext, and MSIE will take over. Here's hoping it will help my organizational problems!

Getting Down to the Nitty Gritty

Note that as you've been going through this FTP site, your choices have gotten narrower—this is how most FTP sites are organized. The site begins with a broad category, such as the computer platform you're currently using, and then narrows your field some more by giving you another page with a limited number of choices, which again require you to narrow your search. Some FTP sites can go on for a few pages like this, but eventually, they all come to a page containing downloadable files that match the requirements you've been asked to choose. If you don't like what you've found at any point, you can just click on the back button at the top of the MSIE browser and just choose a different hypertext category.

Chapter in Review

In this chapter, you've learned how to find and retrieve files from FTP sites, and from Microsoft. There's no big secret to finding files on the Internet, it's as easy as point and click. And MSIE makes it easy to store them wherever you want on your hard drive, so you can find it (or delete it) later on.

There are files out there for everyone in the family, so don't limit yourself to just looking for games. If you look hard, you can find cookbooks, programs to help you organize your stamp or record collection, software that will teach you another language, and even software to help you write more software. If you can't find them using the FTP search engines, try using one of the search engines we discussed in Chapter 10. More often than not, they'll help you find what you're looking for.

Other Useful Sites

Along with the sites reviewed in this chapter, the sites listed here are a starting point for finding interesting items to download. There are plenty of places left, however, for you to explore on your own.

http://www.u-net.com/axiom/links/net
This site contains a number of freeware programs, as well as interesting screensavers. Check out the one from British Columbia!

http://www.gamesdomain.com/freebies/index.html
This site's URL pretty much speaks for itself.

http://www.tucows.com
This site calls itself the world's largest site for Winsock software. This is the place to go to download Internet-related programs, such as chat software, browsers, and more.

http://hoohoo.ncsa.uiuc.edu
This site calls itself the Monster FTP Sites List, so it's a good bet that this is the place to start looking for FTP sites.

Microsoft Internet Mail 14

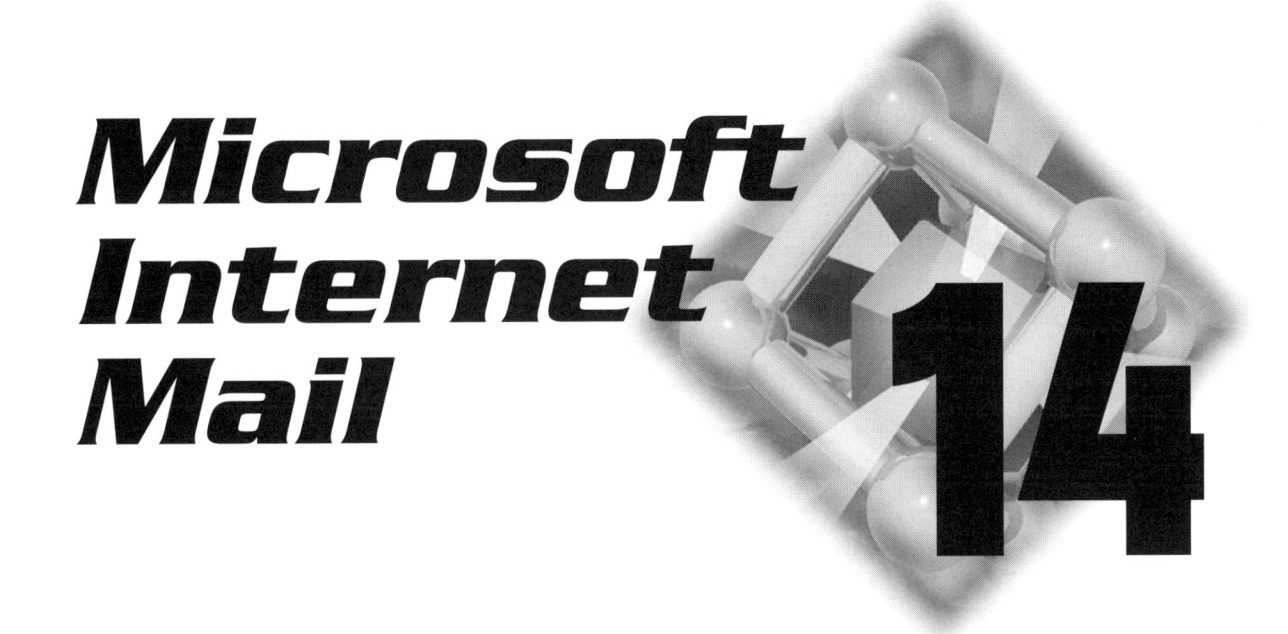

Email is the fastest-growing communications tool around. Learn how to use it to keep in touch with your friends, family, and business associates.

With the tips in this chapter, you'll master Mail's functions and learn more than just the basics. Plain and simple—email is easy to understand and master. As long as you've typed the address correctly, or correctly placed it in the Address Book, your message will get to where it's supposed to go. But beyond these basics, there's a lot more you can do with Microsoft Internet Mail. You can share shortcuts with friends, participate in Listservs, send messages with hyperlinks, and expand your Internet imagination.

Better than the daily visit from the postman is the instant access to email through the Internet Mail client. At any time of the day or night, there's a good chance I (and you, too, once you get up to speed) have mail waiting.

A little elementary stuff. Before you read this section, make sure you have the Mail and Newsgroup clients ready. I keep them as shortcut icons on my desktop for super-quick access, as shown in Figure 14.1, but, as with many Microsoft products, you have choices. If you like Windows 95 shortcuts, you can launch the Mail icon on your desktop. To add the Internet

Mail icon to your desktop, use Start|Find, select "Files or Folders" and type "Mail". As the software versions change, yours may be identified as Mail or as Internet Mail. Just right-click on the icon and select Create Shortcut. A dialog box will ask if you would like the shortcut placed on the desktop. Select the Yes button.

If you keep your Internet Service Provider's Dialup Networking icon on your desktop, you might start with that. Neatniks with organized desktops might prefer to clear all icons from the desktop and start the program by selecting the Mail icon found under My Computer. Yet another option resides under the Start button. If that's your choice, select Programs|Internet Mail. Finally, if you're in MSIE, you can choose Go|Read Mail.

Using the Microsoft Internet Mail Service

If you're like me, the first thing you do each day is check to see if you have any mail. If someone were to run a study of email users, I would guess that

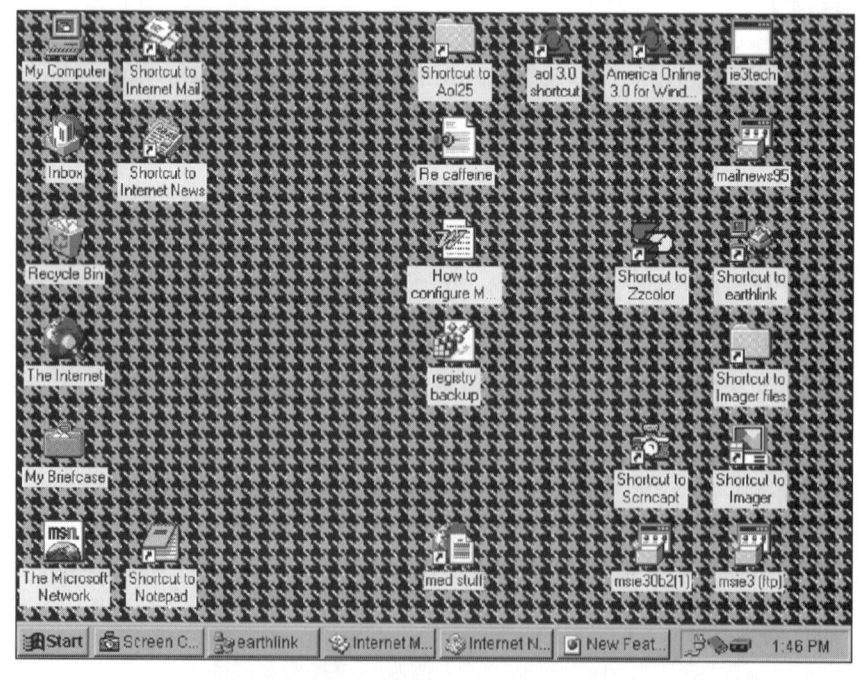

Figure 14.1 My desktop is a bit like my closet—somewhat organized. Explorer, Mail, News, and Earthlink (my ISP) are easily accessible.

99 out of 100 Internet users find email to be addictive. When my email friends travel without a laptop, they refer to that time as having gone cold turkey! So let's add another addict to the bunch. Choose your preferred launch, start Mail, and let's go.

Let's take a quick spin at sending a message. I'm going to walk you through by using the large icons on the top of the Mail window. If yours don't appear, look under the View menu and select Toolbar. To open a new message window, select the icon for New Message. In the top line, next to the Rolodex card, type the Internet Address. It's OK to use mine: **LuanneO@earthlink.net**. The keyboard command, Tab, will move your cursor to the next line, or you can just use your mouse to click in each space. Add the Subject and complete your note in the body of the message. When complete, just select the icon from the Toolbar that looks like an addressed and stamped envelope, and then select the Send and Receive icon. Your mail is on its way to me.

Redialing Made Easy

Dialup Networking (DUN) is a feature that can be set to quickly redial a number that is busy. To take advantage of redialing with DUN, select My Computer|Dialup Networking|Connection|Settings. At this point, check Redial, and set the number of times you would like DUN to retry the number and the time to wait between redial attempts. So the next time you can't get in touch with your ISP, let DUN do the redialing work for you.

What I just described is the most simple way to send email. As we progress through this chapter, I'll show you many of the options that you can utilize to make the most of Microsoft Internet Mail. The Address Book will aid efficiency, and "automation" can be added to save steps along the way.

The Toolbar

The toolbar is the best feature of Internet Mail. Right-click on the toolbar and you will discover a new world of options by selecting the most appropriate buttons, determining the alignment, and choosing to show the icon buttons with or without text. Select Customize the Toolbar and you will be greeted by a window that carries a list of available buttons on the left and the current toolbar buttons on the right, as shown in Figure 14.2. The toolbar arrives with New Message, Reply to Author, Reply to All, Forward, and Send and Receive. The original buttons can be removed (or kept) and eleven other buttons can be added. My screen holds eight buttons comfortably and yours may hold a few more.

To reorganize the left to right display of the buttons on the toolbar, use the Move Up and Move Down buttons in the Customize Toolbar window. The leftmost toolbar button on the Internet Mail window corresponds to the top toolbar button on the list.

Flex the Toolbar

With the first launch, the toolbar appears at the top of the Internet Mail window. If you'd prefer to have it on the left, right-click on the toolbar. A window will pop up, and you can select Align|Left, and the toolbar will move to the left of the screen.

Addressing Mail

My Internet address is **LuanneO@earthlink.net**. Earthlink is my Internet Service Provider (ISP). *LuanneO* is my user name and *earthlink.net* is the domain name. You'll find a similar address for each of your online friends. When sending email, you must use the entire address. Don't trust your memory, add the complete user name and domain name to the Address

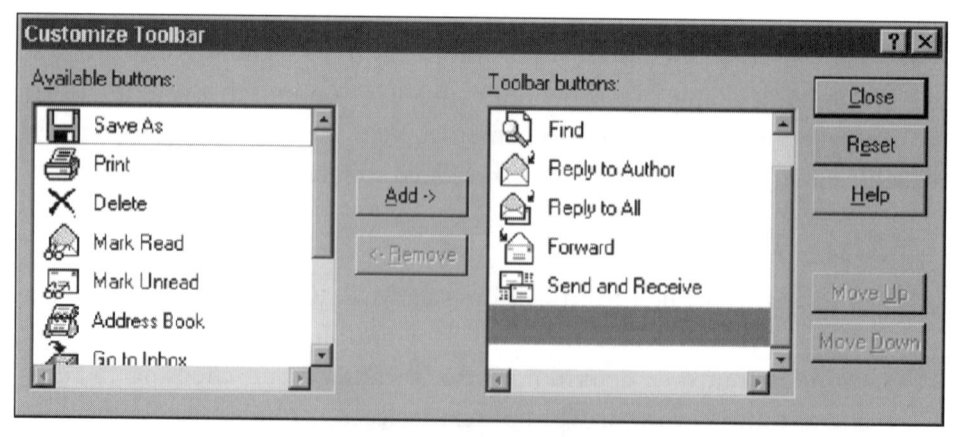

Figure 14.2 Customize the toolbar to make Mail work for you.

Book (see the next section). When you are replying to a message, however, you don't need to enter the address, just click on Reply, and Mail will return your email note to the proper address.

Generally, it only takes a few minutes for your Internet mail to reach its destination, but your letter to your old flame may get delayed at a few points along the way. It is possible, but not likely, that there will be a delay leaving your ISP. Mail is more likely to be delayed entering an online service, than leaving its destination. If your mail is going to another online service, there may be a delay due to the volume on their servers. But, trust me on this one, as long as it is addressed properly, it will always beat the U.S. Postal Service!

Using the Address Book

The Address Book is used to store the addresses of your online pals. You can enter addresses at your leisure by accessing the Address Book through the File menu. That way, when you begin a new mail message, you can simply plop the address into the message by selecting the Pick Recipient icon from the toolbar.

To make an entry in the Address Book, select the Address Book from the File menu and then select New Contact. As indicated on screen, complete the lines for First Name, Middle Name, Last Name, and E-Mail Address; then click Add and OK. You'll see that you can add multiple addresses for each contact. If you wish to review or edit entries, select a name and then select Properties.

There's an easy way to add someone to your Address Book once you receive an email from them. Double click to open the mail, right click on the "From" name, and a box will pop-up. With one click on Add To Address Book, your selection will be made. You can also make this selection under the File menu. Unfortunately, this little timesaver does not work in the Preview mode.

The Address Book can be sorted by Name (first or last), E-Mail Address, Business Phone, or Home Phone. No matter which column is selected for the sort, you may also arrange the entries in ascending or descending order. Simply click on the column to indicate your preference, or look under View|Sort by.

When you are writing an email, you have four ways to access the Address Book. The first option is to type the name as you know it. Second, if you are unsure or like to double check your work, use the Check Names selection to verify or correct the entry. Another option is to select the icon labeled Pick Recipients. The fourth method, and my preferred choice, is to double click on the Rolodex card, which will bring up the Address Book. It can also be accessed under the File menu.

Microsoft has made it easy to update transfer addresses from Windows Messaging (formerly known as Exchange) or other email clients. For more information, refer to the sections on Importing and Exporting later in this chapter.

You can also access the Pick Recipients and Check Names options from the Mail menu or an active email window. Check Names can be thought of as a spell-checker for your addresses. If you manually enter an email address and then select Check Names, the program will verify if it matches an address in the Address Book, or if it is in the format of an Internet address. Once recognized as valid, it will appear with an underline.

Quick Adds

To quickly add a recognized name to your Address Book, right click on the name.

GROUPS OF FRIENDS

Just prior to travel, I'll often send a copy of my itinerary to friends or family. With the Groups feature of the Address Book, I can preset groups of mail recipients. I've set up a group called "Friends" for my favorite email correspondents, "MSIE Project" for my correspondents at Coriolis, and others for relatives on both sides of the family.

You can set up a group by selecting File|Address Book|New Group. Group members are selected from those already appearing in your Address Book. As you add individuals, they are added to the Address Book and then added to the group.

Let's walk through the creation of a new group for the MSIE Project. With the Address Book open, select the icon for New Group. In the next screen, enter the Group Name: MSIE Project. Select Add; this will bring up a window with the Address Book list. Select from the left column, and use the Add button to move the selected names to the Members column on the right. If a name does not appear on the list, use the New Contact button to add the individual to the Address Book. I'd previously entered both Mary and Toni, so it's easy to move their entries to the Members list on the right. Next, select OK, review the group, and select OK again. As shown in Figure 14.3, the group is now complete and available in the Address Book.

When you need to modify a group, names can be deleted from the group or from the Address Book list. When an individual name is deleted from the Address Book, it is also removed from any group.

Setting View Options

Let's take a quick tour through some of the options offered by Microsoft Internet Mail.

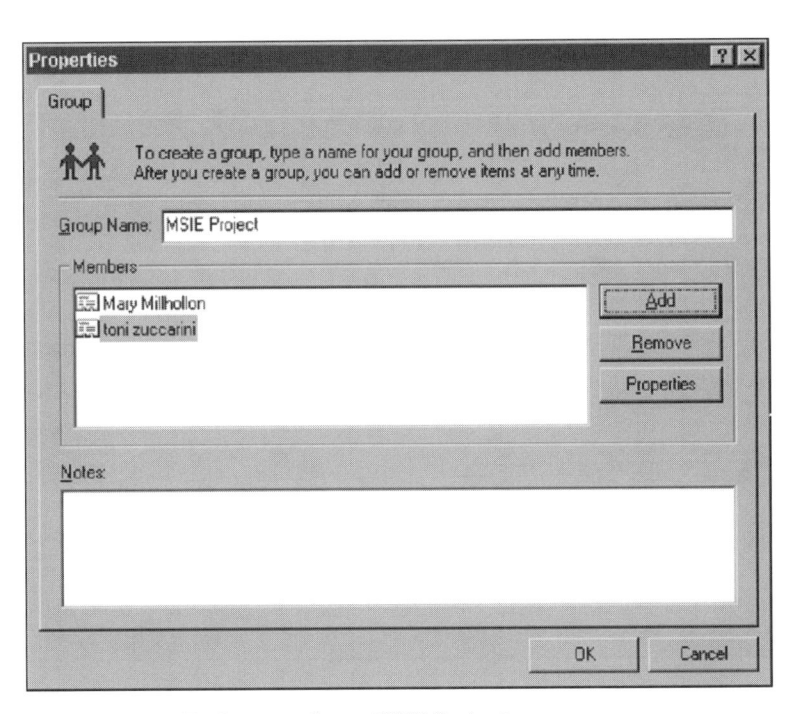

Figure 14.3 **Mary and Toni appear in my MSIE Project group.**

Previewing Your Mail

My favorite feature is Preview. It lets me speed read through my email. I average 30 inbound messages per day and I need help managing my mail. A good deal of help!

To set up Preview, select View|Preview Pane. At this point, you can use the arrow keys to move up and down the list, displaying the contents of each piece of mail in the adjacent window. The Preview Pane can be divided horizontally from the Mail List (Mail List at the top, Preview Pane at the bottom), or the sections can be divided vertically (Mail List on the left, Preview Pane on the right). To expand or reduce the size of either the Preview or Mail List, simply rest the cursor on the dividing line until the cursor becomes a double-pointing arrow, and then click and hold your right mouse button and slide to resize the panes. In Figure 14.4, the Preview Pane options are shown. You can also choose to suppress the display of the Preview Pane altogether when you need the full view of the mail list.

Preview works for all mail folders so that you will be previewing the messages in your Inbox, Outbox, and all designated folders.

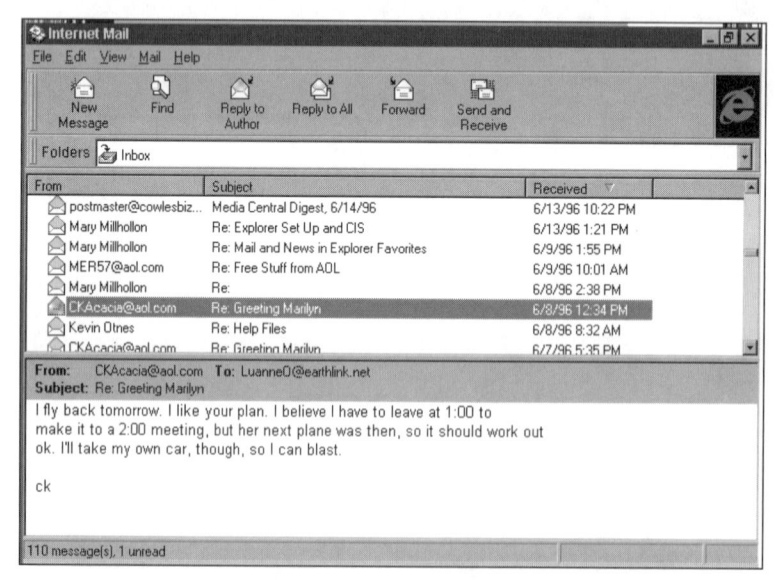

Figure 14.4 CK's message is shown with the horizontal Preview option.

I am on four email groups that are not set up as Listserv mailing lists. We'll discuss Listservs in detail later in this chapter. What this means is that messages from my email groups arrive with 60 screen names or Internet addresses in the header. (Thank goodness I can now use the Groups feature in the Address Book for outbound mail!) Such large headers can obscure the text in the Preview Pane. To minimize that agonizing and painful scroll list, and to keep my Previews efficient, I have selected the option *not to show* the message headers in the Preview. Should I need to see the header, I can double click to select the mail to be read, and it will open with the full header information. To show or hide header information in the Preview Pane, simply select View|Preview Pane|Header Information. From there, you can toggle Header Information on and off.

Another way to clean up your view is to delete the status bar and toolbar by selecting the View menu and deselecting the appropriate option. I choose to show the toolbar. I don't like to have too much real estate on my screen occupied by various toolbars, and Mail makes it easy for me to customize the screens to the way I work.

Sorting Your Mail

Under the View menu, Sort By is your key to selecting how you would like to view your mail. I have selected to sort by the date received, in descending order (ascending order is also available), with the most recent mail appearing at the top of the list, as shown in Figure 14.5. When I look at the list, there are two indications that I have unread mail: The subject line appears in boldfaced text, and it is preceded by the addressed envelope. Conversely, if the subject is not in boldface and the envelope is open, the mail has been read.

Click the column heading to change from ascending to descending. Prefer it the other way? Click again! You can also sort alphabetically by author and alphabetically by subject. In case you were wondering, RE and FW are disregarded when the list is alphabetized.

Just as with Preview, you can resize the columns' width by placing the cursor on the vertical line between the headers. When the arrow becomes double-pointed, you can click and hold to resize the columns.

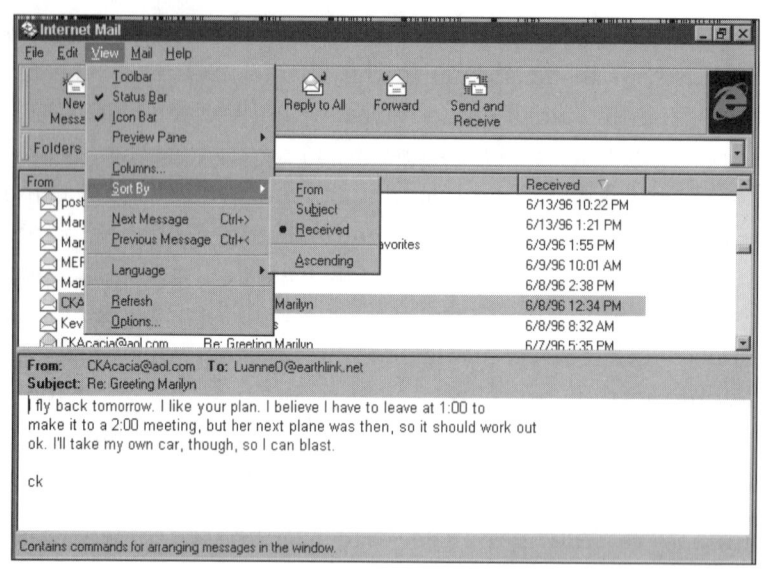

Figure 14.5 Use Sort By to rearrange Mail to work best for you.

Making Mail Work for You

Whenever I move to a new city (and that's about every two years), I want to learn how to get around town safely. After that, I start learning shortcuts. The same can be said for any new computer program I work with. First, I want to know the safest way to get things done, and then I want to know the fastest route around. Lucky for me (and you), Microsoft Internet Mail provides several options to make the most of my time. Let's take a look at just what Mail can do for you.

Customizing Your Replies

If you aren't on top of your mail situation (which can easily happen if you find yourself disconnected due to travel), your replies to old messages may seem out of the blue to the receiver. In fact, this happened to me just the other day, only I was on the receiving end. I received a one-liner to a message I had written weeks ago. The message didn't make any sense to me. I had to call the sender and ask what the heck he meant. Microsoft remedies this situation by allowing you to include the original message in your reply. Using Mail|Options|Send, you can make selections so the program will grab all of the text in the previous message and place it in your reply. If you are only replying to one paragraph or to selected text, cut the excess text from the reply before sending. In the world of Internet etiquette, it is considered a bit lazy, wasteful, and even unkind to include a long message if you are only replying to a small portion. Let's hope my friend reads this section and remembers to enable this feature in the future!

Checking Mail Automatically

With Microsoft Internet Mail, it's quite easy to set the program to automatically check your mail. You can even decide how often you'd like it to check your mail. If your system is not signed on, it will sign on and check your mail at the frequency you designate.

To set this option, select Mail|Options|Read, and then set Mail to check your incoming mail as often as you wish, as shown in Figure 14.6. When you are signed on, you'll know background checking is active because an icon and status message will appear just above the clock in the lower-right corner of the screen.

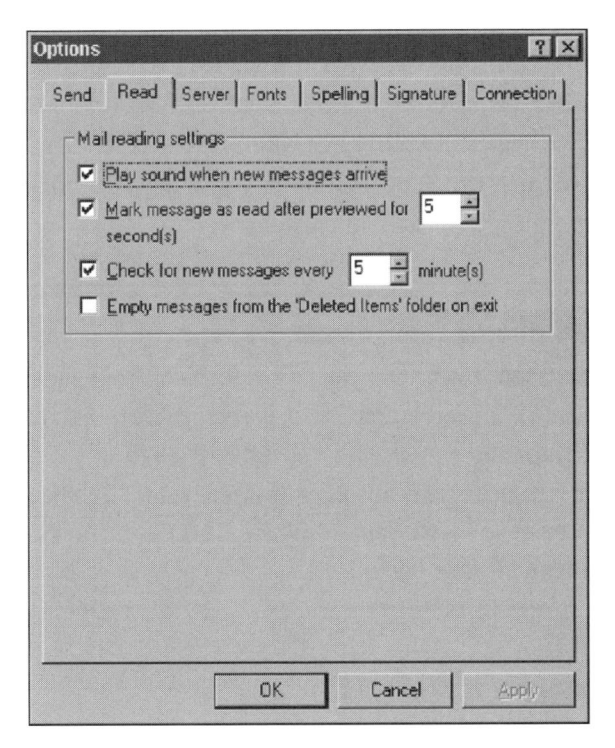

Figure 14.6   Use this tab to make Mail work for you.

I personally think that automatic mail checking is the best thing to come around the pike since the online community started rolling. In fact, I set Mail to check my mail every five minutes! Of course, you don't need to be quite this excessive. Remember, if you don't have a flat-rate account, you will be charged a connection fee each time you are signed on by the program

Composing Mail Offline

One feature I'm always amazed that more people don't take advantage of is the ability to compose mail offline. Most online mail services and Internet email packages, including Microsoft Internet Mail, allow you to do this. As you are probably well aware, in the online community, time is definitely money; the more time you spend online, the thinner your pocketbook becomes! Because I often ponder as I write messages, I find it quite thrifty to compose my mail offline. To compose your mail offline, select New Message or Reply. When the message is complete, click the envelope icon. When all messages have been written, select Send and Receive to transmit your message. Many folks have problems with an automatic signon that are due to programming issues with their ISP. To have Mail automatically sign off after Send and Receive, select Mail|Options|Connection and check the box that indicates "Disconnect when finished sending and receiving". You'll want to turn off Send Immediately when composing mail offline. You'll find more on that later in this chapter.

Always Spell Check Your Messages

Microsoft has made it easy for you to spell check your messages if you are working with the 32-bit version of Office, Works, or Word. Internet Mail interacts with their dictionaries so you can consistently spell check your documents. After a new message or reply has been drafted, select Check Spelling from the Mail menu, or select F7 from your keyboard. This option only appears when you have an outbound message open.

Volumes of Mail

By now you know I receive a lot of email. I have accounts and email addresses at Earthlink, The Coriolis Group, Microsoft Network, CompuServe, and

America Online, but I prefer to have mail sent to me at my America Online account. If you also have multiple accounts, and get tired of checking all of them every day, you will appreciate Mail's ability to allow you to designate a particular reply address, as indicated in Figure 14.7. Choose Mail|Options|Server|Advanced Settings and enter your preferred address in the Reply To text box.

But if you want to receive any mail at all, you must heed the Internet parable that states, "Those who receive must also send."

Sending and Receiving Mail

After writing a message, the next action is to send it, right? After you click on the Send Mail icon, you may be greeted by a notice, shown in Figure 14.8, that the message has been placed in the Outbox folder, ready to be sent the next time you choose the Send and Receive command. (At this point, you can mark the check box: Don't show me this message again.)

I tend to write messages in batches, and I'm afraid that I'll forget to choose Send and Receive Mail. Two options for Send and Receive are shown in Figure 14.9. The best alternative for me is to set the frequency for Mail to

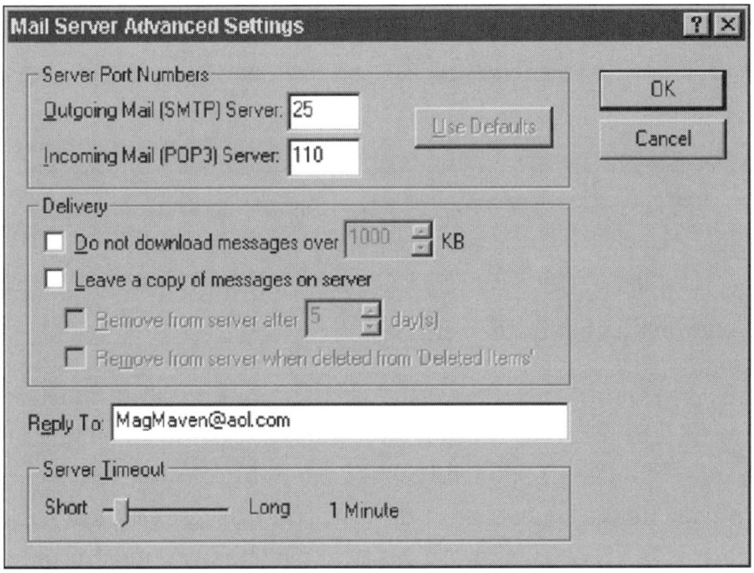

Figure 14.7 All replies to my messages are sent to my alias, MagMaven.

Figure 14.8 Hopefully, you'll only see this once.

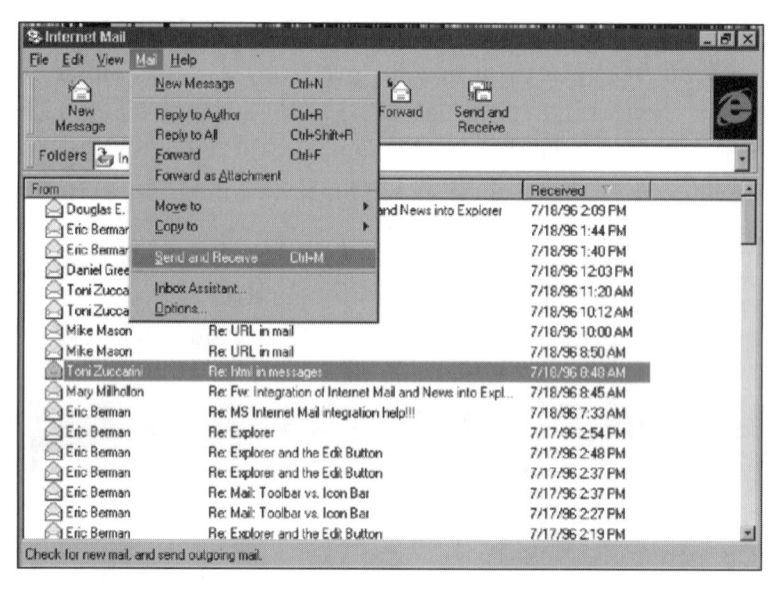

Figure 14.9 The large Send and Receive button is my preferred choice.

"Send and Receive" messages every 5 minutes (see *Checking Mail Automatically* earlier in this section).

There are two other ways to verify whether your outbound messages have been sent. The first is to check the Outbox. If it is empty, all messages have been sent. If you're still not convinced, take a look in the Sent Items folder. Once your message appears on the list, you can rest easy knowing that it has been sent. Of course, the only way to truly know that your message was received is when you receive an email in response. The online services have credible "receipt" functions, but you won't find one yet for the Internet.

Sending Mail Immediately

To send messages immediately, there's one more, albeit hidden, option. Choose Mail|Options|Send|Advanced Settings. Notice the highlighted check box labeled Send Messages Immediately in Figure 14.10. If you write most of your messages online, you may want to check this box to make sure you remember to get your message off immediately. If you write messages offline, Mail will sign on and off each time you compose a message, providing you have a ready and available phone line and your password entered by default.

Setting Your Priorities

Microsoft Internet Mail has a great little feature for setting priorities for mail you send (and mail you receive). Clicking on the postage stamp icon

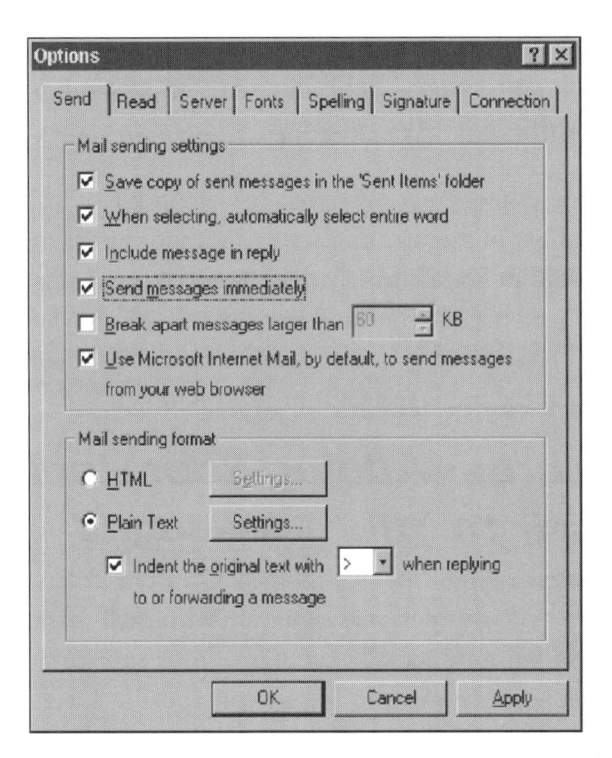

Figure 14.10   There's nothing better than to send your messages immediately.

in the upper-right corner of your outbound message header allows you to set the priority of your message—High, Normal, or Low. The receiver of your message (providing they are also using Microsoft Internet Mail or another Microsoft mail package) will know the priority you have assigned to the message by the icon that accompanies the message. High priority mail is accompanied by an exclamation point icon, normal priority is iconless, and low priority is accompanied by a blue downward-pointing arrow. Of course, every message to my co-authors, Mary and Toni, is accompanied by an exclamation point!

Keeping Your Mailroom Neat

Because I get so many messages every day (don't worry, I'm not complaining), I sometimes find my hard drive overwhelmed with mail. Determined to get organized, I decided to take action! As soon as I look at a message for five seconds, Mail marks the message as read. It will stay in the Inbox until I move it to Deleted items or another designated folder. Some days, I want all messages deleted immediately, and I elect to empty messages from my Deleted Items folder automatically when I exit the program. Simply select Mail|Options|Read to make all of these changes to your Mail client.

Of course, sometimes you only have a few seconds to check your mail. On these occasions, you might come across an important item, but don't have the time to read it. You definitely don't want to delete this mail, you want to be able to read it again. In this situation, select Edit|Mail| and manually mark the mail as unread (you can also double-click to manually select the option to open the message again for reading now).

Signatures: Adding Your John Hancock to Your Messages

Microsoft Internet Mail includes a speedy feature called Signatures that allows you to add your personal signature with each message and posting that you send without actually typing it. Your signature can be used to close Internet Mail messages and newsgroup postings. Figure 14.11 shows a sample signature and the window where it is defined.

Many users apply signatures to add a friendly identification label, others use signatures to include their professional credentials, phone numbers, fax numbers, preferred email address, and even the URL for their Web site. To add your name in the Signature block, select Mail|Options|Signature, and then select to add the signature at the end of all outgoing messages. You can use the default of no signature or specify for Mail to use a particular file. A simple text signature will suffice for most of us, but you even could scan your real signature into a file and use that.

In order to keep you from going astray, I consulted my Internet Netiquette FAQ in regard to signatures. Long signatures are frowned upon. They consume the recipient's time, and they waste Internet bandwidth. Try to keep your signature to a maximum of four lines. If you feel that your signature is part of your person, your creativity, or your innermost self, keep it short and change it often. Regular readers of your email or newsgroup postings will certainly find you more creative if your signature changes on a regular basis. Before too long, you'll be able to select a signature from your collection.

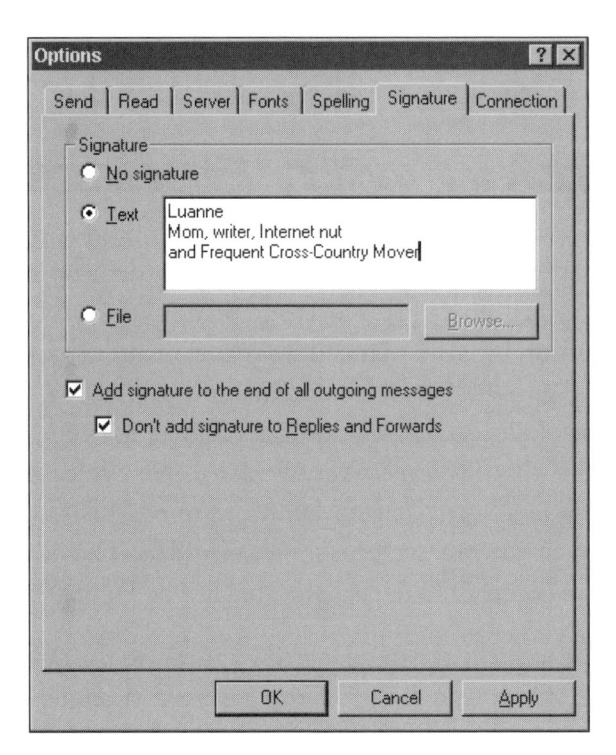

Figure 14.11 Signatures identify you to the world.

On the Signature Card, you can select to have your signature added to all messages, Replies, and Forwards. If you've not indicated an automatic signature selection, you have to click one more button—the small pen icon. Alternatively, you can select Signatures from the Insert menu.

SIGNATURES WITH A TWIST

Many Internet Mail users include the URL for their personal Web page in the signature block. With the integration of Mail and Explorer, you are able to click on the URL (as are your recipients) and be transported to the indicated Web site. This works for URLs listed anywhere in the email message, although the signature box is a favorite location. This is a little tricky because the URL won't be highlighted on the message while you're preparing it. To verify that it was correctly defined as a hot link, open Sent Mail and take a look at the message again. The hotlink becomes activated once the mail is sent.

Another interesting little gem is that any URL and email address sent from any email program will automatically be rendered as a Hot Link when read with Internet Mail. Internet Mail does all of the work for you.

Organizing with Folders

Everyone knows that the key to organization lies in some sort of filing system. Whether you're working on a wooden desktop or an electronic one, I'm sure you'll agree that folders add organization and depth to a filing system. Microsoft Internet Mail's filing system includes four default folders, as shown in Figure 14.12: Deleted Items, Inbox, Outbox, and Sent Items. You have the ability to create additional folders for your own workstyle. I've added one that I've called Very Personal. New folders can be created under File|Folder|Create. Select Mail|Move to or Mail|Copy to when you need to move or copy messages among the folders. The functions to delete folders and to compact folders are located at File|Folder.

Just under the toolbar, a triangular arrow appears to the right of the current folder name. Click and hold on the inverted triangle, and the folder collection appears for your selection.

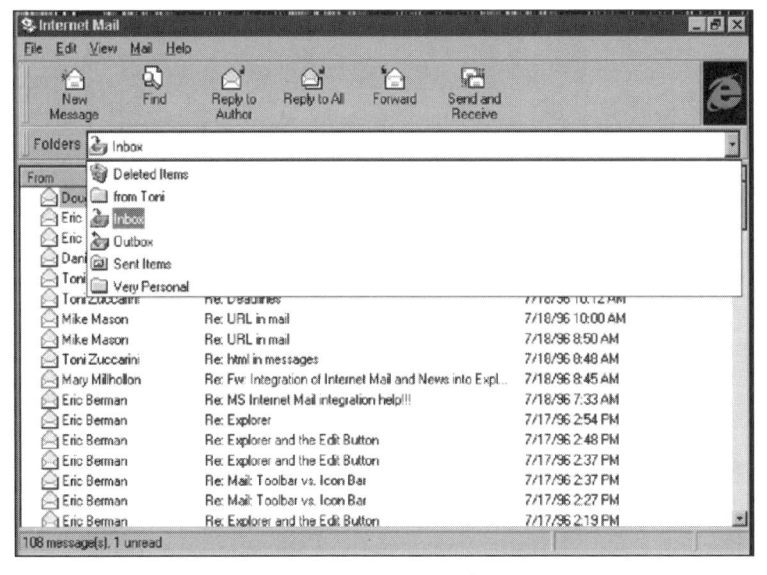

Figure 14.12   The four default folders, plus my personal folders.

What's That Strange Message?

Messages that you send from Microsoft Internet News will appear in Microsoft Internet Mail's Sent Items folder.

Inbox Assistant

Do your coworkers surreptitiously read what's on your computer screen before you can invoke your screen saver? Mine do. I often keep Internet Mail's Inbox open on my screen. I know that I like to keep some of my mail hidden from public view, and I can do so by designating that mail from certain friends is sent straight to my Very Personal folder.

Once you've established your Very Personal folder (or whatever you choose to call it) select Mail|Inbox Assistant|Add. Indicate the criteria in the boxes labeled To, CC, From, or Subject. For example, if your current crush is George Clooney, put his email address in the From line, as seen in Figure 14.13, and any mail from him will be sent straight to your Very Personal folder. In the Move To box, select the inverted triangle and the list will display the Deleted Items folder and any custom folders you have added.

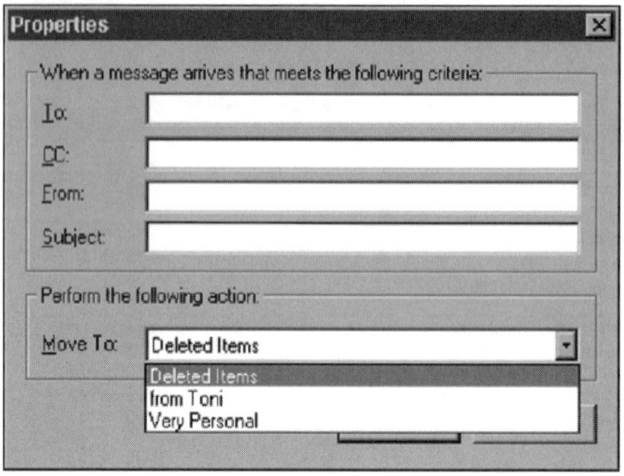

Figure 14.13 Inbox Assistant is here to help!

So why would you designate Mail to the Deleted Items folder? I get a lot of mail offering new Internet accounts with free Web site space. I'm a bit tired of the junk mail, so I designate mail with "Free Web site" in the subject line to take the detour to the electronic recycling bin.

HTML

Hypertext Markup Language (HTML) is a nifty innovation that allows you to add creative fonts and colors to enhance your messages. Those who are enthralled by all things multimedia are impressed by this. Unfortunately, HTML-enhanced messages slow down Internet transmission times. I suppose those of you with T1s, ISDNs, and cable infrastructure (coming soon to a town near you) won't mind the slowdown, but the rest of us would appreciate it if you would reserve your HTML-heavy messages for special occasions like birthdays, holidays, and major announcements (like telling your Mom that you're getting married this weekend in Las Vegas), rather than for everyday correspondence. As the Internet further develops, HTML will play a major role in the further integration of Mail, News, and Explorer—eventually allowing you do such fancy things as read mail with your browser and include complex images, hypertext, and other HTML effects within an email message.

To enhance all of your messages with HTML, select Mail|Options|Send and select HTML, Apply, and OK. If you prefer to designate individual messages for HTML formatting, select Format|HTML from the message window.

Sending Attachments in Internet Mail

Once upon a time, it was very difficult to send attachments with Internet mail. Microsoft has made it much easier. When you compose a message that should include an attachment, simply select the paper clip icon to insert an attachment. The icon appears at the bottom of the message screen, indicating that the attachment has been added. (You can also select the Insert pull-down menu while you're composing a message.) I tested this feature by attaching two files to one message, which I then sent to another account of mine. When I retrieved the mail, both documents were present in the body of the email. The mail system at the receiving end may present the document either as an attachment or within the body of the email. A variation on this idea is to send an attachment as its own file, not as part of the email message. To do this, select Mail|Forward as Attachment. In this case, the open message becomes the attachment. Merely selecting the Forward as Attachment command brings up a new outbound message window with the prior message window collapsed as an attachment. The file to be attached appears as an icon at the bottom of the email message, as shown in Figure 14.14. If you wish to keep the attachment (and discard the email message), you can move the icon to your desktop or to your preferred folder.

To display or run an attachment from the Preview pane, select the attachment icon (paper clip) in the preview pane header and then click on the file name.

Whether or not you can send attached files from another service to your Microsoft Internet Mail account depends on the criteria of the originating service. When I sent attached files with Mail from my Internet account to America Online, they worked with great ease. The reverse did not work; the mail was sent with the attachment but only the header arrived at the ISP account. With the availability of Microsoft Internet Explorer through America Online, I anticipate these kinks will be worked out of the system.

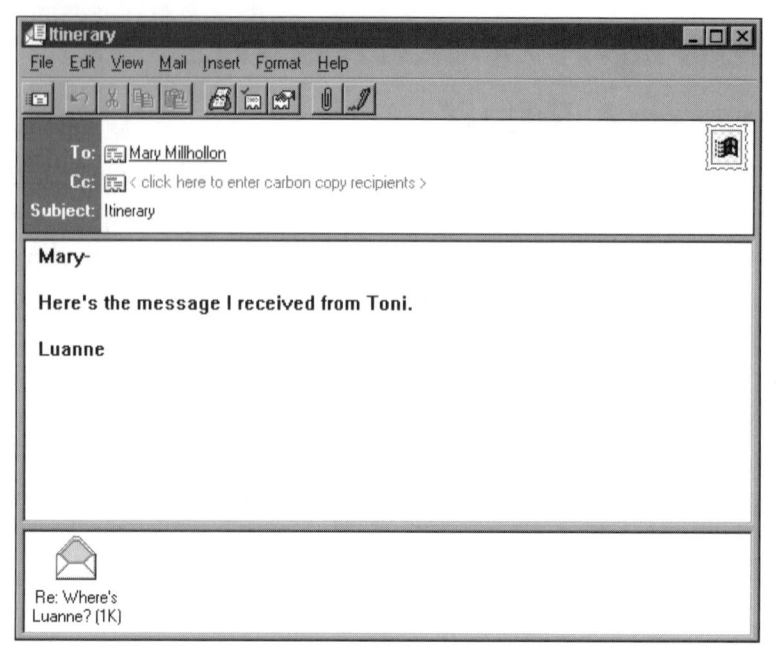

Figure 14.14 Forward stands ready to advance the news in your mail.

Import

The Import function, located in the File menu, allows you to move Address Book content or message files from other programs into Microsoft Internet Mail. You can select to import messages from all folders or from selected folders, as shown in Figure 14.15. When you choose to import an Address Book, you'll be asked how to handle imported names that match existing entries.

Export

The Export function, located under the File menu, allows you to send messages from Microsoft Internet Mail to Microsoft Messaging (Exchange). You can select to Export all folders or selected folders.

Message Formats

In order for messages to move over the Internet, they have to be encoded in a format that the Internet can read. The two dominant message format standards supported by Microsoft Internet Mail are MIME and UUEncode.

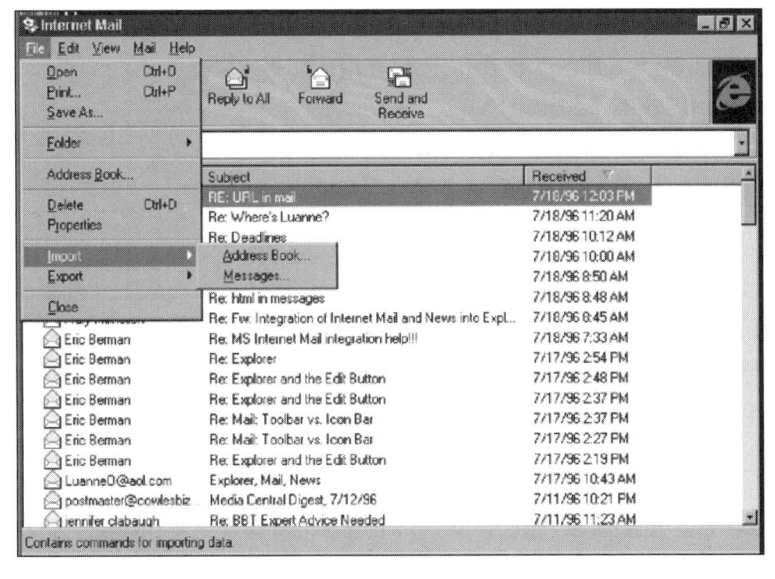

Figure 14.15 Importing and exporting start here.

The MIME and UUENCODE settings only apply to binary file attachments and how they are encoded. Since SMTP is only a 7-bit protocol, the mailer must first change your binary file back into text. That is what MIME and UUEncode do. They both accomplish the same thing, but use different methods.

MIME, which stands for Multipurpose Internet Mail Extensions, is the default setting for message transmission in Mail. MIME beefs up the capability of electronic mail and allows for the transmission of multimedia email messages with fonts and pictures. MIME is a specification, not a program, and MIME messages can include pictures, sounds, and PostScript images. Not all of your correspondents will be able to receive MIME messages, so you may have to change to UUEncode for selected recipients by selecting Mail|Options|Send|Plain Text|Settings. Stick with MIME unless you are informed that you need to use UUEncode.

UUEncoding is an Internet standard process for transferring files over the Internet. You can send and receive Internet mail with attachments if the attachments have been UUEncoded. Unfortunately, your correspondents on other commercial online services may not be able receive or read your messages if their mail system does not support UUEncoded attachments.

When it comes to everyday email, you can pretty much ignore this section. Concerns about file encoding generally only come into play with large emails and attached files.

Simple Shortcuts

It seems to be easier to explain Shortcuts to Macintosh users than to Windows users. Let me switch hats (and operating systems) to give this a try. Those who know the Mac operating system will find shortcuts to be very similar to aliases. A shortcut can be an Internet address, a direct link to a file, or a program starter that resides anywhere you put it. Shortcuts are a great customization tool for Windows and you can use drag and drop to move them around. When I think of shortcuts, I generally think of the shortcut icons I have placed on the desktop for fast access to my programs. They can also represent Internet URLs, as seen in Figure 14.16, or links to files. To share a shortcut in your email message, begin by creating the shortcut. Next, open the email or bulletin board message in which you want to embed the shortcut, then drag and drop the shortcut onto the message.

The shortcuts are represented by icons and can be transmitted in your email. If your correspondent has Microsoft Internet Mail, when he receives the message, he can click on the icon to go straight to whatever Internet address the shortcut designates.

Alternatively, you can include an icon representing a document, and the document will travel as an attachment with your mail. Generally, both of these features can be used only when both the sender and recipient have Windows 95 and Microsoft Internet Mail. It is possible that you can send a UUENCODED attachment to someone who has an Internet account and Windows 95. Again, Microsoft sets the standard for compatibility.

Working with Listservs

When you are no longer excited by those notes from your cousin in Montana, it's time to explore *listservs*. Also known as mailing lists, listservs are basically newsgroups or bulletin boards that arrive in your mailbox.

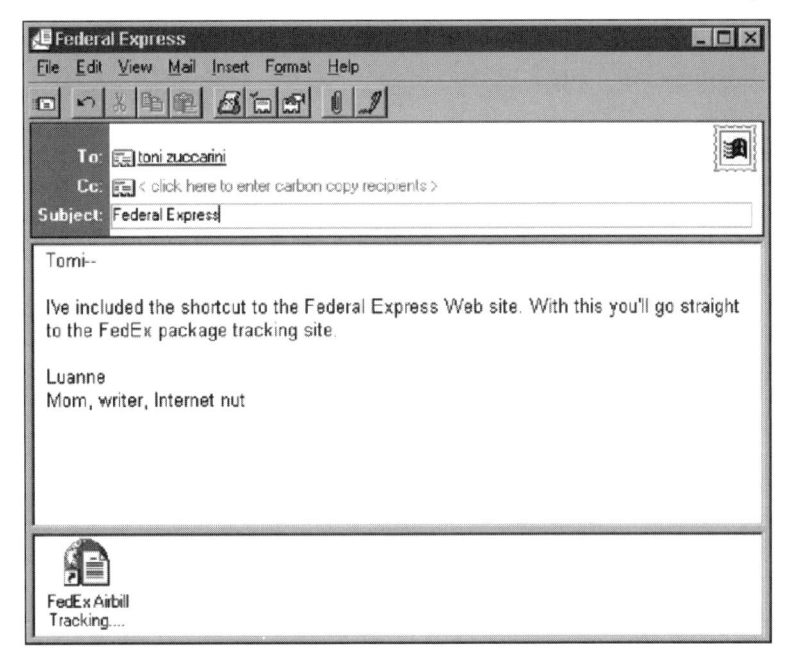

Figure 14.16 This shortcut transmitted perfectly to Toni, and she enjoyed her visit at FedEx.

Hundreds of mailing lists abound with topics ranging from *Mad About You* to *The Brady Bunch*. When a list member sends an email to the list, it is automatically redistributed (by the server) via email to all list subscribers. On one list, I was inundated by 70 to 80 pieces of mail a day (and that's too much, even for me!), so I requested a digest, which compacts the information into a single, albeit long, email message.

Most mailing lists are open to anyone interested in the topic. Some lists have membership restrictions, and others have restrictions on message content. Another type of mailing list, called a moderated list, requires that a moderator review and approve messages before they are sent off to subscribers.

Roadmap to Mailing Lists

If you're in the market for a good mailing list, launch Explorer and check out the Publicly Accessible Mailing Lists Web page, which is located at **http://www.neosoft.com/Internet/paml**. However, if you're not in the mood to use Explorer, you still have a few options.

You can use Mail to obtain a comprehensive list of mailing lists by sending email using these instructions:

```
To: mail-server@rtfm.mit.edu
Body of message: send usenet/news.answers/mail/mailing-lists/*
```

For an even larger list with hundreds of pages and 5,000 lists, send email using these instructions instead:

```
To: listserv@bitnic.bitnet
Body of message: LIST GLOBAL
```

Notice that I didn't include a subject line in my instructions. Mail servers do not generally read the subject line. However, you might find it helpful (as I do) to enter a subject line to quickly locate such messages in your Sent Items folder.

Once you select and register for a list, I advise you to carefully read the content of the "welcome" message for tips to help you with the list in the future. I highly recommend that you follow the instructions in the welcome message, and request the digest version of the list. With the digest version, you will get one fairly long post per day containing all of the messages sent by members in the prior 24 hours. Otherwise, you may receive 100 or so individual messages per day, which believe it or not, can get a bit tedious and damper your excitement for electronic mail.

Still another alternative to finding mailing lists is to use the infamous Usenet newsgroups news.lists and news.answers. You can access these newgroups with your newsreader, which is covered in detail in Chapter 15.

Microsoft Internet Mail vs. Windows Messaging

Windows Messaging is the primary mail client for the Microsoft Network (MSN) and is bundled with Windows 95. In its original incarnation, Windows Messaging was known as Microsoft Exchange. It may still be known as Exchange on your system, if you have not visited the site for Windows 95 updates on the Web, at **http://www.microsoft.com/windows/software/exupd.htm**.

At this point, Windows Messaging is necessary to access the mail you have been waiting to be read on MSN; Microsoft Internet Mail can't access this mail. You can use Windows Messaging for Internet mail through MSN, but Mail is integral to Explorer. For many of us, this really boils down to whether we use MSN. If so, you'll need to have Windows Messaging. If you are not an MSN subscriber, Mail, News, and Explorer contain everything you need.

Microsoft has forecast that MSN will support SMTP/POP3 in the future, and when they do, it will be possible to use Mail with MSN, rather than being forced to use Windows Messaging.

Changing to Microsoft Internet Mail

If your mail client is Windows Messaging instead of Microsoft Internet Mail, you'll need to change your setup. To do this, you'll need to open Microsoft Internet Explorer, select View|Options|Programs and review or change the mail service listed in the top box. Use this setting to define Microsoft Internet Mail as your default mail client. In Microsoft Internet Mail, select Mail|Options|Send to check the box indicating to "Use Microsoft Internet Mail, by default, to send messages from your Web browser." You will have to have an account established with an ISP because, as we learned above, MSN is not compatible with Microsoft Internet Mail.

For each ISP, you'll need to know the POP3 address (for incoming mail) and the SMTP address (for outgoing mail). Contact your ISP if you can't find these mail server addresses listed in material from your service provider.

Who's on First?

I like full interactivity when I am online. The busier, the better. I am always forwarding newsgroup messages to friends, checking my email, and locating the best Web sites (that I just *must* share immediately). I generally keep Mail, News, and Explorer open-but-minimized at the bottom of my screen. All are handy for easy access, and I can "hear" new mail arrive in my Inbox. To hear your Mail arrivals check Mail|Options|Read and check "Play sound when new messages arrive."

You can send mail from Explorer, as well. Try this at your favorite Web page: Go|Read Mail. The Mail program will load and an email window will open. Compose and address your message and you can send Mail from Explorer.

Another faster way to send an email from Explorer is to type "mailto:" followed by the Internet address in the Address line. For example, if you want to send mail to me at my MSN account, you would type **mailto:LuanneO@msn.com**. That will bring up a Mail message screen with no finagling. Simply typing "mailto:" in the browser's address line will bring up a Mail window with full access to the Address Book.

Chapter in Review

Whew! Boy, we covered a lot in this chapter. Microsoft Mail, with all its bells and whistles, sure makes electronic mail a serious endeavor. Not only have you seen how to create basic mail, but you've also seen how easily you can make the Mail system fit your personal habits, how to send attachments, how to enhance your messages with HTML, how to find and subscribe to mailing lists, and even how to locate your long lost friends on the Internet! With all these skills tucked neatly under your belt, you're bound to strike up some great pen pal relationships online.

Now, why don't you send me some mail and let me know how you're doing!

Microsoft Internet News 15

With Microsoft's Internet Newsreader, users have access to Usenet newsgroups and multiple news servers, and the ability to read news offline.

Usenet newsgroups (or simply, *newsgroups*) can be thought of as international message boards, similar to the BBSes or Message Boards on an online service. Figure 15.1 shows a typical newsgroup. They allow subscribers to communicate their thoughts and ideas on topics of interest. Usenet newsgroups number in the thousands (17,000 to be specific!), with topics ranging from auto mechanics to holistic health care. And each group has its own personality and style.

The best feature of newsgroups is that you can share your knowledge and experiences with a much wider group of people than you might find on an online service. For example, I'm quite interested in groups pertaining to parenting, kids' health, and medicine. The other members of the newsgroups have shared their stories of diagnoses and treatments in ways that have led me to be a better medical consumer. And best of all, through the newsgroups, I've even learned how to purchase prescription drugs from overseas at greater than 50 percent savings.

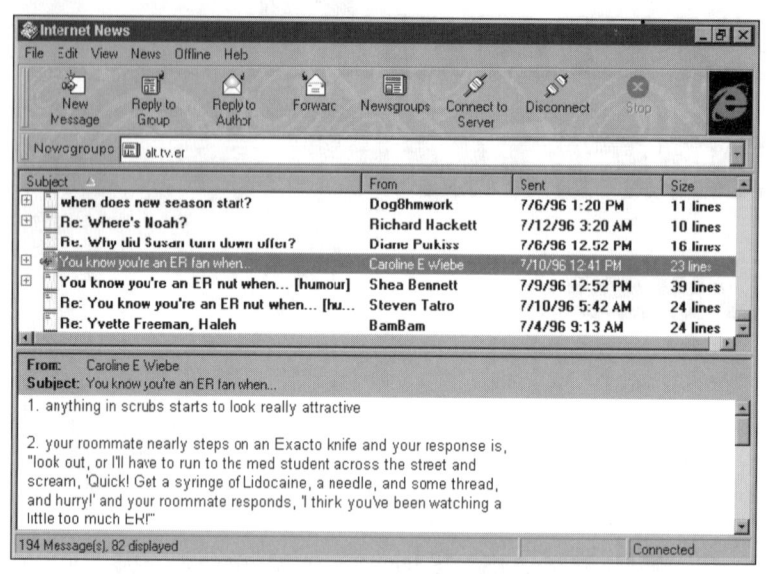

348 *Microsoft Internet Explorer 3.0 FrontRunner*

Figure 15.1 The ER newsgroup with status bar, toolbar, and the Preview pane.

You'll recognize newsgroups by their distinctive domain names: alt, misc, comp, news, rec, sci, soc, and talk. These domain names and a description of what they cover are shown in Table 15.1. The traffic volume on newsgroups can be quite heavy. It's not unusual for a newsgroup to have 100 to 200 messages posted in a 24-hour period. Once you subscribe to a newsgroup (don't worry, it's free), it's considered good etiquette to monitor the goings on for a few days before posting anything. Regulars find it frustrating to be asked the same questions over and over again by "newbies." Many groups have a FAQ—a document of Frequently Asked Questions about the mission or topic of the group—that you can access to answer many of your basic questions. Before you post any opinions or open discussion on the topic of the newsgroup, first ask whether the group maintains a FAQ and how you can obtain a copy. For more information on FAQs, see *Just the FAQs, Ma'am* later in this chapter.

Microsoft Internet News makes it easy to access newsgroups. Let's get you up and running so that you, too, can start immersing yourself in the wonderful world of mass information.

Table 15.1 Newsgroup Classifications

Classification	Description	Example
comp	Computer science and information on hardware and software systems	comp.os.ms-windows
misc	Groups with themes not easily classified under other headings	misc.kids
news	Groups associated with the Usenet news network	news.answers, news.groups
rec	Groups oriented toward the arts, hobbies, and recreational activities	rec.crafts.winemaking
sci	Discussions marked by special and practical knowledge, relating to research or applications in established sciences	sci.space.science
soc	Discussions of social issues	soc.women
talk	Debate-oriented groups	talk.politics
alt	Alternative to the "big seven" listed previously in this table	alt.tv.er, alt.tv.mad-about-you, alt.fan.rush-limbaugh

Getting Started with Microsoft Internet News

Just as in Chapter 14, where we covered Microsoft Internet Mail, there are also several ways to launch Microsoft Internet News. The installation process places the Mail and News icons on the Start|Programs menu. The program can either be launched from there, or copied and moved to the desktop. If you like Windows 95 shortcuts, you can launch the News icon or your Internet Service Provider's Dialup Networking icon from your desktop. From the browser, you'll find quick access to News under the Go menu.

The first time you run Microsoft Internet News you will be asked for:

- The name of your news server. You may need to contact your ISP if their literature does not include the address for the news server. If you have access to multiple servers, you may find that you have different newsgroup choices on each, as shown in Figure 15.2. To change your news servers go to News|Options|Server and select the appropriate button to add, remove, or review the properties of a server. To set the default server, highlight the server name, select Properties, and then click Set As Default. You can switch between servers while reading your newsgroups, and all subscribed newsgroups are listed together.

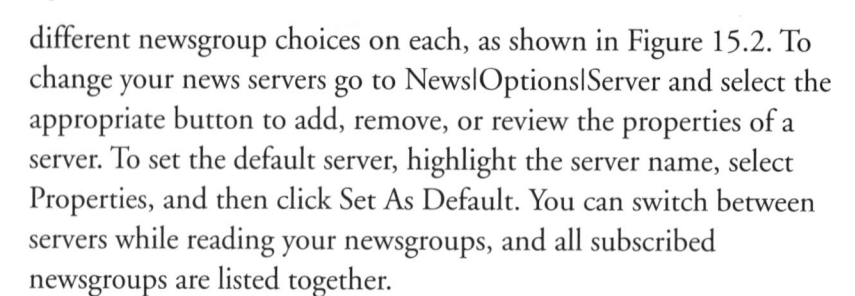

- Your account name and password on each server, if needed.
- Your full email address (this is the address that people should use when responding to a message that you post on a newsgroup, for example, **LuanneO@earthlink.net**).

If you do not know all of this information, contact your Internet Service Provider (ISP) or your mail administrator.

Troubleshooting

If you have problems getting News going, first check your connection to your ISP by selecting News|Options|Server and checking the settings against those provided by the ISP. When I am ready to pull my hair out, I'll even take the archaic step of calling the ISP's modem to the tone to make sure I hear the modem mating noises before I call the ISP's tech support line; in the evenings, I sometimes get an "all circuits busy" message instead of a tone. Another way to check the procedures is to use the Troubleshooter function located at Start|Help|Troubleshooting.

Depending on your settings and work preferences, you can either establish the connection to your ISP manually before reading News, or double click on News to bring up the dialer.

Searching for Topics

As I mentioned before, there are about 17,000 newsgroups in existence, and dozens are added every day. Select News|Options|Read and mark the check box that says, "Notify me if there are any new newsgroups".

News also makes it easy for you to search out your favorite topics. Let's do a quick search for newsgroups on Disney—a topic everyone loves! Select

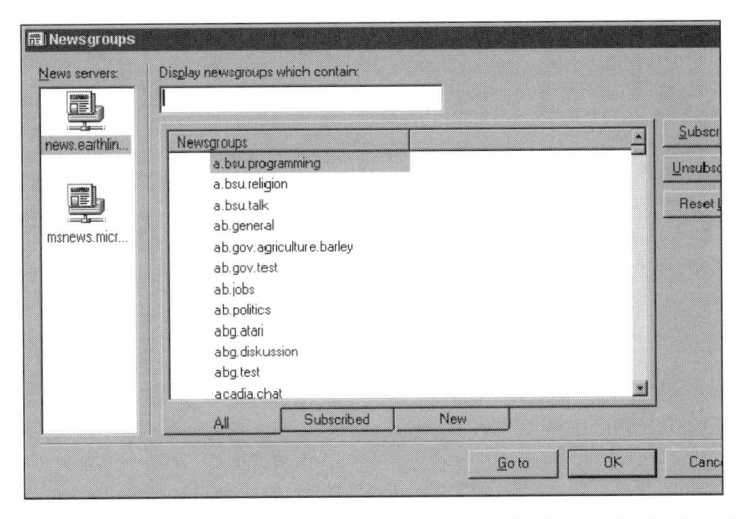

Figure 15.2 The newsgroup locator lists the groups available on the Earthlink server.

News|Newsgroups. If your toolbar is active, you can also select the Newsgroups icon on the top of the screen. (To activate your toolbar, Select View|Toolbar.)

First you'll need to select the appropriate server, and for this example, the msnews server will not be appropriate. Enter *Disney* in the search field. As indicated in Figure 15.3, 14 newsgroups appeared on my list. At this point, you can subscribe to one or more of the newsgroups. To read a newsgroup before subscribing, select it and click the Go To button. Once you view a newsgroup and then leave, News will ask whether you want to subscribe to the newsgroup. If you think you'll want to visit again, click on Yes. My subscribed newsgroups are shown in Figure 15.4. To exit without subscribing, simply click OK.

Finding the Microsoft Newsgroups

Microsoft, in typical Microsoft fashion, has a huge number of newsgroups listed on the msnews.microsoft.com server. You'll find topics ranging from specific Microsoft products to business areas such as banking, manufacturing, insurance, and even childcare. There's even a newsgroup for Microsoft Internet News (microsoft.public.internet.news).

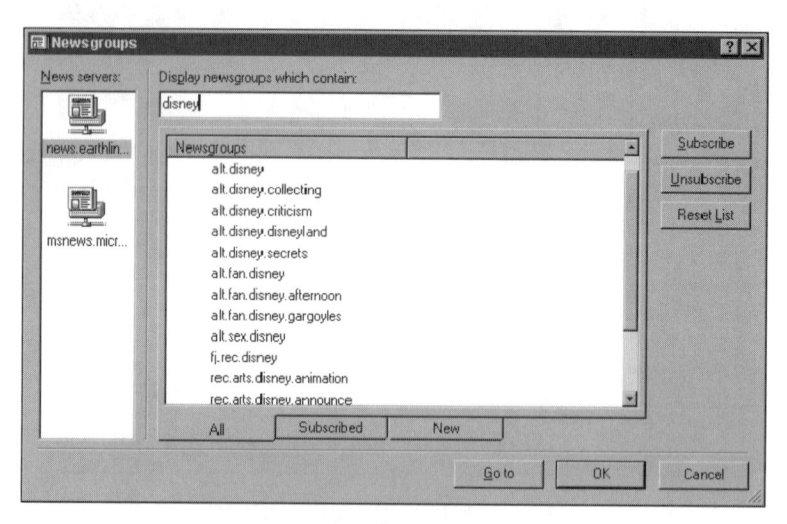

Figure 15.3 All things Disney, as found on Earthlink's server.

I highly recommend that you subscribe to keep track of your favorite newsgroups. You'll save time because you'll no longer have to locate a newsgroup from the master list, and it helps you to manage newsgroups.

Whenever you wish to delete a newsgroup, select it so that it is active, and then choose News|Unsubscribe from this Group. The Unsubscribe command only appears when a newsgroup is active. The best way to do

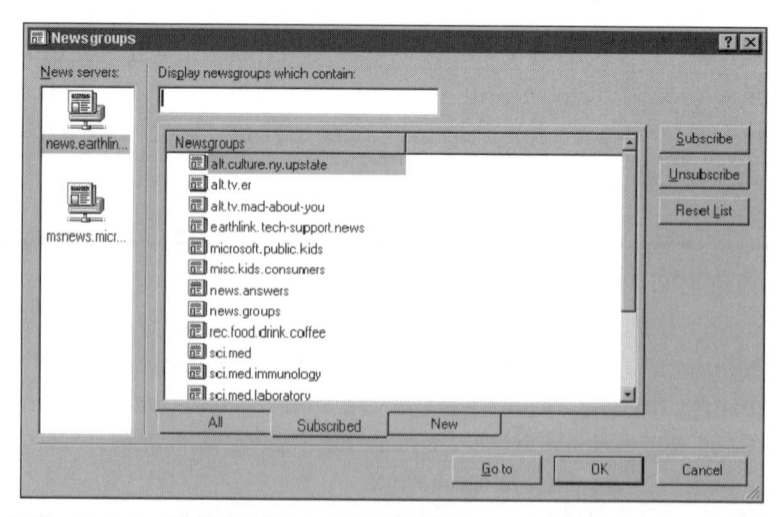

Figure 15.4 My list of subscribed newsgroups indicates I like TV, kids, and medical newsgroups.

multiple newsgroup pruning is to select News|Newsgroups|Subscribed. Take a good look at your list, highlight, and unsubscribe.

Viewing Subscribed Newsgroups

When the newsgroup client is launched, the most recently viewed newsgroup will appear in the large bar. You can't miss it! Click-and-hold on that bar and a drop down menu will list newsgroup servers and newsgroups. The servers are listed in alphabetical order, and the newsgroups for each server are also listed in alphabetical order. Move the cursor to the desired group name, and the group will load into your newsgroup screen. Use this technique each time you wish to switch newsgroups.

Newsgroup Netiquette

As I mentioned earlier, proper etiquette requires you to read a newsgroup for a week or so before posting new messages. You'll be keystrokes ahead of the game by reviewing the questions and answers posted by others. You can learn a great deal this way, and your first posting will undoubtedly be well-written and pertinent to the newsgroup topic.

Another no-no is posting unsolicited advertisements to any newsgroup. Although such postings are often veiled under the guise of information dispersal, they go strictly against newsgroup netiquette. Don't ever advertise in a newsgroup (no matter how much you think the members will benefit from your words) or you will be shunned (and not always politely).

I'd like to add one caution here. Please re-read your messages and replies, and take one last deep cleansing breath before selecting the Send or Post icon. Confirm that what you've written is what you intended. Make sure that the addressee is correctly designated. I once witnessed a post to a group that never should have occurred. It was meant to be a private exchange between two women, and it contained negative comments about a third woman.

There is one way to get a message back once it has been transmitted, but you're taking a risk that the message will be read by others before you can cancel it. To cancel your message, highlight it on the newsgroup list and select File|Cancel. (You might have to wait a few minutes until the message appears on the newsgroup list.) The confirmation will appear as in Figure 15.5 Please be careful and remember there are real people reading the messages you write.

Previewing Messages

Just as you can take advantage of the Preview pane in Microsoft Internet Mail, you can also use the feature with News. Select View|Preview Pane to split your screen either vertically or horizontally. The message list will appear in one area and the Preview pane in the other.

I find that Preview lets me make a faster decision about which messages to view. However, Preview slows the loading of each newsgroup. For the fastest newsgroup loading with Preview, go to News|Options|Read and uncheck Automatically the Preview Pane. When a message is selected, press the spacebar to view it. That's just as fast as turning off Preview.

Waiting for newsgroups has become a bit of a cosmic experience. The images on your screen will appear to be inactive for what seems like minutes. In the status bar, you should see the notation "Connected". And if you stare at the modem icon in the lower-right corner, near the clock, you may see the modem lights change from red to green. Eventually the progress bar will appear. It's just my opinion, but this is a feature that could be improved. It takes a while to know if any messages are coming my way. The highest volume newsgroups take the longest to load.

Managing the News

When you subscribe to multiple newsgroups, you're going to quickly find the need to manage the enormous amount of messages you receive. In this section, we'll take a look at some of the options.

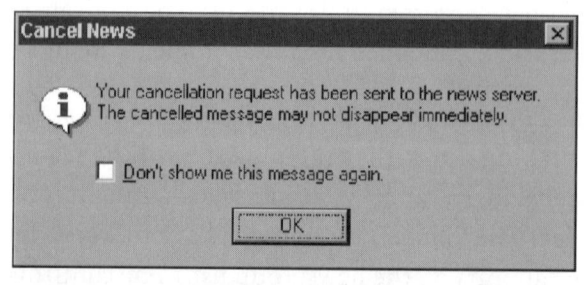

Figure 15.5 This confirms the cancellation of a newsgroup post.

Sorting Posts

Sorting is one way—and a very easy way—to manage the deluge of posts from your newsgroups. Using View|Columns you can determine which columns should be included: Size, Subject, From, and Sent are available. As shown in Figure 15.6, I have selected Subject, From, and Sent (date). Using the Move Up and Move Down buttons, I have chosen the order in which the columns appear. Subject is at the top of the list, and it appears as the first column when the messages are listed. Once your columns are aligned, select View|Sort By and then choose the column you want the sort to be based on. In sequential steps, you can select Ascending or Descending order and whether you wish to have messages grouped by thread (topic). Alternatively, you can simply click on the heading for the column you wish to sort by.

I prefer to have new messages appear at the top of the list, so my newsreader has been set in descending order.

Reorganizing Your View

To reorganize the news, you'll find it helpful to first undo the Preview pane so you can visualize your options. To display the most current messages first, click on the Sent header indicating the time and date for messages that have been posted to the newsgroup. When the arrow is pointing downward, the most current messages appear at the top. This carries through for all newsgroups, not just the one that is open at the time of the change. At other

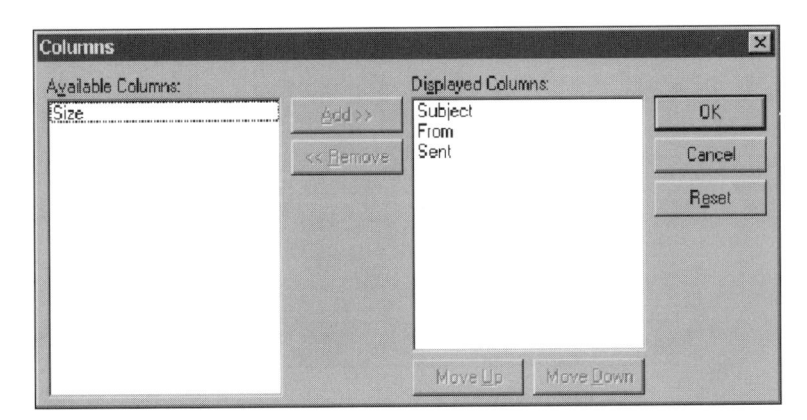

Figure 15.6 *Selecting Columns for the newsgroup presentation.*

times, you might want to sort by alphabetical order or by the author of the post (From). If you are looking for posts or replies from a specific person, selecting the From column can certainly save time. Go ahead and experiment until you find the organizational system that works best for you.

Speed Reading

After you become familiar with newsgroups, you'll see that not every posting is applicable or of interest to you. Of course, you'll want to zoom through those messages as quickly as possible. Generally, after just a few seconds you can tell if the message is worth your time. News provides an option that allows you to set how long a message should be open before being marked as read. Select News|Options|Read and choose the amount of time that suits your habits. Figure 15.7 shows the place to go to customize your speed reading option.

Newsgroups and their content multiply faster than rabbits in springtime. If not "pruned" often, your newsgroups can quickly become overwhelming.

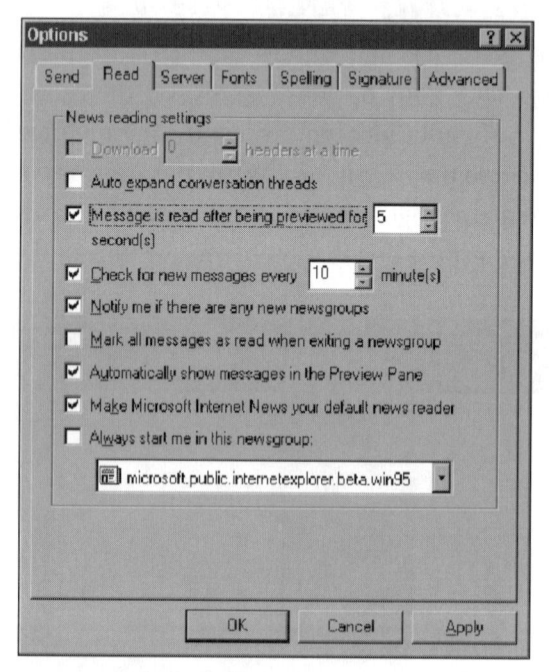

Figure 15.7 Making News suit your habits.

As you sift through the posts each day, you read topics that interest you; the others you probably don't bother with. Unfortunately, these messages will continue to show as new messages each time you access the newsgroup unless you read them or have News mark them as read. To have News list only those messages that have been posted since your last session select News|Options|Read, and then select the Mark all messages as read when exiting a newsgroup option.

If you prefer to make this change each time, simply select Edit|Mark All as Read before you exit. For a single message, select Edit|Mark as Read. To reactivate a message, select Edit|Mark as Unread. And to remove a particular thread, select Edit|Mark Thread as Read. If you want to view an entire newsgroup again, select View|All Messages.

Internet News Folder

Microsoft Internet News has a hidden feature—three folders to help you keep track of saved messages, posted messages, and sent messages. Specifically, they are called Outbox, Posted Items, and Saved Items.

Messages are designated to go to the Outbox when you have not elected to Send Messages Immediately in Microsoft Internet Mail. In that case, when Mail is open, selecting Post Message will send your message to the Mail Outbox, where it will wait for the next Send and Receive Command.

The Posted Items folder holds copies of messages you have posted to newsgroups. I know that sometimes I actually forget what I have posted (can you believe it?) so I'll check posted messages to verify my recent requests for information or my replies to others' posts. Replies to Author can be found in Internet Mail's Sent Items folder.

And what about Saved Items? You can elect to save specific messages for further reference in your own folder. Busy newsgroups may only keep messages for a week or two, but the Saved Items folder allows you to keep them as long as you'd like, because they'll be stored on your hard drive. When you find a newsgroup post that you'd like to save, select File|Save Message. A confirmation message will tell you that the message has been placed in your Saved Items folder. You may also save your outbound message in the Saved Items folder, but that will just duplicate the messages in the Posted Items folder.

What are those "+" signs?

In the message list, you'll see small icons with "+" and "-" signs. If you click on the "+", the topic will expand and you'll see all replies. You'll only see "-" when you've chosen to Auto expand topics under News|Options|Read, or when you click on the plus sign to expand the topic.

Posting to Newsgroups

Friends all over the world know when I'm online because they get messages from me. Lots of messages. If I'm reading a newsgroup and find a post of interest, I'll forward it to a friend. If I get a new idea, I'll start a new thread. I'll even freely respond to the newsgroup if my comment is of interest to many, or just to the author if I wish to keep my opinion a bit more private.

Let's take a look at the options you have for posting to a newsgroup. All of these options are shown in the toolbar in Figure 15.8, except two that are found only in the News pull-down menu: "Reply to Newsgroup and Author" and "Forward as Attachment."

The New Message option allows you to introduce a new topic or question not currently being addressed by the group.

The Reply to Group option allows you to send a response to the entire group. Use this option when you can answer a question or add to the discussion underway. I highly advise you not to send a reply that merely says, "Me, too!" Think of how you'd feel if you received a bunch of "Me, too!" messages to sift through! If you absolutely have to send a "Me, too!" reply, please send it to the author using the Reply to Author option. It's possible that only the author really cares. Or you might like to keep some privacy to your reply. There really are topics that your Mom might not find appropriate for you to be sharing with millions of Internet subscribers. Perhaps it is your inclination for boxers or briefs?

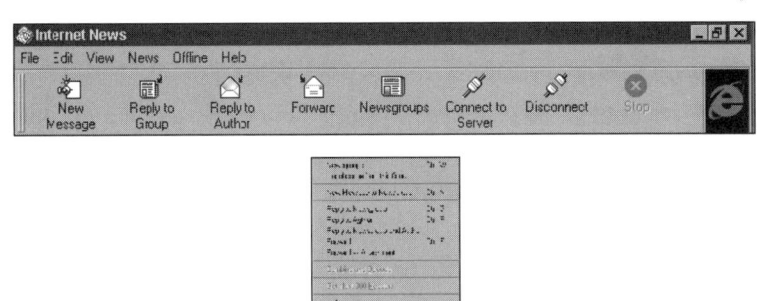

Figure 15.8 I prefer to use the Reply options from the toolbar; others prefer to use the selections from the menu bar.

Reply to Newsgroup and Author is a very handy option. You may have a time critical answer that the post's author needs, and most of us do check our mail more frequently than we check the newsgroups. Newsgroup readers may find your post to be a newsworthy addition to the thread, and Reply to Newsgroup and Author allows you to contribute to everyone, with only one message from you.

Use the Forward option if you find something that will interest someone who doesn't have access to the newsgroup. If I find a posting about George Clooney on alt.tv.er, I can forward it to my friend Julie—a big George fan. I know that some friends, like Julie, don't have time to surf newsgroups, and I forward the best tidbits to her.

When the Reply to Author and Forward Options Don't Work

If Reply to Author and Forward are not working correctly, make sure that you have set Internet News as your default mail client. Select News|Options|Read and check the box to "Make Microsoft Internet News your default newsreader". Once you've done this, clicking on the Reply to Author or Forward button should bring up Internet Mail correctly.

The last option is Forward as Attachment. When you select this option, the opened message is forwarded as an attachment to an email message. The post is represented as an icon at the bottom of the email message.

Always Spell Check Your Posts and Replies

Microsoft has made it easy for you to spell check your posts and replies if you are working with Office, Works, or Word. Internet Mail and News interact with the word processors' dictionaries so you can consistently spell check your documents. After a new message or reply has been drafted, select Check Spelling from the News menu, or push F7 on your keyboard. This option only appears when you have an outbound message open.

Quotes in Posts

As I discussed in Chapter 14, when you set Mail to include the original message in the reply, the entire contents of the original message will be quoted. This function can also be set for News, as shown in Figure 15.9. The full quote of the prior message may be a bit more information than you need to make your point, so you should manually omit the non-critical text. It is very easy to be a lazy newsgroup poster, but including long, unnecessary text is considered impolite, or even rude. As a matter of fact, Microsoft will give you an error message to tell you when the quoted information exceeds 80 percent of the message length. You will get this message after you click the Post message icon. Heed the warning, shorten the message, and post it successfully.

Select News|Options|Send to access the command center for marking quotes in message replies. You can choose to automatically select entire words, include the original message in the reply, and identify the indentation character to use to mark the quote when replying to or forwarding a message.

POSTING AND SENDING

If Mail is not active, use the Post Message action to send your message. If Mail is open, selecting Post Message will send your message to the Mail Outbox, where it will wait for the next Send and Receive Command. If you want to make sure that all messages you send are sent immediately, start Microsoft Internet Mail, select Mail|Options|Send|Advanced Settings, and then click on the "Send messages immediately" check box.

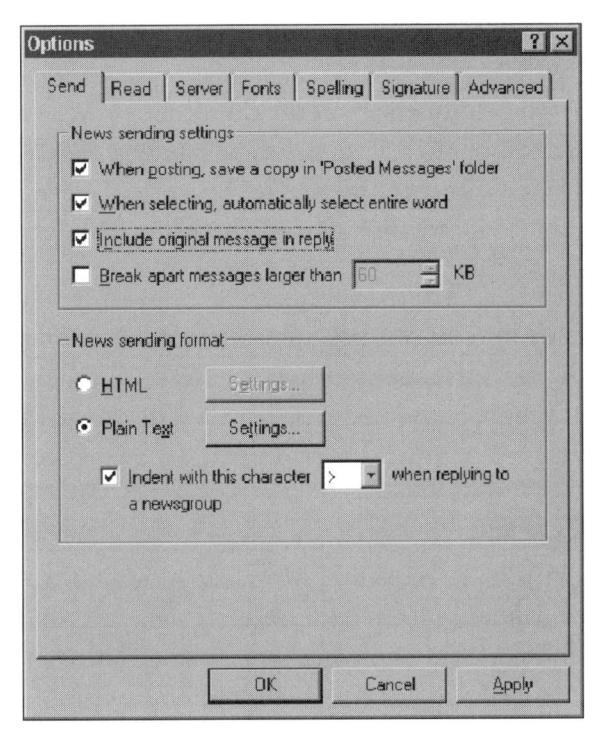

Figure 15.9 Quoting the prior message helps readers and writers to stay on the topic at hand.

To keep track of the messages that you have posted to your newsgroups, select News|Options|Send and select "When posting, save a copy in 'Posted Messages' folder." Your posted messages can be accessed through the Newsgroups pull-down menu. Click on the inverted triangle and scroll to the bottom of the list to find the Posted Messages folder.

If you are looking for a Reply to Author (in response to a newsgroup posting), look in the Sent Items folder of Microsoft Internet Mail. You'll find replies saved there, along with copies of email that you have sent.

How to Decode Messages

When you encounter multipart binary messages that need to be combined and decoded, select the appropriate messages on the message list, then select News|Combine and Decode. In the decode order list, drag the messages into the correct order and click OK.

News vs. Mail

You might be a bit confused about the difference between Mail and News. The line is actually not as clear cut as you might like. Mail is generally private, while News is generally open to the world. Generally is a *key* word in this instance. It is certainly possible for your friends to forward your mail to someone else.

The commands for the two programs are complementary, and changes made to one may affect the other. These options are found in the News|Options commands in both programs. The primary features that are different in each program are covered in the following sections.

Signature

You can be Dr. Jekyl in News and Mr. Hyde in Mail. If you would like to have two personalities, you can create separate signatures for Mail and News. Your signature may be as simple as your name. The most creative news posters include URLs to favorite Web sites, quotes, employers' addresses, or even professional credentials. You can have great imaginative fun with your signature, but remember that your name and email address may still identify you.

Reply Address

Between my PC and my Power Mac, I can access newsgroups through my Internet account, plus CompuServe, America Online, and Microsoft Network. It can get awfully confusing as I often post messages from whatever service I happen to be on. Microsoft has added one tool that is particularly good for people like me. Newsgroup messages sent from News can be marked so that any replies will be sent to one designated address. For example, I can post messages from my Internet account and receive the replies at my America Online account. When a reader on the newsgroup wants to Reply to Author, the message will arrive in your designated email account. You can change the Reply Address at News|Options|Server. A separate Reply Address can be designated for email, and you can review those procedures in Chapter 14.

Include Original Message in Reply

This setting determines reply formats for both email and newsgroup replies to newsgroup posts. Your selection is made independently in either Mail or News. Perhaps you prefer to include quotes in newsgroup messages (for the continuity of the thread), but you and your email correspondents don't need the quotes to stay on top of the message topic. When the selection is made in News it will affect all messages sent from the newsreader, whether you are posting a reply to a message or sending an email response to a message author.

Read, Check for New Message Every X Minutes

One feature that works independently in the two programs is the option for setting a time period for automatically checking for new messages—email or newsgroup posts. You can have News check for newsgroup updates every 10 minutes if you wish, and have Mail seek updates at a different interval.

Offline News

When I don't want to tie up the phone line, I can retrieve newsgroup posts, sign off, read and compose responses, write news posts, and sign back on to send. The first thing you need to do is to prevent News from connecting when you launch the program. Select News|Options|Server|Properties and make sure Automatically Connect to this Server is unchecked.

To facilitate newsgroup reading offline, right click on the Toolbar, select Customize Toolbar, and Add the Next Unread Message button to the Toolbar. You may need to delete another Toolbar button so that you can see all selected buttons on the screen. I omitted the Stop button because I rarely interrupt newsgroup downloads. When you omit buttons, you can continue to access the commands through the menu bar. The next step is to get ready to download headers. Select Offline|Mark Newsgroups, and then select All Subscribed Newsgroups or Selected Newsgroups. If you choose Selected Newsgroups, you'll need to specify them by clicking on the plus sign to show all newsgroups on the server, and then selecting the requested newsgroup from that server. You can download posts from groups on more than one server. For example, I can choose groups from both the msnews server and from the Earthlink server.

Make sure "Download headers only" is selected. Click on Download Now. The first time it may take awhile, so feel free to browse the Web while you are waiting. Go through the newsgroups and select interesting messages by selecting Offline|Mark Message for Download. A new icon with a green downward arrow confirms your selection.

When you have completed your selections and you are ready to download messages, select Offline|Post and Download. Check the box to sign off when the transmission is complete. When the transmission is completed, you can go back through the newsgroups and read messages marked with the push pin. Make sure to verify that the transmission has been completed or your modem will continue to be occupied.

As you compose responses, they are sent to the News Outbox, where they stay until you next select Offline|Post and Download. When message responses are ready to be posted, and new posts have been composed, select Offline|Post and Download to complete the cycle.

As you test this, you'll see that there are other alternatives, such as downloading all messages at once, or downloading selected threads. These options are pictured in Figure 15.10.

Cross-Posting Your Messages

When you've learned the term cross-posting, you're ready for a sports car on the information speedway. Cross-posting allows you to post a message to similar newsgroups within the same hierarchy. This helps you to cover all the bases at once. For example, the following message (crazy as it sounds) is begging for advice in multiple areas (breastfeeding, vacationing with kids, kids and computers, kids and medicine) within the same hierarchy (kids):

"I am pregnant and breastfeeding, and I don't know if it is safe to take my kid's computer on vacation, and besides, I'm not sure if the car seat will fit

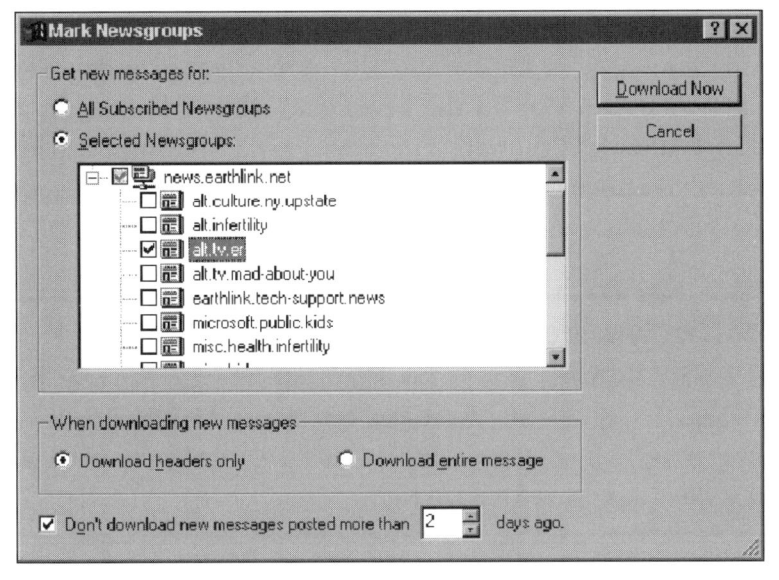

Figure 15.10 Select Offline|Mark Newsgroups to take advantage of the offline newsreading options.

on the airplane, and my kid might get an ear infection from swimming in the ocean. What should I do?"

Before entering the loony bin, this writer might cross-post this message to misc.kids.breastfeeding, misc.kids.computer, misc.kids.consumers, misc.kids.health, misc.kids.info, misc.kids.pregnancy, and misc.kids.vacation. Of course, this is a bit on the extreme. There's rarely an instance where you truly need to cross-post to more than three groups. The people who share your interests are likely to be reading several of the same groups that interest you. Please don't overpopulate groups with redundant messages. Given the volume of traffic on most newsgroups, you are likely to get a prompt response to your query.

Excessive cross-posting is called *spamming*. By definition, a spam is a post sent to more than 20 newsgroups. Spamming is unwelcome no matter what the message content is: Advertising, 1-900 numbers, multilevel marketing, and chain mail are equally and universally disliked.

If you are ready to cautiously practice cross-posting, select News|New Message to Newsgroup or the New Message icon. In the Newsgroups box, enter the names of any other groups—separated by semicolons—you'd like to send the message to. You can also add the newsgroups by double-clicking on the Newsgroup icon in the newsgroup address line of the message window. Figure 15.11 shows that the message will be cross-posted to alt.tv.er and alt.tv.mad-about-you. If you wish to see the entire list of newsgroups on the server, click on Show only subscribed newsgroups.

Accessing Newsgroups through Explorer

There's more than one way to use Microsoft Internet Explorer to access newsgroups. In Explorer's address line, type "news:" followed by the name of the newsgroup. I tried news:misc.kids, and it correctly launched Microsoft Internet News and opened misc.kids.

Just the FAQs, Ma'am

Frequently Asked Questions files, also known as FAQs, set out to answer the questions newbies often have in a newsgroup. Members who read FAQs before asking questions save other members from the major headaches of answering the same questions over and over again. A crafts newsgroup might

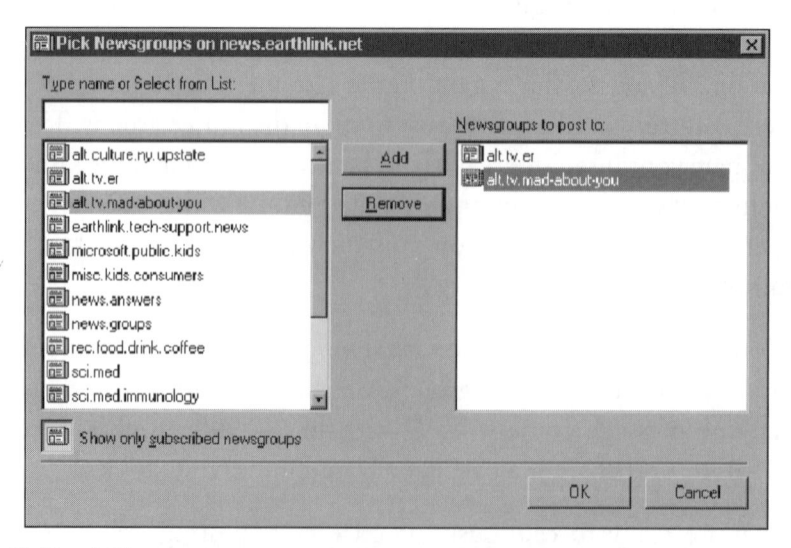

Figure 15.11 Adding newsgroups to the list for cross-posting.

maintain a list of suppliers on their FAQ. A sports newsgroup might keep a list of URLs to obtain sports scores on the Internet. Misc.kids.health may have a review of thermometers.

To obtain a newsgroup's FAQ, ask the newsgroup first. If no one responds, check the newsgroup news.answers, which is shown in Figure 15.12.

With Explorer, you can check the news.answers archive maintained at Ohio State. It's a whopper of a URL (**http://www.cis.ohio-state.edu/hypertext/faq/usenet/top.html**), but worth the effort.

MIT maintains a FAQ document server. Use an FTP program to connect to **rtfm.mit.edu** and then look in **/pub/usenet/news.answers**.

If the site at MIT is too busy to let you in, check the following sites:

- **ftp.uu.net/usenet/news.answers**
- **mirrors.aol.com/pub/rtfm/usenet**
- **ftp.seas.gwu.edu/pub/rtfm**

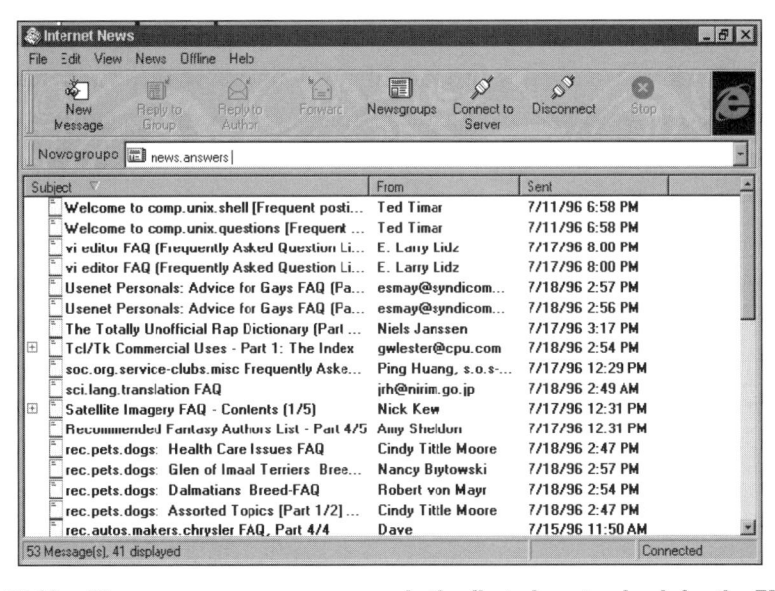

Figure 15.12 The news.answers newsgroup is the first place to check for the FAQs.

When you know the name of the FAQ, you can obtain it via email by sending a message in the following format:

```
To: mail-server@rtfm.mit.edu
Subject: <this line is ignored>
Body: send <filename>
```

Filename is the name of the specific FAQ you are seeking.

Chapter in Review

Newsgroups can keep you up to date on the topics that interest you most. They are a truly unique feature of cyberspace, linking people of similar interests but different perspectives, from locations all around the world. You never know what you'll find.

Internet News offers many of the same features as Internet Mail, and many of the changes you make in one client are reflected in the other. Take time to explore the functions in both clients to familiarize yourself with the potential of each. You can't hurt anything, and you just might discover something I haven't been able to!

One final note: Be sure to follow the rule of netiquette when working with newsgroups. Check FAQs thoroughly and always send posts with a clear head. No one wants to read a nasty message...no matter how warranted you feel it is!

Multimedia, MSIE, and the Web 16

Not long ago, text-based documents ruled the Net. Today, the Internet is a world of images, sound, animation, three dimensional graphics, and interactive games.

*A*s the Net world rapidly expands into a universe, keeping abreast of new developments can prove difficult. You have to keep your eyes (and ears) open to catch the latest technologies. As Internet technologies evolve, MSIE runs more and more Internet applications automatically—but not all of them. We have to undertake the responsibility ourselves to understand what's available; we have to hunt down the applications we need if MSIE doesn't hand them to us.

This chapter introduces you to some hot Internet tools—tools that will help you get the most out of your Internet explorations and get a jump on today's technologies. Some tools are bundled with MSIE, others you'll have to download. I suggest you download the applications you need now, because a year from now, you'll be on your own (unless, of course, we meet again in the next edition of this book).

Let's start this chapter's multimedia discussion slowly, reviewing frames and audio applications first. Then, we can pick up some speed as we check out video and mixed-media applications. After that, I suggest we take an introductory look at Java and ActiveX—programming applications sure to change the way we use the Internet for years to come. Finally, let's close out the chapter with an exploration of the world of virtual reality and 3D programs.

Frames

Before we dive headfirst into the flashing lights and sirens of the Net, we need to address *frames*—one of the newest Internet features. Frame technology allows Web pages to be divided into several panes called *frames*. Each frame displays a different HTML page with a unique URL, so you can view a number of different Web pages at once. Figure 16.1 shows Microsoft's sample page for using frames. To test the linking capabilities of frames, let's go to the sample page at **http://www.microsoft.com/ie/showcase/howto_3/ volcano3.htm** (*Note:* Microsoft has updated the Volcano Coffee Company site with a later version, but I'm leaving Figure 16.1 here because it's a good example of how frames and links interact. Microsoft has left past versions of their Volcano Coffee Company sample pages online, so you should be able to access this page as you read this book.)

If you click on the Ancient Art, Gift Packs, or Catalog link, the frame to the right of the links displays the resulting information. As you can see, MSIE supports borderless frames, as well as frames without scroll bars. The elimination of borders and scrollbars on frames allows for a seamless, almost magazine appearance to Web pages.

While frames add a graphic elegance to Web pages, they are also extremely useful. Frames allow Web pages to offer sophisticated layouts that can mix a variety of sounds, video, animation, and background colors and patterns in one place. Plus, with multiple frames, information can be organized more effectively. For example, Figure 16.1 illustrates how menu links in one frame can display linked information in a separate frame.

Floating Frames

Another frame innovation available with MSIE is the *floating frame*. Floating frames essentially enable you to open a browser within a browser—a window

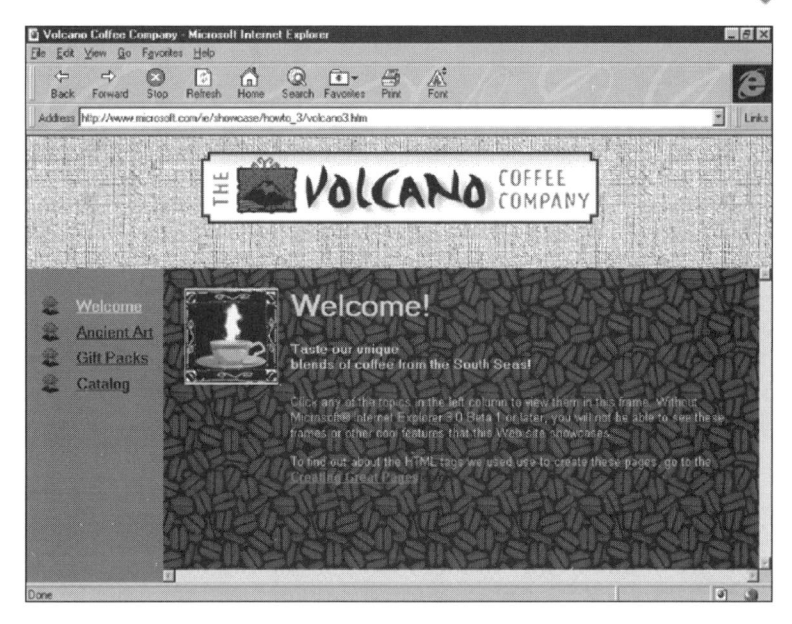

Figure 16.1 Frames allow you to view multiple Web pages at once.

to the Net within your browser's window. Floating frames can appear anywhere images can appear, and they can be designed to display in any size, with or without borders. Microsoft's example of a floating frame displays in Figure 16.2 and can be found at **http://www.microsoft.com/ie/htmlext/samples/fframeex.htm**.

You can click on a hypertext cinema link, as shown in Figure 16.2. Clicking on a cinema link displays movie times in the floating frame, while leaving the remainder of the page unchanged. In the previous example, I clicked on the Renton Cinema link to display the movie times for that theater. This example is very simplistic, but you get the idea.

Pop-up Frames

Yet another frame feature supported by MSIE is the capability for Web designers to include pop-up menus on Web pages. Microsoft provides an example of pop-up menus in its latest version of the Volcano Coffee Company sample page, as shown in Figure 16.3.

In Figure 16.3, clicking on the image of a Volcano Coffee product, such as the coffee cup, results in a pop-up menu that you can use to order the

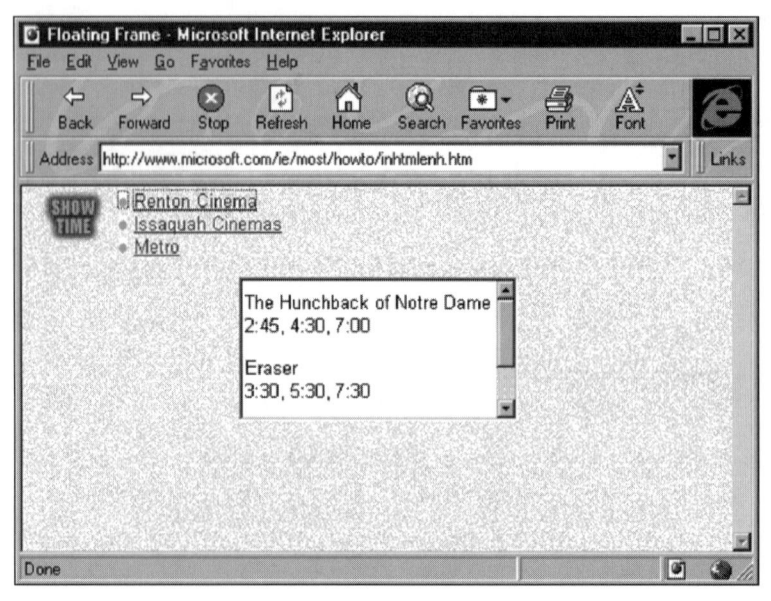

Figure 16.2 MSIE supports floating frames, which act as a browser within the browser.

product. The most recent version of the Volcano Coffee Company site is a good place to look for some of the latest frame innovations running today.

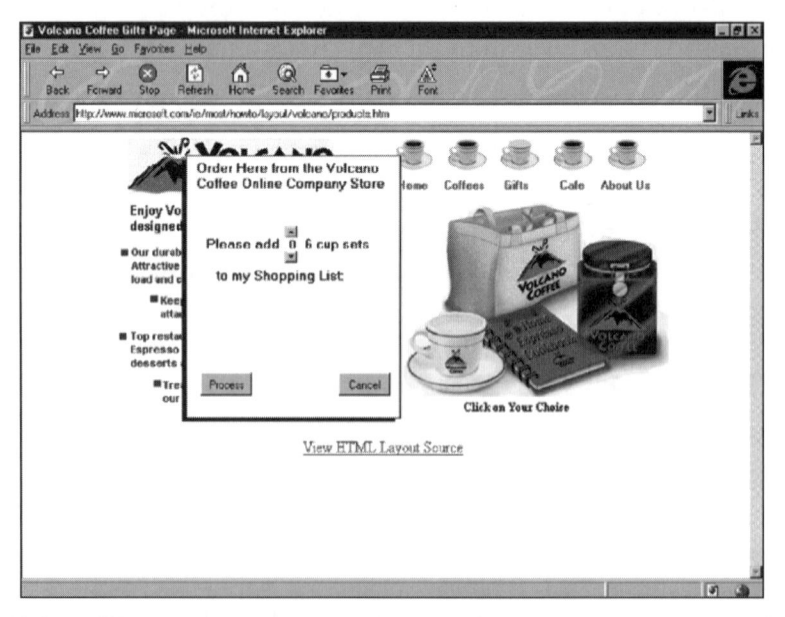

Figure 16.3 MSIE supports pop-up menu frames, which act as Web site dialog boxes.

You can visit the latest Volcano Company site at **http://www.microsoft.com/ie/most/howto/layout/volcano/Volcano.htm**.

Frame Exploration

Exploring frames is similar to exploring basic Internet pages. You can click on links, refresh, and go backwards and forwards within the frame. Depending on the design of a page, clicking on links within a frame might take you to another page within the same frame, or it might change the display in another frame on your screen. To refresh a particular frame (as opposed to refreshing the entire page), right-click in a frame and select the Refresh command. To go backward or forward within a frame, click in the frame, then press the Backspace key to go backward or press Shift+Backspace to move forward.

Don't worry if you get lost while exploring frames. Over time, you will become comfortable with them. Soon enough, everyone will take frames for granted, but in the meantime, rest assured that frames are a new exploration tool for even the most veteran surfers.

Audio: Surfing with Sound Waves

Before you can listen to audio files, your system has to be the proud owner of a sound card. Most systems sold today come with sound cards, so running audio files shouldn't be a problem. I'm going to introduce you to three types of sound applications: MIDI files, sound clips, and RealAudio.

MIDI Files

Think back to Chapter 5. Remember when we were setting up the MSN start page, and we had the option to play background music? That background music came in the form of a Musical Instrument Digital Interface (MIDI) file. MIDI files are digitized computer music files, usually carrying the file extension .MID. The popularity of MIDI files stems from the fact that the files are fast and small compared to other sound formats. MSIE comes already equipped to play MIDI files. Some MIDI files play automatically when a page opens, others have to be opened or downloaded.

374 Microsoft Internet Explorer 3.0 FrontRunner

If a MIDI file plays as part of a Web page, you probably won't see a MIDI recorder. However, if you are opening or downloading a MIDI file, you'll probably see a recorder similar to Figure 16.4.

Saving MIDI Files to Disk

If you happen upon a MIDI file that you like, you can save it to disk. After you are finished listening to the recording, open your cache file (C:\Windows\Temporary Internet Files). Your cache file saves a copy of the MIDI file as a cached document, which you can then copy to another directory. From that point, you can rename and manipulate the file to suit your needs.

Basically, the MSIE MIDI recorder consists of a Pause button, a Stop button, and a File Meter (the bar showing how much of the MIDI clip has played). You can adjust the music loudness by adjusting your system or speaker volume controls. There are a couple good sites with lists of links to MIDI files. I'm willing to bet that you can find enough links to meet your MIDI needs at **http://www.flexfx.com**, **http://xraent.uel.ac.uk**, and **http://www.tst-medhat.com/midi**. (Choose to view this last site with frames, and you'll get a nice sampling of frame technology along with your MIDI file exploration.)

Sound Clips

Sound clips are similar to MIDI files in that they are music files, and you might have to download the file before you can listen to it. Usually sound clips carry the extensions .AU, .AIFF, .SND, and .WAV. Samples of sound clips can be found everywhere. Remember in Chapter 12 when we visited the Froggy Page (**http://www.cs.yale.edu/homes/sjl/froggy.html**) and listened to frog noises? Those were AU sound clip files. Sound clips differ from MIDI files because sound clips can be much more than digitally synthesized music.

Figure 16.4 The MIDI file recorder displays when you open or download a MIDI file.

MSIE recognizes sound clips automatically—you don't need to add any special features to your browser to play a sound clip. Most of the time, MSIE displays a recorder complete with a File Meter and Play, Pause, Stop, and Done buttons when you click on a sound clip, as shown in Figure 16.5.

As with MIDI files, you can adjust the volume using your system or speaker volume controls. Sound clips are not as compact as MIDI files, so you might have to wait while your computer downloads the files. There are a couple good sites to visit to listen to sound clip samples. For example, check out the WWW TV Theme Songs home page at **http://ai.eecs.umich.edu/people/kennyp/tv2/tvtemp.html** for a great collection of AU files. And for hundreds more AU audio file samples, check out **http://sunsite.unc.edu/pub/multimedia/sun-sounds**.

RealAudio

I've saved the most advanced audio system for last—RealAudio. RealAudio enables you to obtain instantaneous feedback from audio files via the Internet. With RealAudio, you can listen to good quality live and recorded music, speeches, newscasts, radio broadcasts, simulcasts, audio greetings, and sound effects. To run RealAudio, you need to have a 14.4 Kbps modem (28.8 Kbps to play music), a 486/33 SX processor or higher, 4 MB of RAM, 2 MB of disk space, and a 16-bit sound card. RealAudio files, which are popping up all over the Net, carry the .RA or .RAM extensions. Fortunately, MSIE already bundles the RealAudio player with your browser. The RealAudio player, shown in Figure 16.6, appears whenever you click on a RealAudio application.

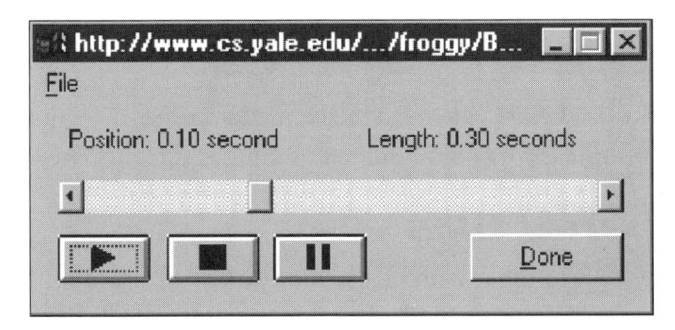

Figure 16.5 **Listening to a sound clip.**

Figure 16.6 Using the RealAudio Player.

Notice the RealAudio player is more advanced than the two audio players we viewed previously. When you use RealAudio, you can play, pause, and stop the player; change the volume; view the status bar; and use the menu bar to change your display settings or go to another RealAudio site.

Along with the CNN Interactive page (which we've viewed previously), there are a couple RealAudio sites worth noting. First, you should visit the RealAudio home page at **http://www.realaudio.com**. This page offers links to ABC and NPR news audio sites, as well as directs you to tips and information about using RealAudio. A second must-hear RealAudio page is AudioNet (**http://www.audionet.com**), shown in Figure 16.7. AudioNet links you to live radio broadcasts from across the nation. Now you can listen to radio news and music while you download files or browse the Web.

There are other audio-streaming technologies out there, but RealAudio is by far the most popular and the easiest to use with MSIE.

Animated Graphics

After audio, but before video and mixed media, comes the animated graphic. The most popular form of animated graphic is the animated GIF file.

Animated GIFs

You're probably familiar with GIFs, because GIF files are common graphic files. *Animated GIFs* are GIF files layered on top of other GIF files to produce the effect of an animation. Animated GIFs are small (averaging around 2 K) and easy to use (you can save and copy them just like graphics). To see

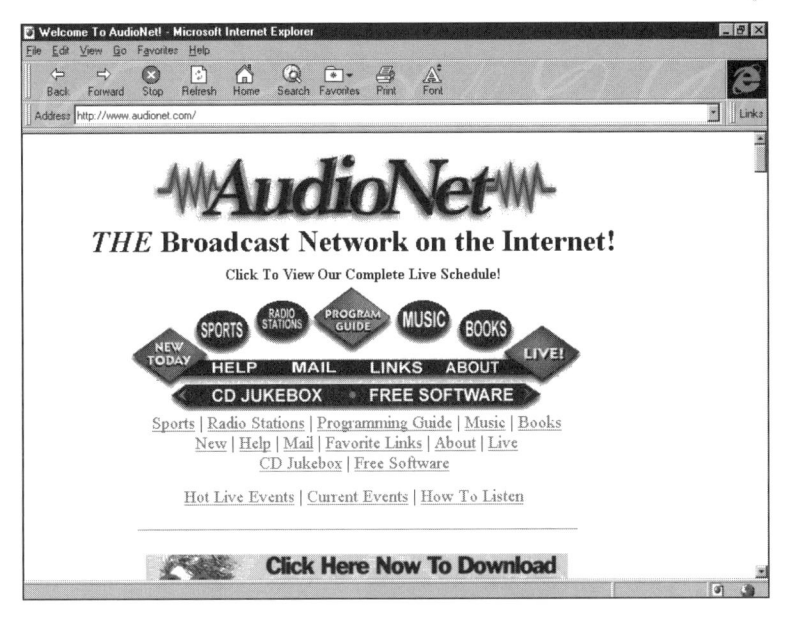

Figure 16.7 Listening to live radio broadcasts using RealAudio.

some examples of animated GIFs, visit the MMMM Animated Icon Browser Web site at **http://www.teleport.com/~cooler/MMMM/giving index.html**.

To view some of the animated GIFs on the MMMM Animated Icon Browser page, click on a topic button, such as the Misc. button near the bottom-left corner of the page. When icons display in the main window, click on an icon and the animated GIF will display in the top-right frame (disregard MMMM's Netscape comment— MSIE can display animated GIFs as well as the next guy). Figure 16.8 displays the Misc. page of animated icons after selecting the dancing skeleton icon.

Your Cursor in the Groove

If you are interested in animated cursors (which are mostly ANI files and animated GIF files), you should visit Dierk's List of Animated Cursors at http://ourworld.compuserve.com/homepages/dierk/moreani.htm. Dierk's page lists over 2500 animated cursors, in addition to instructions on how to download, install, and create animated cursors. While you are strolling through Dierk's park, check out his Cool Links—he's listed over 700 cool sites for you to visit!

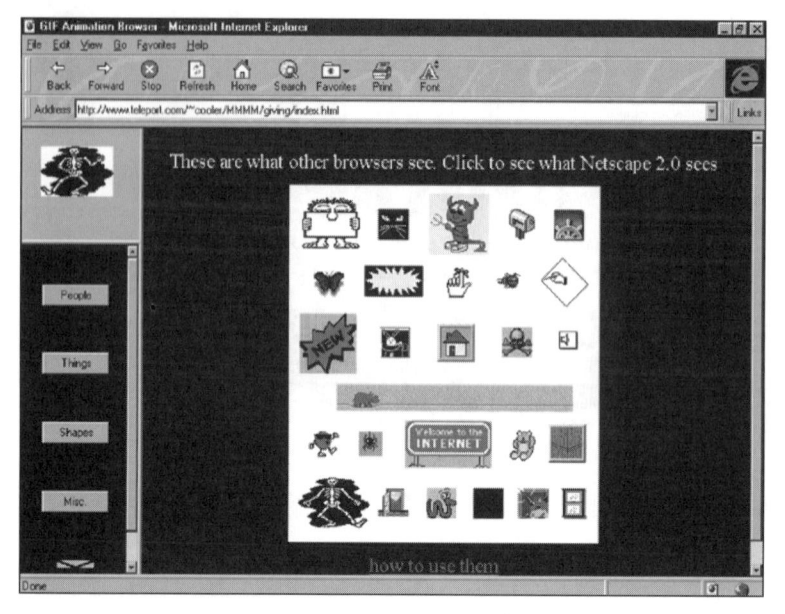

Figure 16.8 Viewing animated GIF files.

Video and Mixed Media

So far you've experienced frames, sound files, and animated graphics. Now comes true multimedia: video and mixed media. MSIE's incorporation of ActiveX and ActiveMovie means your multimedia experiences are simplified. No more downloading plug-ins if you don't want to (and if you don't know what plug-ins are—don't worry; you won't need to mess with plug-ins as long as you surf the Net using MSIE).

ActiveMovie

As an MSIE user, ActiveMovie will serve many of your video, audio, and multimedia needs. ActiveMovie is Microsoft's innovative approach to incorporating the best of today's multimedia offerings by providing integrated video and audio services. Best of all, ActiveMovie is built into your version of MSIE. Because of Microsoft's new ActiveMovie technology, you can play popular media formats on the Web efficiently, including MPEG audio and video, AVI, QuickTime, AU, WAV, MIDI, and AIFF. In addition, ActiveMovie includes MPEG playback for full-screen, television-quality video on mainstream computer systems; playback and streaming of all popular media types on the Internet; and a flexible, extendible architecture so future technologies can be integrated easily. To find out more about ActiveMovie, check out Microsoft's Interactive Movie Technologies home page at **http://www.microsoft.com/imedia/activemovie/activem.htm** shown in Figure 16.9.

Shockwave

An extremely popular application, Shockwave enables users to view animation, movies, and other types of multimedia presentations on the Internet. Using Shockwave, designers can deliver rich multimedia Internet experiences to viewers by adding animation, buttons, links, digitized video movies, sound, and more to their Web sites.

Shockwave, brought to you by the folks at Macromedia, works in conjunction with MSIE to bring you the fabulous world of multimedia. To see how your shocked version of MSIE works, visit the Macromedia site (**http://www.macromedia.com/shockwave**), shown in Figure 16.10. I suggest you go directly to the game page to see the best Shockwave action around.

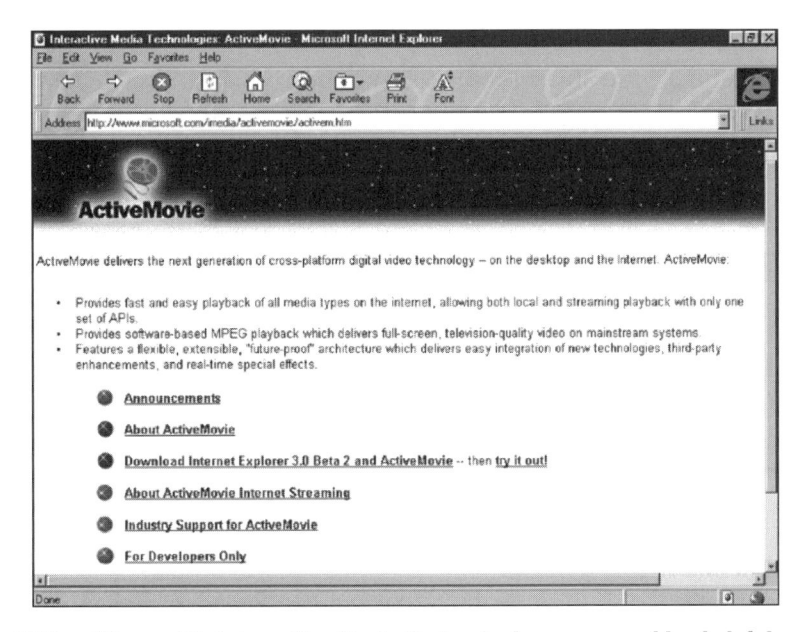

Figure 16.9 Microsoft's Interactive Movie Technologies page provides helpful information about ActiveMovie.

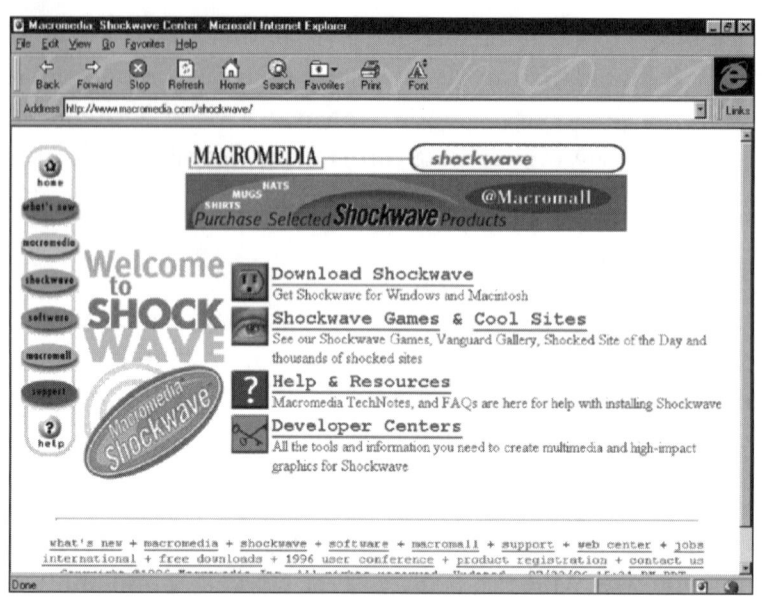

Figure 16.10 The Macromedia Shockwave page.

QuickTime

QuickTime is another application supported by MSIE's integrated ActiveMovie feature. Quicktime provides full-motion video with digitized sound. QuickTime, from Apple Corporation, enables you to view movies inside Web pages. To try out a QuickTime application, visit the QuickTime home page at **http://quicktime.apple.com/qt/qthome.html**. I suggest you click on the *Samples* icon to view some of the cool sites using QuickTime.

VDOLive

VDOLive offers realtime (streaming) video and audio over the Internet, and, as an added bonus, MSIE can play VDOLive applications without any tweaking on your part. All you have to do is click on a video link—no downloading or configuring plug-ins required. Web sites proffering VDOLive links go beyond static Web page design and advance into Internet video broadcasting. VDOLive is used for a wide range of applications, including news services, vacation tours, music videos, movie premieres, and corporate communications, and it can handle video clips ranging from several seconds to several hours, serving both Internet and intranet users.

VDOLive enables Web site designers to incorporate video into their pages and eliminates lengthy download times for users. To get your fill of information on this new technology, visit the VDOLive home page at **http://www.vdo.net**. Click on the VDOLive Gallery graphic link to view some cool VDOLive sites.

Multimedia Programming Tools

If you've surfed the Net, you've heard the news—multimedia programming is hotter than the streets of Arizona in July. With the advent of Java and ActiveX programming tools, multimedia elements on the Web have become more dynamic and interactive than ever. By this time next year, you'll be wondering how you ever managed without the instant interactivity that is about to descend upon you within the next few months. From the user's perspective, Java and ActiveX give you more, while you do less (sounds too good to be true, but that's the nature of this beast). Java and ActiveX open up a whole new realm of programming tools, enabling programmers and designers to hold a stronger reign over their creative endeavors. Let's take a quick look at Java and ActiveX. Don't expect to become programmers from reading this section—this is strictly an introduction to the terms, so you'll know what people are talking about when they drop some techno-jargon on you.

Java

If you've ever surfed before, you've heard about Java. Java is a new multimedia programming tool that allows you to see and interact with animation built into Web pages. Using Java technology, icons wave at you, game pieces move on your screen, and realtime charts and graphs update automatically (popular with Wall Street stock market sites). Java, created by Sun Microsystems, uses applets, which are mini programs embedded in Web sites. The MSIE browser comes Java enabled, so you don't have to do anything extra to view a Java applet. (In fact, you've probably already seen a lot of applets without even knowing it.) When you go to a site that has Java, MSIE temporarily transfers the applet to your computer for your use. Visit Sun Microsystems (**http://www.javasoft.com**), the creators of Java, for more information.

You can also read about Java in the Java World online magazine, located at **http://www.javaworld.com** and shown in Figure 16.11.

Finally, the best way to see Java's presence on the Internet is to visit sites sporting Java applets. A great site with a full supply of Java applets is the Gamelan Java directory at **http://www.gamelan.com**, a major source of Java links and information.

Gamelan provides all kinds of links to cool Java applets. You could start your tour by clicking on the Special Features link. Next, and this isn't just a cheap excuse to fool around, I suggest you scroll down the page and click on the Our Favorite Games link. Games provide an excellent illustration of Java capabilities. In addition, I've provided a little more play-and-learn encouragement by listing a couple Java games appearing on the Gamelan site (not all of them are listed on the Our Favorite Games list). Figure 16.12 displays a recent Pick-of-the-Week game called Iceblox.

Iceblox—**Penguins playing with fire**
http://www.tdb.uu.se/~karl/java/iceblox.html

Figure 16.11   Reading up on Java in the Java World online magazine.

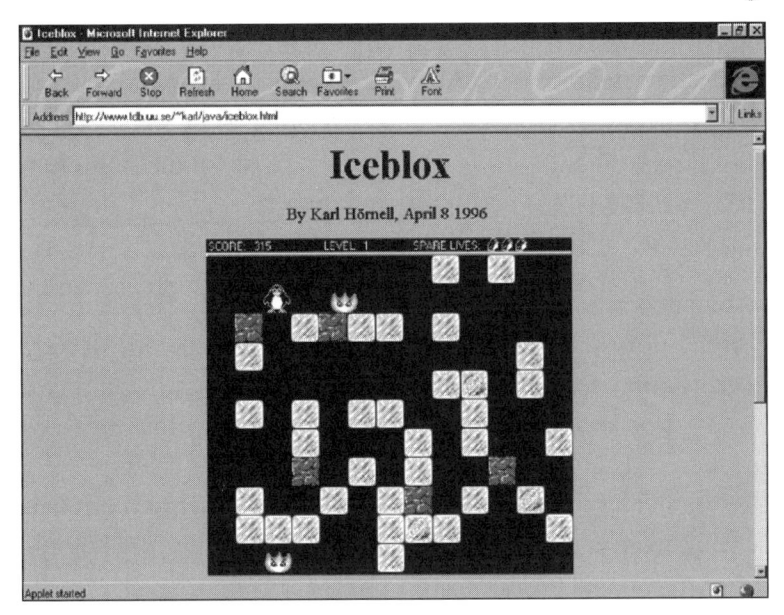

Figure 16.12 Playing Iceblox—a Java-enabled game.

Tetris—The traditional falling blocks game
http://www.lookup.com/Homepages/96457/blocks.html

Flip—A well done version of Othello
http://www.theglobe.com/fungames/flip/flip.html

NetCell—Competition Solitaire on the Net (May be addictive!)
http://www.cd.com/netcell

Crossword—Updated every night at midnight
http://www.starwave.com/people/haynes/xword.html

ActiveX

ActiveX is Microsoft's step beyond Java. ActiveX incorporates Internet interactivity with application interactivity, enabling hassle-free local and Internet access to all types of applications and files. Are you wondering what that just meant? OK, here are some examples of how ActiveX technology might affect you. ActiveX enables you to view QuickTime files (as we just saw) even though you don't have the QuickTime application on your system. ActiveX controls Java applets, so that Java applets—like all

ActiveX components—can be supported by any application, not just MSIE and other Internet browsers. ActiveX allows non-HTML content, such as spreadsheets, to be inserted into HTML files, enabling Internet accessibility to non-HTML documents. It may seem very convoluted right now, but as you see what happens with Internet interactivity, you'll understand the flexibility gained with ActiveX.

Now, back to the techie-side of things. ActiveX is a stripped-down implementation of *OLE* (Object Linking and Embedding) technology designed to run over slow Internet links (a.k.a. telephone modems). OLE allows an editor, such as Word, to "farm out" part of a document to another editor, such as Excel, then reimport it. ActiveX uses the same technology on the Internet level. When ActiveX is fully implemented, you will be able to use your browser to run HTML documents as well as other applications. In addition, you will be able to run Internet files, such as Java and HTML documents, in your desktop applications. You will be able to use your browser to open a spreadsheet on the Web, complete with its own toolbar, or you will be able to browse the Internet from your local spreadsheet application. Fortunately, MSIE enables ActiveX controls to install automatically when you download documents and applications. Once installed, the ActiveX controls run the Web page contents. You will not need to download any additional files or applications.

ActiveX is a dramatic step toward Microsoft's vision of complete interactivity; netizens sit (in front of their monitors) in anticipation of the changes sure to accompany ActiveX. Eventually, Microsoft envisions users moving from desktop, to Internet, to intranet without noticeable transition—sounds good to me! For more information on ActiveX, Microsoft provides a number of sites. You can visit the Active X pages offered on the Internet Explorer site at **http://www.microsoft.com/ie/ie3**. Or, you can check out Microsoft's new Site Builder Workshop at **http://www.microsoft.com/workshop**.

Better yet, run a search on ActiveX using SavvySearch or the Microsoft Search engine, and you'll pull up all kinds of information on this hot new technology.

The Future: Surfing in 3D

Beyond interactive application technology lies the possibility of entirely new worlds. You've probably heard of virtual reality. The Internet brings us its version of virtual reality using Virtual Reality Modeling Language (VRML). In turn, MSIE enables you to exist in virtual reality by supporting the full integration of VRML, without opening a separate browser. VRML is the language used to create digitized virtual realities. 3D virtual realities are starting to pop up on the Internet, and no doubt they will be commonplace before long. WorldView and Alpha World are two 3D applications that seem to stand out at the moment (keep in mind, as with most Internet technologies, statements like that can fall apart in a matter of hours). Regardless of the Internet's rapid change, I'm including this short discussion on 3D applications because, whether WorldView or Alpha World specifically makes it, 3D technology is here to stay and will influence future Internet technologies.

WorldView

WorldView is a VRML application that allows you to navigate through virtual reality sites as a standalone application or through Microsoft's Internet Explorer. WorldView is the first browser to incorporate Microsoft's powerful Reality Lab 3D software, which enables realtime manipulation of 3D objects on the Internet. The WorldView home page, shown in Figure 16.13, is located at **http://www.webmaster.com/vrml**.

Netizens entering the dimension of WorldView experience realtime, full-color, 3D "worlds" over the Internet. WorldView is simple to use and offers fast and accurate rendering for average complexity 3D objects. Other features include:

- Easy navigation through fully rendered, 3D VRML worlds
- Smooth, fully controllable movements
- Easy access to your designated home world
- Controllable image quality
- Variable speed of movement

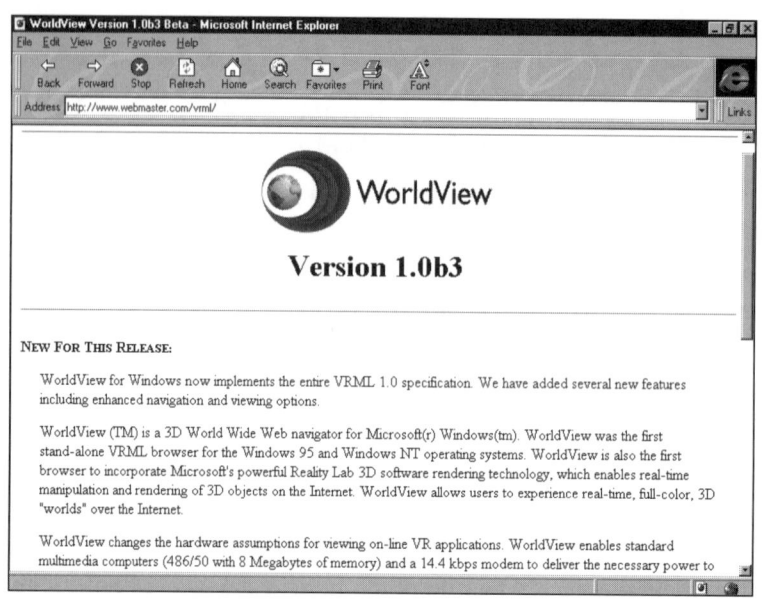

Figure 16.13 Entering the dimension of WorldView.

- A helpful Information Center
- Controllable lighting
- User-designated background color or texture
- The ability to save different camera views
- A hot list of favorite places
- Animation control

Microsoft recently licensed WorldView technology to be included in the new multimedia toolkit BlackBird. Through this license, WorldView potentially may become the most widely available and used 3D application on the market.

Alpha World

Alpha World, a virtual world on the Web, is the latest project of the people who developed Worlds Chat. Alpha World utilizes VRML to create an interactive world that allows visitors to manipulate it as they wish. Alpha World, displayed in Figure 16.14, is located at **http://www.worlds.net/alphaworld.**

In Alpha World, residents build their own environments and interact with each other. Residents can acquire and develop property, assume online personas, and interact in and with a living, breathing, multiuser community. Alpha World is not a preprogrammed simulation—it is as unpredictable and unique as the residents who create it. As of this writing, Alpha World isn't completed yet, and it only appears as a beta release. The good news is that membership is free while beta testing continues. Unless you're using a 28.8 Kbps modem, be prepared for long download times and jerky motion.

Chapter in Review

Well, we've come to the end of the chapter. As you've probably learned, the more you play on the Net, the greater your astonishment. Additionally, the more you learn, the more you sense the continual flux of the Internet's evolution. That's okay—in fact, it's good, because that's what makes it all so exciting. Maybe we can talk about it in a virtual world sometime, sipping coffee while we shoot the breeze and watch Net activities march past our virtual window.

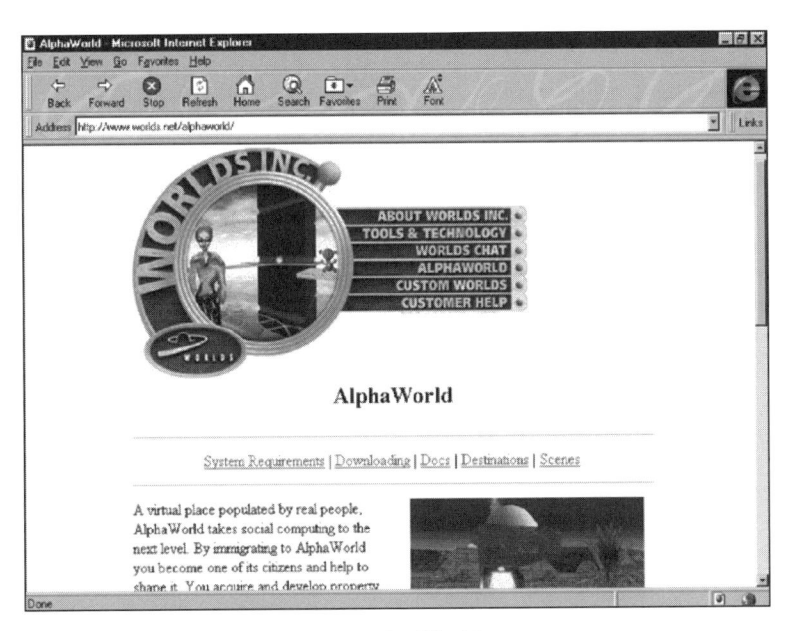

Figure 16.14   Visiting the residents in Alpha World.

As it is, we've merely caught a glimpse of the Internet's parade (in which the majorettes have barely begun to march). With the rapid advancement of ActiveX and Java technologies, the way you use your computer is about to change. Soon your movement from desktop to disk, to Internet, to local area networks will be so fluid and efficient, that you won't give your file manipulation efforts a second thought. One minute, you'll be viewing a file that's at least a five-hour flight away; the next minute, you'll be copying a file to your desktop from the server down the hall; and to top it off, your email will be running while you're writing a report on your desktop, illustrated with Java applets and links to the Internet. Of course, high-quality videos and realtime sound effects will compliment your seamless explorations throughout the day. And from the sounds of the drums, that day isn't too far away. The best thing you can do now is to grab a good spot on the curb—that way you'll be ready to join the parade when it gets to your block.

Creating Your Own Web Page 17

Now that you've explored the Internet, it's time to learn how to make your own home page.

*N*ow that you've gotten comfortable with navigating the Internet, you've probably seen a lot of interesting (and not-so-interesting) sites. After surfing for a few weeks, it becomes inevitable—that probing question on every Web surfer's mind, "How can I make my own home page on the Internet?" In this chapter, we'll show you how to make a simple Web page with a few interesting graphics.

Because we only have twenty or so pages to explain everything you need to know, this chapter will not help you create a masterpiece—we'll be focusing on the basics. For more in-depth Web page creation, see the Appendix.

Introducing HTML

HTML stands for Hypertext Markup Language. Don't worry, it's not as scary as it sounds. It's just the basic language for creating Web pages. HTML is not like other computer languages, such as C++ or Pascal. Instead, it's a formatting language.

If you've ever used WordPerfect (which is not a Microsoft product), you're probably familiar with the Reveal Codes function, which you use to see the formatting codes within a document. HTML coding works in a similar way to WordPerfect codes. In most instances, the formatting command (such as <BOLD>) will appear before the text to be bolded, and then another command (such as </BOLD>) will appear, indicating the end of the bolded text. Yes, HTML is, in general, really that simple.

There are other languages that you can use to enhance your Web pages, such as Perl scripts when you're creating forms, and Java when your creating a more interactive Web site. However, all the pages that you've ever seen on the Web start with basic HTML, and you can do a lot with it.

Microsoft Internet Explorer even supports extensions to HTML that other browsers, such as Netscape Navigator, can't see. This is both an advantage and a disadvantage. As an MISE owner, it means you can see everything a page designer includes in her page. On the other hand, using the extensions means that other browsers might not be able to see all the effort you've put into your page. I encourage you to be sparing with your use of the Microsoft-only HTML commands. Including these commands won't make your Web page unreadable; other browsers simply ignore what they don't understand. Eventually, the other browsers will catch up to MSIE, and then Microsoft will probably come up with new extensions...it's a vicious cycle!

HTML Editors

Before you begin writing HTML code, you need to acquire an HTML editor. Basically, an HTML editor provides you with built-in HTML commands, so you don't have to memorize and enter commands every time you need to use them. There are an incredible number of HTML editors available for downloading on the Internet. Some of the most popular are Hot Dog, HTML Notepad, and HTML Editor. I'll be using HTML Notepad—my favorite HTML editor—to demonstrate techniques in this chapter. However, if you already have Microsoft Internet Assistant, you can simply click on the Edit button that's on the toolbar. If you don't have IA, you won't have the Edit button, so you'll have to use a different editor.

Now let's get down to the nitty gritty—learning the HTML commands you need to create your own home page!

Writing HTML

As I said earlier in this chapter, HTML is, in general, very simple. Most HTML commands, which are also called *tags*, come in pairs, such as <B>...</B>, <TITLE>...</TITLE>, and <CENTER>...</CENTER>. Table 17.1 shows some of the most common paired HTML commands.

While the HTML tags listed in Table 17.1 are by no means comprehensive, they are among the most used of HTML commands. Again, for a much more detailed list of HTML commands, see the Appendix.

Writing Good Code

You might have noticed that I've written all the HTML code so far in all capital letters. Personally, I prefer all caps, because it makes it easier to find code after you've written a long HTML document, but it's not necessary. <CENTER>, <Center>, <center>, and <CenTEr> will all perform the same task: centering a line of HTML text. Some people prefer to have the opening half of a tag in all caps, and the closing in lowercase; use whatever you think will make writing and reading HTML easier for you.

Using the few tags we've learned, let's start creating our HTML document. You can create a Web page on almost any topic imaginable; I've decided to do our example page on a topic near and dear to my heart: travel.

Table 17.1 Paired HTML Commands

Tag Opening	Tag Close	Description
<BODY>	</BODY>	Defines the body of the document
<TITLE>	</TITLE>	Creates a title at the top of the browser window
<B>	</B>	Bolds the text enclosed within the tags
<I>	</I>	Italicizes the text enclosed within the tags
<U>	</U>	Underlines the text enclosed within the tags
<CENTER>	</CENTER>	Centers the text enclosed within the tags

Let's start by opening up your favorite HTML editor and starting a new HTML document.

Note: All the instructions in this book will be geared toward HTML Notepad. Other editors should behave in a similar fashion.

As you'll see in Listing 17.1, a new HTML document should start with **<HTML>** and end with **</HTML>**, which defines everything between those tags as an HTML document. HTML Notepad also provides **<HEAD>…</HEAD>** and **<BODY>…</BODY>** tags. The text within the **<HEAD>** tags will be the heading for your document. However, I prefer to use **<H (1-6)>** tags. The numbers in parentheses simply mean that the heading size can be set from 1 to 6, with 1 being the largest heading and 6 being the smallest. In Listing 17.1, I used a level 1 head for a large heading at the top of the page. The **<BODY>** tags simply mean that everything between the tags is the body of the document. As a final touch, I'm going to add **<CENTER>** tags to the heading, so it will be centered at the top of the page. Figure 17.1 shows the results of our first HTML outing.

LISTING 17.1 OUR FIRST HTML OUTING

```
<HTML>
<!-- Created Using HTML Notepad, Copyright (c) cranial software 1995-->
<!-- This file created by cranial software change initial.htm to do
  your own-->
<H1><CENTER>HTML Example</CENTER></H1>
<BODY>

</BODY>
</HTML>
```

Notice that HTML Notepad also has text between <!--> and <-->. This text is called *comment text* and is used for notes to the author or other people reading the HTML code. Anything between the tags is not readable by any HTML browser.

Now, that wasn't too hard…but it's not too interesting looking, either. Let's add just a few more tags to make things a little more flashy.

Creating Backgrounds

During your Internet travels, you may have noticed that very few pages have flat gray backgrounds like the one in our first example. Most pages

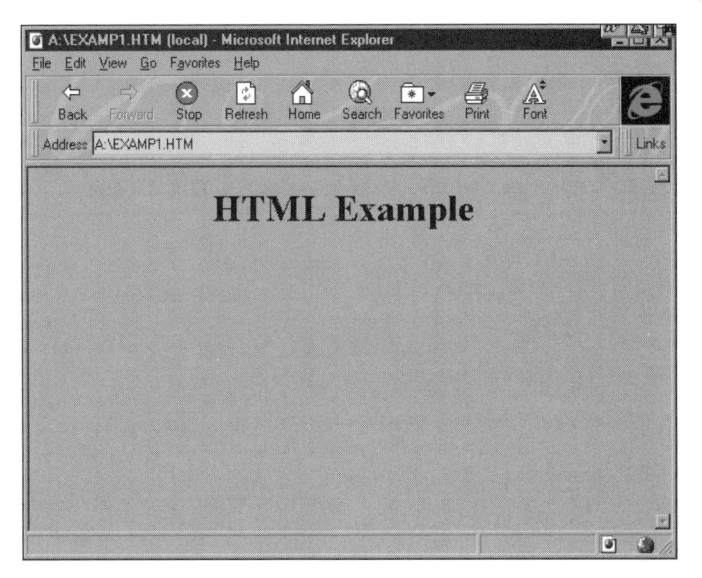

Figure 17.1 Our first attempt at HTML.

have one of two types of backgrounds: a single background color or a patterned background. Both make a home page much more attractive, and with very little work. Let's talk about single-color backgrounds first.

ADDING BACKGROUND COLOR

The background of our sample Web page is gray because that's the default color chosen by MSIE for pages that don't specify a color or design. Adding a color to the background is easy, but you have to make sure that you don't pick a color that makes a page hard to read. I don't know how many interesting looking pages I've skipped over, because the background was so bright, it made my eyes hurt.

To change the background color for a page, you simply add the command **BGCOLOR=** inside the <BODY> tag. After the equal sign is where things get difficult. The good news is that 16 simple word commands, such as black, red, blue, and white, are now available for you to designate the color; this is a new HTML standard (which only is visible to people using MSIE), and it makes life a lot easier. The bad news is that unless you want one of those specific colors, you'll have to list the color in a six-number hexadecimal format. Basically, what this means is that it's too complicated for you and me. Included in the Appendix is a list of some of the most popular colors in hexadecimal format; from there you can experiment for yourself by changing around a few numbers. Listing 17.2 shows our sample HTML code with background color added, and Figure 17.2 shows the resulting document.

LISTING 17.2   ADDING A BACKGROUND COLOR

```
<HTML>

<H1><CENTER>HTML Example</CENTER></H1>
<BODY BGCOLOR=blue>

</BODY>
</HTML>
```

Unfortunately, what you can't see in a black and white picture is that this blue background is really bright (remember what I said about trying not to hurt people's eyes?). You can change this color to whatever suits you.

ADDING BACKGROUND IMAGES

Another way to spruce up your Web page is to add a background image. The patterns you see behind most Web pages are actually comprised of just one small GIF (image) file. Again, all we have to do is add a single command to the **<BODY>** tag: **BACKGROUND=**. After the equal sign, you simply add the name of a small GIF file that you've downloaded from the Internet

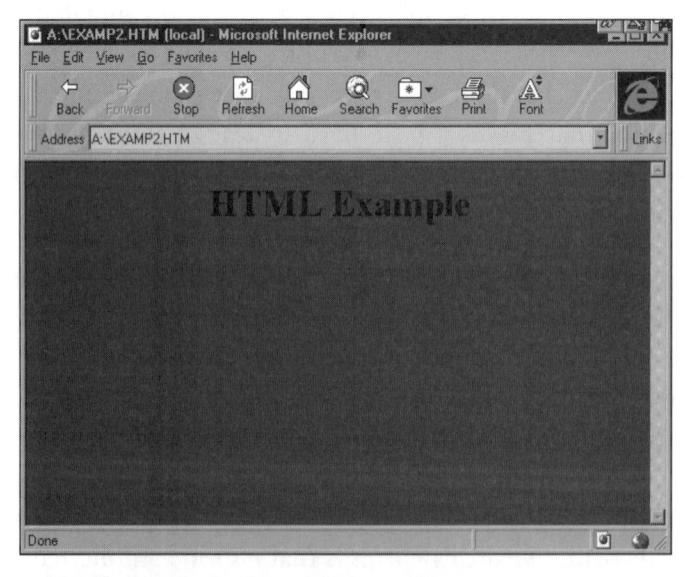

Figure 17.2   A blue background spices things up a bit.

or drawn yourself (if you're the artistic type). Remember, again, you don't want to turn someone off with a busy background, so be careful what types of images you use. Trial and error is the best method to figure out what looks good in an HTML document.

Microsoft maintains a great site for developers to explore and find ideas and image files for their Web pages, at no charge. The address for the site is **http://www.microsoft.com/workshop/design/mmgallry**. Let's go there now and take a look around.

As you can see, Microsoft has made it easy to find the types of images you're looking for. The site is divided into 16 categories; and look, there's even one for travel! Let's poke our noses around there and see what we can find. Simply click on the hypertext Travel link. Look at all the images we have to choose from. Not only are there four different background images, there are also four sounds, horizontal rules, banners, controls, and general images. This place is really a great resource for you when you're just starting to build your own Web pages (more resources are listed at the end of this chapter).

Personally, I really like the clouds as a background for a travel page, so let's use that one. To copy any graphic that you like from any Web page, simply position your cursor over the image, and click the right mouse button. You'll see a list of choices, as shown in Figure 17.3. The option we're interested in is Save Picture As. (For more information on the options available on this menu, see Chapter 12.)

Scroll down to Save Picture As and click with your left mouse button. MSIE will provide a standard Save As dialog box, so you can choose where to download this image. I suggest keeping all the files for each HTML project in one folder, so you don't get confused and go chasing files all over your computer. Feel free to change the name of the graphic to something you'll remember, so it will be easier for you when you go looking for it later. I'm going save the file as "cloudback".

Notice that MSIE saves this image using the JPEG file type. JPEG and GIF are the two most common image file types on the Internet and are widely accepted by all but the oldest browsers. JPEG files are usually quite

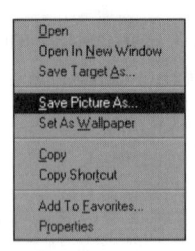

Figure 17.3 The menu of choices provided by right-clicking with your mouse.

detailed or are actual photographs, unlike GIFs, which are usually created with a computer graphics program.

Saving Space

I don't know about you, but when I come across a graphics-heavy page that will take forever to load, I usually just say forget it, consider it their loss, and point my browser in another direction. Don't let this happen to you! Keep track of how many megabytes of graphics you're putting on your page, and don't let the number get above 100 MB at the most. To find out how many megabytes a graphic has, simply right-click on the image before downloading and choose Properties. After you download, you can simply look in Windows Explorer. Choose your graphics wisely!

Now let's add this background to our travel page. As I said earlier, all you need to do is add the command **BACKGROUND=** to the **<BODY>** tag and enter the name of the file you want to use as the background, in this case, cloudback. Listing 17.3 shows you what the HTML code will look like.

LISTING 17.3 ADDING A BACKGROUND IMAGE TO OUR TRAVEL PAGE

```
<HTML>

<H1><CENTER>Welcome to the Travel Source</CENTER></H1>
<BODY BACKGROUND=cloudback.jpg>

</BODY>
</HTML>
```

Notice that I called the file cloudback.jpg, although the file doesn't seem to have a .jpg extension if you look at it in Windows Explorer. The extension identifies the file type to MSIE, so it knows what type of object it's dealing with.

Figure 17.4 shows how much more attractive our travel page looks, now that it's got an interesting background. (Trust me, it looks even better in color.) You can also see that I've changed the title of our page from "HTML Example" to something a bit more meaningful—"Welcome to the Travel Source".

Now it's time to move on to the next part of our project, adding some more titles and some actual text, so our page says something.

Text Formatting

To add basic sentences to our HTML document, we can simply start typing anywhere beneath the first <BODY> tag. However, there are a few tips to text formatting that you should know about. First of all, any tabs or excess spaces will be ignored, so you can't create columns or extra space between words (for that you need tables, which are too complex to include in this chapter—be sure to look at the Appendix for more on HTML table commands). Any hard returns will also be treated as just a simple space; so how do you end one paragraph and start a new one?

Figure 17.4 **Flying high with our travel page's background.**

There are a number of formatting commands that will allow you to easily break up text. The **
** tag (which stands for Break) will break a line wherever it's inserted and start a new one flush left. The **<P>** tag (Paragraph) will also break text, but it will start a new indented paragraph, with extra space between the two paragraphs. Finally, the **<HR>** tag will place a line (Horizontal Rule) across the screen. You can further specify the height, width, and alignment of the line. **SIZE=** specifies the thickness of the line in pixels (the default is 2). **WIDTH=** specifies the width of the line, either in pixels or a percentage of the screen (default is 100%). **ALIGN=** aligns the line to the left, right, or (the default) the center of the screen.

You can also change the sizes and style of the font you're using. To make the type smaller or larger, simply use the tag **<FONT SIZE=>** followed by a + or - and the desired number to make it larger or smaller than the default size. Enter the **</FONT>** tag when you want to go back to the default size. For example, to make some words appear larger, you would simply use the command **<FONT SIZE=+3>**, which would make the words appear three times larger than the default.

Listing 17.4 shows how I've added some text, with the help of these formatting tools, so our page actually says something. Because our page is going to be about different kinds of travel information, I'm also going to create some more headings to break up our page. Figure 17.5 shows the end result.

LISTING 17.4 ADDING FORMATTED TEXT TO OUR TRAVEL PAGE

```
<HTML>

<H1><CENTER>Welcome to the Travel Source</CENTER></H1>
<BODY BACKGROUND=cloudback.jpg>

<H2><CENTER>Expanding Your World</H2></CENTER>
<HR SIZE=4>

Thanks for stopping by the Travel Source. The goal of this site is to
 give you important links and information regarding the places
 <B>you</B> want to go.<P>
We've organized the information on this site into four
 categories:<BR>
```

```
* Airlines<BR>
* Other Transportation<BR>
* Hotels<BR>
* Other Travel Resources on the Web<BR>
<P>
Enjoy your stay at the Travel Source!<BR>
<BR>

<FONT SIZE=+3 Color=red>Airlines</FONT>

</BODY>
</HTML>
```

All the tags that I mentioned in the last paragraph were used in Listing 17.4. The spaces in between the lines have no effect on the layout of the page, but I find them useful to separate commands so they don't all run together. That way, if I need to make changes later on, it'll be easier to find whatever lines I'm looking for.

Now look at the third line from the bottom of the code listing. Notice that I included another modification within the <FONT SIZE=> tag: **COLOR=**.

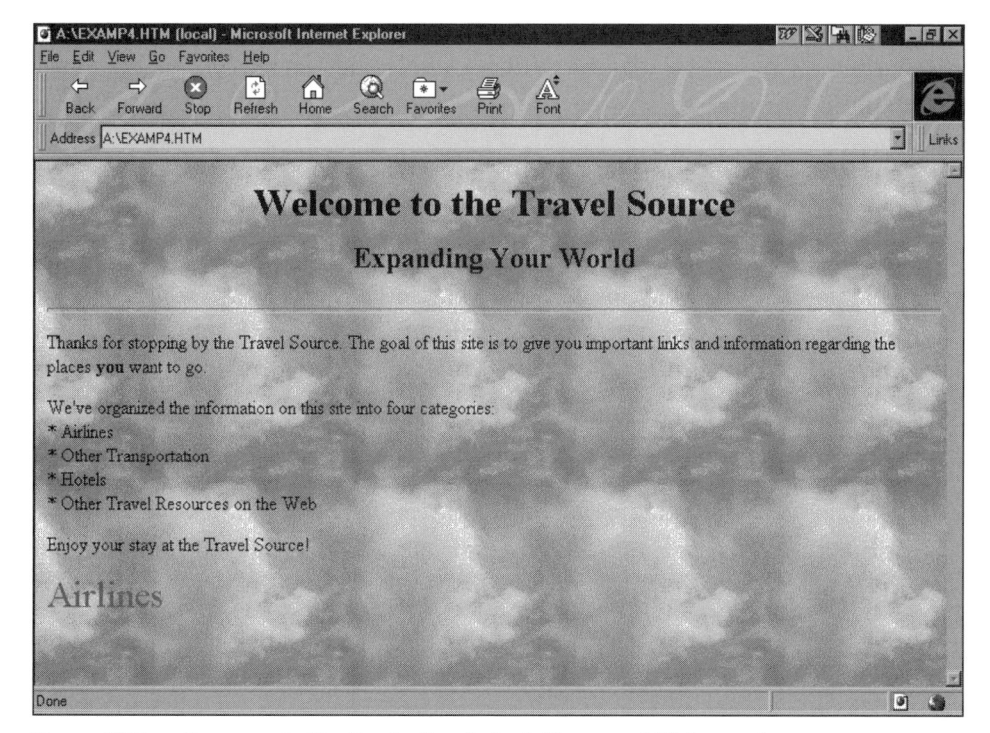

Figure 17.5 Our page is finally starting to look like a real Web page!

The same color specifications that can be used for the background of the page can now be given to any words you want within the text. If you don't want to change the size of your text, just the color, you can simply use the **<FONT COLOR=>** command. I think it's good to use it for emphasis, but a whole page filled with red type can be hard on the eyes. One good use for colored type is if you're using a very dark or black background; you can use white type to make it easier for users to read your page.

Creating Links to Other Sites

What does every Web page have that our page doesn't have yet? That's right, hypertext links. Don't you think it's about time we add some to our page? Let's go, then!

The basic command tags that are used to insert a hypertext link into an HTML document are **<A HREF=>** and **</A>**. (**HREF** stands for Hypermedia REFerence.) Following the **HREF=** command, you simply insert the URL of the site that you want to link to. More advanced linking information can be found in the Appendix. (Have I mentioned the Appendix enough yet? Well, it's really an important resource if you want to go further with HTML…so use it!) Everything between the two tags will appear as an underlined hypertext link.

Let's add some links under the Airline title in our document. Most of the major airlines (and some airlines that I've never heard of) have sites on the Web, so let's connect to them. You can link your page to any page you want; you don't have to ask permission. Now, to get someone to link their page to yours…well, that you have to ask for (and most major corporations won't do it). Listing 17.5 shows how we added links to our page, and Figure 17.6 shows what those links look like.

LISTING 17.5 ADDING HYPERTEXT LINKS TO OUR TRAVEL PAGE

```
<HTML>

<H1><CENTER>Welcome to the Travel Source</CENTER></H1>
<BODY BACKGROUND=cloudback.jpg>

<H2><CENTER>Expanding Your World</H2></CENTER>
<HR SIZE=4>
```

```
Thanks for stopping by the Travel Source. The goal of this site is to
  give you important links and information regarding the places
  <B>you</B> want to go.<P>

We've organized the information on this site into four
  categories:<BR>

* Airlines<BR>
* Other Transportation<BR>
* Hotels<BR>
* Other Travel Resources on the Web<BR>
<P>
Enjoy your stay at the Travel Source!<BR>
<BR>

<FONT SIZE=+3 Color=red>Airlines</FONT>
<BR>
<A HREF=http://www.aircanada.com>Air Canada</A><BR>
<A HREF=http://www.alitalia.it>Alitalia</A><BR>
<A HREF=http://www.amrcorp.com>American Airlines</A><BR>
<A HREF=http://www.british-airways.com>British Airways</A><BR>
<A HREF=http://www.delta-air.com>Delta Airlines</A><BR>

</BODY>
</HTML>
```

Adding links is as simple as that. To find the sites that you want to link to, simply search for the topic you're interested in (Chapter 10 gives you pointers on how to do a search) and include the addresses in your site. You can even link to other pages that you've created, so everything isn't located on one page. For instance, you could create a different page for each of the topics that we've listed, as well as your own personal page, so everything isn't squished into one page. It's good to not have too much information on one page—a good rule of thumb is to keep each page to two full screens; after that, it's time to start thinking about multiple pages.

Our little travel page is really starting to take shape now. But you know what it needs to start spicing it up? Some cool graphics!

Using Images

Inserting graphics is, again, done with one simple command: **<IMG SRC=>**. After the equal sign, you insert the name and location of the image file you want included on your HTML page. It's also considered polite to use the

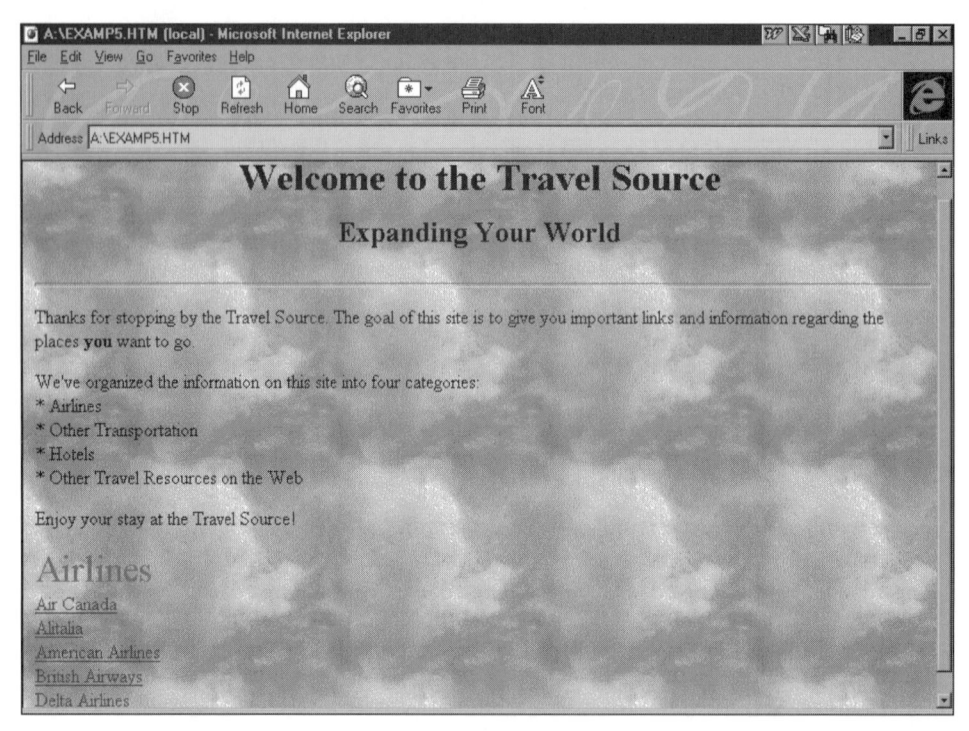

Figure 17.6 Linking to other sites is simple!

ALT= command, which gives your image a name. Leave a space after the **SRC**= URL, and then type in **ALT**= and what you want to call the figure, followed by the end bracket (>). That way, if someone using a text-only browser, or a browser with the images turned off, they'll see a symbol indicating that an image is there, and what the image is. A list of some of the commands associated with <**IMG**> is shown in Table 17.2.

Table 17.2 The <IMG> Tag Commands

Command Name	Use
SRC	Specifies the location of the image file
ALT	Names the image; helpful for non-image browsers
ALIGN	Aligns the image with text on the same line; choices are top, middle, bottom, left, right, texttop, absmiddle, baseline, and absbottom
HEIGHT	Specifies the height of the picture in pixels
WIDTH	Specifies the width of the picture in pixels
BORDER	Specifies the size of a picture's border in pixels

Believe it or not, these are not all the commands associated with <IMG>. You know where to look for the rest.

Earlier, in the section on backgrounds, we learned how to copy images from elsewhere for our own use. I copied another picture from the Microsoft page while I was there, and I think it would go perfectly on our travel page. Listing 17.6 shows how the image was inserted on the page, while Figure 17.7 shows our nearly completed page.

LISTING 17.6 INSERTING AN IMAGE ON OUR TRAVEL PAGE

```
<HTML>

<H1><CENTER>Welcome to the Travel Source</CENTER></H1>
<BODY BACKGROUND=cloudback.jpg>

<H2><CENTER>Expanding Your World</H2></CENTER>
<HR SIZE=4>

<CENTER><IMG SRC=worlds1.gif ALT=old world map></CENTER><BR>
<BR>

Thanks for stopping by the Travel Source. The goal of this site is to
  give you important links and information regarding the places
  <B>you</B> want to go.<P>
We've organized the information on this site into four
  categories:<BR>

<IMG SRC=bluecube.gif ALT=bluecube> Airlines<BR>
<IMG SRC=bluecube.gif ALT=bluecube> Other Transportation<BR>
<IMG SRC=bluecube.gif ALT=bluecube> Hotels<BR>
<IMG SRC=bluecube.gif ALT=bluecube> Other Travel Resources on the
  Web<BR>
<P>
Enjoy your stay at the Travel Source!<BR>
<BR>

<FONT SIZE=+3 Color=red>Airlines</FONT>
<BR>
<A HREF=http://www.aircanada.com>Air Canada</A><BR>
<A HREF=http://www.alitalia.it>Alitalia</A><BR>
<A HREF=http://www.amrcorp.com>American Airlines</A><BR>
<A HREF=http://www.british-airways.com>British Airways</A><BR>
<A HREF=http://www.delta-air.com>Delta Airlines</A><BR>

</BODY>
</HTML>
```

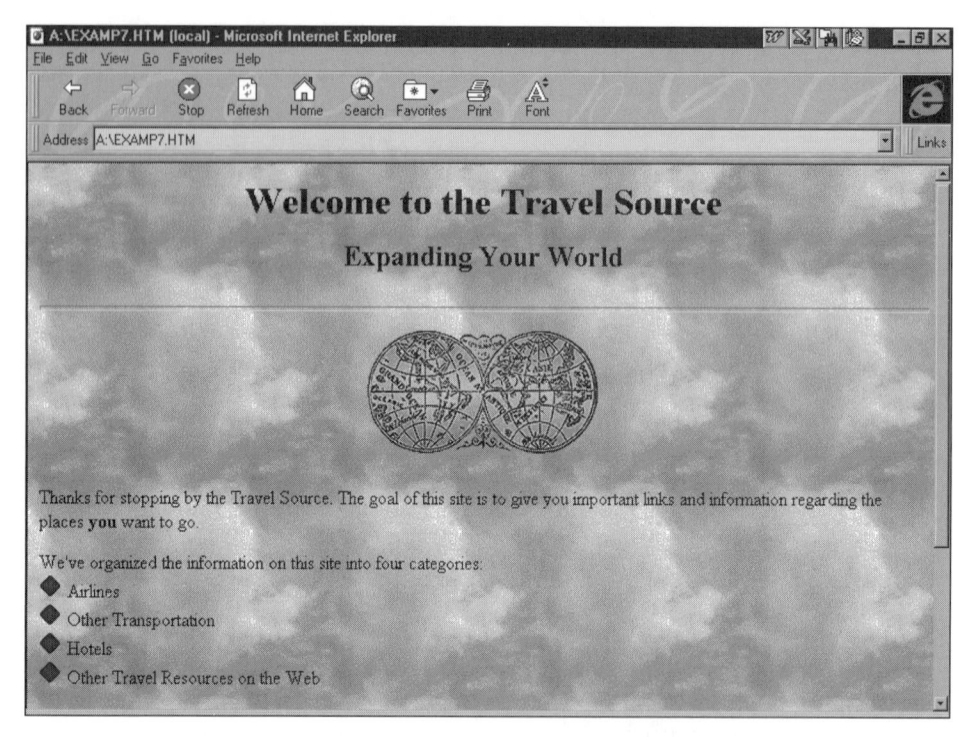

Figure 17.7 Images can really make a page look more interesting.

Notice that I used the <CENTER>...</CENTER> tags to center the picture on the page, which I think looks a lot better than just having it sit to the left side, which is the default. I also included some cubes to the side of the list near the top of the page. Bullets, cubes, and the like help to make the points of a list stand out. If you wanted to, you could also put different bullets next to the links in the Airlines list. You can even include the bullets as part of the link, by rewriting the code to look like this:

```
<A HREF=http://www.alitalia.it><IMG SRC=bluecube.gif ALT=blue
 cube>Alitalia</A>
```

Now the bullet will be designated as part of the link, because it, too, will be outlined.

Linking an Image

Remember before how I warned you about not putting too many large pictures on one page, because it takes too long to load? Well, if you have a lot of pictures you want to display, you can use very small versions of the picture, and have them link to another, larger picture on a separate page. That way, if people are interested in seeing a larger version, they can, but if they aren't interested in graphics, the page will still load quickly. Just use <A HREF= (URL of page with just image on it)><IMG SRC=(image file name)></A>. A blue line will appear around the picture, showing it's a link.

Well, our page is really pretty complete now. It needs some more links and categories, but I'll leave it to you to fill in those blanks. There's just one more piece of HTML code that I want to tell you about. It's a new extension created by Microsoft, and it hasn't been picked up by Netscape yet (at least at the time this book went to print).

Adding Marquees

One of Microsoft's new extensions, the marquee, is used to display a line of text or images that scroll across the screen. Normally, moving images on a screen requires a non-HTML programming language, such as Java. That's why the <MARQUEE> command is so interesting. You can specify the background color of the marquee, using the same colors specifications as backgrounds and text colors, so it doesn't clash with the background you're using. Unfortunately, a marquee's background can't be made to match a graphic that you've used for the background of your page...yet. To specify a background color, simply use the **BGCOLOR=** command. Listing 17.7, our last listing, shows the code added to our HTML page, and Figure 17.8 shows our completed HTML page.

LISTING 17.7 LIGHTING THINGS UP WITH A MARQUEE

```
<HTML>

<H1><MARQUEE BGCOLOR=white>Welcome to the Travel Source</MARQUEE></
   H1>
<BODY BACKGROUND=cloudback.jpg>

<H2><CENTER>Expanding Your World</H2></CENTER>
```

```
<HR SIZE=4>

<CENTER><IMG SRC=worlds1.gif ALT=old world map></CENTER><BR>
<BR>

Thanks for stopping by the Travel Source. The goal of this site is to
 give you important links and information regarding the places
 <B>you</B> want to go.<P>
We've organized the information on this site into four
 categories:<BR>

<IMG SRC=bluecube.gif ALT=bluecube> Airlines<BR>
<IMG SRC=bluecube.gif ALT=bluecube> Other Transportation<BR>
<IMG SRC=bluecube.gif ALT=bluecube> Hotels<BR>
<IMG SRC=bluecube.gif ALT=bluecube> Other Travel Resources on the
 Web<BR>
<P>
Enjoy your stay at the Travel Source!<BR>

<BR>

<FONT SIZE=+3 Color=red>Airlines</FONT>
<BR>
<A HREF=http://www.aircanada.com>Air Canada</A><BR>
<A HREF=http://www.alitalia.it>Alitalia</A><BR>
<A HREF=http://www.amrcorp.com>American Airlines</A><BR>
<A HREF=http://www.british-airways.com>British Airways</A><BR>
<A HREF=http://www.delta-air.com>Delta Airlines</A><BR>
<BR>
For questions, contact: <a
 href=mailto:toniz@coriolis.com>toniz@coriolis.com</a>
</BODY>
</HTML>
```

Trust me, it looks more interesting on the screen than in a still picture. The text in the marquee scrolls across the screen from right to left in an infinite loop. If you want, you have the option of having it stop at the edge of the screen, or of bouncing back and forth at the top of the screen. You can even specify how long it runs. You know where to look for more info.

You might have noticed the one piece of code at the bottom of Listing 17.7 that we haven't discussed yet—the text that starts with "for questions, contact...." The HTML code after that allows the viewer to send you an email message by simply clicking on the hyperlinked text. Figure 17.9 shows you the bottom half of the Web page, and Figure 17.10 shows the email box that appears.

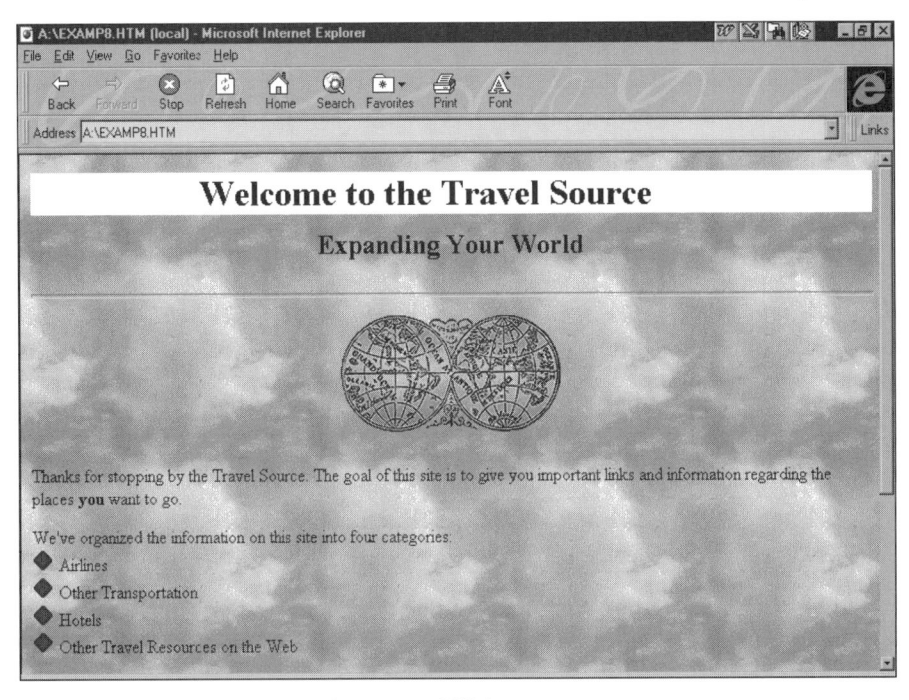

Figure 17.8 The final version of our travel Web page.

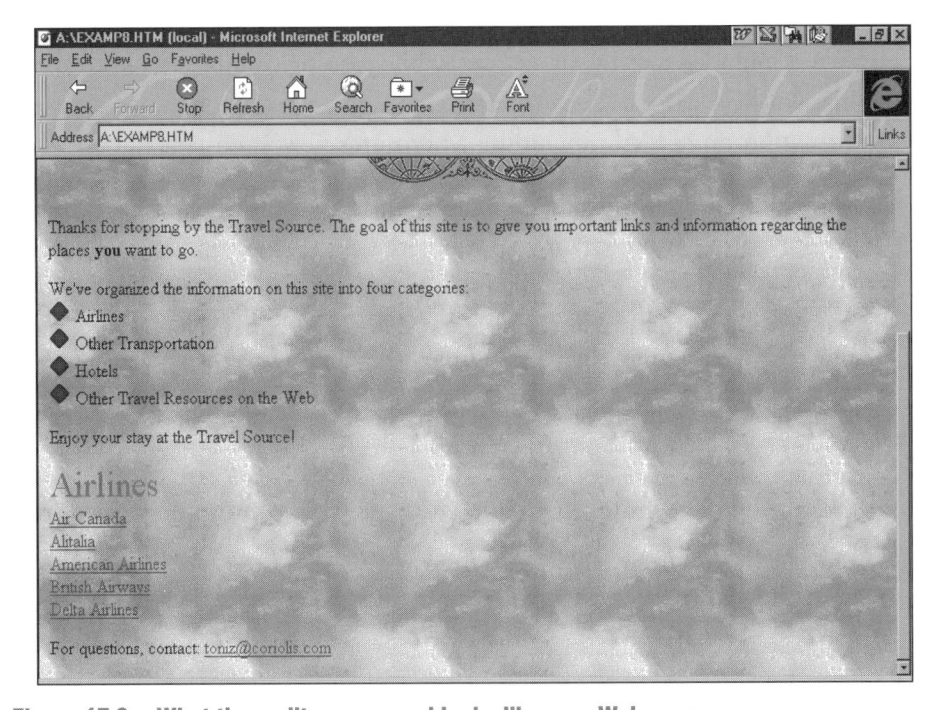

Figure 17.9 What the mailto: command looks like on a Web page.

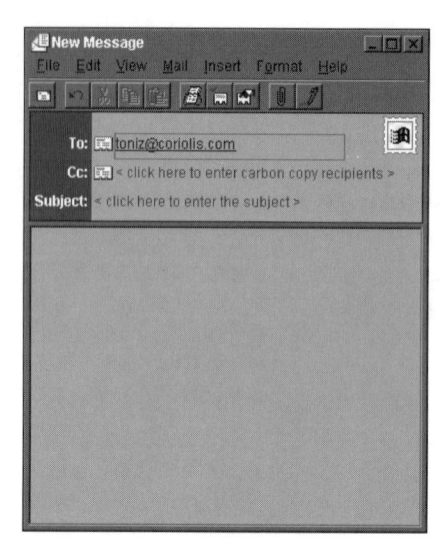

Figure 17.10 The results of clicking on the mailto: link.

Chapter in Review

I realize that this chapter has been a bit of a whirlwind lesson in HTML, but I tried to cover the most useful and attractive features of the language. This was intended to get your feet wet, while piquing your interest in creating your own Web pages. The Appendix will give you much more detailed information on HTML, including Microsoft's newest enhancements.

Don't feel bound by my subject matter, you can create a Web page about anything you're interested in. Some of the best pages on the Web were created by non-professionals who had a passion about a subject and wanted everyone to share that passion. So go ahead and be creative. May the creative muses be with you!

Other Resources

I've listed only a few sites that contain images that you can download free of charge. Stop by a few and see if they've got what you want. If not, just do a search for icons, or gifs, or images, or...you get the idea.

http://www.pentagon-ai.army.mil/images/image_libraries.html
This site is maintained by the Army Intelligence unit, but the graphics that can be found here include lines, balls, bullets, and a variety of other types of art.

http://www.netset.com/~wyatt/user/art
The beauty of this site is that it makes it easy to find what you're looking for.

http://www.mcs.com/~loch/www/index1.html
This site has a seemingly inexhaustible supply of images, ranging from the standard lines and balls, to images of all the characters on The Simpsons.

Writing Great HTML

*U*nderneath the slick point-and-click user interface of a Web browser such as Microsoft Internet Explorer lies an ASCII "markup language" that can easily be composed and edited with any Windows or DOS editor. Although we covered some of the basic features of creating Web pages with HTML in Chapter 17 of this book, this appendix provides a useful guide to most of the HTML features supported by leading Web browsers. As you spend more time creating Web pages, you'll find that this appendix will help you use the HTML tags.

HTML—The Language of the Web

HTML commands are enclosed in angle brackets, like <this>. Most commands come in pairs that mark the beginning and end of a part of text. The end command is often a repetition of the start command, except that it includes a forward slash between the opening bracket and the command name. For example, the title of an HTML document called "Habanero-Mango Chutney" would look like this:

```
<TITLE>Habanero-Mango Chutney</TITLE>
```

Similarly, a word or phrase that MSIE shows in **bold** type, would look like this:

```
<B>bold</B> type.
```

HTML Basics

All HTML files consist of a mixture of text to be displayed and HTML tags that describe how the text should be displayed. Normally, extra *whitespace* (spaces, tabs, and line breaks) is ignored, and text is displayed with a single space between each word. Text is always wrapped to fit within a browser's window. Line breaks in the HTML source are treated as any other whitespace, and must be specified with a *line break* tag, **
, or a *paragraph break,* **<P>, tag.

Tags are always set off from the surrounding text by *angle brackets* or the less-than and greater-than signs. Most tags come in "begin" and "end" pairs: for example, <I> ... </I>. The end tag includes a slash between the opening bracket and the tag name. There are a few tags that require only a start tag; I'll take particular care to point out these tags as they come up.

HTML is *case insensitive*: <HTML> is the same as <html> or <hTmL>. However, many Web servers run on Unix systems, which *are* case sensitive. This will never affect HTML interpretation, but will affect your hyperlinks: My.gif is not the same file as my.gif or MY.GIF.

Some begin tags can take *parameters*, which come between the tag name and the closing bracket like this: **<DL COMPACT>**. Others, like description lists, have optional parameters that will alter their appearance, if your reader's browser supports that option. Still others, such as anchors and images, require certain parameters and can also take optional parameters.

The Structure of an HTML Document

All HTML documents have a certain standard structure, but MSIE and most other Web browsers will treat any file that ends in .HTML—.HTM on PCs—as an HTML file, even if it contains *no* HTML tags. All HTML text and tags should be contained within this tag pair:

```
<HTML> ... </HTML>
```

<HEAD> ... </HEAD> Tag

All HTML documents are divided into a *header* that contains the title and other information about the document and a *body* that contains the actual document text.

While you should not place display text outside the body section, this is currently optional since MSIE will format and display any text that's not in a tag. Also, while you can get away with not using the **<HEAD>** tag pair, it's strongly recommended.

<BODY> ... </BODY> Tag

The body of the document should contain the actual contents of the Web page. The tags that appear within the body do not separate the document into sections. Rather, they're either special parts of the text, like images or forms, or they're tags that *say something* about the text they enclose, like character attributes or paragraph styles.

HEADINGS AND PARAGRAPHS

In some ways, HTML text is a series of paragraphs. Within a paragraph, the text will be wrapped to fit upon the reader's screen. In most cases, any line breaks that appear in the source file are totally ignored.

Paragraphs are separated either by an explicit paragraph break tag, **<P>**, a line break, **
**, or by paragraph style commands. The paragraph style determines both the font used for the paragraph and any special indenting. Paragraph styles include several levels of section headers, five types of lists, three different "block formats," and the normal, or default paragraph style. Any text outside of an explicit paragraph style command will be displayed in the normal style.

<ADDRESS> ... </ADDRESS> Tag

The last part of the document body should be an **<ADDRESS>** tag pair, which contains information about the author and, often, the document's copyright date and revision history. While the address block is not a required part of the document in the same way that the header or the body is, official style guides urge that all documents have one. In current practice, while many documents don't use one of the **<HTML>**, **<HEAD>**, or **<BODY>**

tag pairs, almost all documents have address blocks—perhaps because the address block is visible.

The format for using the **<ADDRESS>** tag is as follows:

```
<ADDRESS>Address text goes here</ADDRESS>
```

Comments

Comments can be placed in your HTML documents using a special tag as shown:

```
<!--Comment text goes here-->
```

Everything between the "<>" will be ignored by a browser when the document is displayed. Be sure to use the exclamation point!

Header Elements

The elements used in the header of an HTML document include a title section and internal indexing information.

<TITLE> ... </TITLE> Tag

Every document should have a title. The manner in which a title is displayed varies from system to system and browser to browser. The title could be displayed as a window title, or it may appear in a pane within the window. The title should be short—64 characters or less—and should contain just text.

The title should appear in the header section, marked off with a <TITLE> tag pair; for example, <TITLE>Lime-Jerked Chicken</TITLE>. MSIE is actually such an "easy-going" browser that the title can appear anywhere in the document, even after the </HTML> tag, but future browsers might not be quite so clever and accommodating. Including a title is important because many Web search engines will use the title to locate a document.

The format for using the <TITLE> tag is as follows:

```
<TITLE>Title text goes here</TITLE>
```

Normal Text

Most Web pages are composed of plain, or *normal*, text. Any text not appearing between format tag pairs is displayed as normal text.

Normal text, like every other type of paragraph style except the *preformatted* style, is wrapped at display time to fit in the reader's window. A larger or smaller font or window size will result in a totally different number of words on each line, so don't try to change the wording of a sentence to make the line breaks come at appropriate places. You'll be in for a big surprise!

 Tag

If line breaks *are* important, as in postal addresses or poetry, you can use the **
** command to insert a line break. Subsequent text will appear one line down, on the left margin.

The general format for this tag is:

```
<BR [CLEAR=Left|Right]>
```

The section listed between the "[]" is optional. This is a feature introduced as an HTML enhancement and supported by newer versions of some browsers.

Let's look at an example of how **
** is used. To keep

```
Coriolis Group Books
7339 East Acoma Drive, Suite 7
Scottsdale, Arizona 85260-6912
```

from coming out as

```
Coriolis Group Books 7339 East Acoma Drive, Suite 7 Scottsdale,
 Arizona
85260-6912
```

you would write:

```
Coriolis Group Books<BR>
7339 East Acoma Drive, Suite 7<BR>
Scottsdale, Arizona 85260-6912<BR>
```

The extended form of the **
** tag allows you to control how text is wrapped. The **CLEAR** argument allows text to be broken so that it can flow around an image to the right or to the left. For example, this tag shows how text can be broken to flow to the left:

```
This text will be broken here.<BR CLEAR=Left>
This line will flow around to the right of an image that can be
 displayed with the IMG tag.
```

<P> Tag

The **
** command causes a line break within a paragraph, but more often we want to separate one paragraph from another. We can do this by ending each paragraph with a **<P>** command. Paragraph breaks may be shown with an extra line or half line of spacing, a leading indent, or both. A **</P>** command exists, but it's optional and rarely used.

Logical and Physical Attributes

Character attribute tags let you emphasize words or phrases within a paragraph. HTML supports two different types of character attributes: *physical* and *logical*. Physical attributes include the familiar bold, italic, and underline, as well as a *tty* attribute for monospaced text.

Logical attributes are different. Logical attributes let you describe what sort of emphasis you want to put on a word or phrase, but leave the actual formatting up to the browser. That is, where a word marked with a physical attribute like **<B>**bold**</B>** will always appear in **bold** type, an **<EM>**emphasized**</EM>** word may be *italicized*, underlined, **bolded**, or displayed in color.

Web style guides suggest that you use logical attributes whenever you can, but there's a slight problem: Some current browsers only support some physical attributes, and few or no logical attributes. Since Web browsers simply ignore any HTML tag that they don't "understand," you run the risk that your readers will not see any formatting at all if you use logical tags!

The standard format for using any of the physical attributes tags is as follows:

```
<tag>text goes here</tag>
```

You can nest attributes, although the results will vary from browser to browser. For example, some browsers can display **bold italic** text, while others will only display the innermost attribute. (That is, **<B><I>**bold italic**</I></B>** may show up as *bold italic*.) If you use nested attributes, be sure to place the end tags in reverse order of the start tags; don't write something like **<B><I>**bold italic**</B></I>**! This may work with some Web browsers but it may cause problems with others.

<BLINK> ... </BLINK>

This is an enhanced tag. Text placed between this pair will blink on the screen. This feature is useful for getting someone's attention, but if you use it too much, it could get rather annoying. The format for this tag is:

```
<BLINK>This text will blink</BLINK>
```

<CENTER> ... </CENTER>

This HTML enhancement makes some Web page authors feel like they've died and gone to heaven. Any text (or images) placed between this pair is centered between the left and right margins of a page. The format for this tag is:

```
<CENTER>This text will be centered between the left and right
 margins</CENTER>
```

<FONT> ... </FONT>

This HTML enhancement allows you to control the sizes of the fonts displayed in your documents. The format for this tag is:

```
<FONT SIZE=font-size>text goes here</FONT>
```

where *font-size* must be a number from 1 to 7. A size of 1 produces the smallest font. The default font size is 3. Once the font size has been changed, it will remain in effect until the font size is changed by using another tag.

<BASEFONT>

To give you even greater control over font sizing, you can use the <BASEFONT> tag to set the base font for all text displayed in a document. The format for this tag is:

```
<BASEFONT SIZE=font-size>
```

Again, *font-size* must be a number from 1 to 7. A size of 1 produces the smallest font. The default font size is 3. Once the base font size has been defined, you can display text in larger or smaller fonts using the "+" or "-" sign with the **<FONT>** tag. Here's an example of how this works:

```
<BASEFONT SIZE=4>
This text will be displayed as size 4 text.
<FONT SIZE=+2>
This text will be displayed as size 6.
</FONT>
This text will return to the base font size—size 4.
```

Headings

HTML provides six levels of section headers, **<H1>** through **<H6>**. While these are typically short phrases that fit on a line or two, the various headers are actually full-fledged paragraph types. They can even contain line and paragraph break commands.

You are not required to use a **<H1>** before you use a **<H2>**, or to make sure that a **<H4>** follows a **<H3>** or another **<H4>**.

Standard format for using one of the six heading tags is illustrated by this sample:

```
<H1>Text Goes Here</H1>
```

Lists

HTML supports five different list types. All five types can be thought of as a sort of paragraph type. The first four list types share a common syntax, and differ only in how they format their list elements. The fifth type, the "description" list, is unique in that each list element has two parts—a tag and a description of the tag.

All five list types display an element marker—whether it be a number, a bullet, or a few words—on the left margin. The marker is followed by the actual list elements, which appear indented. List elements do not have to fit on a single line or consist of a single paragraph—they may contain <P> and <BR> tags.

Lists can be nested, but the appearance of a nested list depends on the browser. For example, some browsers use different bullets for inner lists than for outer lists, and some browsers do not indent nested lists. However, MSIE and Netscape, which are the most common browsers, *do* indent nested lists; the tags of a nested list align with the elements of the outer list, and the elements of the nested list are further indented. For example:

- This is the first element of the main bulleted list.
  - This is the first element of a nested list.
  - This is the second element of the nested list.
- This is the second element of the main bulleted list.

The four list types that provide simple list elements use the *list item* tag, <LI>, to mark the start of each list element. The <LI> tag always appears at the *start* of a list element, not at the end.

Thus, all simple lists look something like this:

```
<ListType>

<LI>
There isn't really any ListType list, however the OL, UL, DIR, and
MENU lists all follow this format.

<LI>
Since whitespace is ignored, you can keep your source legible by
putting blank lines between your list elements. Sometimes, I like to
 put the &lt;li&gt; tags on their own lines, too.

<LI>
(If I hadn't used the ampersand quotes in the previous list element,
the "&lt;li&gt;" would have been interpreted as the start of a new
list element.)

</ListType>
```

Numbered List

In HTML, numbered lists are referred to as *ordered lists*. The list type tag is <OL>. Numbered lists can be nested, but some browsers get confused by the close of a nested list, and start numbering the subsequent elements of the outer list from 1.

Bulleted List

If a numbered list is an ordered list, what could an unnumbered, bulleted list be but an *unordered list?* The tag for an unordered (bulleted) list is <UL>. While bulleted lists can be nested, you should keep in mind that the list nesting *may* not be visible: Some browsers indent nested lists; some don't. Some use multiple bullet types; others don't.

List Extensions

Unordered List with Extensions

When, for instance, Netscape displays the different levels of indentation in an unordered list, it uses a solid disc (level 1) followed by a bullet (level 2) followed by a square (level 3). You can use the **TYPE** feature with the <UL> tag to override this sequence of bullets. Here's the format:

```
<UL TYPE=Disc|Circle|Square>
```

For example, here's a list defined to use circles as the bullet symbol:

```
<UL TYPE=Circle>
<LI>This is item 1
<LI>This is item 2
<LI>This is item 3
</UL>
```

Ordered List with Extensions

When most browsers display ordered (numbered) lists, it numbers each list item using a numeric sequence—1, 2, 3, and so on. You can change this setting by using the **TYPE** modifier with the <OL> tag. Here's how this feature is used with numbered lists:

```
<OL TYPE=A|a|I|i|1>
```

where **TYPE** can be assigned to any one of these values:

A Mark list items with capital letters
a Mark list items with lowercase letters

I   Mark list items with large roman numerals
i   Mark list items with small roman numerals
1   Mark list items with numbers (default)

Wait, there's more. You can also start numbering list items with a number other than 1. To do this, you use the **START** modifier as shown:

```
<OL START=starting-number>
```

where *starting-number* specifies the first number used. You can use the feature with the **TYPE** tag. For example, the tag

```
<OL TYPE=I START=4>
```

would start the numbered list with the Roman numeral IV.

Inline Images

Using only text attributes, section headers, and lists, you can build attractive looking documents. The next step is to add pictures.

<IMG> Tag

The **<IMG>** tag is a very useful HTML feature. It lets you insert *inline images* into your text. This tag is rather different from the tags we've seen so far. Not only is it an empty tag that always appears alone, it has a number of *parameters* between the opening **<IMG** and the closing **>**. Some of the parameters include the image file name and some optional modifiers. The basic format for this tag is:

```
<IMG SRC="URL" ALT="text"
     ALIGN=top|middle|bottom
     ISMAP>
```

Since HTML 3.0 has emerged and additional extensions have been added, this tag has expanded more than any other HTML feature. Here is the complete format for the latest and greatest version of the **<IMG>** tag:

```
<IMG SRC="URL" ALT="text"
     ALIGN=left|right|top|texttop|middle|absmiddle|
           baseline|bottom|absbottom
     WIDTH=pixels
```

```
HEIGHT=pixels
BORDER=pixels
VSPACE=pixels
HSPACE=pixels
ISMAP>
```

The extended version allows you to specify the size of an image, better control image and text alignment, and specify the size of an image's border.

Every **<IMG>** tag *must* have a **SRC=** parameter. This specifies a *URL*, or Uniform Resource Locator, which points to a GIF or JPEG bitmap file. When the bitmap file is in the same directory as the HTML document, the file name is an adequate URL. For example, **<IMG SRC=MySmilingFace.gif>** would insert a picture of my smiling face.

Some people turn off inline images because they have a slow connection to the Web. This replaces all images, no matter what size, with a standard graphic. This isn't so bad if the picture is incidental to your text, but if you've used small inline images as "bullets" in a list or as section dividers, the placeholder graphic will usually make your page look rather strange. Some people avoid using graphics as structural elements for this reason; others simply don't worry about people with slow connections; still others include a note at the top of the page saying that all the images on the page are small, and invites people with inline images off to turn them on and reload the page.

Keep in mind that some people use text-only browsers, like Lynx, to navigate the Web. If you include a short description of your image with the **ALT=** parameter, text-only browsers can show *something* in place of your graphic. For example, **<IMG SRC=MySmilingFace.gif ALT="A picture of the author">**.

Since the **ALT** parameter has spaces in it, we have to put it within quotation marks. In general, you can put any parameter value in quotation marks, but you only need to do so if it includes spaces.

Mixing Images and Text

You can mix text and images within a paragraph; an image does not constitute a paragraph break. However, Web browsers like earlier versions of Netscape did *not* wrap paragraphs around images; they displayed a single line of text to the left or right of an image. Normally, any text in the same paragraph as an image would be lined up with the bottom of the image, and would wrap normally below the image. This works well if the text is essentially a caption for the image, or if the image is a decoration at the start of a paragraph. However, when the image is a part of a header, you may want the text to be centered vertically in the image, or to be lined up with the top of the image. In these cases, you can use the optional **ALIGN=** parameter to specify **ALIGN=top**, **ALIGN=middle**, or **ALIGN=bottom**.

USING "FLOATING" IMAGES

With the extended version of the <IMG> tag, you can now create "floating" images that will align to the left or right margin of a Web page. Text that is displayed following the image will either wrap around the right-hand or left-hand side of the image. Here's an example of how an image can be displayed at the left margin with text that wraps to the right of the image:

```
<IMG SRC="limage.gif" ALIGN=left>
This text will be displayed to the right of the image
```

SPECIFYING SPACING FOR FLOATING IMAGES

When you use floating images with wrap-around text, you can specify the spacing between the text and the image by using the **VSPACE** and **HSPACE** modifiers. **VSPACE** defines the amount of spacing in units of pixels between the top and bottom of the image and the text that is displayed. **HSPACE** defines the spacing between the left or right edge of the image and the text that wraps.

SIZING IMAGES

Another useful feature that has been added to the <IMG> tag is image sizing. The **WIDTH** and **HEIGHT** modifiers are used to specify the width and height of an image in pixels. Here's an example:

```
<IMG SRC="logo.gif" WIDTH=250 HEIGHT=310>
```

When a browser like MSIE displays an image, it needs to determine the size of the image before it can display a placeholder or *bounding box* for the image. If you include the image's size using **WIDTH** and **HEIGHT**, a Web page can be built much faster. If the values you specify for **WIDTH** and **HEIGHT** differ from the image's actual width and height, the image will be scaled to fit.

USING MULTIPLE IMAGES PER LINE

Since an image is treated like a single (rather large) character, you can have more than one image on a single line. In fact, you can have as many images on a line as will fit in your reader's window! If you put too many images on a line, the browser will wrap the line and your images will appear on multiple lines. If you don't want images to appear on the same line, be sure to place a <BR> or <P> between them.

DEFINING AN IMAGE'S BORDER

Typically, an image is displayed with a border around it. This is the border that is set to the color blue when the image is part of an anchor. Using the **BORDER** modifier, you can specify a border width for any image you display. Here's an example that displays an image with a five pixel border:

```
<IMG SRC="logo.gif" BORDER=5>
```

ISMAP Parameter

The optional **ISMAP** parameter allows you to place hyperlinks to other documents "in" a bitmapped image. This technique is used to turn an image into a clickable map.

Horizontal Rules

The <HR> tag draws a *horizontal rule*, or line, across the screen to separate parts of your text. It's fairly common to put a rule before and after a form, to help set off the user entry areas from the normal text.

Many people use small inline images for decoration and separation, instead of rules. While using images in this manner lets you customize how your pages look, it also makes them take longer to load—and it makes them look horrible with inline images turned off.

The original **<HR>** tag simply displayed an engraved rule across a Web page. A newer version of the tag has been extended to add additional features, including sizing, alignment, and shading. The format for the extended version of **<HR>** is:

```
<HR SIZE=pixels
    WIDTH=pixels|percent
    ALIGN=left|right|center
    NOSHADE>
```

The **SIZE** modifier sets the width (thickness) of the line in pixel units. The **WIDTH** modifier specifies the length of the line in actual pixel units or a percentage of the width of the page. The **ALIGN** modifier specifies the alignment for the line (the default is center) and the **NOSHADE** modifier allows you to display a solid line.

As an example of how some of these new features are used, the following tag displays a solid line, five pixels thick. The line is left justified and spans 80 percent of the width of the page:

```
<HR SIZE=5 WIDTH=80% ALIGN="left" NOSHADE>
```

Hypermedia Links

The ability to add links to other Web pages, or to entirely different sorts of documents, is what makes the Web a *hypermedia* system. The special sort of highlight that your reader clicks on to traverse a hypermedia link is called an *anchor*, and all links are created with the anchor tag, **<A>**. The basic format for this tag is:

```
<A HREF="URL"
   NAME="text"
   REL=next|previous|parent|made
   REV=next|previous|parent|made
   TITLE="text">

text</A>
```

Links to Other Documents

While you can define a link to another point within the current page, most links are to other documents. Links to points within a document are very similar to links to other documents, but they are slightly more complicated, so we will talk about them later. (See the section, *Links to Anchors*.)

Each link has two parts: the visible part, or *anchor*, which the user clicks on, and the invisible part, which tells the browser where to go. The anchor is the text between the <A> and </A> tags of the <A> tag pair, while the actual link data appears in the <A> tag.

Just as the <IMG> tag has a **SRC=** parameter that specifies an image file, so does the <A> tag have an **HREF=** parameter that specifies the **hypermedia reference**. Thus, "<A HREF=SomeFile.Type>click here</A>" is a link to "someFile.Type" with the visible anchor "click here".

Browsers will generally use the linked document's file name extension to decide how to display the linked document. For example, HTML or HTM files will be interpreted and displayed as HTML, whether they come from an http server, an FTP server, or a gopher site. Conversely, a link can be to any sort of file—a large bitmap, sound file, or movie.

IMAGES AS HOTSPOTS

Since inline images are in many ways just big characters, there's no problem with using an image in an anchor. The anchor can include text on either side of the image, or the image can be an anchor by itself. Most browsers show an image anchor by drawing a blue border around the image (or around the placeholder graphic). The image anchor can somehow be a picture of what is being linked to, or it can just point to another copy of itself:

```
<AHREF=image. gif><IMG SRC=image.gif></A>.
```

THUMBNAIL IMAGES

One sort of "picture of the link" is called a *thumbnail* image. This is a tiny image, perhaps 100 pixels, which is either a condensed version of a larger image or a section of the image. Thumbnail images can be transmitted quickly, even over slow lines, leaving it up to the reader to decide which larger images to request. A secondary issue is aesthetic: Large images take up a lot of screen space, smaller images don't.

Many people turn off inline images to improve performance over a slow network link. If the inline image is an anchor for itself, these people can then click on the placeholder graphic to see what they missed.

USING MANY ANCHORS IN AN IMAGE

The <IMG> tag's optional ISMAP parameter allows you to turn rectangular regions of a bitmap image into clickable anchors. Clicking on these parts of the image will activate an appropriate URL. (A default URL is also usually provided for when the user clicks on an area outside of one of the predefined regions.) While forms let you do this a bit more flexibly, the ISMAP approach doesn't require any custom programming—just a simple text file that defines the rectangles and their URLs—and this technique may work with browsers that do not support forms. For more information about how to create and use image maps, go to:

http://sunsite.unc.edu/boutell/faq/imagemap.htm

LINKS TO ANCHORS

When an HREF parameter specifies a file name, the link is to the whole document. If the document is an HTML file, it will replace the current document and the reader will be placed at the top of the new document. Often this is just what you want. But sometimes you'd rather have a link take the reader to a specific section of a document. Doing this requires two anchor tags: one that defines an *anchor name* for a location and one that points to that name. These two tags can be in the same document or in different documents.

DEFINING AN ANCHOR NAME

To define an anchor name, you need to use the NAME parameter: <A NAME=AnchorName>. You can attach this name to a phrase, not just a single point, by following the <A> tag with a </A> tag.

LINKING TO AN ANCHOR IN THE CURRENT DOCUMENT

To then use this name, you simply insert an <A HREF=...> tag as usual, except that instead of a file name, you use a # followed by an anchor name. For example, <A HREF=#AnchorName> refers to the example in the last paragraph.

Names do not have to be defined before they are used; it's actually fairly common for lengthy documents to have a table of contents with links to names defined later in the document. It's also worth noting that while tag and parameter names are not case sensitive, anchor names *are*; <A HREF=#anchorname> will not take you to the AnchorName example.

Linking to an Anchor in a Different Document

You can also link to specific places in any other HTML document, anywhere in the world—provided, of course, that it contains named anchors. To do this, you simply add the # and the anchor name after the URL that tells where the document can be found. For example, to plant a link to the anchor named "Section 1" in a file named complex.html in the same directory as the current file, you could use <A HREF="Complex.html#Section 1">. Similarly, if the named anchor was in http://www.another.org/Complex.html, you'd use <A HREF="http://www.another.org/Complex.html#Section 1">.

<BASE> Tag

One drawback of local URLs is that if someone makes a copy of your document, the local URLs will no longer work. Adding the optional <BASE> tag to the <HEAD> section of your document will help eliminate this problem. While many browsers do not yet support it, the intent of the <BASE> tag is precisely to provide a context for local URLs.

The <BASE> tag is like the <IMG> tag in that it's a so-called empty tag. It requires an **HREF** parameter—for example, <BASE HREF=http://www.imaginary.org/index.html>—which should contain the URL of the document itself. When a browser that supports the <BASE> tag encounters a URL that doesn't contain a protocol and path, it will look for it relative to the base URL, instead of relative to the location from which it actually loaded the document. The format for the <BASE> tag is:

```
<BASE HREF="URL">
```

Preformatted and Other Special Paragraph Types

HTML supports three special "block" formats. Any normal text within a block format is supposed to appear in a distinctive font.

<BLOCKQUOTE> ... </BLOCKQUOTE> Tag

The block quote sets an extended quotation off from normal text. That is, a <BLOCKQUOTE> tag pair does *not* imply indented, single-spaced, and italicized; rather, it's just meant to change the default, plain text font. The format for this tag is:

```
<BLOCKQUOTE>text</BLOCKQUOTE>
```

<PRE> ... </PRE> Tag

Everything in a *preformatted* block will appear in a monospaced font. The <PRE> tag pair is also the only HTML element that pays any attention to the line breaks in the source file: Any line break in a preformatted block will be treated just as a <BR> elsewhere. HTML tags can be used within a preformatted block, thus you can have anchors as well as bold or italic monospaced text. The format for this tag is:

```
<PRE WIDTH=value>text</PRE>
```

The initial <PRE> tag has an optional **WIDTH=** parameter. Browsers won't trim lines to this length; the intent is to allow the browser to select a monospaced font that will allow the maximum line length to fit in the browser window.

<ADDRESS> ... </ADDRESS> Tag

The third block format is the address format: <ADDRESS>. This is generally displayed in italics and is intended for displaying information about a document, such as creation date, revision history, and how to contact the author. Official style guides say that every document should provide an address block. The format for this tag is:

`<ADDRESS>`*text*`</ADDRESS>`

Many people put a horizontal rule, <HR>, between the body of the document and the address block. If you include a link to your home page or to a page that lets the reader send mail to you, you don't have to include a lot of information on each individual page.

Using Tables

Features like lists are great for organizing data; however, sometimes you need a more compact way of grouping related data. Fortunately, some of the newer browsers like MSIE have implemented the proposed HTML 3.0 specification for tables. Tables can contain a heading and row and column data. Each unit of a table is called a *cell* and cell data can be text and images.

<TABLE> ... </TABLE> Tag

This tag is used to define a new table. All of the table specific tags must be placed within the pair <TABLE> ... </TABLE>, otherwise they will be ignored. The format for the <TABLE> tag is:

```
<TABLE BORDER= number in pixels
       WIDTH= percentage of page or number
       cellspacing= number in pixels
       cellpadding= number>
table text</TABLE>
```

The **BORDER** tag allows you to define the width of the table's border in pixels. If **BORDER** is not defined, the default setting is no border. **WIDTH** defines the width of the table within the page, as either a percentage of the page or a defined number. It's better to use a percentage, as different people have different sized browser windows, so a defined number may not look right on their screen.

Like it sounds, **CELLSPACING** is the amount of space inserted between individual cells in a table, defined in pixels. The default spacing is 2. **CELLPADDING** is the amount of space between the border of the table cell and the contents of that cell. Setting the **CELLPADDING** at zero is not a good idea, because text from one cell could run into text from the next.

CREATING A TABLE CAPTION

Creating a title or caption for a table is easy using the <CAPTION> tag. This tag must be placed within the <TABLE> ... </TABLE> tags. Here is its general format:

```
<CAPTION ALIGN=top|bottom>caption text</CAPTION>
```

Notice that you can display the caption at the top or bottom of the table. By default, the caption will be displayed at the top of the table.

DEFINING HEADINGS FOR CELLS

In addition to displaying a table caption, you can include headings for a table's data cells. The tag for defining a heading looks very similar to the <TD> tag:

```
<TH ALIGN=left|center|right
    VALIGN=top|middle|bottom|baseline
    NOWRAP
    COLSPAN=number
    ROWSPAN=number>
text</TH>
```

CREATING TABLE ROWS

Every table you create will have one or more rows (otherwise it won't be much of a table!). The simple tag for creating a row is:

```
<TR ALIGN=left|center|right
    VALIGN=top|middle|bottom|baseline>
text</TR>
```

For each row that you want to add, you must place the <TR> tag inside the body of the table (between the <TABLE> ... </TABLE> tags).

DEFINING TABLE DATA CELLS

Within each <TR> ... </TR> tag pair come one or more <TD> tags to define the table cell data. You can think of the cell data as the column definitions for the table. Here is the format for a <TD> tag:

```
<TD ALIGN=left|center|right
    VALIGN=top|middle|bottom|baseline
    NOWRAP
```

```
        COLSPAN=number
        ROWSPAN=number>
text</TD>
```

The size for each cell is determined by the width or height of the data that is displayed. The **ALIGN** parameter can be used to center, left, or right justify the data displayed in the cell. The **VALIGN** parameter, on the other hand, specifies how the data will align vertically. If you don't want the text to wrap within the cell, you can include the **NOWRAP** modifier.

When defining a cell, you can manually override the width and height of the cell by using the **COLSPAN** and **ROWSPAN** parameters. **COLSPAN** specifies the number of columns the table cell will span and **ROWSPAN** specifies the number of rows to span. The default setting for each of these parameters is 1.

Frames

One of the newest HTML features is the ability to have separate frames within a document. Each frame is separate from the others and is controlled independently. Frames are a way to completely change the look of your Web site, without having to learn another, more complicated language.

<FRAMESET>...</FRAMESET>

When you define a set of frames, you enclose your frame code inside the <FRAMESET> tags. The <FRAMESET> tag replaces the normal <BODY> tag and helps to alert MSIE that the file is a frame file that will set up the overall layout of the screen. Within the <FRAMESET> tag you can have a number of tags, such as:

```
<FRAMESET ROWS="row info, row info, row info..."
          COLS="col info, col info, col info...">
```

The **ROWS** and **COLS** attributes use a comma-separated list of values, either specific pixel values, percentages of the screen (1 to 100), or a relative scaling value. The scaling value is used to divide a section of the screen into separate frames divided into rows or columns. If you leave out the **ROWS** attribute, MSIE assumes that you're dealing with a single row and it will automatically size the row to fit. The same applies to **COLS**.

Within the <FRAMESET> tags, you can have a number of <FRAME> attributes, which define each frame that is being created. The tag for creating a frame is:

```
<FRAME SRC="url"
       NAME="window_name"
       MARGINWIDTH=value
       MARGINHEIGHT=value
       SCROLLING="YES|NO|AUTO"
       NORESIZE>
```

First, the <FRAME> tag specifies a source URL (**SRC=**), which tells MSIE which HTML file or picture to load into the frame. **NAME** gives the frame an internal source, so you can refer to the frame later in your HTML code. **MARGINHEIGHT** and **MARGINWIDTH** define how much of a border you want between the displayed document and the actual borders of the frame. This value is specified in pixels and can range from 0 up to completely filling the frame. These settings are optional. If you don't use them, MSIE will set the appropriate margin width automatically.

When you define a frame, you can choose to have it scroll or not scroll. The default setting is **AUTO**, which allows the browser to scroll if the document loaded to that frame is bigger than the frame size allows. If you set the scrolling attribute to **YES**, the scroll bar will always appear. If you assign it **NO**, it won't show up. And finally, adding **NORESIZE** to the **FRAME** tag denies the user the ability to resize the frame.

The <TARGET> Tag

The **TARGET** attribute is the main resource MSIE offers to direct exactly which frame is updated by a specific user action. **TARGET** uses the following basic syntax:

```
TARGET="window_name"
```

TARGET can be used in conjunction with several tags, including the <A>, <BASE>, and <FORM> tags. Adding the **TARGET** attribute to the <A> tag directs the hyperlink to load the document into a specific frame. Here's an example:

```
<A HREF="myhtml.html" TARGET="mywindow">update my window.</A>
```

You can use the <BASE> tag to establish your own default target that is only overridden by other specified targets. This is a good way to set up a list of pictures in one frame that is reserved just for that. Here's an example:

```
<BASE TARGET="pictureframe">
```

When you activate a form using the <FORM ACTION> tag, you can add **TARGET** to it to tell MSIE which frame gets the result from the submitted form, as shown below:

```
<FORM ACTION="/process.cgi" TARGET="verification_window">
```

All **TARGET** names need to begin with an alphanumeric character to be valid, except for four, _blank, _self, _parent, and _top, which MSIE calls "magic **TARGET** names."

Java Applets

To allow Java applets to be played in Java-enabled browsers like MSIE, a new <APPLET> ... </APPLET> tag pair has been added. The format for this tag pair is:

```
<APPLET CODE = "appletclassfile"
         WIDTH = pixelwidth
         HEIGHT = pixelheight
         CODEBASE= "URL"
         ALT = "alternatetext"
         NAME = symbolicname
         ALIGN =
 left|right|top|texttop|middle|absmiddle|baseline|bottom|absbottom
         VSPACE = vertspace
         HSPACE = hortspace
         <PARAM NAME = parametername VALUE = parametervalue> >
```

When this tag is encountered, the Java-enabled Web browser loads the applet having the name *appletclassfile*. This will usually be the applet name with the extension .class at the end. In Java, all applets are created using Java classes. The applet class file that is loaded must be a compiled Java file. To load an applet, you must also specify the width and height of the area you want to run the applet in. These values must be specified in units of pixels.

Here's an example:

```
<APPLET CODE ="TickerTape.class"
            WIDTH = 300
            HEIGHT = 100
            ALIGN = left>
```

If you look closely at the <APPLET> tag, you'll see that it includes a <PARAM> tag. This tag provides information about optional parameters that can be passed to an applet. For each parameter that is passed to an applet, a separate <PARAM> tag must be provided. The **NAME** attribute specifies the name of the parameter and the **VALUE** parameter specifies the value assigned to the parameter. Here's an example of an <APPLET> instruction that includes a couple <PARAM> tags:

```
<APPLET CODE="TickerTape.class" WIDTH=600 HEIGHT=50>
<PARAM NAME=TEXT VALUE="The Java TickerTape Applet...">
<PARAM NAME=SPEED VALUE="4">
</APPLET>
```

MSIE Extensions

Microsoft has created a number of HTML extensions that enhance standard HTML. For example, in Chapter 17, we used the <MARQUEE> tag in our examples. While you're creating your Web pages, however, you'll want to keep in mind that, as of this book going to press, only Microsoft Internet Explorer can "see" these tags. Other browsers, like Netscape, will ignore the tags, so no harm will be done, but the effects you're looking for on your page might not show up for many Web browsers. For now, I suggest using these tags and parameters sparingly, until browsers like Netscape begin recognizing them.

A final note before we begin: MSIE accepts a list of 16 color names, as well as the standard hexadecimal codes. These colors are: black, white, green, maroon, olive, navy, purple, gray, red, yellow, blue, teal, lime, aqua, fuchsia, and silver.

<MARQUEE>Ö</MARQUEE>

Let's start with an HTML tag that was created by Microsoft. Here are the various parameters for the tag:

```
<MARQUEE
  BGCOLOR=HEXADECIMAL NUMBER OR ACCEPTED COLOR
  ALIGN=TOP, MIDDLE, BOTTOM
  BEHAVIOR=SCROLL, SLIDE, or ALTERNATE
  BGCOLOR=HEXADECIMAL NUMBER OR ACCEPTED COLOR
  DIRECTION=LEFT or RIGHT
  HEIGHT=n or n%
  HSPACE=n
  LOOP=n or INFINITE
  SCROLLAMOUNT=n
  SCROLLDELAY=n
  VSPACE=n
  WIDTH=n or n%>
</MARQUEE>
```

As you can see, <MARQUEE> gives you a lot of options to choose from. **BGCOLOR**, obviously, lets you choose the background color of the marquee, so it can either stand out or blend in with the background of your page (white is the default). **ALIGN** specifies that the text around the marquee should align with the top, middle (the default), or bottom of the marquee. **BEHAVIOR** specifies how the text in the marquee should behave. **SCROLL** (the default) means start completely off one side, scroll all the way across, and then start again. **SLIDE** means start completely off one side, scroll in, and stop as soon as the text touches the other margin. **ALTERNATE** means bounce back and forth within the marquee. **DIRECTION**, obviously, controls the direction in which the marquee scrolls, with left being the default. **HEIGHT** specifies the height of the marquee, either in pixels or as a percentage of the screen height. **HSPACE** and **VSPACE** define the left and right, and top and bottom margins, respectively, in pixels. **LOOP** specifies the number of times the marquee will loop, or it can loop infinitely. **SCROLLAMOUNT** specifies the number of pixels between each successive draw of the marquee text, while **SCROLLAMOUNT** tells the marquee how many milliseconds to wait before starting across the page again. Finally, **WIDTH** specifies the width of the marquee in pixels or as a percentage of the screen.

By no means do you need to use all (or even most) of these parameters when you use the <MARQUEE> tag. These extra options are provided so you can fine tune the look of your marquee. Don't let the number of parameters scare you from using what can be a very effective tag.

<BGSOUND>

Another Microsoft creation, **<BGSOUND>** allows you to add background sounds that will automatically play when a visitor enters your page. However, you will need to have a sound file that you can use within the tag. The parameters of the tag are:

```
<BGSOUND
  SRC= URL
  LOOP=n or INFINITE>
```

SRC specifies the URL where the sound is located. For faster loading of the background sound, I suggest you keep the sound file on your site; however, you can link to a sound located on another site. **LOOP** defines how many times the sound file will loop when a person enters the page. Try to use background sound sparingly, because it can become annoying after a while. You might want to skip looping altogether. To stop a background sound when you are at a page, you can simply press the Esc key on your keyboard.

New Parameters

The two HTML tags mentioned above are the complete creation of Microsoft. However, Microsoft has added some new parameters to a number of familiar tags that are worth mentioning.

<FONT>

Microsoft has added two important attributes to this tag: **COLOR** and **FACE**.

COLOR sets the color of the font, so different words can be different colors. For instance:

```
The last word of this sentence will be<FONT COLOR=red>red</font>
```

This is a great way to draw attention to certain words or sentences within your Web page, without resorting to using the often annoying **<BLINK>** tag.

FACE allows you to use a particular font on your page. Three fonts are available: Arial, Lucida Sans, and Times Roman. You can even specify a list of font names, so if the first font is available on the system, it will be used, otherwise the second will be tried, and so on. If none are available, a default font will be used.

<HR>

The one attribute added by Microsoft is **COLOR** which allows you to make a line any color you want.

<TABLE>

The final new parameters we'll be covering in this book are those associated with <TABLE>. The new parameters include:

- **ALIGN=LEFT** or **RIGHT**—Specifies that the table or the text can be left- or right-aligned. The default is left-aligned for **TABLE, TR,** and **TD**. The default is center-aligned for **TH**.

- **BACKGROUND=url**—Specifies a background graphic. The picture is tiled behind the text and graphics. This parameter can be used for the whole table, a row, or even just one cell.

- **BGCOLOR=hexadecimal number** or **color name**—Sets background color. Can also be used for the entire table, a row, or a cell.

- **BORDERCOLOR=hexadecimal number** or **color name**—Sets border color and must be used with the **BORDER** attribute.

- **VALIGN=TOP** or **BOTTOM**—Specifies that the text can be top- or bottom-aligned. The default is center-aligned.

Index

A

Accessing Web page menus, 289
Active Content options, 89
ActiveMovie, 59, 60, 378
ActiveX, 56, 58, 383
Add to favorites command, 283
Adding links to Web page, 401
Address Book, 319, 321, 323, 321–27
    adding groups, 324
    adding names, 323
    Pick Recipients command, 324
    sorting, 323
Address box, 35
    moving, 35
    pasting information, 29
    Quick Menu, 278–80
Addresses
    mail, 322
    printing a links table, 28
    sharing, 28
Advanced card, 90, 92
    additional options, 95
    cryptography, 95
    ratings, 91
    temporary Internet files options, 92
Advanced Research Projects Agency (ARPA), 4–5
Advertising, 227
    in newsgroups, 353, 365
AIFF, 59
Alpha World, 385, 386
Alta Vista, 135, 233, 234–36
Amazon.com Books, 269
America Online (AOL), 6, 9–10, 125, 331, 339, 362
    buddy lists, 143
    case sensitivity, 136
    checking billing, 145
    downloading, 126
    favorite places, 136
    file transfer protocol (FTP), 139
    find file feature, 129
    flash sessions, 143
    free areas, 145
    getting online support, 142
    hyperlinks, 142
    installing
        from CD, 128
        from downloaded program, 129
    integration with MSIE, 138
    keywords, 132
    mail, 139
    multiple page access, 138
    navigating with keywords, 126
    newsgroups, 140
    parental controls, 144
    restricting access, 145
    search function, 133
    setting browser preferences, 133
    software search, 136
    toolbar, 131
    world wide web icon, 132
Animation
    animated GIF, 59
    cursors, 377
    graphics, 376
    interrupting display, 78
ANS, 72
Applets, 382
Application sharing, 62
Apply button, 78, 80
Archie, 45
Area and country codes link, 183
Army Intelligence unit graphics site, 407
Art & Architecture Thesaurus link, 198
Art links, 218
Arts & Entertainment, 216, 218
    Louvre, 219
    Mr. Showbiz, 219
    Ticketmaster Online, 219
    UnitedMedia, 219
ASCII, 8
AT&T's online 800 Directory, 181
AU, 59
Audio conferencing, 63
Audio files, 373–376

MIDI, 373
RealAudio, 375
sound clips, 374
AVI, 59

B

Background
 adding and changing, 291
 bitmap, 80
Bartelby Library link, 194
Bartlett's Quotations link, 194
BBSes, 347
Berners-Lee, Tim, 8
BET link, 226
Billennium, The, 222
BlackBird, 386
Book review, 220
Boolean searches, 233
Browsers
 address box, 35
 client, 10
 customizing settings, 75
 multiple windows, 308
 setting preferences, 133
 window, 24
Buddy lists, 143
Business & Finance, 216, 219
 business news, 219
 doing business on the internet, 219
 government resources, 219
 personal finance, 219
 small business, 219
Business Numbers link, 182
Buttons, 34
 apply, 78
 international, 81
 reassigning, 35

C

C|Net, 220, 221
Caching, 30, 56, 70, 93
 amount of disk space, 94
 clearing cached files, 95
 controlling, 133
 proxy gateways, 72
 refreshing, 70
 setting options, 93
 viewing cached files, 94
Canceling newsgroup posts, 353

Car Talk, 222
Cards
 connection, 81
 general, 77
 navigation, 83
Case sensitivity in AOL, 136
Catapult, 72
CERN, 6, 8, 10, 44
Certificates, 89
Character sets
 non-English, 65
Check Spelling. *See* Spell Check.
Cinemania Online, 199
CIS Download directory, 149
Clear History button, 86
Client authentication, 69
Client/server
 model, 9
 systems, 44
Client/server model, 8–9
CMP Technology Magazine Search, 197
Code certificate, 69
Colleges, finding, 174
Colors
 adding to Web pages, 393
 customizing display, 78
Comic strips link, 114
Commands, 29-33
Comment text, 392
Communications
 connection card options, 81
 security protocols, 69
 via MSIE, 61
Composing mail offline, 330
CompuServe Information Systems (CIS), 6, 147, 330, 362
 access charges, 154
 access number, 151
 changing providers, 160
 checking for WinSock, 157
 connection tips, 160
 dial-up scripting tool, 155
 downloading Explorer, 152
 establishing PPP connection, 154
 getting support online, 162
 home page, 158
 installing Explorer, 151
 setting up Explorer, 148
 signing off, 163
 with Mosaic, 150

Computers & Technology, 216, 220
Conferencing, 62
 application sharing, 62
 Internet audio, 63
 multipoint communications, 63
 whiteboard, 63
Connection card, 81
 dialing options, 81
 proxy server options, 83
Connection Wizard, 23
Content Advisor cards, 91
Cookies, 88
Copy shortcut command, 283
Coriolis Group, The, 330
Creating links, 400
Cross-posting messages, 364
CryptoAPI, 70
Cryptography, 95
Cultural information database link, 198
CultureFinder, 203
Custom options pages, 102
Custom start options
 personal preferences, 104
 service options, 106
Custom start page. *See* Microsoft Network (MSN).
Cyber Atlas, 219

D

Dangerous Creatures, 306
Day planner, 316
Decoding messages, 361
DejaNews, 136
Deleting
 items in Microsoft Internet Mail, 336
 newsgroups, 352
Demodulation, 55
Desktop Links, 297–300
 in folders, 299
Development tools, 220
Dialup Networking, 349
 CIS, 151
 DUN, 320
 redial, 321
Digital telephone lines, 55
Dilbert, 219
Disclaimer, 228

Index   441

Display
　controlling content, 65
　disabling pictures, 77
　disabling videos, 77
　local file directory, 48
　previous sites, 31
　rapid redisplay, 70
　speeding up display time, 31
DNS. *See Domain Name System.*
Document
　as a shortcut, 342
　pointers (links), 268
Doing Business on the Internet, 219
Domain name system, 23
Domains
　error messages, 51
　name, 40, 322
　table of abbreviations, 15
Download headers command in Microsoft Internet News, 364
Downloading
　code safety, 68
　expediting, 114
　files, 303–17
　finding downloaded files, 23
　non-English character sets, 65
　progressive rendering, 57
Drag-and-drop, 296, 342

E

Earthlink, 23, 149, 322, 330. *See also Internet Service Provider.*
Easter Egg Surprises, 280
Edit menu, 29
Email, 61, 319–46
　domain name, 322
　features, 61
　finding addresses, 185
　flash sessions in AOL, 143
　receipts, 333
　user name, 322
Embedded programs, 59
Enable/Disable Ratings button, 91
End-to-end connectivity, 56
Error messages, 50
Essentials directory, 124, 165-212
　accessing, 166
　address lookup, 180
　business phone numbers, 182
　environmental directory, 170

　financial information, 175
　home maintenance, 169
　home reference, 168
　music, 201
　travel tips, 186
　writer's reference, 190
Exchange, 324
Excite, 135, 233, 236–38
　accuracy, 237
Executable file links, 22
Expert Add, 141
Explorer. *See Microsoft Internet Explorer.*
Extensions. *See Hypertext Markup Language.*

F

FAQ. *See Frequently Asked Questions.*
Fast text mode, 57
Favorite links, 120
Favorite places (AOL), 136
Favorites, 275. *See also Shortcuts.*
　creating Favorites folders, 300
　locating, 297
Favorites folder, 33, 254, 259
　adding links, 259
　creating hierarchies of favorites, 265
　creating subdirectories, 266
　default location, 261
　deleting links, 271
　importing Netscape bookmarks, 273
　Internet shortcut card, 264
　moving links to subdirectories, 267
　organizing, 33, 261
　property sheet, 263
　renaming links, 270
　viewing, 261
File compression, 304
　self-extracting file, 304
　WinZip, 304, 309
File Manager, 307
File menu, 26-29
File Transfer Protocol. *See FTP.*
Files
　downloading, 303–17. *See also Downloading files.*
　open command, 307

　save to disk command, 307
　temporary, 307
　viewing cached files, 94
Finance, 219
FinanceHub, 220
Financial Information link
　information about a business, 178
　IRS information, 176
　track a package, 178
Find a college link, 174
Find a vacation spot link, 186
Find File feature, 129
Finding people on the Internet, 251
Fixed-width fonts, 80
FlashSessions, 143
　activating, 144
Flight Times link, 186
Floating frames, 371
Folders in Microsoft Internet Mail, 336
FOLDOC site, 261
Fonts
　choosing, 80
　fixed-width, 80
　proportional, 80
　selecting for viewing, 30
Food & Drink, 220
　Internet Epicurean, 220
Formatting, 397
　codes, 390
　command, 390
　commands, 398
　language, 389
　tools, 398
Forward as Attachment
　in Microsoft Internet News, 359
　in Microsoft Internet Mail, 339
Frames, 370
　borderless, 370
　floating, 370
　pop-up, 371
　refreshing, 373
Free areas in AOL, 145
Free stuff, 33
Freeware, 304
　defined, 305
　program site, 317
　search engine, 313
Frequently Asked Questions (FAQs), 366
　newsgroups, 348
　obtaining via email, 368

FTP, 42, 139, 303, 308
   Monster FTP Sites List, 317
   search engines, 243
   site, 316
   software libraries
      Garbo, 308
      WinSite, 308
Fun. *See Games.*
Fun & Interests, 216, 220

G

Games, 220, 382
   download files, 313
   files, 316
   Flip game, 49
   program site, 317
Garbo, 308
Gateways, 71
General card, 28, 77
   appearance, 78
   font options, 80
   international button, 81
   multimedia, 77
   toolbars, 80
Getty Information Institute site, 198
GIFs, 394, 395, 396
   animated, 376
Go menu, 31-32
Gopher, 43, 139
   search engines, 243
Government Publication Search, 198
Government Resources, 219
Graphics
   adding to Web pages, 401
   progressive rendering, 57
   quick menu, 277
Graphics site
   Army Intelligence unit, 407

H

Hard drive properties, 97
Harvest Broker, 313
Health, 221
Health information link, 173
Help menu, 33
History folder, 300

   clearing, 86
   forward arrow button, 255
   options, 85
History list, 32, 254, 257
   viewing, 258
Home Entertainment links, 218
Home Maintenance link, 169
Home page, 12
   accessing, 41
   designing a travel page, 395
   personal, 389
Home Reference link, 168
   environmental directory, 170
   find a college, 174
   health information, 173
   plant and garden information, 170
Host name, 40
Hot Dog, 390
Hot link, 336
HTML. *See Hypertext Markup Language.*
HTTP
   format, 41
   Keep-Alive protocol, 57
HTTPS protocol, 42
Hyperlink, 12
   anchor, 13
   in AOL, 142
   reference, 13
Hypermedia documents, 8
Hypermedia reference (HREF), 400
Hypertext, 8, 79
   link, 306
   links quick menu, 277
Hypertext Markup Language (HTML), 8, 11, 40, 389–406
   comment text, 392
   defined, 389
   editors, 390
   extensions, 390, 405
   in email, 338
   marquees, 405
   notepad, 392
   paired commands, 391
   tags, 391
   text formatting, 397
   viewing, 31
Hypertext Transport Protocol (HTTP), 14, 39

I

Icons
   heart icon (AOL), 136
   Internet links, 138
   on newsgroup message lists, 358
IETF, 69
Import
   in Microsoft Internet Mail, 340
   Netscape bookmarks, 273
Inbox in Microsoft Internet Mail, 336
Inbox Assistant in Microsoft Internet Mail, 337
Infoseek, 135, 233, 238–40
Inktomi, 135
Installation, 22
   contacting the Internet Connection Wizard, 23
   downloading, 22
Integrated Services Digital Network. *See ISDN.*
Intellicast weather, 116
Interactive Movie Technologies home page, 379
Internal Revenue Service (IRS), 219
International button, 81
International extensions, 37, 63, 64
Internet, 16
   addresses, 39
   communication, 61
   connection wizard, 23
   defined, 2
   domain name, 322
   history of, 1, 4
   mail, 336. See also Microsoft Internet Mail.
   news, 62
   newsgroups, 46
   protocol (IP), 5
   ratings card, 91
   resources, 39
   searches options, 117
   security, 293
   services, 166
   shortcut card, 264
   Sleuth, 118
   traffic, 11
   users, 3

Index 443

user name, 322
using NetMeeting, 62
Internet Engineering Task Force.
  See IETF.
Internet Epicurean, 220
Internet Searches Option, 117
  favorite links, 120
  great sites, 119
  search engine settings, 118
Internet Service Provider (ISP).
  See also ISP.
  automatic signon problems, 330
  Earthlink, 322
Investments. See Business &
  Finance.
IRS information, finding, 176
ISDN, 55
ISP, 23
  checking current settings, 82
  dialing options, 82

J

Java, 8, 381, 405
  applets, 382
  compiler in MSIE, 58
  enabling JIT compiler, 96
  games sites, 382
  in Web page design, 390
  logging, 96
JPEG, 59, 395

K

Keep-Alive protocol, 57
Keepers links, 216–18
Keyboard Commands, 293–96
  assigning shortcut keys, 295
  tabbing, 293
Keywords, 233
  in AOL, 126
  in the Essentials Directory, 169
  searching using AOL, 135
Kids
  area, 226
  fun stuff for, 220
  link option, 105

L

Language capabilities, 63
Linking images
  on a Web page, 405
Links, 8, 12. See also Shortcuts.
  acronyms, 193
  address information, 38
  assigning links to folders, 122
  button, 24, 35
  changing the color for printing, 28
  contents, 123
  creating, 33
  custom start options, 103
  customizing display, 78
  customizing the toolbar, 85
  desktop, 297
  displaying, 26
  document pointers, 268
  essentials directory, 165
  essentials services directory, 124
  favorite, 120, 254
  favorites folder, 33
  health information, 173
  highlighting when clicked, 96
  kids, 105
  magazine, 198
  maps, 188
  movie essentials, 199
  MSN Investor, 107
  MSNBC, 108, 111, 124
  music, 110
  navigating with, 49
  options, 79
  preview, 124
  printing a links table, 28
  reassigning buttons, 35
  shortcuts, 27
  site of the day, 119
  status bar, 37
  stock market update, 108
  stopping access, 30
  Surf Stories page, 124
  today's links, 32
  toolbar, 30, 56
  travel tips, 186
  try MSN, 123
  turning off underlines, 79
  tutorial, 123
  weather information, 115
Links toolbar
  moving, 35

reassigning buttons, 35
services, 166
Listservs, 327
  digest version, 344
  membership restrictions, 343
  moderated list, 343
  Publicly Accessible Mailing
    Lists, 343
Local files
  format for URL, 47
  menus, 34
  properties, 96
Lycos, 135, 233, 240–43
  descriptive abstract, 242

M

Magellan, 135, 233, 243–45
  related topic, 244
  reviewed sites, 243
Mail
  flash sessions in AOL, 143
Mail client, 344
  default, 345
Mailing lists, 342. See also
  Listservs.
  digest version, 344
  locating, 343
Map link, 188
Marquees
  adding to Web pages, 405
MCI service provider, 23
Members Helping Members,
  142, 145
Memory requirements, 56
Menu bar, 24, 217
  file menu, 25
Message
  formats, 340
    MIME, 340
    UUencode, 340
  priority, 334
Message Boards, 347
Microsoft, 35, 36, 37, 48
  free product downloads, 305
  home page, 14, 227
  Internet Explorer
    home page, 227
  Keeper sites, 215
  More Links, 216

newsgroups, 351
search page, 228
site for Web page developers, 395
Web picks, 215
Word, 360
Works, 360
Microsoft Essentials Directory, 229
Microsoft Exchange. See
  Windows Messaging.
Microsoft Internet Explorer (MSIE)
  accessing newsgroups, 366
  ActiveMovie, 378
  address box, 24
  advantages over browsers, 54
  browser window, 24
  caching, 70
  cryptography, 70
  downloading, 23
  edit menu, 29
  email features, 61
  essentials directory, 165
  fast text mode, 57
  favorites folder, 259
  favorites menu, 32
  file management features, 76
  go menu, 31
  help menu, 33
  history list, 254
  importing Netscape bookmarks, 272
  installing, 22, 129
  international extensions, 63
  ISDN support, 55
  Links, 213, 215, 225, 226
  local files menus, 34
  mailto command, 346
  menu bar, 25
  MIDI recorder, 374
  multilingual capabilities, 63
  multimedia functions, 58
  multitasking, 57
  multithreading, 57
  opening a second window, 26
  parental control software, 67
  progressive rendering, 57
  proxy gateways, 71
  Quick Links toolbar, 277
  RealAudio player, 375
  scripting support, 56
  search feature, 217
  search page, 231, 232
  sending mail from, 346
  shortcuts, 276
  smooth scrolling, 54
  sound clips, 374
  support for Java, 58
  title bar, 277
  Today's Links, 213
  toolbar, 34
  using ActiveMovie, 60
  using ActiveX, 60, 384
  using NetMeeting, 62
  view menu, 29
  windows compatibility, 54
  with CompuServe, 152
  with Shockwave, 379
Microsoft Internet Mail, 319–46. See also Email.
  address book, 319, 321, 323
  addressing mail, 322
  automatic signoff, 330
  checking automatically, 329
  compared to Microsoft Internet News, 362
  compared to Windows Messaging, 345
  composing mail offline, 330
  creating a new group, 324
  creating folders, 336
  deleted items, 336
  folders, 336
  hotlinks in email, 336
  inbox, 326
  inbox assistant, 337
  including previous message in reply, 328
  message formats, 340
  message priority, 334
  outbox, 326, 331-332, 336
  preview, 326
  sending messages immediately, 333
  sending mail, 321, 331
  sent items
    from Microsoft Internet News, 361
  sent items folder, 336
  shortcuts, 319
  signatures, 334
  Sort by command, 327
  spell check, 330
  status bar, 327
  toolbar, 327
  use of Outbox in Microsoft Internet News, 357
Microsoft Internet News, 347–68
  accessing from Explorer browser, 349, 366
  automatic message checking, 363
  canceling newsgroup posts, 353
  changing servers, 349
  compared to Microsoft Internet Mail, 362
  cross-posting messages, 364
  decoding messages, 361
  deleting newsgroups, 352
  Download headers command, 364
  icons on newsgroup lists, 358
  launching, 349
  locating newsgroups, 350
  New message command, 358
  news outbox, 364
  news server address, 349
  Posted Items folder, 357
  posting messages, 358, 360
  preview, 354
  quoting original message in reply, 363
  reading and writing offline, 363
  reply address, 362
  Reply to Group command, 358
  saved items folder, 357
  sending, 360
  sent items in Microsoft Internet Mail, 361
  shortcuts, 319
  signatures, 362
  sorting posts, 355
  speed reading messages, 356
  spell check, 360
  subscribing to newsgroups, 351
  troubleshooting, 350
  unsubscribing, 352
  use of Microsoft Internet Mail Outbox, 357
  using multiple servers, 349
Microsoft Network (MSN), 226, 227, 233, 330, 344, 362
  Best of the Web, 213
  cartoon link, 219
  custom start page setup, 226
  international links, 230
  Investor, 220, 229
  Keepers, 216–18
  More Links, 216–23
  Pick-of-the-day, 215
  Preview link, 226
  Sitemap, 217, 224, 226, 230
  Stale Surf, 216, 223–24
  Start Page, 226, 228, 229, 305
  Surf Stories, 213, 214

Index   445

More Links section, 215
Today's Pick, 214
This Week's Picks, 218
Today's Links, 213, 214
trial offer, 226
Microsoft pages
  accessing, 33
Microsoft Word, 296
MIDI
  files, 373
  saving to disk, 374
MIME, 340
MIT FAQ document server, 367
Modems, 55
Moderated list, 343
Modulation, 55
Monster FTP Sites List, 317
Mosaic, 11
Movie & Theater links, 218
Movie Essentials link, 199
Movies
  ActiveMovie, 378
  at MSN page, 199
  link, 200
  using ActiveMovie, 60
MPEG, 59
MSN, 226
MSN Essentials Directory, 36
MSN home page, 101
MSN Investor, 107
MSNBC News, 224, 226
Multimedia
  ActiveMovie, 378
  option selection, 77
  programming tools, 381
  QuickTime, 380
  Shockwave, 379
  streaming, 60
  support, 59
  suppressing download, 31
  toolkit, 386
Multiple browser Windows, 308
Multiple servers
  with Microsoft Internet News, 349
Multipoint communications, 63
Multipurpose Internet Mail Extensions. *See MIME.*
Multitasking, 57
Multithreading, 3, 57
Music
  category link, 201
  clip option, 105
  links, 218
Music Central, 110, 202
Musical Instrument Digital Interface. *See MIDI.*

N

NASA Information Services, 221
National Science Foundation (NSF), 5
Navigation
  smooth scrolling, 54
Navigation card, 83
  customize options, 83
  history folder, 85
Netiquette
  newsgroup, 353
  signatures, 335
NetMeeting, 62, 63
Netscape, 11, 72, 390
  extensions, 405
Network, 2
New Message command, 358
News and Entertainment Options, 111-115
News Outbox, 364
News sites
  MSNBC, 108
news.answers archive, 367
Newsgroup domain names, 348
Newsgroups, 46, 62, 140, 235, 347
  accessing FAQs, 367
  canceling newsgroup posts, 353
  cross-posting messages, 364
  locating, 350
  netiquette, 353
  news.answers archive, 367
  offline reading, 141
  posting messages, 358
  quotes in posts, 360
  reading offline, 363
  searching for in AOL, 136
  spamming, 365
  speed reading, 356
  subscribing to newsgroups, 351
Newsreader. *See Microsoft Internet Mail.*

O

Object Linking and Embedding. *See OLE.*
OLE, 384
Online publications
  C|Net, 221
  Time, 227
Online Services, 9–10, 17, 323
  America Online (AOL), 6, 10, 331, 362
  CompuServe (CIS), 6, 10, 331, 362
  Microsoft Network (MSN), 362
Open History Folder command, 255
Option cards, 75
Outbox in Microsoft Internet Mail, 336
Outdoor Sports. *See Sports Information.*

P

Pages
  customizing MSN start page, 101
  displaying start page, 31
  home vs. start, 102
  printing, 28
  refreshing, 30
  saving to disk, 27
  searching, 31
  setting up, 27
  start, 31
  suppressing display of items, 31
  with ActiveX, 58
Parental controls in AOL, 144
Peanuts, 219
Perl scripts in Web page design, 390
Personal Finance, 219
Personal Home Page, 407
Phone & Address Look-Up Services, 181
Pick-of-the-day section, 215
PICS, 65
Pictures
  disabling display, 77
  hiding, 78
  placeholder text, 29
Plant and garden information, 170
Platform for Internet Contact Selection. *See PICS.*
Pollstar home page, 202
POP3 address, 345
Pop-up frames, 371

Ports, 42
Posted Items folder, 357
Posting and Sending in Microsoft Internet News, 358, 360
PostScript, 8
PPP connection to CompuServe, 154
Preferences
 customizing start pages, 104
 kids link, 105
 music clip, 105
 who are you?, 104
Pregnancy and Child Care, 226
Preview, 339
 in Mail and News, 326
Preview link, 124
Preview Pane in Microsoft Internet News, 354
Previous Picks, 216, 217, 218
Primenet, 23
Printing, 28
Priority. *See Message priority.*
Privacy options, 88
Private Communication Technology, 69
Product updates button, 36
Programming files, 316
Programs card, 86
 mail and news, 86
 viewers, 86
Progressive rendering, 57
Properties, 29
 button, 91
 command, 292
 sheets (for favorites), 263
Proportional fonts, 80
Protocols
 file, 15
 FTP, 42
 Gopher, 43
 HTTP, 41
 HTTPS, 42
 of a URL, 39
 omitting in URLs, 56
 security, 69
 Telnet, 45
Proxy gateways, 71
Proxy server, 72, 83
Public domain, 304
Publications Search page, 197
Publicly Accessible Mailing Lists (PAML), 343

Q

Quick Go button, 140
Quick Menus, 277, 276–93
 address box, 278
 Graphic, 286
 Hypertext, 281
 Text, 280
 Title bar quick menu, 277
QuickTime, 59, 380
Quotes in newsgroup posts, 360
Quoting in email replies. *See Microsoft Internet Mail.*

R

Rating
 obtaining, 66
 options, 91
 sample rating chart, 67
 setting levels, 91
 systems, 65
Read Offline option, 141
RealAudio, 59, 375
Receipts for email, 333
Recreation links, 222
Recreational Software Advisory Council, 66
Refresh command, 373
Refresh toolbar button, 292
Refreshing pages, 30, 70, 109, 292
Reply
 to Author command, 358
 to Group, 358
 to Newsgroup and Author command, 359
Reply address for newgroup posts, 362
Right-click quick menus. *See Quick Menus.*
RSAC, 66

S

Safety Level button, 90
Save as file option, 27
Save Web page, 27
 as HTML, 283
 as text, 283
Saved items folder, 357
SavvySearch, 85, 118, 247
Science, 220
Scripting tool (CIS), 155
Search engines, 118, 231–52, 308–16
 Alta Vista, 233, 234
 boolean, 233
 downloadable software files, 308
 Excite, 233, 236
 Featured Search of the Day, 232
 government publications, 198
 Harvest Broker, 308
 Infoseek, 233, 238
 Internet Explorer Search page, 232
 keywords, 233
 Lycos, 233, 240
 magazines, 197
 Magellan, 233, 243
 SavvySearch, 247
 shareware.com, 308
 Telnet, 243
 Usenet newsgroups, 235
 WhoWhere?, 251
 WinSite, 314
 Yahoo, 233, 245
Search Page link, 228
Search the Internet option, 135
Searches, 31
 customizing, 84
 SavvySearch site, 118
 Sleuth, 118
 topics in Microsoft Internet News, 350
 using AOL, 133
Second window, opening, 26
Secure Sockets Layer, 69, 72
Security, 29, 67, 293
 authentication, 69
 channel protocols, 69
 cryptoAPI, 70
 downloading code, 68
 Internet Engineering Task Force, 69
Security card, 87-89
Self-extracting file, 304
Send Messages Immediately command, 333
Send to command, 27
Sending attachments in email, 339

Index   447

Sending Mail. *See Microsoft Internet Mail.*
Sent Items in Microsoft Internet Mail, 336
Servers, 7, 9, 17
   authentication, 69
   proxy server options, 83
Services button, 36
Services Quick Link button, 174
shareware, 304
   defined, 304
   registration, 305
   WinZip, 304
shareware.com search engine, 308, 309
Shockwave, 379
Shortcuts, 302, 342
   copying, 283
   copying desktop links, 297
   creating, 28
   defined, 275
   drag-and-drop, 296
   from History folder, 300
   in email, 342
   renaming, 296
   representing a document, 342
   sending a file, 27
Show Picture, 78
Signatures, 334, 362
   in Microsoft Internet Mail, 334
   in Microsoft Internet News, 362
   netiquette, 335
   with URLs, 336
Simpsons, The, 407
Site Builder Workshop, 60, 384
Sitemap page, 123
Sites
   button, 89
   history, 32
Smart caching, 70
Smooth scrolling, 54
   setting, 96
SMTP address, 345
SMTP/POP3, 345
Software, 220
   code certificate, 69
   conferencing, 62
   installing MSIE, 22
   parental control software, 67
Sound clips, 374
   differences from MIDI, 374
   interrupting play, 78

Source file viewing, 31
Space Flight, 221
Spamming, 365
Spell Check, 330
   in Microsoft Internet News, 360
Sports & Health, 216, 221
   Sports Illustrated, 221
   Sportsline USA, 221
Sports information, 109
   scores and statistics, 108
   SportsZone, 109
Stale Surf, 223–24
Standard text quick menu, 277
Star Trek: Continuum, 226
Start menu
   placing shortcuts in, 298
Start page customizing, 102
   assigning links to folders, 122
   Internet searches, 117
   linking selected sites, 121
   music, 110
   news and entertainment options, 111
   personal preferences, 104
   service options, 106
   setting location, 83
   setting to a blank page, 84
   stock market update, 108
Status bar, 30, 37
   in file downloads, 307
   in Microsoft Internet Mail, 327
   multitasking, 57
   sample, 38
Stock quotes, 176, 220
Stopping a process, 30
Subscribing to newsgroups, 141, 351
Sun Microsystems, 381
Surf Stories page, 32, 124, 229, 255 *See also Microsoft Network (MSN).*

T

Tabbing
   keyboard commands, 293
Tags. *See Hypertext Markup Language.*
Tax forms, 176
TCP/IP, 5, 151
Telephone connection, 55
Telnet, 45
   search engines, 243

Temporary files, 307
Temporary Internet files, 70
   setting options, 92
Text editor, 296
Text formatting in HTML, 397
Text Quick Menu, 280
Ticker symbols, selecting, 108
TicketMaster Online, 219
Time, 227
Time Warner Publication Search, 197
TIS Gauntlet, 72
Title bar, 24
Title bar quick menu, 277
Today's Favorite Web Pick, 214
Today's Links, 225. *See Microsoft Network (MSN).*
   button, 36, 112
   option, 255
Toolbar, 24, 30, 34
   back arrow button, 255
   buttons, 34
   customizing, 35
   forward arrow button, 255
   hiding, 34
   in Microsoft Internet Mail, 321, 327
   links button, 35
   standard, 80
   using AOL, 131
Top-level domain, 40
Tracer, 72
Track a Package link, 178
Travel Information Services
   flight information, 186
   weather forecasts, 189
Troubleshooting in Microsoft Internet News, 350
Tutorial, 33, 123

U

U.S. Small Business Administration (SBA), 220
United Media Comic Strips, 114
United States Postal Service, 323
United States Government, 4
UnitedMedia, 219
Universal Resource Locator. *See URLs.*
Unzip. *See File compression.*

URLs, 14, 52. *See also Web Sites.*
   accessing a home page, 41
   address, 38, 40
   avoiding typos in, 280
   case sensitivity, 41, 257
   directory path, 40
   favorites folder, 254
   format for HTTP, 41
   forward slash, 41
   FTP format, 42
   Gopher, 43
   hints for locating, 61
   HTTPS format, 42
   in Microsoft Internet News, 362
   in signatures, 336
   local file format, 47
   omitting protocols, 56
   partial, 48
   port, 42
   protocol, 39
   references, 52
   show friendly option, 96
   Telnet format, 45
   Usenet format, 47
Usenet, 46
Usenet newsgroups, 235. *See also Microsoft Internet News.*
   news.answers, 344
   news.lists, 344
User name, 322
UUEncode, 340
   attachments in email, 342

V

VDOLive, 59, 380
Video, 378
   disabling display, 77
View Files button, 95
View menu, 29-31
View|Option command
   advanced card, 90
   connection card, 81
   general card, 77
   navigation card, 83
   programs card, 86
   security card, 87
Viewers options, 87
Virtual Hospital, 173
Virtual Reality Modeling Language. *See VRML.*
Virtual Software Library, 309
Viruses, 306
   scanner, 306
Visual Basic files, 316
VRML, 59, 385

W

Wallpaper
   from Web page graphics, 286
WAV, 59
Weather forecast link, 115, 189
Web
   address. See URLs.
   Best of the, 213
   tutorial, 33, 36
Web pages 11-14, 389
   accessing menus, 289
   adding background color, 393
   adding graphics, 401
   adding links, 401
   creating links, 400
   home page, 12
   how to create, 389
   linking images, 405
   personal home page, 389
   quick menu, 277
   refreshing, 292
   resources, 407
   save as HTML, 283
   save as text, 283
WebCrawler, 135
Webster's link, 191
Whiteboard and Chat features, 63
WhoWhere?, 251
WinCIM, 148
   technical support, 162
Windows 95, 276, 344
   Dangerous Creatures background, 306
   foreign language support, 65
   opening a second window, 26
   shortcuts, 276, 319, 349
   sizing buttons, 24
   tricks, 297
Windows Explorer, 304, 307, 396, 397
Windows Messaging, 324, 344
   compared to Microsoft Internet Mail, 345
WinGate, 72
WinSite, 308
   search engine, 314, 316
WinSock, 157
   software site, 317
WinZip, 304, 309
Wiretap, 6
Wizard, 23
Word for Windows files, 316
WordPad, 296
WordPerfect, 389
Working with Listservs, 344
World Wide Web, 1, 7-9
WorldView, 385
Writer's Reference link, 190
   acronyms, 193
   global encyclopedia, 192
   quotations, 194
   Shakespeare, 195

Y

Yahoo, 233, 245-47
   category lists, 246

Z

Ziff-Davis, 115
   ZDNet, 221
ZIP code information, 183
Zipping programs, 304. *See also File Compression.*
Zone link, 172